JAVA

with

OBJECT-ORIENTED

PROGRAMMING

Second Edition

Paul S. Wang
Kent State University

THOMSON

BROOKS/COLE

Australia • Canada • Mexico • Singapore • Spain
United Kingdom • United States

THOMSON

BROOKS/COLE

Editor: *Kallie Swanson*
Senior Editorial Assistant: *Carla Vera*
Technology Project Manager: *Burke Taft*
Marketing Director: *Tom Ziolkowski*
Marketing Assistant: *Darcie Pool*
Advertising Project Manager: *Laura Hubrich*
Project Manager, Editorial Production: *Kelsey McGee*
Print/Media Buyer: *Vena M. Dyer*

Permissions Editor: *Sue Ewing*
Production Service: *Matrix Productions*
Copy Editor: *Frank Hubert*
Cover Image and Design: *Cassandra Chu*
Cover Printing, Printing and Binding:
 Transcontinental Printing–Louiseville
Composition and Illustration:
 TEX Consultants/Arthur Ogawa

Printed in Canada

1 2 3 4 5 6 7 05 04 03 02

For more information about our products, contact us at:
Thomson Learning Academic Resource Center
1-800-423-0563

For permission to use material from this text, contact us by:
Phone: 1-800-730-2214
Fax: 1-800-730-2215
Web: http://www.thomsonrights.com

Library of Congress Control Number: 2002102847

ISBN 0-534-39276-8

Brooks/Cole–Thomson Learning
511 Forest Lodge Road
Pacific Grove, CA 93950
USA

Asia
Thomson Learning
5 Shenton Way #01-01
UIC Building
Singapore 068808

Australia
Nelson Thomson Learning
102 Dodds Street
South Melbourne, Victoria 3205
Australia

Canada
Nelson Thomson Learning
1120 Birchmount Road
Toronto, Ontario M1K 5G4
Canada

Europe/Middle East/Africa
Thomson Learning
High Holborn House
50/51 Bedford Row
London WC1R 4LR
United Kingdom

Latin America
Thomson Learning
Seneca, 53
Colonia Poianco
11560 Mexico D.F.
Mexico

Spain
Paraninfo Thomson Learning
Calle/Magallanes, 25
28015 Madrid, Spain

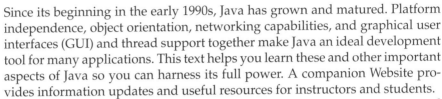

Preface

Since its beginning in the early 1990s, Java has grown and matured. Platform independence, object orientation, networking capabilities, and graphical user interfaces (GUI) and thread support together make Java an ideal development tool for many applications. This text helps you learn these and other important aspects of Java so you can harness its full power. A companion Website provides information updates and useful resources for instructors and students.

Object-oriented design (OOD) and programming (OOP) concepts and techniques are integrated with the Java presentation so that you'll learn Java and OOP at the same time. Topics are covered in detail and illustrated by realistic examples with object-oriented structures. The goal is to give a comprehensive and in-depth introduction to Java and OOP in a concise and practical manner.

Update

The Java language itself has been stable, but the class libraries that support major Java features have been evolving. This text updates, expands, and reorganizes *Java with Object-Oriented Programming and World Wide Web Applications*, published in 1998, to include new materials and emphasize OOP and OOD. The companion Website offers information updates and hands-on experiments to use with the latest version of Java.

OOP and OOD

OOP is the dominant modern programming paradigm; complete understanding of OOP is a must for any serious programmer. The integration of theory with practice makes OOP principles concrete and provides reasons for Java constructs. Many complete examples demonstrate how different Java constructs and individual OOP techniques combine to achieve results in practice. Java provides excellent support for OOP. But, simply using Java constructs does not automatically lead to well-organized object-oriented programs. On the contrary, without a good design created with an object-oriented view, the resulting program will most likely be a procedure-oriented program written in Java. Worse yet, it could be such a program bent out of shape to give rise to classes!

OO concepts and techniques are introduced early and integrated tightly with Java coverage. You'll learn OOP and practice it as you make progress through the text. Chapter 13 is devoted to OOD concepts, methods, and patterns. The OO design of major examples is shown with Unified Modeling Language (UML) class diagrams to reinforce object-oriented thinking. UML diagrams use the following graphical symbols:

———▷ extends, inherits   ———▶ calls   ◇—— aggregates
- - -▷ implements   - - -▶ instantiates   ◆—— composes

To distinguish them from classes, interface names are marked by the symbol «interface» and italicized.

GUI

Graphical user interfaces are great for making programs easy for end users. But GUI adds complexity and sophistication to a program. The Java Foundation Classes (JFC) provide an infrastructure and predefined components, or *widgets*, for GUIs. The Swing package is an important part of the JFC. Swing and its effective application are covered in depth to get you started with GUI programming for *applets* and stand-alone applications alike.

Event-Driven Programming

GUI requires a programming style that handles *events* at run time. Instead of following a prescribed execution path, *event-driven programs* react to *external events* whose occurrence is unpredictable. Event-driven programming techniques are introduced and put to use in GUI and applet programming.

Comprehensive Coverage

Both basic and advanced topics are covered, with emphasis on OOP and realistic applications.

- Basics—Java language constructs, classes, objects, using objects to solve problems, OOP tips, Java program structure, compilation, execution, error handling, and debugging
- OOD and OOP—extending programs by inheritance, superclass and subclass, method overriding, plug-compatible objects, polymorphism, abstract superclasses, interfaces, uniform public interface planning, object cloning, iterators, design patterns, the model-view-controller (MVC) pattern in Java
- Generic and Polymorphic Programming—writing and using programs that are type independent or applicable to a hierarchy of objects; the Java collections framework
- GUI—using Swing widgets to construct graphical user interfaces for programs

- Applets—writing and deploying Swing-based applets, the Java plug-in
- Threads—concepts, techniques, and applications of multithreading
- Advanced topics—networking with URL and sockets, writing server-side and client-side code, remote method invocation (RMI), multithreading, understanding concurrent programming and its challenges, mutual exclusion, scheduling, coordination of concurrent activities, animation as application of multithreading, class as objects, introspection and reflection, dynamic loading of objects, interfacing to *native programs* (C, C++, f77) through JNI, the security manager, signed programs

Examples illustrate concepts, constructs and usages, and show how Java features combine to achieve useful purposes. Yet, comprehensive coverage, numerous full examples, good appendices, and a thorough index do not translate into a huge volume. In fact, the book is no thicker than a regular textbook.

Flexible Usage

The text is designed for a semester course at the upper college or beginning graduate level. Students should know C or C++ already. However, the book is self-contained, and it is entirely possible for a motivated student with less C/C++ knowledge to manage with extra effort. The book is suitable for an *Introduction to Java*, *Java with OOP*, or *Principles of OOP with Java* course. It can also be used as an auxiliary text for a *Theory of OOP*, *Networking*, *Graphical User Interface Design*, *Web Programming*, or *Concurrent/Parallel Programming* course.

The text can also be used for custom training courses for industry. A shorter course may omit chapters 10–12, as appropriate. An advanced course may assign most of Chapters 1 and 2 for reading and select more substantial programming projects from the exercises.

After a course, the text can be used as a valuable reference.

Web Site

The text has a companion Web site at

```
http://sofpower.com/java
```

Information updates, on-Web examples, hands-on exercises, instructor notes (in PDF), articles, FAQ, links to documentation, and other resources can be found on the site.

Throughout the book, concepts and usages are thoroughly illustrated with examples. Instead of using contrived examples, however, every effort is made to give examples with practical value and to present them as complete programs, ready to enter into the computer. The entire set of examples is available for download at the site. Follow simple instructions on the inside back cover to set up these examples.

Easy Reference

Information is organized and presented in a way that facilitates quick and easy reference. There are ample appendices, including *Major Differences between Java and ANSI C/C++* and *The Java Debugger:* `jdb`, a list of classes with section cross-references, and a thorough and comprehensive index. This book will be a valuable aid for working with Java.

Acknowledgments

This text evolved from the author's *Java with Object-Oriented Programming and World Wide Web Applications* book. It also benefited from two custom training courses conducted by the author at Westfield Companies, Westfield Center, Ohio. Sincere thanks go to Alex Sykes at Westfield and Kelli Baxter at Kent State campus for setting up the training courses and to the participants for their feedback. The draft manuscript was put to classroom trial in Spring 2002. Students of the *Theory of OOP* class found typos and made suggestions for improvements. Yinghong Sun helped design the Web site for the book. I am grateful to them. Appreciation also goes to reviewers of the manuscript who provided valuable comments and suggestions:

Iyad A. Ajwa of Ashland University
Hristina Galabova of HBO/Information Technology
Ralph Grove of James Madison University
Sridhar Narayan of the University of North Carolina at Wilmington
Denise Sargent-Natour of California State University at Hayward
Carolyn J.C. Schauble of Colorado State University
Daniel Spiegel of Wright State University
T. Andrew Yang of Indiana University of Pennsylvania

I would also like to thank Kallie Swanson and Carla Vera at Brooks/Cole and Merrill Peterson at Matrix Productions, Inc., for their support and able management of this project, and Arthur Ogawa at TeX Consultants, who did an excellent job of typesetting the manuscript and re-creating the figures. It helps when the compositor also understands the technical content of the book. I am grateful to Arthur. Finally, and most of all, my deep appreciation to my wife, Jennifer, and my children, Laura, Deborah, and David, for their support and encouragement.

Paul S. Wang
Kent, Ohio

Contents

APPENDICES

Introduction

Since its introduction by Sun Microsystems™ (Sun) in 1995, the Java™ programming system has gained worldwide acceptance with unprecedented speed. The rapid acceptance is due primarily to Java's object orientation, platform independence, graphical user interface support, and Internet/Web capabilities.

At the center of Java are the innovative Java programming language and the *Software Development Kit*[1] (SDK). The general-purpose Java language is totally object oriented. You program by building *software objects*. *Object-oriented programming* (OOP) makes software easier to build, maintain, modify, and reuse. The SDK includes a rich set of code libraries and tools. Together, the language and the SDK make programming convenient, efficient, and effective.

Platform independence is an important reason for Java's success. Java programs are compiled into *Java bytecode* that runs on any computer with a *Java interpreter* or *Java Virtual Machine* (JVM) that provides a run-time environment for executing Java programs. The bytecode is architecture and operating system independent. Thus, Java programs can be written and compiled once and then transmitted to run anywhere. Java interpreters from many vendors also include just-in-time compilation of bytecode into native machine code for increased execution speed. Using Java, software developers are freed from the busy work of porting programs and can concentrate on producing high-quality software that will run on computers from any vendor.

JAVA COMPONENTS

Tools and software for Java are available from many companies worldwide. Java from Sun includes these components:

- Java programming language—supports OOP and comes with *core class libraries* for I/O, strings, multithreading, and exception handling.
- Java compiler—compiles Java source code into Java bytecode.
- Java Virtual Machine—interprets and executes Java bytecode.
- JFC (*Java Foundation Classes*)—support event-driven and graphical user interface (GUI) programming.

---

[1] Also known as JDK, the Java Development Kit

1

- Applet and Servlet support—aids development of client-side and server-side programs for the Web.
- Java documentation generator—automatically produces, from Java source files, application programming interface (API) documentation in HTML.
- JAR (*Java Archive*)—packs and unpacks files for fast and efficient transfer across a network.
- JDBC (*Java Data Base Connectivity*)—interfaces Java front-ends to existing databases.
- RMI (*Remote Method Invocation*)—enables access to Java objects on remote computers across a network.
- Java debugger—helps you locate and fix bugs in Java programs.
- Java disassembler—extracts source code information from compiled bytecode.
- Java header generator—creates header (.h) files needed for extending Java code with C, C++, or FORTRAN programs.
- JNI (*Java Native Interface*)—provides interface to C and C++ code.
- Java documentation—covers demos, tutorials, guides to topics, usage of tools, APIs, and other information. You can access Java documentation on the Web.

Most items in this list are included in the *Software Development Kit* (SDK) that Sun distributes.

New tools and software are being introduced at a fast pace. We shall focus on the Java language and core classes. Many examples illustrate OOP in Java for regular, GUI, applet, and networking applications.

APPLET AND GUI PROGRAMMING

The Web is fueling the explosive growth of the Internet. It is increasingly important for institutions, corporations, and individuals to retrieve and disseminate information on the Web. A Java *applet* is a special form of Java code that can supply *executable content* in Web documents. Web browsers can use *Java plug-ins* to execute applets on local computers. The Java applet is one way to add moving images, sound effects, and responsive user interactions to a Web page.

Java also has excellent support for graphical user interfaces and event-driven programming. You can make applications easy to use by adding interactive window-mouse oriented graphical interfaces. The *Java Foundation Classes* (JFC) provide for widgets (window objects), event handling, graphics drawing, image displaying, and dynamically selectable look and feel. Applet support is part of the JFC.

WHAT IS OOP?

OOP is the modern programming paradigm of choice. The central idea of *object-oriented programming* is to build programs using software *objects*. An object can be considered as a self-contained computing entity with its own data and programming. On modern computers, windows, menus, and file folders, for example, are usually represented by software objects. But objects can be applied to many kinds of programs. An object can be an airline reservation record, a bank account, or even an automobile engine. An engine object would include data (called *fields*) describing its physical attributes and programming (called *methods*) governing how it works internally and how it interacts with other related parts (also objects) in an automobile.

A payroll system would have employee records, time cards, overtime, sick leave, taxes, deductions, and so on, as objects. An air traffic control system would have runways, airliners, and passenger gates as objects. Thus, in OOP, the software objects correspond closely to real objects involved in the application area. This correspondence makes the computer program easy to understand and manipulate. In contrast, traditional programming deals with bytes, variables, arrays, indices, and other programming artifacts that are difficult to relate to the problem at hand. Also, traditional programming focuses mainly on step-by-step procedures, called *algorithms*, to achieve the desired tasks. For this reason, traditional programming is also known as *procedure-oriented* programming.

OOP Advantages

A large computer program is among the most complex constructs ever built. The cost of design, implementation, verification, maintenance, and revision of large software systems is very high. Thus, it is important to find ways to make these tasks easier. In this direction, OOP has enormous potential.

For reasons that will become clear, OOP offers the following main advantages:

- Simplicity—Because software objects model real objects in the application domain, the complexity of the program is reduced and the program structure becomes clear and simple.
- Modularity—Each object forms a separate entity whose internal workings are decoupled from other parts of the system.
- Modifiability—It is easy to make minor changes in the data representation or the procedures used in an OO (object-oriented) program. Changes within an object do not affect any other part of the program provided that the *external behavior* of the object is preserved.

- Extensibility—Adding new features or responding to changing operating environments can be a matter of introducing a few new objects and modifying some existing ones.
- Flexibility—An OO program can be very flexible in accommodating different situations because the interaction patterns among the objects can be changed without modifying the objects.
- Maintainability—Objects can be maintained separately, which makes locating and fixing problems and adding "bells and whistles" easy.
- Reusability—Objects can be reused in different programs. A table-building object, for instance, can be used in any program that requires a table of some sort. Thus, programs can be built from prefabricated and pretested components in a fraction of the time required to build new programs from scratch.

OOP Concepts

The breakthrough concept of OOP technology is the attachment of program procedures to data items. This concept changes the traditional segregation between data and programs. The wrapping together of procedures and data is called *encapsulation*, and the result is a software object. In Java, all procedures are encapsulated and they are called *methods*. For example, a window object (Figure 1) in a graphical user interface system contains the window's physical dimensions, location on the screen, foreground and background colors, border styles, and other relevant data. Encapsulated with these data are methods to move and resize the window itself, change its colors, display its text, shrink it into an icon, and so on. Other parts of the user interface program simply call upon a window object to perform these tasks by sending well-defined

Figure 1   A WINDOW OBJECT

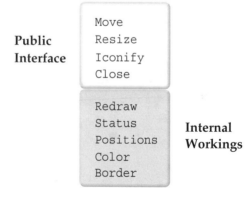

messages to the object. It is the job of a window object to perform appropriate actions and to keep its internal data updated. The exact manner in which these tasks are achieved and the structures of the internal data are of no concern to programs outside the object. The *public interface* formed by the different kinds of messages understood by an object completely defines how to use that object. This public interface is the *application programming interface* (API) of the object. The hiding of internal details makes an object *abstract*, and the technique is sometimes referred to as *data abstraction*.

The separation of *public interface* from *internal workings* is not difficult to understand. In fact, it is common practice in our daily lives. Consider a bank teller, for example. Customers go to any bank and talk to any teller using the same set of messages: account number, deposit, withdrawal, balance, and so on. The way each bank or teller actually keeps records or performs tasks internally is of no concern to a customer. These tried-and-true principles simplify business at all levels and can bring the same benefit to organizing programs. As an OO program executes, objects are created, messages sent, and objects destroyed. These are the only allowable operations on objects. The internal (*private*) data or methods in an object are off limits to the *public*. The decoupling of the private mechanisms in objects from routines outside the objects significantly reduces the complexity of a program.

It is often the case that more than one object of the same type is needed. For example, multiple windows often appear on workstation screens. Normally, objects of a given type are *instances* of a *class* whose definition specifies the private (internal) workings of these objects as well as their public interface. Thus, in OOP, a class would be defined for each type of object required. A class becomes a blueprint for building a particular kind of object. A class definition and appropriate *initial values* are used to create an instance (object) of the class. This operation is known as *object instantiation*.

The OOP technology also calls for easy ways to construct objects on top of other objects. There are two principal methods, *composition* and *inheritance*. Composition allows existing objects to be used as components to build other objects. For instance, a calculator object may be composed of an arithmetic unit object and a user interface object. Inheritance is a major OOP feature that allows you to extend and modify existing classes without changing their code. In Java this is done through class extension. A *subclass* can *inherit* code from its *superclass* and also add its own data and methods. For example, a graphics window, a text window, and a terminal emulator window can all be extended from a basic window class. Also, a check, an invoice, and an application form can all be extended from a basic business form class. Inheritance allows the extraction of commonalities among similar or related objects. It also allows classes in OO software libraries to be used for many different or unforeseen purposes. Inheriting from one class is *single inheritance* and from several classes is *multiple inheritance*.

Furthermore, OOP allows *polymorphism*, the ability for a program to work with different objects as interchangeable *black boxes*. Polymorphism allows the creation of compatible objects that are interchangeable. Modifying and improving a polymorphic program can be simply a matter of plugging in updated objects.

Obviously, OOP has many powerful concepts. Java provides a set of well-designed language mechanisms to help achieve these goals. Only through actual programming can the many implications of these concepts be fully understood.

JAVA FEATURES

Java is very popular and useful for many reasons. Some important features are summarized here:

- Object orientation—Java is totally object oriented. There are no unattached functions in a Java program. All methods are within classes. Primitive data types, such as integers and doubles, have class wrappers. Classes are objects themselves, allowing program manipulation of classes.

- Simplicity—Java syntax is similar to ANSI C and C++ and, therefore, easy to learn. But Java is much simpler and smaller than C++. Java eliminates header files, preprocessor, pointer arithmetic, multiple inheritance, operator overloading, struct, union, and templates. Also, Java performs automatic *garbage collection*, making explicit memory management unnecessary.

- Compactness—Java is designed to be small. The most compact version can be used to control small appliances. The Java interpreter and basic class support are kept small by packaging other libraries separately.

- Portability—Java programs are compiled into architecture-neutral bytecode and will run on any platform with a Java interpreter. The Java compiler and other tools are written in Java. The Java interpreter is written in ANSI C. The Java language specification has *no implementation-dependent features* whatsoever.

- Network friendliness—Java has built-in facilities for network communication, Web applets, and client-server applications, as well as remote access to database, methods, and programs.

- GUI support—The Java Foundation Classes make it simple and easy to write event-driven GUI.

- Dynamic incremental loading and linking—Java classes are linked dynamically at load time. Thus, adding new methods and data fields to a class does not require recompilation of client classes. In C++, for example, a modified header file requires recompilation of all client files. Furthermore, applications can execute statements to look up fields and methods and then use them accordingly.

- Internationalization—Java programs are written in *Unicode*, a 16-bit character code that includes alphabets from most of the world's widely used languages. The manipulation of Unicode characters and support for local date/time, and so on, make Java welcome worldwide.
- Threads—Java provides multiple control flows that execute concurrently within a Java program. Threads allow your Java program to undertake several computing tasks at once, a feature that supports event-driven, networking, and animation programs.
- Security—Java security measures include restrictions on Java applets, redefinable socket implementations, and user-defined security manager objects. They make applets trustworthy and allow applications to implement and enforce customized security rules.

OOP in Java

Java is thoroughly object oriented. A Java program consists of one or more classes. Classes can be organized into *packages*. The Java class defines software objects by enclosing data members (*fields*) and function members (*methods*). Members can be designated *private*, *protected*, *package*, or *public*, providing a convenient way to define the public interface and the private domain of an object.

The Java mechanism for inheritance is *class extension*, which achieves both type relations and code reuse. Only single inheritance is allowed. *Dynamic method overriding* supports polymorphism and enables building of interchangeable objects conforming to a uniform interface. The Java *abstract superclass* helps you plan uniform interfaces for, and supply common code to, a set of plug-compatible objects.

You can specify *interfaces* in Java. An interface specifies methods required for any class to function for certain purposes. For example, a *sortable* interface can specify the behavior of any objects that can be sorted into order. You make a class conform to an interface by implementing the required methods. A class may implement any number of interfaces, so its objects support certain prescribed behaviors.

A *generic container* is a data structure in which you can place objects of any type. The *Java Collections Framework* provides a well-designed architecture to support the representation, manipulation, and interoperability of many kinds of generic containers.

Networking

The *Internet* is a global network that connects networks using the *Internet Protocol* (IP). The activity of linking computer networks is called *internetworking*, hence the name Internet. The Internet links all kinds of organizations around the world—universities, government offices, corporations, libraries, supercomputer centers, research labs, and even individual homes. The Web is a big part of the Internet and uses HTTP (*Hypertext Transfer Protocol*). The number of connections on the Internet and the number of Web sites are large and growing rapidly.

On the Web, resources and services are identified by URLs (Uniform Resource Locator). Java provides convenient class libraries for networking with URLs, allowing easy access to standard Internet services. Java also supports Internet *sockets* that use the lower-level Internet protocols TCP/IP or UDP/IP.

Multithreading

Programs written in languages such as Fortran, C, or C++ execute a single flow of control. These are *single thread* programs. Java allows multiple threads to exist and execute independently within a program. The multithreading capability brings many benefits, including decoupling time-consuming computations and handling events responsively.

With multiple threads, you can organize tasks to execute concurrently or in parallel within a program. To harness the power of parallelism, you need to overcome a number of challenges associated with managing and coordinating activities that take place simultaneously.

OBJECT-ORIENTED DESIGN

Without a design created with an object-oriented view, a program can easily become a procedure-oriented program written in Java. Worse yet, it could be such a program bent out of shape to give rise to classes! Object orientation requires its own approach to software design. Basic *object-oriented design* (OOD) techniques include decomposition approaches, UML (Unified Modeling Language) class and use case diagrams, the CRC method (Classes, Responsibilities and Collaborators), and design patterns.

WEB SITE AND ORGANIZATION OF MATERIAL

This book has a Web site that offers useful resources, an example package ready to download, and hands-on experiments to enhance learning:

```
http://www.sofpower.com/java
```

The text introduces Java, effective OOP, applets, GUI and event programming with Swing, the Java collections framework, networking, multithreading, and basics of object-oriented program design. It provides comprehensive and in-depth coverage of many important topics.

A thorough introduction of Java is integrated with OOP concepts and techniques. Many examples of practical value illustrate not only individual features but, more importantly, how they combine effectively. All code examples are available on the Web (http://www.sofpower.com/java). The appendices complement the chapters with background and reference material.

A number of advanced topics important in practice are presented in Chapter 12. These include reflection, run-time class loading, document generation via javadoc, interface with native programs (C, C++, f77), clipboards, security management, signed applets, and interapplet communication.

Chapter 13 overviews the basics of OOD, gives the CRC design of a pocket calculation simulation program, and explains the MVC (model-view-controller) architecture of the Swing package in Java. An instructor may choose to cover some OOD material from this chapter earlier in a course.

The text is designed for a semester course at the upper-division undergraduate or beginning graduate level. It is also suitable for custom training courses for industry. A shorter course may omit Chapters 10 to 13, as appropriate. An advanced course may proceed at a faster pace, cover early parts of Chapter 13 sooner, and select more substantial programming projects from the exercises.

Knowledge of C or C++ is a prerequisite for this course. The materials remain interesting and challenging even for people with some exposure to basic Java. Appendix K supplies basic Java backgound, so a motivated student with less C/C++ programming experience can still manage with extra effort.

## CHAPTER ONE

Classes and Objects

The best way to learn a new language is to write programs in it. A collection of basic Java constructs and OOP concepts are introduced to get you started quickly. Early topics include program structure, classes, methods, and basic data types. Beginners with insufficient background can find supplemental material on basic Java constructs (very similar to C/C++) in Appendix K.

The class is a key Java construct that supports *data abstraction* through *encapsulation*. A bank account example illustrates these concepts in a clear and intuitive manner and shows how classes are defined and how objects are created and used.

Problem solving with objects involves modeling interacting entities in a solution. The methodology is demonstrated by solving a simple problem in plane geometry with Vector2D objects. A complete Java program is given.

Objects interact in a program through method calls that pass arguments and receive results. Argument passing is explained, making clear how primitive data, arrays, and objects are passed in method calls. The way a Java program receives *command-line arguments* is also described. This information helps you in writing programs that receive arguments and options from the command line.

OOP requires a way of thinking that is different from the traditional *flow charting* of solution steps. Tips on object-oriented thinking provide a new perspective on effective program writing.

1.1 JAVA PROGRAM STRUCTURE

A program is a set of instructions, written in a programming language, to solve a given type of problem or to achieve well-defined goals. A Java program consists of one or more *classes*. Classes describe *objects*, software entities that interact at run time to achieve specific tasks. Objects are used to closely model actual or logical entities in the problem domain. One important aspect of OOP is identifying these entities and their interactions in the solution process.

A class is a blueprint for objects. It describes an object's data structures and their associated operations. After a class is defined, objects belonging to the class can be declared and used in a program. A class usually contains *members* that are *fields* and *methods*. *Fields* are variables that store data and objects.

Methods are functions that codify operations. A method receives *arguments*, performs predefined computations, and returns results.

In Java, all methods must be contained in classes. Unattached methods or functions are not allowed. You activate (or *invoke*) a method in an object by naming the object and the method and by specifying any arguments for the method. A method may produce a *return value*. Objects interact by invoking methods.

A class provides a name under which members are collected into one unit. By the use of objects, a large program can be built with many small, independent, interacting units. Object orientation can significantly reduce program complexity, increase flexibility, and enhance reusability. A Java program can define its own classes, use Java built-in classes, and utilize classes created by others. Classes can be organized into named *packages*. Each package may contain one or more source code files.

1.2   A FIRST PROGRAM

To begin, let's consider a very simple program with only one class that contains a single method:

```
///////    Average.java    ///////

public class Average                                // class name
{
   public static void main(String[] args)    // a method
   {   int i = 11, j = 20;
       double a = (i + j) / 2.0;
       System.out.println("i is " + i + " and j is " + j);
       System.out.println("Average is " + a);
   }
}
```

The source code is stored in the file Average.java. First, compile this program with a Java compiler

javac Average.java

to produce the Average.class file containing machine-independent Java bytecode executable by any Java interpreter. Then, run the program by

java Average

Note, the argument to **java** is Average, the name of the class containing the method main you wish to run, not Average.class, the name of the compiled file.

The interpreter **java** loads the given class (Average.class in this case) and any other classes the program requires, and begins execution by invoking the main method of the given class, Average. The following output is produced:

```
i is 11 and j is 20
Average is 15.5
```

Appendix A contains more information on the Java compiler. Now, let's take a closer look at this program. The first line is a *comment*, from // until the end of the line. Then you have the definition of the class Average. Simple class definitions follow this general form:

```
[ public ] class Name        (class header)
{
      members                (class body)
}
```

A member given in the class body can be a *field* (data) or a *method*. To declare a class public, use the modifier public at the beginning of the class header. Otherwise, the class is used only inside its package.

Class members declared public are accessible to all parts of a program that can access the class. A main method is public so it can be invoked by the Java interpreter. The parameter args of main receives arguments given on the command line that invoked the program. More will be said about *command-line arguments* when we put them to use.

A class member is either an *instance member* or a *classwide member*. A member is an instance member unless declared static, which makes it a classwide member. The main method of a class is always declared static. When you program, simply use the same header for main as shown in Average all the time. The distinction between instance and classwide members and their usage will be explained fully in Section 2.6.

1.3 DEFINING METHODS

A *method* is a computation procedure defined in a class. Each method contains *statements* that specify a sequence of computing actions to be carried out, and *variables* that are used to store values needed and produced during the computations. Some of the variables may be objects, and the computing procedure usually involves interactions among objects.

A method takes arguments as input, performs a sequence of programmed steps, and returns a result of the declared type. A method can call other methods in the course of its computation.

A *method definition* consists of a *method header* and a *method body*. The method header states the method name and the type of the return value. The header also specifies variables, known as *formal parameters*, which receive the incoming arguments. These formal parameters are used in the method body to perform computations.

The method body consists of a sequence of *declarations* and *statements* enclosed in braces, {}. A declaration supplies information to the Java compiler, and a statement specifies actions for execution. Many basic declarations and statements can be found in Appendix K.

Simple methods follow this general form:

```
valuetype name ( type arg1, type arg2, ... )     (method header)
{                                                 (body begin)
    declarations and statements
}                                                 (body end)
```

The `valuetype` specifies the type of the value returned by the method. If the method does not return a value, then its `valuetype` is given as `void`.

Depending on the number of arguments needed, the method header may specify zero or more *formal parameters*. If there are no formal parameters, the parameter list is given as an empty list `()`. Furthermore, the method body may contain zero or more declarations and statements. (Appendix K gives more information on statements.) The return type of an entry-point `main` is always `void`.

In our example, the method body begins with the declarations

```
int i = 11, j = 20;
double a = (i + j) / 2.0;
```

establishing the variables i, j, of type `int` (32-bit integer) and a of type `double` (64-bit floating-point number). A variable must be declared before it is used. A simple declaration consists of a *type name* followed by a list of variable names separated by commas and terminated by a semicolon. Each variable may also be given an optional *initializer* after an equal sign (=). The expression

```
(i + j) / 2.0
```

is evaluated and the resultant value is used to initialize the variable a. There are different kinds of expressions. An *arithmetic expression* involves arithmetic operators such as +, -, *, and /. Generally, an *expression* is a constant, a variable, or expressions connected by operators.

Here are a few more variable declarations:

```
int age = 8;
float rate, speed;
char c, d;
boolean flag = false;
```

These declare the variable age of type `int`, rate and speed of type `float` (32-bit floating-point number), c and d of type `char` (a single character), and flag of type `boolean` (`true` or `false`).

Variables, such as i, j, and a, declared in a method body, are used within the method and will not conflict with any variable with the same name used elsewhere. Therefore, such variables are said to be *local* to the method.

The example continues with two output statements using the output object System.out, which is provided by the Java run time environment. The dot (.) is the *member-of operator*, and out is a static member of the System class. The object System.out implements the println method that outputs its argument to the display, followed by a platform-dependent line terminator (NEWLINE on UNIX and NEWLINE RETURN on Win32). The System.out.print method is the same but does not supply the line terminator.

A special function of the + operator in Java is to conveniently append the string representation of many other Java data types to a string:

```
System.out.println("Average is " + a);
```

A *string constant* is given as a sequence of characters enclosed in double quotes. Use \" to include a double quote character in a string constant. In Java, strings are objects of the built-in class String (Section 1.7).

1.4 DATA TYPES AND VARIABLE DECLARATIONS

Unlike most other languages, Java's data types are uniformly defined across all platforms. The *primitive data types* for Java are listed in Table 1.1.

The effects of all Java operators on the primitive types are defined by the language.

Table 1.1   JAVA PRIMITIVE DATA TYPES

Primitive Type	Description
boolean	true or false
char	16-bit Unicode character ('\u0000' to '\uffff')
byte	signed 8-bit integer (-2^7 to $2^7 - 1$)
short	signed 16-bit integer (-2^{16} to $2^{16} - 1$)
int	signed 32-bit integer (-2^{31} to $2^{31} - 1$)
long	signed 64-bit integer (-2^{63} to $2^{63} - 1$)
float	32-bit floating point (IEEE 754-1985)
double	64-bit floating point (IEEE 754-1985)

Data Type `char`

Most programming languages use the ASCII (American Standard Code for Information Interchange) character set, and their source code is composed of 7-bit ASCII characters. In short, most programs are in ASCII.

Java, on the other hand, adopts *Unicode*—an international character set standard. Unicode uses 16-bit characters, providing enough range to represent characters in all the world's major languages. Java source programs are written in Unicode. For example, $A\pi x\alpha7$ is a valid Java identifier. To create programs in Unicode, you need to use a Unicode text editor. Because ASCII code, when padded with a zero leading byte, is a subset of Unicode, programs written in ASCII are acceptable by Java.

Consistent with this international approach, the Java `char` type is a 16-bit quantity representing the Unicode of a character. Like `'A'` and `'Z'`, character constants are given between single quotes. A few special characters are specified by *escape sequences*. For example, `'\n'` is NEWLINE and `'\u03C0'` is π[1]. Table 1.2 lists all escape sequences.

Integer Types

Java provides `byte`, `short`, `int`, and `long` integer types using signed twos complement representation (Table 1.1). An integer constant is a sequence of octal, decimal, or hexadecimal digits. A leading `0` (zero) denotes an octal number. A leading `0x` or `0X` denotes a hexadecimal number. Otherwise, the constant is decimal. An integer constant is `int` unless it ends in L or l, which makes it `long`. An `int` constant in the valid range can be assigned to (or used as an initializer for) a `byte` or `short` variable directly.

Floating-Point Types

A floating-point constant is a sequence of decimal digits with an optional decimal point, followed by an optional exponent and ending in an optional f (F) or d (D). Table 1.3 shows some examples. A number is `double` (64-bit) unless it ends in f (F) for `float` (32-bit). Assigning a `double` value to a `float` variable requires explicit *type casting* (Section 2.12).

Floating-point classes `Double` and `Float` provide `static` fields:

```
Double.POSITIVE_INFINITY    +∞
Float.POSITIVE_INFINITY     +∞
Double.NEGATIVE_INFINITY    −∞
Float.NEGATIVE_INFINITY     −∞
```

---

[1]Unicode charts are extensive and available on the Web. Try http://www.unicode.org/charts

Table 1.2   CHARACTER ESCAPE SEQUENCES

\n	NEWLINE	\r	RETURN
\t	TAB	\f	FORMFEED
\'	SINGLE QUOTE	\"	DOUBLE QUOTE
\\	BACKSLASH	\b	BACKSPACE
\ooo	char in octal	\uhhhh	char in hexadecimal

They are produced as a result of floating-point arithmetic overflow. Their inverses are 0.0 and -0.0 respectively. The symbols Double.NaN (not a number) and Float.NaN result from invalid floating-point operations, such as dividing zero by zero or taking the square root of a negative number. The constants are testable using methods in the classes Double and Float. Java implements a subset of the IEEE-754 floating-point arithmetic standard.

Variables and Identifiers

A variable is an *identifier* referring to a memory location holding a value. There is more to an identifier than just naming the variable. It can be a class name, a method name, a field name, and so on. Java identifiers start with a Unicode letter (including _ and $) followed by any number of Unicode letters and digits. Thus, an identifier can be entirely in Chinese or Greek, for example. A mixture of characters from different languages is possible, but less useful. Java has a list of *reserved keywords*, such as class, double, public, and static, that cannot be used as identifiers. See Appendix B for a list of Java reserved keywords.

As mentioned before, the data type of a variable must be declared before it is used in a program. When a variable is declared it can also be initialized. For example:

```
int i = 7;
float x = 1.2f;
double pi = 3.141592653589793D;
```

Table 1.3   INTEGER AND FLOATING-POINT CONSTANTS

-9876	int	-9876L or -9876l	long
025	Octal int	0xFFF	Hex int
025L	Octal long	0XFFFL	Hex long
3.14159	double	314e-2 or 314E-2	(3.14) double
3.1416f or 3.1416F	float	314e-2d or 314E-2D	double

In general, a variable can be initialized with an arbitrary expression involving constants, other variables, and method calls. The types of expressions are described next.

In Java, a variable of primitive type holds values of that type. But an array variable (`type[] var;`) or an object variable (`ClassName var;`) holds values that refer to an array or an object. Such a value is called a *reference*.

1.5 DATA ABSTRACTION AND ENCAPSULATION

In programming, data structures represent quantities and attributes in a problem-solving process. The programming language construct that represents a data structure is called a *data type*. A data type is *concrete* when its exact structure and representation are known and subject to unrestricted manipulation. Traditional programming approaches make heavy use of concrete data types, often leading to unmanageable program complexity.

Data abstraction is the concept of defining data types and using them only through a set of allowed operations, barring direct manipulation of their representations. Thus, an *abstract data type* becomes a *black box* that provides *interface operations* to access and manipulate internal structures that are hidden and protected from direct access and alteration.

Hence, we know only about the *external behavior* of an abstract data type, not its internal representation. For example, not knowing details of the construction of a car, one can still drive it effectively, knowing behaviors such as "steering clockwise makes it turn right." This leaves the implementation of steering to the black box, which could use one of several alternatives: regular, power-assisted, rack-and-pinion, and so on.

In OOP, the *class* construct supports data abstraction. A class *attaches* interface operations to data to form a protected unit, hiding the internal data structures, representations, and code from disallowed access. The technique is called *encapsulation*. You write a class to define a new data type and use the class to create *objects* of that type. For example, an `Address` class gives you objects for different addresses.

Objects are thus self-contained and autonomous entities with well-defined behaviors. The external behavior of an object is an *interface contract* between the object and its *clients*, programs that use the object. The interface contract consists of data/operations made available by an object to external clients and documentations on their precise meaning.

In OOP, a program consists of classes and objects that are largely independent and interacts only through available interface operations. This organization significantly reduces overall complexity and helps the quality of the program in many different ways.

1.6 CLASSES AND OBJECTS

The Java *class* construct supports data abstraction through encapsulation. A class describes the construction of an object and serves as a blueprint to build objects. It specifies the inner workings as well as the public interface of an object. A class specifies *members* belonging to the class that may be *fields* (data) and *methods* (functions). Once a class is defined, the class name becomes a new data type and is used to declare variables of that type and create objects of that type.

First, a simplified class representing bank accounts is presented. BankAccount introduces our first example class for building objects. It illustrates how procedures are attached to data and how objects are established once a class is defined.

```java
///////    BankAccount.java    ///////

public class BankAccount      // class name
{
    public BankAccount(int id, String ss, double amt) // constructor
    {   acct_no = id;
        owner = ss;
        acct_bal = (amt > 0) ? amt : 0.0;
    }
    public double balance()
    {   return acct_bal;    }

    public void deposit(double amt)
    {   if ( amt > 0 ) acct_bal += amt; }

    public boolean withdraw(double amt)
    {   if ( amt <=0 || amt > acct_bal ) return false; // failure
        acct_bal -= amt;
        return true;                                   // success
    }

    public int id()
    {   return acct_no;    }

    public String owner()
    {   return owner;    }

    private int    acct_no;   // account number
    private String owner;     // owner ss
    private double acct_bal;  // current balance
```

```
// other members ...
}
```

Using *capitalized nouns* as class names is a style recommended and followed in this book. Here the class BankAccount is declared following this general form:

```
[ public ] class Name
{
        class body
}
```

The class body defines data members, method members, or both. The class BankAccount contains the data members

```
private int      acct_no;          // account number
private String   owner;            // owner ss
private double   acct_bal;         // current balance
```

the account number, owner social security number, and current balance of a bank account. Method members define functions or procedures in a class. For the BankAccount class the methods

```
public void deposit(double amt)
public boolean withdraw(double amt)
public double balance()
public String owner()
```

perform obvious tasks. In BankAccount, the identifier owner is used both as a field name and as a method name. There is no conflict.

Information Hiding and Member Access Control

An object can be thought of as an independent computing agent (a tiny computer) with its own storage and instruction set. The field members provide the storage, and the methods form the instruction set.

The Java class construct also specifies access control to its members. In a class, members are declared public, private, or package to achieve information hiding.

- *Public members* can be accessed by any code that can access the class.
- *Private members* can be accessed only by methods in the same class.
- *Package members* can be accessed freely by code in the same package. A member with no access specifier is a package member.

All a *client* of a class needs to know is the public interface (Figure 1.1). As long as the public members are well-documented, there is no need to know any implementation details. In the case of deposit, all that matters is putting the given amount amt into the account. Thus, knowledge of internal details

Figure 1.1   AN OBJECT

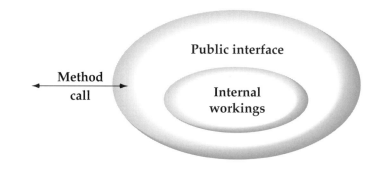

is confined to member methods. The class now provides BankAccount as an *abstract data type*.

An object embodies the abstract data item. Values stored in an object constitute its internal *state*, and public members of an object form its interface to the outside (other classes and objects). Thereby, an object *encapsulates* (envelops) a set of fields and methods. The encapsulating object is called the *host object* of its members.

Although all members, method or field, are thought of as being contained within each individual object, Java achieves this effect without having to replicate the member methods. The memory required for each object is essentially for storing the fields.

The BankAccount fields acct_no, owner, and acct_bal are declared private so their access is limited to member methods such as id() and balance(). No operations other than those specifically provided by the BankAccount class can be performed on these private members. In designing a class, you, the OO programmer, must design the public/private designations to support effective use and to maximize information hiding.

Creating Objects

Once a class is declared, objects of the class can be created. The class definition is the blueprint to build objects, and the objects are known as *instances of the class*. The class name becomes a type name and can be used to declare variables. A variable is either primitive type or reference type:

- Primitive variable—holds the value of a primitive quantity such as an int, a double, and so on
- Reference variable—holds the reference (memory address) to an object (Figure 1.2) or an array

Figure 1.2   CLASS, REFERENCES, AND OBJECTS

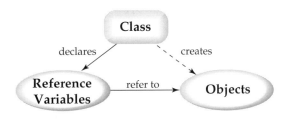

Thus a class or array variable is a *reference variable*. A reference is called a pointer, or a memory address in other languages. A reference variable can also hold the value null, which represents an invalid reference. For example, the code

```
BankAccount jack;          // no initial value
BankAccount susan
           = new BankAccount(105551234, "042-33-1212", 600.0);
```

declares two class-type variables jack and susan. The variable jack has no value yet. The value of susan references a newly created BankAccount object (Figure 1.3) with the given account number and a beginning balance of 600.

The Java operator new allocates space dynamically (at run time) and is used for creating objects (Section 3.10). The assignment

```
jack = new BankAccount(105556789, "024-00-4231", 540.0);
```

gives jack an object to reference. In Java, all objects are created at run time with the operator new.

Figure 1.3   CREATING OBJECTS

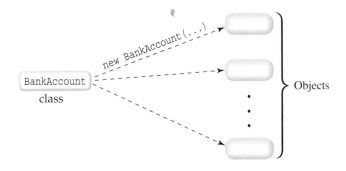

Constructors

In the `BankAccount` class, the member `BankAccount` is special. In general, a method with the same name as the class itself is called a *constructor* and is treated differently from other methods. The purpose of a constructor is to initialize fields in an object when it is created. For example, the expression

```
new BankAccount(105556789, "024-00-4231", 540.0);
```

allocates space for a `BankAccount` object and passes the values in parentheses to this constructor:

```
BankAccount(int, String, double)
```

The value returned by `new` is an *object reference*, which can be assigned to a variable such as `jack`. Thus, the constructor

```
public BankAccount(int id, String ss, double amt) // constructor
{   acct_no = id;
    owner = ss;
    acct_bal = (amt > 0) ? amt : 0.0;
}
```

provides the desired initialization of the fields `acct_no`, `owner`, and `acct_bal`. No return type of any kind is allowed in declaring a constructor, which should never return a value.

Member Access Notations

Once objects are built, they can be used to perform computations by accessing their methods and/or fields. It is understood that not every member of an object is accessible from the outside. Members of an object are accessed (referenced) with the *dot* (.), or *member-of*, operator. For example:

```
susan.deposit(25.60);        // deposit into BankAccount object susan
double bal = susan.balance(); // retrieve balance of susan
susan.withdraw(25.0);        // take 25 out of susan
from.acct_bal -= amt;        // decrease from's balance          (1)
to.acct_bal += amt;          // increase to's balance            (2)
```

Because `acct_bal` is a private member, the assignments on lines 1 and 2 are possible only inside a method of `BankAccount`.

Clearly, the general syntax to reference a member is as follows:

object . *member*

This notation does not work for a constructor, which is not considered a method in a class.

Figure 1.4   INSTANCE METHOD AS COMPUTATION UNIT

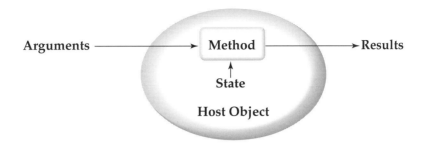

Methods

Let's look at the methods in the class BankAccount. Note that the method

```
public void deposit(double amt)
{    acct_bal += amt;    }
```

takes only one argument, the amt to be deposited. There is no mention of the target account to which the deposit is made. But the method deposit is always attached to a specific account when it is called. In OOP, methods are not pure procedures but a procedure attached to a host object, like an accelerator to a car. There is never a need to worry about which car you are driving when you depress the accelerator. Because objects are instances of classes, methods attached to objects are known as *instance methods* (Figure 1.4). Unless otherwise designated, a method in Java is always an instance method.

Because deposit is a member method, it can access other members in the host object (acct_bal for example) directly without using the *object.member* notation. All members in a class are accessible by member methods.

At this point, you should have enough information to read the methods withdraw and balance.

1.7 STRING BASICS

A string is a sequence of characters. Java provides a built-in class String to deal with character strings. A String object represents a string and is sometimes simply referred to as a string. You have already seen strings used in System.out.println calls and in the argument of main(). The statement

```
String msg = "Happy Birthday";
```

initializes msg with a reference to a String object (allocated by new) containing the given string. Each string has a length() method that returns the number of characters in the string. Individual characters in a string are accessible by indexing. For example, `msg.charAt(0)` is `'H'` and `msg.length()` returns 14.

In Java, a variable of primitive type holds values of that type. A variable of a user-defined type (a class, for example), however, holds a *reference to an object of that type*. For example, a string variable can hold a reference to any string object. Therefore, it is possible to assign another `String` reference to the variable `msg`:

```
msg = "Many happy returns";
```

However, a string object itself is *read-only*, or *immutable*, after creation. To make a copy of a string object use:

```
String s2 = new String(s1);
```

The code `(str1 == str2)` tests whether the two variables refer to the same object. The `String` method

```
str1.equals(str2)
```

tests whether the two strings contain the same characters. The method call

```
str1.compareTo(str2)
```

returns positive, zero, or negative if `str1` is greater than, equal to, or less than `str2`.

String Concatenation

The operator + can be used to concatenate two strings, creating a new string. The example `Average` has applied this feature already. You can also concatenate a string with a primitive type or an object. For example:

```
System.out.println("Ans= " + factorial(n));
```

When one operand is a string, the + operator automatically converts the other argument to a string and concatenates them. The conversion also takes place when += is used with a string left-hand argument (e.g., `str += 3;`). Thus, the code

```
msg = "" + var;
```

can be used to easily obtain the string representation of `var`.

Whereas a `String` is read-only, a `StringBuffer` is a *mutable* string and provides methods for building and modifying the string. More details on `String` and `StringBuffer` are described in Section 2.9.

String Representation of Objects

Java knows how to convert any value of primitive type to a string. But, it depends on the toString method to convert an object to its string representation. The toString method also makes displaying objects in a class easy.

For example, add the following to BankAccount

```
public String toString()
{    return acct_no + ":" + owner + ":" + acct_bal;
}
```

and you can display BankAccount objects v with the following:

```
System.out.print("Account=" + susan);
System.out.println(jack);
```

Thus, when you define the method toString appropriately in a class, objects of that class can be converted to strings automatically and displayed easily.

1.8 ARRAYS

In Java, an array is an object that contains a number of consecutive memory locations, *array cells*, each of which holds data of the same type. For example,

```
int[] b = new int[10];        (creating an array)
```

declares an array reference variable b and initializes it with the address of an int array. Here, the operator new creates an array of 10 cells, b[0] through b[9], each just large enough to hold an int, and returns a reference to the newly created array.

Each array object has a field length recording the array's length at the time of creation. For example, b.length is 10. In Java *arrays are always created with new and array index goes from zero to the length minus one*. This is important to keep in mind. Here are some typical usages:

```
int n, i = 0;
for (i = 0 ; i < 10 ; i++) b[i] = 0;
n = b[i + 1] - 13;
```

The array p can be declared and initialized to hold the first 10 prime numbers as follows:

```
int[] p = {2,3,5,7,11,13,17,19,23,29};
```

The construct after the = is an *array initializer*. It is a shorthand for creating the array with new and then assigning values to the cells. Figure 1.5 provides a graphical representation of the array p.

Figure 1.5   **INTEGER ARRAY p**

p[0]	p[1]	p[2]	p[3]	p[4]	p[5]	p[6]	p[7]	p[8]	p[9]
2	3	5	7	11	13	17	19	23	29

Once an array is created, its cells can be used to store and retrieve data of a given type. Cells are accessed using the index notation p[i] where each array cell can be thought of and treated as a separate variable. Thus, an array can be viewed as a set of subscripted variables.

The simple declaration

```
int[] arr;
```

declares arr as an array variable but does not allocate cells for it. Array cells must be allocated before they can be accessed. The assignment

```
arr = b;
```

makes arr refer to the same object as b. The assignment

```
arr = new int[30];
```

assigns the reference to a newly allocated array object with 30 cells to arr.

Putting arrays to use, an AccountManager object holds an array of bank accounts and provides various management functions.

```
///////    AccountManager.java    ///////

public class AccountManager
{   AccountManager(BankAccount[] acc)
    {   accounts = acc;    }

    void display()
    {   for (int i = 0; i < accounts.length ; i++)      // (1)
            System.out.println( accounts[i] );          // (2)
    }

 // other methods not shown

    private BankAccount[] accounts;
}
```

For simplicity, we show only a display method to list the accounts. A for loop uses the array length conveniently to display each account (line 1) through the toString method of BankAccount (line 2).

The following test program puts `AccountManager` to use:

```
public class TestAcc
{ public static void main(String[] args)
  { BankAccount[] arr = new BankAccount[3];                      // (3)
    arr[0] = new BankAccount(233445678, "043-22-1004", 32.0); // (4)
    arr[1] = new BankAccount(143741234, "055-11-4546", 98.0);
    arr[2] = new BankAccount(453850357, "011-23-4567", 66.0); // (5)
    AccountManager am = new AccountManager(arr);                 // (6)
    am.display();                                                // (7)
  }
}
```

The `main` method establishes a reference variable `arr` and initializes it with a `BankAccount` array of length 3 (line 3). Three accounts are put into the array (lines 4–5), by calling the method `displayAccounts` (line 4). An `AccountManager` object is instantiated with the array (line 6) and is told to display the accounts (line 7).

Running this program produces the following output:

```
233445678:043-22-1004:32.0
143741234:055-11-4546:98.0
453850357:011-23-4567:66.0
```

An array, once created, has a fixed dimension. The `java.util` package provides an `ArrayList` class that functions as an *extensible array* of objects. In addition to being extensible automatically, an `ArrayList` can also hold *any type object*. Coverage of this nice utility can be found in Section 4.19.

1.9 METHOD INVOCATION AND ARGUMENT PASSING

For writing methods and calling them to perform computations, a fundamental understanding of how methods are called and arguments passed is essential.

Java supports *method overloading*, defining multiple methods with the same name. Overloaded methods must be different in the arguments they take (Section 3.9). For example, the `System.out.println` method is overloaded and it can take a string, an int, a double, and so on. The Java compiler knows which one of the multiple versions of an overloaded method to call by examining the call's arguments. Overloading simplifies method naming and eliminates the need to invent different names for methods that do the same thing but take different arguments.

A method is always encapsulated in a class. The method header specifies the number and type of *formal parameters* required. Java does not support optional or variable-length parameters. Within a class, a method is identified not only by its name but also by its formal parameter list. Thus, the same method name may be *defined more than once* with different formal parameters to achieve method overloading.

When calling a method, the correct number and type of arguments must be supplied. The arguments in the method call are known as the *actual arguments* or simply *arguments*. The BankAccount method deposit has a formal parameter amt. In the method call bob.deposit(x), the variable x becomes the actual argument. When a method call is executed, the value (primitive data or object reference) of an actual argument is passed to the corresponding formal parameter so the value can be used in the body of the method. This activity is called *argument passing*. When a method with more than one argument is called, arguments are evaluated sequentially from left to right as they are passed.

Parameters in a method header are formal in the sense that any name can be used for them without changing the meaning of the method. The same situation is found in mathematics where the notations $f(x) = x^2$ and $f(y) = y^2$ define the same function. Formal parameters are local to a method.

When calling a method, the formal parameter receives *a copy of the value of the actual argument*. Consider a primitive type variable abc_arg passed to a parameter abc_par. The increment abc_par++ will not change the value of abc_arg. Now, consider a reference variable (Section 1.6) jack, of type BankAccount, say. The variable jack holds only a reference to an object, not the object itself. Passing jack in a method call passes a copy of the reference value. The receiving parameter account, say, will reference the same object. The operation account.deposit(50.0) will cause the balance of jack to increase. Thus, both of the following statements are true:

1. *In Java, arguments are always passed by value.*
2. *In Java, primitive data are passed by value and objects (including arrays) are passed by reference.*

The called method can do anything to the passed value (a copy) without affecting the value of the argument in the caller. But if the state of a passed object is changed by the called method, the object in the calling method is changed because it is the same object (Figure 1.6).

Figure 1.6   PASSING OBJECTS BY REFERENCE

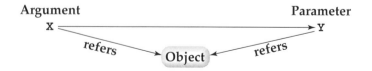

1.10 STANDARD I/O

For every Java program, there are three *standard I/O streams*:

Standard input: The standard input stream reads from the keyboard and is represented by the built-in I/O object `System.in`. The `System.in.read()` call returns a single byte (value 0–255) as an `int` or `-1` upon end-of-file.

Standard output: The standard output sends output to the display and is represented by the built-in I/O object `System.out`. The `System.out.write(int c)` method outputs the low byte of c to standard output. The `System.out.println( str )` call outputs the given string *str* followed by a platform-dependent line terminator. The `System.out.print( str )` call outputs without the end-of-line. The two methods also display any Java primitive data and any object that can be automatically converted to a string.

Standard error: The standard error output stream (`System.err`) is just like the standard output stream. However, standard error is used for displaying error or diagnostic messages that should come to the immediate attention of the user.

1.11 COMMAND-LINE ARGUMENTS AND main

The `main` method is special in a Java class; properly declared, it marks a starting point for program execution by the Java interpreter. A `main` method also receives arguments specified on the command line when a Java program is executed. The *command-line arguments* are passed as strings to `main` in the class whose name appears on the command line.

The Java interpreter expects a `main` method to be declared as:

```
public static void main(String[] args)
```

The number of command-line arguments is `args.length`. The first argument is `args[0]`, the second `args[1]`, and so on. If the command line is

java *Xyz arg1 arg2*

the `main` of class *Xyz* is passed two arguments:

`args.length`	is 2
`args[0]`	is the string *arg1*
`args[1]`	is the string *arg2*

Besides being called by the Java interpreter in the beginning, a `main` method can also be called by your own code just like any other static method.

Now consider a program that receives command-line arguments. To keep it simple, all the program does is echo the command-line arguments to standard output:

```
class Echo
{   public static void main(String[] args)
    {   for (int i = 0; i < args.length; i++)
            System.out.print(args[i] + " ");
        System.out.println();   // outputs line terminator
    }
}
```

The program displays each entry of args. To separate the strings, the program displays a SPACE after each args[i], and the last argument is followed by a line terminator.

Let's consider the factorial program and make it receive a command-line argument *n* and display *n*!:

```
//  Computes n factorial.
//  Usage:  java Factorial n

public class Factorial
{   public static void main(String[] args)
    {   if ( args.length != 1 )
            System.err.println("Usage: Factorial n");
        int n = Integer.parseInt(args[0]);
        if ( n >= 0 && n < 13 )
            System.out.println(factorial(n));
        else
            System.err.println("Factorial("+ n +")?");
    }

    /* put factorial method here */
}
```

The first statement in main checks the number of command-line arguments supplied. The object System.err is used to send error output to the display. The first argument supplied on the command line, args[0], is converted into an int value by:

```
Integer.parseInt(args[0]);       // converts string to int
```

The parseInt method in the Integer class knows how to obtain an int from its string representation.

Integer is an example of Java *wrapper classes* (Double, Float, etc.) for primitive types (Section 3.3). Wrapper classes allow you to convert primitive type data to/from objects easily. They also supply other useful methods.

To detect a specific command-line argument, use the `equals` method of `String`. For example:

```
if ( args[0].equals("-verbose") ) // Is 1st arg -verbose?

if ( args[1].equals("-debug") )   // Is 2nd arg -debug?
```

Note that the return type of `main` is `void`, and the Java interpreter expects no return value from `main`. The Java interpreter generates an *exit status*, made available to the interpreter's invoking environment, to indicate whether the program executed successfully and terminated normally. For example, on UNIX systems a zero exit status indicates successful or normal execution of the program, while a nonzero (usually positive) exit status indicates abnormal termination. The code

```
System.exit(status);
```

can be used explicitly by your program to abort execution and return an exit status.

1.12   PROBLEM SOLVING WITH OBJECTS

With OOP you solve problems with interacting objects. To illustrate what this means in a simple way, consider a problem from plane geometry: "Given four vertices A, B, C, and D in the x-y plane, determine whether $ABCD$ is a rectangle."

Clearly one direct way to make the determination is to decide whether the neighboring sides of $ABCD$ are all mutually perpendicular. An ad hoc procedure can be written for this purpose to solve the problem, but that is the traditional procedure-oriented approach.

The OO approach first identifies the interacting objects in the problem domain. Here the objects are the vertices and the sides. The sides are determined by the vertices, and the orthogonal properties of neighboring sides lead to the solution. A little more analysis leads to the identification of two-dimensional vectors as the object needed because they can represent a vertex or a side. Thus, for the OO solution of the given problem, a `Vector2D` class is first established.

A Simple Vector2D Class

Vectors in 2-D space are familiar geometric objects. A vector **v** has an x-component and a y-component:

$$\mathbf{v} = (x, y)$$

This vector can represent a point at coordinates (x, y). The vector difference

$$\mathbf{v}_3 = \mathbf{v}_2 - \mathbf{v}_1$$

gives $\mathbf{v}_3$, representing the line from $\mathbf{v}_1$ to $\mathbf{v}_2$ (Figure 1.7). Vectors have many well-defined arithmetic and other kinds of operations.

Next, a class Vector2D is defined to model 2-D vectors:

```
//////// Vector2D.java //////////

public class Vector2D
{    public Vector2D() {}

    public Vector2D(float a, float b)
    {   x = a;
        y = b;
    }
    public boolean equals(Vector2D v)
    {   return  x == v.x && y == v.y ; }

    public boolean nonzero()
    {   return ( x != 0.0f || y != 0.0f ); }

    public float inner(Vector2D a)
    {   return x*a.x + y*a.y; }

    private static float delta = 0.00000001f;
    private float x, y;
 // additional members ...
}
```

For the class Vector2D, the two private fields

```
private float  x, y;
```

Figure 1.7   2D VECTORS

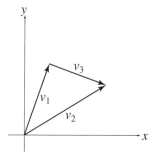

represent the *x* and *y* direction components of a vector. In addition there are several public methods. The method `inner`

```
public float inner(Vector2D a)
```

receives a `Vector2D` object argument and returns a `float` value. Again, because `inner` is a class member, it is allowed to access the private members x, y (in the host object) and a.x, a.y (in object a). For example,

```
Vector2D u = new Vector2D(2.0, 3.0);
Vector2D v = new Vector2D(4.0, 5.0);

u.inner(v);
```

computes the inner product of the vectors u (host object of `inner`) and v (argument to `inner`). Here the `Vector2D` v is passed to the method `inner` of the object u. Because the data in the host object (u in this case) are already available, `inner` requires only one argument. The methods `nonzero` and `equals` are simple.

The Null Constructor

The `Vector2D` constructor is overloaded, as constructors usually are. The version

```
public Vector2D(float a, float b)
{   x = a;
    y = b;
}
```

provides the desired initialization of the fields x and y.

The other constructor of `Vector2D` takes no arguments. A constructor that takes no arguments, called a *null constructor*, must be present to allow the usage

```
new Vector2D()
```

where no argument is passed to the constructor. Such a constructor is also known as a *no-args constructor*. In this example, as in many other occasions, the null constructor happens to do nothing. However, the body of a no-args constructor does not have to be empty.

A null constructor that does nothing is sometimes automatically supplied for a class:

- If a class defines no constructor at all, a null constructor that does nothing is supplied automatically.
- If a class defines any constructor, a null constructor is not automatically supplied. This is fine if the null constructor is not needed. However, if it is needed, an appropriate one must be given explicitly.

This is why the null constructor that does nothing is sometimes also known as the *default constructor*.

Additional `Vector2D` Methods

The `Vector2D` method `minus` supplies a procedure for subtracting any given `Vector2D` from the host object and returns a `Vector2D` that is the difference:

```
public Vector2D minus(Vector2D a)
{   Vector2D tmp = new Vector2D();
    tmp.x = x - a.x;
    tmp.y = y - a.y;
    return tmp;
}
```

To subtract vector w from v, use `v.minus(w)`. The `Vector2D` method

```
public boolean isPerpendicular(Vector2D b)
{   return ( nonzero() && b.nonzero()
                  && Math.abs(x * b.x + y * b.y) < delta );
}
```

determines whether the given vector b is perpendicular to the host vector. Because the operation involves floating-point arithmetic, a tolerance of `delta` is used. The `static` method abs in the `java.lang.Math` class computes the absolute value. The `Math` class supplies a set of static fields and methods useful for common mathematical computations (Appendix H). All basic Java language classes in the package `java.lang` can be used directly in your Java program.

For object display, add to `Vector2D` this method:

```
public String toString()
{   return( "(" + x + ",  " + y + ')' );
}
```

The `Vector2D` class will allow the formulation of a nice OO solution to the *rectangle problem* originally posed.

1.13 SOLUTION VIA OBJECTS

The `Vector2D.java` file is now in place. A solution for the given plane geometry problem that makes use of `Vector2D` objects can then be constructed. The approach is simple:

1. Represent the given vertices *A*, *B*, *C*, and *D* as four `Vector2D` objects.
2. Subtract neighboring vertices to get the sides that are again `Vector2D` objects.
3. Determine perpendicularity through inner product of neighboring sides.

With the `Vector2D` class, the task at hand is reduced to reading the four vertices from the user and testing whether the neighboring sides (as vectors) are all perpendicular. Writing a class `Rect` accomplishes this.

```
///////    Rect.java    ///////
import java.io.*;  // import classes from java.io package as needed

class Rect
{  public static Vector2D getPoint(int i)
        throws IOException
    {   String s; float x = 0.0f, y = 0.0f;
        BufferedReader in = new BufferedReader(          // (A)
            new InputStreamReader(System.in));
        System.out.print("x" + i + "= ");
        System.out.flush();  s = in.readLine();          // (B)
        x = Float.parseFloat(s);                         // (C)
        System.out.print("y" + i + "= ");
        System.out.flush();  s = in.readLine();
        y = Float.parseFloat(s);
        return new Vector2D(x,y);
    }

  //  main listed later
}
```

The declaration

```
import java.io.*;
```

tells the compiler to *import* any classes in the *package* `java.io` supplied by Java as needed. It is a good idea to include this line at the beginning of any `.java` file that performs I/O. The wildcard * matches any class name[2] in the package. Use a specific class name instead of * to import a particular class. Classes in the `java.lang` package are basic and do not need importing. Java packages and their use are discussed in Section 6.1.

The `getPoint` methods first create a `BufferedReader` object connected to standard input (line A). The `readLine` method of a `BufferedReader` object is most convenient for reading input text lines (Section 6.11). To prompt for user input, we use `System.out.print`, which does not send a line terminator at the end that normally forces the output. Hence, we use `System.out.flush()` to force output. Then the program reads a line from standard input (line B) and converts the string into a proper `float` value (line C). The x and y values are used to create a new `Vector2D`, which is returned. A well-formed string can be converted to any target primitive type, using the technique shown on line C.

---

[2]A simple class name not containing the . character

With the getPoint method, a main method can be written to provide the desired solution.

```
public static void main(String[] args)
        throws IOException
{   int i;
    System.out.println("Enter vertices 0, 1, 2, 3");
 // input four points
    Vector2D[] point = new Vector2D[4];                    // (1)
    for ( i = 0; i < 4; i++) point[i] = getPoint(i);
    for ( i = 0; i < 4; i++)
        System.out.print(point[i] + "   ");
 // check sides for perpendicularity
    Vector2D v;
    Vector2D u = point[1].minus(point[0]);                 // (2)
    for ( i = 0; i < 3; i++)
    {   v = point[(i + 2) % 4].minus(point[i + 1]);    // (3)
        if ( ! u.isPerpendicular(v) )
        {   System.out.println("No, not a rectangle.");
            return;
        }
        u = v;
    }
    System.out.println("Yes, a rectangle.");
}
```

After reading in the coordinates for the four vertices (in sequence), four Vector2D objects are in the array point (line 1). Then a vector u (line 2) representing one side of the quadrilateral is calculated by subtracting the vectors representing the two end points. Vector subtraction is by the minus method (line 2). A second Vector2D object v is made for an adjacent side (line 3). The perpendicularity of u and v is checked. After checking all sides, the right conclusion can be made.

Assuming the file Vector2D.class has already been produced, compile Rect.java and run the program to give it a try. Following is a sample run:

java Rect

```
Enter vertices 0, 1, 2, 3
x0= 0
y0= 0
x1= 0
y1= 1
x2= 1
y2= 1
x3= 1
```

```
y3= 0
(0,  0) (0,  1) (1,  1) (1,  0) Yes, a rectangle.
```

Because in this instance one is able to work with vectors that correspond to real geometric objects, the solution is stated simply and elegantly with geometric concepts and it is very simple to explain and understand. More importantly, the Vector2D class can help in many other situations in plane geometry. Hence, the class has potential for reuse.

Furthermore, the object-based solution is easily adaptable to changes in the problem specification. For instance, determining whether $ABCD$ is a parallelogram involves almost no change to the program. Just add a method isParallel(Vector2D b) to Vector2D if it is not already there.

1.14 OBJECT-ORIENTED THINKING

The traditional approach to program design involves breaking down a given problem into a number of steps. Each step is either simple and straightforward or has to be broken down further into finer steps. Sequences of steps form procedures that combine to solve the problem. This approach is known as *procedure-oriented decomposition*.

Object orientation involves a whole new way of thinking. Program design begins with identifying the interacting entities, or objects, in a given problem. In a banking application, for example, objects can be accounts, customers, credit records, monthly statements, and so on. The key is thinking in terms of concepts and items present in the problem domain rather than programming artifacts in the computer language domain. An object may represent a physical item such as a monthly statement or a logical item such as a transaction. Objects must be self-contained and must correspond to well-understood concepts in the problem domain. Thinking with the *language of the problem*, not the language of the computer, is essential. Some objects may have to be further broken down into smaller constituent objects. This approach is known as *object-oriented decomposition*. Objects thus identified lead to software objects, defined by classes, that simulate real ones in the problem domain.

The interactions among the problem-domain objects must then be considered carefully to define the external behavior of the objects and their interdependence. After that, class definitions of the objects can be coded. The set of all public fields and methods forms the *public interface* of objects in a class. The public interface must support the intended external behavior precisely. It determines how objects are used by other parts of the program. Hiding behind the public interface are internal workings kept from outside access. Thus, object orientation decouples the internal workings of objects from the rest of the program and significantly reduces program complexity. Internal fields and methods can be modified without affecting other parts of the program as long as the public interface is preserved.

A good OO design takes into account features such as generalizations of the given problem, possible future extensions, reuse of existing code, ease of modification, and so on. The ideas discussed here will become more concrete as you become more familiar with OOP mechanisms and their proper use under Java. Chapter 13 contains more information on object-oriented design (OOD), and it may be advantageous for readers to take a look at the early sections there as well.

1.15 CODE ORGANIZATION

Note the following points about managing your Java programs:

- Java source code files use the `.java` suffix.
- Compiling Java source files with the compiler **javac** produces bytecode files with the `.class` suffix.
- There are no C/C++-style header files in Java.
- A program consists of one or more classes in one or more files.
- A public class *Abc* must be in its own file named *Abc*.`java`.
- Source code files can be organized into *packages* (Section 6.1).
- Classes with no explicitly declared package names are in the package unnamed.
- A file can use classes from other files directly. To use a class from a different package, the class name must be qualified by its package name. Classes from the basic `java.lang` package can be used directly.
- A file can *import* one or more classes from another package and then use those classes with their simple names.

1.16 PROGRAMMING TIPS

Following are some basic programming tips to make writing Java programs easier:

- Import `java.io.*` if you use more than simple standard I/O.
- Always terminate a declaration. A class definition has no terminating semicolon.
- A simple statement must be terminated by a semicolon, but this is not true for a compound statement.
- The `main` method of a class is declared:

```
public static void main(String[] args)
```

The `main` method does not return a value and receives `args.length` command-line arguments in `args[0]`, `args[1]`, and so on.

- Array and object variables have reference values. A variable must first be given a value, either through initialization or assignment, before being used.
- Arrays and objects are created dynamically with the operator `new`, which returns a reference to the newly created object.
- Use zero-based indexing for arrays. An array of length 100 is indexed from 0 to 99. Remember that `arr.length` gives the length of the array `arr` and `str.length()` returns the length of the string `str`.
- Use `System.in`, `System.out`, and `System.err` for standard I/O.
- Arguments are always passed by value in method calls.
- Loops in Java use continuation conditions. The iteration ends when the condition becomes false.
- Use the operator + to concatenate all types of data with strings.
- Learn useful idioms such as `for ( ;; )` (infinite loop), `for(int i=0 ; i < j ; i++)`, `while(i-- > 0)`, and `while( (c=System.in.read()) != -1 )`. (Idioms will be pointed out throughout the book.)
- Always access an instance method or field through a host object (e.g., `susan.deposit(45.50);`).
- The call `System.exit(status);` aborts program execution and returns an *exit status*.
- Use `boolean`, not zero/nonzero, values in logical expressions.

Class Style

Recommended also is a consistent set of conventions for defining classes, as follows:

- Use capitalized nouns for class names. `BankAccount` and `Vector2D` are examples. Multiple words can be concatenated with each word capitalized, as in `BankAcct` and `GroupLeader`.
- Declare a class `public` if it may be used by other programs.
- Place a public class in a file whose name coincides with the class name.
- Group public members in the beginning of a class, methods before fields. (Note: class members can be given in any order.) Document public members for application programming and nonpublic members for code maintenance.
- If a class has an explicitly defined constructor, it normally should also have a null constructor.

Program examples in this book follow these conventions closely. However, because explanations are usually included in the text, the examples tend not to have extensive comments.

1.17 SUMMARY

A Java program consists of one or more classes in one or more files. A class is a blueprint for building objects. Members in a class are either *methods* (procedures) or *fields* (data or objects). All methods and fields must be contained within classes.

Java source files use the `.java` suffix, and compiled (bytecode) files use the `.class` suffix. You use the compiler **javac** to compile and the interpreter **Java** to run a program. Given a class to run, the Java interpreter automatically loads all necessary `.class` files, then calls the `main` method of the given class.

Java is a language with strong typing. Every quantity has a type, and the compiler and the loader check for type correctness in a program. Java has eight primitive types: `byte`, `char`, `short`, `int`, `long`, `float`, `double`, and `boolean`. Sizes of these types are predefined and machine-independent.

Operators, expressions, declarations, statements, flow/iteration controls, and method definition are similar to ANSI C (or C++). Important differences include the following:

- Java primitive type sizes are platform-independent.
- Java uses 16-bit Unicode characters.
- Java uses `true`/`false` instead of nonzero/zero.
- Java has no `unsigned` declaration, and all integer types use signed twos complement representation.
- Java strings (`String`) and arrays are objects.
- Java supports both `>>` and `>>>` shift operators.
- Java allows `break`/`continue` to a labeled outer loop.
- Java requires explicit casting from `int` to `char`.
- Java methods must be enclosed in classes.
- A method uses a `throws` clause to specify an exception that may result from a call to the method.

Appendix C provides a more detailed list of such differences. Appendix K gives basic background material for Java.

An object encapsulates methods and fields to form an independent computing unit. It hides internal workings and is used only through its public interface, achieving data abstraction. The isolation of object internals from the rest of a program greatly reduces the complexity of a program. A class describes the structure of an object and controls outside access to class members, which can be primitive data, methods, and other objects. Member access specifiers include `public`, `private`, and `package`.

Once defined, a class name becomes a user-defined type and can be used to: (1) declare reference variables of that type, and (2) create objects of that type (with the operator `new`). An object is the host of its members, and the members are accessed via the host object with the `.` operator. In a class, a member is an instance member unless declared `static`, which makes it a classwide member.

Arrays and strings are objects in Java. The length field (length() method) of an array (a string) gives the length of the object.

Java methods can be overloaded, and the exact method to call is determined by the arguments supplied. When calling a method, arguments are always passed by value. The actual arguments are evaluated sequentially from left to right. Because object-type variables have reference values, arrays, strings, and other objects are effectively passed by reference. The static main of a class can receive arguments supplied on the command line.

Using objects to solve problems is natural and effective. An object-oriented solution involves identifying the interacting objects in the problem domain and building classes to model their behavior. A sequence of interactions among the objects can represent the solution to a given problem. A different sequence of interactions can solve other similar problems in the same problem domain. The *rectangle* example drives these points home.

EXERCISES

Review Questions

1. What is data abstraction? Encapsulation? What Java construct achieves data abstraction? Through what means?

2. How do you declare a class-type variable? Create an object of that class? Show sample code.

3. What notation is used to call an instance method? What is the significance of the host object to an instance method?

4. What is a constructor? A null (default) constructor?

5. Tell, in your own words, the significance of solving problems with objects.

6. Examine the method definition

```
static int myabs(int a)
{   if (a >= 0)
    {   return a; };
    else
    {   return -a; };
}
```

and spot any syntax problems. Enclose it in a class, compile it, and see what your Java compiler says. Explain in detail the source of any error.

7. Certain identifiers are *keywords* reserved by Java and cannot be used for other purposes. Name 15 Java keywords.

8. When reading from standard input, end of file is normally reached when the user types CTRL-D (or CTRL-Z, or some other system-dependent character) at the beginning of a line. Find out what it is on your system.

9. Consider class member method definition and invocation. Can the deposit method be used with the notation BankAccount.deposit(400.0); to deposit 400.0? Why or why not?

10. Consider the BankAccount class given in Section 1.6. Are the declarations or statements

```
BankAccount paul;
BankAccount mary();
new BankAccount jennie();
new BankAccount charlee(100312345, "Charles Williams", 500.00);
```

grammatically correct? Are they possible? Please explain.

11. Consider the null constructor of Vector2D

```
Vector2D() { }
```

Is there a missing semicolon at the end? Why?

12. Consider the following:

```
BankAccount sally
            = new BankAccount(100312345, "034-54-3210", 540.60);
```

Is the call sally.BankAccount(100367890, "304-56-1234", 1000.00) possible? Why or why not?

13. How do you read standard input one line at a time?

14. How do you take a string representation of a Float and turn that into a Float value?

15. In a Java program, how do you determine the number of command-line arguments supplied to the program?

16. Is it possible to run a Java program with multiple classes having main methods? If so, how is the entry point to the program determined?

17. What is CLASSPATH? How do you set and use CLASSPATH for compiling or running a Java program? (Hint: See Appendix A.)

Programming Assignments

1. Write a simple `main` method to display some single characters, strings, integers, and floating-point numbers using the `System.out` object.

2. Explain why calling `factorial(j)` repeatedly with j being $0, 1, 2, \ldots$ is very inefficient. Write a more efficient method to produce a list of factorial values. Also in this method, use `short` for the formal parameter and `long` for the answer.

3. Write a method `void octalDisplay(int n)` that displays the integer n in octal notation.

4. Consider the `octalDisplay` method in the previous problem. Rewrite the method to use bitwise operations to achieve the modulo 8 and the divide by 8 operations.

5. Write a method `isLeapYear` that takes an integer year and returns a `boolean`. (Hint: Use the % operator.)

6. A *bitonic* sequence of integers consists of one monotonic sequence of zero or more elements followed by another. For example, 2,2,3,4,3,2 and 4,3,1,2,7 are both bitonic. Using the `monotonic` method in Appendix K as a model, write a `bitonic` method.

7. Add a member method `transfer` for the `BankAccount` class that transfers a given amount from another account to the host account.

8. Write a reverse echo program that takes all words on the command line and displays them in reverse order and with each word backwards, character by character.

9. Add a method `public void enterAccount()` to the class `AccountManager` (Section 1.8) that prompts the user and retrieves information from standard input (the keyboard) to create one or more new `BankAccounts` and add them to the array of accounts in the `AccountManager` object.

10. Add the member method

    `isParallel(Vector2D v)`

    to the `Vector2D` class to test whether a vector v is parallel to the host vector. Given any four points, use `Vector2D` objects to determine whether they form a parallelogram.

11. Modeling after `Vector2D`, write a `Vector3D` class. Be sure to include a `crossProduct` method, a `toString` method, and an `equals` method.

## CHAPTER TWO

Java Features and Constructs

Introductory material in the first chapter allows you to write simple programs and use objects. Here we begin to cover many subjects in depth and to show the usage of important Java features and constructs:

- I/O—standard and file I/O, with simple error and exception handling. An example demonstrates ASCII character I/O.
- Identifiers—name spaces and scoping rules.
- Instance and static members—definition, access, and initialization.
- Array usage—applications and multidimensional arrays.
- String and StringBuffer classes—understanding and effective use of these basic objects.
- Type conversions—implicit conversions by the compiler and explicit conversion by casting.

A class can include *instance members* and *class-wide members*. The important distinction between an *instance member* and a *class-wide member* is explained clearly. Examples show how class-wide members are useful.

Many examples are given to illustrate the concepts and constructs. A Fraction class shows both instantiation control and display through string conversion. A Matrix class illustrates two-dimensional array usage.

2.1 ASCII CHARACTER I/O

To illustrate ASCII character (byte) input and output, two of the most basic operations, we can write a complete program that does the following:

- Reads ASCII characters from standard input
- Converts uppercase characters into lowercase characters
- Writes all characters to standard output

```
///////    Lowercase.java    ///////
import java.io.IOException;

class Lowercase
{   public static void main(String[] args)
        throws IOException                          // throws clause    (A)
    {   int i;
        while ( (i = System.in.read()) != -1 )
                                                    // input ASCII char (B)
        {   i = Character.toLowerCase( (char) i);
            System.out.write(i);
        }
    }
}
```

The `System.in.read` method (line B) reads a single character and returns either the positive integer code of the character or −1 to indicate end of input. `System.out.write(i)` outputs the low byte of i. The `while` loop in this example will repeat until end of input is reached. When input is from the keyboard, a system-dependent convention is used to signify the end of input. For example, on UNIX systems type ^D (CTRL-D) at the beginning of a line. On PCs, use ^Z (CTRL-Z) instead.

The static method `toLowerCase` of the class `Character` returns the lowercase equivalent of the given character. If it has no lowercase equivalent, the character itself will be returned.

Please note that character I/O using

```
System.in.read()
System.out.write(int i)
```

works only for ASCII characters. Java provides facilities for convenient text I/O based on a platform-specified character encoding. A program using `InputStreamReader`, `OutputStreamWriter`, and `PrintWriter` (Section 6.11) for character I/O will work in either the ASCII or the Unicode environment.

A `throws` clause (line A), as part of a method header, specifies that a certain error or *exception* may result from a call to the method. In this example, it is because `System.in.read()` may throw an `IOException`. We will return to this topic in Section 2.3.

Compile and run `Lowercase.java`. Type a mixture of upper- and lowercase characters on the keyboard and press RETURN. You should see the same line displayed, with all uppercase characters turned into lowercase characters. Type as many input lines as you like, then terminate the input properly.

2.2 FILE I/O

Section 1.10 mentioned `System.in`, `System.out`, and `System.err`, three ready-made objects for I/O. These objects are *instances* of classes supplied by the Java I/O stream library (package `java.io`).

While these standard objects take care of terminal I/O, there are occasions for direct I/O from/to a specific file. This can be done by setting up new I/O objects connected to the desired files. For example, use

```
FileInputStream myin = new FileInputStream("mydata");
FileOutputStream myout = new FileOutputStream("myresult");
```

to establish the object `myin` to read the existing file `mydata`, and the object `myout` to write the new file `myresult`. If `myresult` exists, it will be replaced.

Thus both the `FileInputStream` class and the `FileOutputStream` class have constructors that take a `String` file name argument. The methods

```
public int read() throws IOException
public void write(int c) throws IOException
```

are used to read and write a byte. Open file streams are automatically closed when your program terminates. An open file can also be specifically closed by calling the method `close()`:

```
myin.close();
myout.close();
```

See the next section for an example involving file I/O. Other input/output facilities provided by the `java.io` package are discussed in Section 6.4.

2.3 BASIC ERROR AND EXCEPTION HANDLING

A very important aspect of programming concerns the handling of possible errors during the execution of a program. Many kinds of errors can occur at run time. The `main` method may receive incorrect arguments. A method expecting a positive argument may be passed a negative value. Arithmetic operations can overflow or underflow. I/O to files may have access permission and other problems. A well-written program should detect errors and take appropriate actions.

Displaying Error Messages

A main method should first check the arguments supplied on the command line for correctness. If the arguments are unacceptable, a clear message should be displayed, stating the nature of the error and its cause (if known). The object

`System.err` should be used for sending error messages so they appear on the display immediately without buffering. A conditional statement such as

```
if (args.length != 2)
{    System.err.println(Progname +
        ": expects 2 args but was given " + args.length);
    System.err.println("Usage " + Progname +
        " input-file output-file");
    System.exit(1);
}
```

checks the number of command-line arguments supplied. Always identify the program unit or subunit displaying the error message. Here `Progname` is the name (a string) of the class of the `main` method in question. When appropriate, a method name further narrows down the error location.

After displaying an error message, a method may continue to execute, return a particular value not produced normally, or elect to abort. The call `System.exit(status)` terminates the execution of a program. For normal termination, `status` should usually be zero. For abnormal termination such as an error, a positive `status`, usually 1, is used.

Simple Exception Handling

Unexpected run-time errors are handled in Java with the *exception* mechanism. A method, built-in or user-defined, can *throw an exception object of some known type* that causes control to return to the nearest method, on the chain of calls, that *catches this type of exception*, or all the way back to the Java interpreter (Figure 2.1).

For example, the `System.in.read` method, like many other I/O related methods in Java, detects I/O errors and can *throw an exception* when an error is encountered. Different *exception objects* are used to represent different kinds of errors. `System.in.read` may throw an `IOException` object. The exceptions a method may throw constitute important information and are always documented clearly.

When you write a method that contains a call to a method that may throw an exception, you must do one of two things:

1. Catch the potential exception and treat the error in the method you write.
2. Not catch the exception and let it pass through to a method higher on the call chain. In this case, you must so indicate by adding a `throws` clause to your method header. A `throws` clause is also needed if your method throws an exception on its own.

Figure 2.1   EXCEPTION THROWING

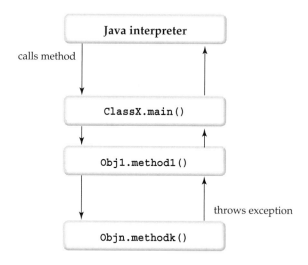

Once an exception is caught, a method can treat the error appropriately. For example, the constructors

```
public FileInputStream(String filename) throws FileNotFoundException
public FileOutputStream(String filename) throws IOException
```

establish objects for file I/O. When you call them, you have to catch the indicated exceptions.

The *try block* construct is used to catch exceptions. Here is a simple form:

```
try
{     statements
}     catch(e-type₁ e)
      {     statements      }
      catch(e-type₂ e)
      {     statements      }
      . . .
```

Exceptions caused by any statement in the `try` part are matched with the exception types listed by the *catch clauses* sequentially. Each catch clause is in the form of a method definition. The exception object is passed to the parameter e of the first matching clause, and the statements are executed. Only matching exceptions are caught. The example in the next section illustrates these remarks. Complete coverage of Java exceptions can be found in Section 6.15.

ASCII Text File I/O and Error Handling Example

Let's improve the class Lowercase so it handles standard I/O and file I/O:

java Lowercase < *infile* > *outfile*   (I/O redirection)
java Lowercase *infile outfile*

The task of converting uppercase characters is performed by the doio method.

```
///////   Lowercase.java   ///////
// Example for text-file I/O
import java.io.*;

class Lowercase
{ public static void doio(InputStream i, OutputStream o)
   {   int c;
       InputStreamReader in = new InputStreamReader(i);    // (1)
       OutputStreamWriter out = new OutputStreamWriter(o); // (2)
       try
       {  while ( (c = in.read()) >= 0 )
          {  c = Character.toLowerCase( (char) c);
             out.write(c);
          }
          out.flush();        // produces all output
       } catch( IOException e )
          {  System.err.println("doio: I/O Problem");
             System.err.println(e.getMessage());            // (3)
             System.exit(1);
          }
   }
  //  main method shown later
}
```

The doio method uses an InputStreamReader object and an OutputStream-Writer object to make textual I/O character-set independent (lines 1–2). It also catches possible exceptions of type IOException caused by in.read() or out.write(c). Note how an exception object contains a message that can be displayed (line 3).

The main method checks for command-line arguments, opens files appropriately, and calls doio.

```
public static void main (String[] args)
{   int argn = args.length;
    if ( argn == 0 )
      doio(System.in, System.out);              // use standard I/O
    else if ( argn == 2 )                        // use files given
    { try
```

```
      { FileInputStream infile =
            new FileInputStream(args[0]);
        FileOutputStream ofile =
            new FileOutputStream(args[1]);
        doio(infile, ofile);
        infile.close(); ofile.close();
      } catch ( FileNotFoundException e )                    // (4)
        { System.err.println(
            "Can't open input file " + args[0]);
          System.err.println(e.getMessage());
          System.exit(1);
        }
      catch ( IOException e )                                // (5)
        { System.err.println(
            "Can't open output file " + args[1]);
          System.err.println(e.getMessage());
          System.exit(1);
        }
    }
    else   // error                                          // (6)
    { System.err.println("Usage: Lowercase infile outfile");
      System.exit(1);
    }
  }
}
```

The `main` method anticipates common errors: failure to open the input file (line 4), inability to open the output file (line 5), and wrong number of arguments (line 6). In the last case, a brief guide to using the program is displayed.

2.4 A CLASS OF FRACTIONS

We are now ready to define a more substantial class. Consider ordinary fractions such as $\frac{3}{4}$ and $\frac{-1}{2}$. A fraction is, of course, the ratio of two integers: a numerator and a denominator. A user-defined type can be built for fractions by the creation of a class `Fraction`. The class supplies a set of necessary operations on fractions and hides implementation details of data representation and internal manipulations.

In designing `Fraction` or any other class to build objects, we first consider these two important aspects:

1. Public interface—The set of public methods and fields forms the public interface and defines the external behavior of objects of the class. This information is important for clients that use the class and its

objects. For `Fraction`, the public interface should support the usual arithmetic, comparison, and logical operations.

2. Internal structures—The internal data representation and manipulation procedures must be efficient and effective. This information, isolated from outside view, is important to developers and maintainers of the class.

Member methods of a class will keep the internal data representation consistent. Outside methods are not allowed to create or modify the internal structures directly. They may do this by calling methods in the class.

Following are some internal representation considerations for `Fraction`:

- A fraction is internally kept as a pair of integers, `num` and `denom`.
- The numerator `num` carries the sign of the fraction and can be positive, negative, or zero.
- The denominator is kept positive and can never be zero.
- Another design decision is whether to allow fractions with the same value in different representations (for example $\frac{1}{2}$, $\frac{2}{4}$, $\frac{3}{6}$) to exist. If not, and if equal fractions must have the same numerator and denominator, all fractions must be reduced to the lowest terms. A data representation in which all equal quantities are represented uniquely is known as a *canonical* representation. Keeping fractions canonical is desirable here, and this will be enforced by the `Fraction` class.
- A fraction can be zero and is represented by `num = 0` and `denom = 1`.

The `Fraction` class can be designed to enforce such conventions, not just to have them as principles that one can choose to follow or ignore. Controlling and protecting internal representations are a big advantage of class encapsulation. The canonical representation conventions are enforced by the `Fraction` constructor.

```
///////   Fraction.java   ///////

public class Fraction
{   public Fraction() { }                // null constructor

    public Fraction(int n, int d)        // constructor, d is not zero
    {   int g;
        if ( d == 0 )
        {   System.err.println(
               "Fraction: fraction with 0 denominator?");
            System.exit(1);
        }
        if ( n == 0 ) {   num = 0;  denom = 1;  return;  }
        if ( d < 0 ) {   n = -n;   d = -d;   }
        if ( (g = gcd(n,d)) != 1 )         // remove gcd
        {   n /= g; d /= g;   }
```

```
        num = n;
        denom = d;
    }
// private data fields
    private int num;                    // numerator
    private int denom;                  // denominator
// other members ...
}
```

This constructor takes the given arguments n and d and constructs a fraction $\frac{n}{d}$. The denominator d should not be zero or negative. The fraction is reduced by removing the gcd (greatest common divisor) between n and d.

The algorithm to compute gcd(*a*, *b*) can be described by the following pseudo-code:

1. If *b* is zero, the answer is *a*.

2. If *b* is not zero, the answer is gcd(*b*, *a* mod *b*).

It is interesting to note that the idea for this simple but effective integer gcd algorithm is credited to Euclid, a Greek mathematician (ca. 300 B.C.).

```
private static int gcd(int a, int b)
{   a = Math.abs(a);
    b = Math.abs(b);
    if ( a == 0 ) return b;      // 0 is error value
    if ( b == 0 ) return a;
    int t;
    while ( b > 0 )
    {   t = a % b;  a = b;  b = t;  }
    return a;
}
```

The member gcd is implemented as a classwide method (static) because it is independent of Fraction instances (Section 2.6). It is declared private because it does not contribute to the public interface of the Fraction class.

Now, a representative set of public methods that manipulate fractions will be examined. Methods such as the following are simple and straightforward:

```
public boolean isZero() { return denom==1 && num==0; }

public boolean isInt() { return denom == 1; }

public boolean equals(Fraction y)
{   return(num == y.num && denom == y.denom); }

public boolean greaterThan(Fraction y)
{   return(num * y.denom > denom * y.num); }
```

Host Object Reference: `this`

For arithmetic operations, let's look at the subtraction of fractions. The call f1.minus(f2) computes $f1 - f2$. If the host object (f1) is zero, a new fraction, which is the negative of f2, is returned. If f2 is zero, the host object is returned. The special symbol

```
this
```

is a *reference to the host object* available in any instance method. Classwide (`static`) methods are not associated with any host object and therefore don't have access to `this`.

```java
public Fraction minus(Fraction y)
{    if ( isZero() )                          // trivial cases
         return makeFraction(-y.num, y.denom);
     else if ( y.isZero() ) return this;
     else                                     // compute difference
         return new Fraction(num * y.denom - y.num * denom,
                             denom * y.denom);
}
```

In an instance method, access to members in the host object is usually done through implicit reference to `this`. For example the code isZero() is really short for this.isZero(). Note, the test num == 0 is more efficient here.

The private method makeFraction initializes a new fraction without the checks in the public constructor and is therefore more efficient. Only trusted member methods can use the private makeFraction, which is called only when no transformation of the given fraction is necessary.

```java
private Fraction makeFraction(int n, int d)
{    Fraction f = new Fraction();
     f.num = n;
     f.denom = d;
     return f;
}
```

For display, here is toString for Fraction:

```java
public String toString()
{    return  num + "/" + denom; }
```

The toString and a version of equals are among a set of standard methods (Section 4.19) recommended for every class.

Testing Fractions

Because a class describes an independent computation unit, you should individually test each class you write to make sure it works. This way, when classes are combined, you can just focus on how objects interact. At that point, you are simply putting working components together.

Following is a simple program to test `Fraction`:

```
///////    TestFract.java     ///////

class TestFract
{  public static void main(String[] args)
   {    Fraction x= new Fraction(1,20);
        Fraction u= new Fraction(-1,60);
        Fraction v= new Fraction(1,30);
        Fraction y;
        y = x.plus(u).minus(v);
        System.out.println(x + " + " + u + " - " + v + " = " + y);
   }
}
```

Compile and run the program with these commands:

javac TestFract.java   (compile)
java TestFract   (execute)

The compilation command automatically compiles `Fraction.java` needed by `TestFract.java` also. Running `TestFract` produces the following output:

```
1/20 + -1/60 - 1/30 = 0/1
```

Appendix I gives an example showing the use of the Java debugger on this program.

2.5 IDENTIFIER SCOPING

Names are identifiers used to refer to entities declared in a Java program: classes, methods, fields, parameters, variables, labels, and so on. Java *keywords* (Appendix B), `null`, `true`, or `false`, cannot be used as identifiers.

To reduce the chance of name conflicts, Java supports multiple *name spaces*. The same identifier can be used in different name spaces without conflict. It is usually safe to assume the following name spaces:

- Package—package names
- Type—class and interface names
- Method—method names in a class
- Field—field names in a class
- Label—statement label names
- Variable—names for parameters of methods and for local variables in a code block

The same identifier can be used as a method name and as a field name in the same class without conflict.

Identifiers are also regulated by *scoping rules*, governing the extent (the parts of the program) to which the names are known. In different scopes, identifiers with the same spelling are actually *distinct*. The different scopes are:

- Local scope—A local variable is known from its point of declaration to the end of its immediate enclosing block or `for` statement.
- Method scope—A formal parameter is known for the entire body of a method, a constructor, or a `catch` clause.
- Class scope—A member is known to the entire extent of a class or interface.
- File scope—A type name introduced by an `import` declaration is known to the entire file.
- Package scope—A class or interface name is known to all parts of the same package.
- Host scope—A package name, introduced by the `package` declaration, is known to all parts of a Java program on the same host computer.

If one scope is enclosed within another, the scopes are *nested*. Examples are: a class in a package, a method in a class, and a block in a method. An *inner scope* identifier hides an *outer scope* identifier with the same name. Consider the following nested blocks:

```
{    double i = 1.5;
     for (int i = 0; i < 5; i++)
     {    System.out.println(i);      // displays 0 through 4
     }
     System.out.println(i);           // displays 1.5
}
```

Each class has its own scope. Enclosed in class scope are field and method members. The name of a class member has *full class scope* and is global to the entire class, independently of where it is declared in the class. For example, the names `acct_no` and `acct_bal` are used like global variables in the member methods of class `BankAccount`. Also, a member method can refer to a field or method declared later in the class definition.

Unless qualified, a class member name is generally not recognized outside its class. For example, neither the method name `deposit` nor the field name `acct_bal` is recognized directly outside `BankAccount`. A classwide (static) member of a class can be accessed from the outside with the *class modifier* notation *ClassName*.*memberName*. The usage `Character.toLowerCase` in the `Lower.java` is an example.

The object member-of notation is another way to qualify a name and to put it in a specific class scope. For example:

```
u.inner(v)          // u, v Vector2D objects
v.delta             // delta is static in Vector2D
sally.balance()     // sally, bob  BankAccount objects
bob.deposit(11.79)
```

The host object reference this can indicate class scope as well. For example, the Vector2D constructor can be coded as

```
public Vector2D(float x, float y)
{   this.x = x;
    this.y = y;
}
```

where the name x in this.x is a class member and will not be confused with the parameter x.

2.6   INSTANCE AND CLASSWIDE MEMBERS

A class is a blueprint for building objects. Thus, each object is known as an *instance* of its class. Conceptually, each object has its own set of members as described by the class. A Fraction f1 has its own num and denom components; so does another Fraction f2. The BankAccount object susan has its own balance() and deposit() methods; so does bob. As another example, a Window class may have location and size fields as well as a move method. But window objects big and small would certainly have their own location and size fields. Thus, big.size is not small.size. Also big.move(...) moves one window and small.move(...) moves another.

Such members are per instance and are known as *instance members*. An instance member is always accessed through its *host object*, using the obj.member notation.

If a member is declared static, it becomes a *classwide member* and is shared by all instances of the class. The field delta of Vector2D is an example:

```
private static float delta = 0.00000001f;
```

In fact, a classwide member exists independently of any instances. A classwide member is accessed by the *ClassName*.member notation. The main method in a class is always declared static, so it can be invoked directly by the Java interpreter. Namely, the shell-level command

java *ClassName*

tells the Java virtual machine to call the method *ClassName*.main after classes are loaded.

Unlike an instance method, a static method has no host object and works independently of any instances in the class (Figure 2.2).

Figure 2.2   CLASSWIDE METHOD AS COMPUTATION UNIT

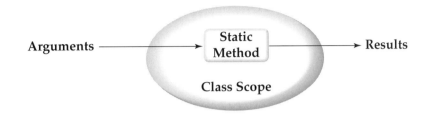

A member in a class is either an *instance member* or a *classwide member*. A member is an instance member unless it is declared `static`, which makes it classwide. An instance field or method is attached to a *host object* and is accessed only through the host. For example, `susan.balance()` returns the balance for the `BankAccount` object `susan`.

Each instance method has a built-in *host object reference* represented by the keyword `this`. In `balance`, the code `return acct_bal` is a shorthand for `return this.acct_bal`. Thus, instance members *live within their host objects* and can access one another freely and directly within the host. A `static` method has neither host object nor access to `this`.

Instance members play an important role in object-based programming: they represent and define the *state and behavior* of an individual object. But there are times when an attribute or operation must transcend the boundaries of individual objects. The error tolerance `delta` in the `Vector2D` class is an example we have seen. A monthly service fee can be part of the `BankAccount` class but not restricted to any individual `BankAccount` object. A classwide member is unique per class and exists independently of any instance (object) of a class. Thus, a classwide field can be used to share information among all objects of the class. In Java, classwide members are declared `static` and are often known simply as static members. A static member is enclosed in the scope of its class but has no host object (Figure 2.3). A static member is under the same access control as any other member.

Figure 2.3   OBJECTS SHARING STATIC MEMBER

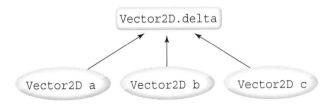

Declare a method `static` when it is a procedure that works independently of any single object in the class. A static method has no host object and therefore no access to `this`, explicitly or implicitly. Hence, a static method cannot reference any instance (nonstatic) members directly. The `gcd` in `Fraction` and `toLowerCase` in `Character` are static methods. The entry method `main` of a class is declared `static`.

A static member can be accessed through any object of the class. Of course, the same static member is reached no matter what instance of the class you use. A static member can also be accessed directly with the notation:

ClassName.staticMemberName

For example:

```
System.in                    // standard input object
System.out                   // standard output object
Integer.MIN_VALUE            // smallest int in Java
Integer.MAX_VALUE            // largest int in Java
Character.toLowerCase(c)
```

When a class has only static members and no instance members, the class is not meant for establishing objects. It becomes a set of methods and/or fields enclosed in a class scope. The `Lowercase` class (Section 2.3) is an example.

Initialization of Static Fields

A field declared `static` is not initialized by the class constructor. An initialization clause can be used for a static field. For example:

```
static float fee = 18.0f;
static float delta = 0.00000001f;
static String year = current_year();
```

A static field initializer cannot invoke a method that has a `throws` clause for exceptions.

For more complicated initialization, a *static initialization block* can be used. Following is an example:

```
///////    Rand.java    ///////
import java.util.*;

class Rand
{   public static int rn[] = new int[8];

    static                              // a static initialization block
    {   Random gen = new Random();
        for ( int i = 0 ; i < rn.length ; i++ )
            rn[i] = Math.abs(gen.nextInt());
    }
```

```
public static void main(String[] args)
{   for ( int i = 0 ; i < rn.length ; i++ )
        System.out.println("rn[" + i + "] = " + rn[i] );
}
}
```

The static initialization block fills the array rn with random integers as the class Rand is loaded. The object gen is a random number generator object (an instance of the Random class in the java.util package).

A static initialization block can be given anywhere in a class. Java initializes static fields and executes static initialization blocks as a class is loaded. Such initializations are done in the order given.

2.7 SYMBOLIC CONSTANTS

It is often desirable to give names to constants and use the names rather than the values in writing programs. It is better to use a constant with a descriptive name than just the constant itself. For example, BUFFER_SIZE and SCREEN_WIDTH are better than 256 or 640. In Java, symbolic constants are declared as final quantities initialized by the values they represent. Some examples follow:

```
public static final float PI = 3.1416;
public static final byte MON = 1;
public static final byte TUE = MON + 1;
public static final byte SUN = SAT + 1;
private final short TABLE_SIZE = 1024;
```

The modifier final makes a quantity's value fixed and final, so it can't change once initialized. Both class and instance variables can be declared final. In Java, declaration modifiers, such as public, static, and final, can be given in any order as long as they precede the type.

If a variable is declared final, it is the value of the variable, not the object it refers to, that is made final. Thus,

```
final Vector2D ORIGIN = new Vector2D(0.0, 0.0);
```

makes ORIGIN final, so it always refers to the given object. However, this does not prevent values contained in that object from changing. The keyword final can also be applied to methods and classes, as we will see later.

2.8 USING ARRAYS: Quicksort

One common use of arrays is to store information for easy retrieval by indexing. Often the array entries are *sorted* into a specified order. Imagine trying to look up (retrieve) a phone number from an unsorted phone book! Among many competing sorting algorithms, quicksort remains one of the fastest.

Consider arranging an array of integers in increasing order with quicksort. The idea is to pick any element of the array as the *partition element*, pe. By exchanging the elements, the array can be arranged so all elements to the right of pe are greater than or equal to pe, and all elements to the left of pe are less than or equal to pe. Now the same method is applied to sort each of the smaller arrays on either side of pe. The recursion is terminated when the length of the array becomes less than 2.

```
///////    Quicksort.java    ///////

public class Quicksort
{   public static void quicksort(int[] arr, int l, int h)
    {   if ( l >= h || l < 0 || h < 0 ) return;
        int k = partition(arr, l, h);
        quicksort(arr, l, k-1);
        quicksort(arr, k+1, h);
    }
// other members
}
```

The method quicksort orders elements in the range given by the lower index l and the higher index h of the array. If h is bigger than l, the method partition is called to select a partition element and to split the array into two parts. The return value of partition is the index of the partition point. The smaller ranges to either side of pe are then sorted by calling quicksort recursively.

The private method partition is used by quicksort to make the left-right partitioning. The arguments to partition are the array arr, the low index l, and the high index h. An array variable is a reference. When arr is passed in the partition call, its value, the reference, is passed. Therefore, the receiving method gets to refer to the same array object. The range of the array from arr[l] to arr[h] inclusive is to be partitioned.

Basically, the middle element is chosen to be the pe. Searching simultaneously from both ends of the range toward the middle, elements belonging to the other side are located. Out-of-place entries are interchanged in pairs. Finally, the searches in opposite directions end when they meet somewhere in the range, pinpointing the location of the partition element.

```
private static int partition(int[] arr, int l, int h)
{   int i=l, j=h;
    // choose middle element as pivot
    swap(arr, (i+j)/2, h);                       // pivot moved to h
    int pe = arr[h];
    while (i < j)
    {   while (i < j && arr[i] <= pe ) i++;   // from left side
        while (i < j && arr[j] >= pe ) j--;   // from right side
```

```
        if (i < j) swap(arr, i++, j);          // switch elements
    }
    if (i != h) swap(arr, i, h);               // pivot element in place
    return i;
}
```

The partition method begins by exchanging the rightmost element with pe. Starting from both ends, the left-to-right sweep locates an element bigger than pe and the right-to-left search finds an element smaller than pe. The two elements located are exchanged. Thereafter, the searches in opposite directions continue. Eventually, no more exchanges are needed and the searches meet somewhere between low and high inclusive. This is the partition spot, and it contains an element greater than or equal to pe. The pe at the rightmost position is now interchanged with the element at the partition position. Finally, the index of the partition element is returned.

Element swapping is performed by the following simple method:

```
private static void swap(int[] a, int i, int j)
{   int tmp = a[i]; a[i] = a [j]; a[j] = tmp;  }
```

Note that quicksort reorders an array *in place*. No auxiliary array is used. The best way to understand how quicksort works is to try an example with fewer than 10 entries by hand.

Following is a simple program to test Quicksort:

```
///////    TestQsort.java    ///////

class TestQsort
{   public static void main(String[] args)
    {   int dim=0;
        if ( args.length == 1 ) dim = Integer.parseInt(args[0]);
        else
        {   System.err.println("Usage: Java Testqsort length");
            System.exit(1);
        }
        int[] a = new int[dim];
        for (int i=0; i < dim; i++) a[i]=(123*i)%dim;
        Quicksort.quicksort(a, 0, a.length - 1);
        System.out.println("sort done");
        for (int i=0; i < dim; i++) System.out.print(a[i]+" ");
        System.out.println();
    }
}
```

2.9 `String` AND `StringBuffer`

Strings are frequently used constructs in programming. `String` objects represent constant character strings, which are not modifiable once created. Modifiable, or *mutable*, strings are supplied by `StringBuffer`, which is described in the next section.

The Java `String` and `StringBuffer` classes supply many useful operations for string manipulations. Familiarity with these classes can make programming easier in many situations.

The `String` class offers many convenient ways to create strings (Table 2.1). This point is underscored by the fact that several of these functions had already been used in previous examples.

Table 2.2 lists some usual string operations where i and j are ints and s is any string. Keep in mind that argument strings are not modified.

The `compareTo` method uses Unicode values for comparing characters. This may not correspond to alphabetical order in some languages. Note also that a Java array supplies a public `length` field for the number of array elements, but Java `String` supports a `length()` method that returns the number of characters in the string. You've seen the use of + and += for string concatenation already.

Table 2.3 shows additional useful `String` methods. The `String` class supports many other methods, including converting strings into and from character (byte) arrays. See the class documentation for more details.

Another frequent operation is reading a text line from standard input to form a string. The `readLine` method of the `BufferedReader` class is convenient for this purpose (Section 6.11).

Table 2.1   STRING CONSTRUCTORS

Constructor	String Created
`String()`	Empty string
`String(String)`	A copy of given string
	Concatenation of nonzero chars—
`String(char[])`	in array
`String(char[], int i, int j)`	in subarray i to j
`String(byte[])`	in given array of bytes
`String(byte[], int i, int n, String code)`	in subarray i to i+n-1 by encoding
`String(StringBuffer)`	in the given string buffer

Table 2.2   STRING OPERATIONS

Method	Returns
`int length()`	Length of the string
`char charAt(i)`	Char at index i
`int compareTo(s)`	$-$, 0, $+$ if host is <, equal to, or > s
`String concat(s)`	String with s appended at the end of the string
`String substring(i [, j])`	Substring from index i to j (inclusive) or the end
`String toLowerCase()`	String converted to lowercase
`String toUpperCase()`	String converted to uppercase
`String trim()`	String with leading and trailing white space removed
`char[] toCharArray()`	A new character array with chars from the string

Table 2.3   STRING MATCHING OPERATIONS

Method	Returns
`boolean startsWith(prefix)`	`true` if the string begins with the given prefix
`boolean endsWith(suffix)`	`true` if the string ends with the given suffix
`int indexOf(int c)`	Index of the first occurrence of the char c or -1
`int indexOf(str [, off])`	Index of the first substring str (from offset off) or -1 (use `lastIndexOf` for the last substring)
`String replace(c1, c2)`	String with all chars c1 replaced by c2

String Tokens

One frequent string operation is the extraction of tokens in a string. In Java, token extraction is supported by the `StringTokenizer` class in the `java.util` package. To extract tokens from a string *str*, first create a `StringTokenizer` object

```
StringTokenizer tk = new StringTokenizer(str, delim);
```

where *delim* is a string of *delimiter characters* that separate tokens. If the *delim* argument is not given, white space (SPACE, TAB, NEWLINE, and RETURN) is used. Once tk is created, you obtain successive tokens, skipping delimiters, by calling

```
tk.nextToken()
```

repeatedly. Do not call `nextToken` after getting all tokens. Table 2.4 shows useful methods for obtaining tokens. See the `StringTokenizer` documentation for more details and Section 6.4 for an application of `StringToken`.

Table 2.4   TOKEN EXTRACTION

Method	Returns
`boolean hasMoreTokens()`	true if one or more tokens remain
`String nextToken()`	Next token in the string
`String nextToken(`*delim*`)`	Next token after switching to new delimiters
`int countTokens()`	Number of tokens remaining

String Buffers

A `String` object is read-only and inefficient for creating strings incrementally by combining characters. The `java.lang` class `StringBuffer` offers a writable character buffer and efficient operations to build and modify a string in the buffer. Typical uses of `StringBuffer` include reading characters to form a string, and building a string from several data items. To get a `StringBuffer` object, use one of the following constructors:

```
StringBuffer()          // empty string buffer
StringBuffer(int)       // with initial capacity
StringBuffer(String)    // with initial string
```

After you get a string buffer sb, you can

```
sb.append(any)          // append at end
sb.insert(i, any)       // insert at position i
```

where *any* is any primitive type or object with a properly defined `toString` method. Once the desired string is built in the buffer, the call

```
sb.toString()
```

returns a `String` without copying the buffer until a later operation tries to modify the buffer again. Table 2.5 lists some useful methods. Java uses a string buffer to implement string concatenation by +. The code

```
"Value =" + x
```

actually turns into

```
new StringBuffer().append("Value ").append(x).toString()
```

Section 3.5 contains an example that puts `StringBuffer` to use.

Table 2.5   STRING BUFFER OPERATIONS

Method	Description
`charAt(int i)`	Returns char at index i
`length()`	Returns char count of the buffer
`setCharAt(int i, char c)`	Sets char at index to c
`setLength(int len)`	Keeps only len characters
`getChars(int i, int j, char[], int k)`	Copies the chars in range (i to j inclusive) into the char array, starting at position k

2.10   TWO-DIMENSIONAL ARRAYS

Up to this point, all of the arrays use a single index or subscript. Such arrays are *one dimensional*. It is possible to have arrays with more than one subscript. For example:

```
int[][] a = {{1, 2, 3, 4}, {5, 6, 7, 8}};   // 2 x 4 int array
double[][] b = {{2.5d, 3.5d, 4.5d}, null }; // 2 x 3 double array
```

Array a is a *two-dimensional* array with the first subscript going from 0 to 1 and the second ranging from 0 to 3. In Java a two-dimensional array is simply an array of arrays of the same length. The entry b[0] is an array of four ints and the entry b[1] is initialized to null, a constant representing an invalid reference.

Two-dimensional arrays are easily created with new:

```
b = new double[4][7];
```

Next we'll see a natural application for two-dimensional arrays.

2.11   A Matrix CLASS

Let's consider writing a simplified Matrix class. The example demonstrates the creation and usage of two-dimensional arrays. It also shows a more complicated toString method for displaying matrices.

```
class Matrix
{   public Matrix(int r, int c)                              // (1)
    {    if ( r > 0 && c > 0 ) mat = new double[nr=r][nc=c];
         else { mat = null; nr = nc = 0; }
    }

    public Matrix(double[][] m)                              // (2)
```

```
{   mat = m;
    nr = m.length;
    nc = m[0].length;
}
```

```
// other methods ...
    private double[][] mat; // the matrix
    private int nr, nc;     // number of rows and cols
}
```

A `Matrix` object can be initialized with just two dimensions (line 1) or a two-dimensional double array (line 2). Public methods to get/set entries and retrieve dimensions are simple:

```
public double getElement(int i, int j)
{   return mat[i][j];   }
```

```
public void setElement(int i, int j, double e)
{   mat[i][j] = e;   }
```

```
public int rows() { return nr; }
public int cols() { return nc; }
```

The method `times` multiplies two matrices. The product of an $r \times s$ matrix A by an $s \times t$ matrix B is an $r \times t$ matrix C. (To appreciate this one, *say the equation*.) Each entry $C_{i,j}$ is given by the inner product of row i of A and column j of B. Here is a simple example:

$$\begin{pmatrix} 1 & 2 \\ 3 & 4 \\ 5 & 6 \end{pmatrix} \cdot \begin{pmatrix} a & b \\ c & d \end{pmatrix} = \begin{pmatrix} a+2c & b+2d \\ 3a+4c & 3b+4d \\ 5a+6c & 5b+6d \end{pmatrix}$$

The matrix multiplication method `times` is implemented as follows:

```
public Matrix times(Matrix b)
{   if ( nc != b.nr ) return null;   // incompatible dimensions
    Matrix p = new Matrix(nr,b.nc);
    for (int i=0; i < nr; i++)
       for (int j=0; j < b.nc; j++)
          p.setElement(i, j, rowTimesCol(i, b.mat, j));
    return p;
}
```

The method `times` multiplies the host matrix with b and returns a product matrix p. Nested `for` loops are used to compute elements of the result. The private method rowTimesCol computes the inner product of row i of the host matrix with column j of b. The result is stored as entry (i,j) in p.

```
private double rowTimesCol(int ri, double[][] b, int ci)
{    double sum=0.0d;
     double[] row = mat[ri];
     for (int k=0; k < b.length; k++) sum += row[k] * b[k][ci];
     return sum;
}
```

The member toString makes displaying matrices easy. A Java StringBuffer object is convenient for building up a string by appending to the end of it. The append method of StringBuffer can take any primitive type or object with a toString method (Section 2.9).

```
public String toString()
{    StringBuffer buf = new StringBuffer();
     for (int i = 0; i < nr; i++)
     {   buf.append("( ");
         for (int j = 0; j < nc-1; j++)
         {    buf.append(mat[i][j]);
              buf.append("    ");
         }
         buf.append(mat[i][nc-1]);
         buf.append(" )\n");
     }
     buf.setLength(buf.length()-1);
     return new String(buf);
}
```

A fully developed Matrix class would have many other methods. The following program can be used to test matrix multiplication and display:

```
public static void main(String[] args)
{    double[][] a = { {1.0,-2.0,1.5}, {1.0,2.4,3.1}};
     double[][] b = { {9.0,0.7},{-2.0,30.5},{-9.0,4.0}};
     Matrix m1 = new Matrix(a);
     Matrix m2 = new Matrix(b);
     Matrix prod = m1.times(m2);
     System.out.println(prod);      // prod.toString()
}
```

The output displayed is:

```
( -0.5    -54.3 )
( -23.7    86.3 )
```

2.12 TYPE CONVERSIONS

Java is a strongly typed language requiring that all quantities be declared types before being used in a program. The compiler uses the type information to check for type compatibility and possible argument passing errors, and to generate efficient running code. Both primitive and user-defined types sometimes have to be converted to a related type before an operation can be performed.

Operations that may involve type conversion include assignment, argument passing, and arithmetic operations. A conversion is sometimes done *implicitly* or automatically. For example:

```
int i = 'A';        // implicit char to int conversion
```

Other times, conversions must be *explicitly* requested. For example:

```
char c = (char) i;  // explicit int to char conversion
```

Implicit and explicit conversions will be described separately.

2.13 IMPLICIT TYPE CONVERSION

Usual implicit conversions in Java include the following:

- Method invocation conversions
- Assignment conversions
- Arithmetic conversions
- String conversions

Method Invocation Conversions

When making a method call, Java makes implicit conversions on the arguments when passing their values to the formal parameters. These conversions are as follows:

- Identity conversions—The type is not converted.
- Widening primitive conversions—A primitive type can be converted to any other primitive type reached by following the arrows in Figure 2.4.
- Widening reference conversions—See Section 4.10.

Figure 2.4   WIDENING PRIMITIVE CONVERSIONS

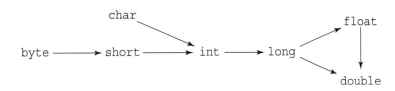

Assignment Conversions

To make an assignment, Java does all the method invocation conversions implicitly. In addition an `int` type constant expression can be assigned to a variable of type `byte`, `short`, or `char` as long as the target type can represent the constant value.[1] For example:

```
int i = 120, j = 250;
byte a, b;
a = i;              // error, requires explicit cast
a = 120;            // fine
b = 250;            // not fine
b = (byte) j;       // b is -6
```

Arithmetic Conversions

For arithmetic expressions, implicit conversions include identity conversions and widening primitive conversions.

String Conversions

In Java, a special implicit conversion to a string is applied when the operator +
is used for string concatenation. Basically, when one of the arguments of + is a
`String`, the other is converted implicitly, if possible, to a string. See Section 2.9
for more details.

---

[1] This is referred to as *narrowing constant* int *conversions.*

2.14 EXPLICIT TYPE CASTS

When an implicit conversion is not possible, often a programmer can request type conversion *explicitly* and force data or reference of one type to become another. The *type cast*

```
( TypeName ) expression
```

converts the value of the given *expression* to the named type.

Examples of explicit casting include: char to short, floating point to integer (dropping fractional part), or a larger precision type to a similar type with smaller precision. A boolean cannot be converted to/from any other type.

With type casting, a round method can be written:

```
public static int round(float f)
{   float fracpart = f - (int)f;          // explicit type cast
    return ( (fracpart < 0.5) ? (int)f    // round down
                      : (int)f + 1 ); // round up
}
```

Upon closer examination, the round method can be implemented simply as:

```
public static int round(float f)
{   return (int) (f + 0.5); }
```

Explicit cast of a *type* to an *extended type* can be made, but care must be taken, as described in Section 4.10.

Java forbids certain type conversions. These include converting boolean to any other type. Except for string conversion, no conversions between primitive and reference types are permitted.

2.15 PROGRAMMING TIPS

- Use

```
System.in.read()
System.out.write(int i)
```

for ASCII characters through standard I/O.
- Use FileInputStream and FileOutputStream for file I/O.
- Use String for read-only strings and StringBuffer for building, manipulating, and altering strings.
- Declare classwide members static. Static methods have no host object and, therefore, no access to this.
- Declare a method static if it does not use any instance members. Such a method operates *independently of the state of any object*.
- Use meaningful names for constants, and declare them static final.

- Access a static method or field through the class name (e.g., `System.out`).
- Define `toString` to make displaying objects and certain other operations easy.
- Explicitly cast an integer to `char` before using it as a character.
- Converting `boolean` to and from any other type will fail.
- Employ a multidimensional array as an array of arrays.

2.16 SUMMARY

Standard and file I/O for characters have been explained. Run-time exceptions are caught with the `try` block and the `catch` clauses. A method either catches an exception or specifies the exception with a `throws` clause.

Constructors control the way objects are initialized. A class such as `fraction` has a constructor for external interface, another for making a copy, and an internal `makeFraction` method for members. The `toString` method makes displaying objects easy. An instance method can access its host through the *host reference* `this`.

To reduce name conflicts, Java identifiers belong to different *name spaces*. The extent to which an identifier is known within a program is limited by its scope. In the same name space, identifiers with the same name but within different scopes are actually distinct. Java keywords and literals cannot be used as identifiers.

Instance and static members are very different. Instance members are accessed only through their host object; static members are class-wide and have no host object. Static members can be accessed through any object in the class or directly through the class name. A `static` method has no host reference and cannot use the symbol `this`.

Use symbolic names for constants in a program by declaring `final` identifiers whose value cannot change after initialization. Constants are often class-wide quantities.

Java arrays are objects, and they are passed by reference in method calls. To pass an array or any other object by value, you must make a copy first. Arrays can be multidimensional. The use of arrays is illustrated by a quicksort program and a `Matrix` class.

A `String` object represents a read-only sequence of characters. The `String` class provides many useful methods for processing strings. `StringBuffer` objects are writable, and characters are easily inserted or appended. Use `StringBuffer` to construct strings; then convert them to `String` objects for general usage. The `StringTokenizer` class offers convenient methods to parse strings into tokens.

In Java, *method invocation conversions*, *assignment conversions*, *arithmetic conversions*, and *string conversions* are made implicitly. Other type conversions must be done with explicit casting. Conversions to and from `boolean` or between primitive and class types are generally not allowed.

EXERCISES

Review Questions

1. Class member names have class scope and are generally not recognized outside the class without qualification. Can you think of any class members that are recognized without being qualified?

2. Consider strings in Java. How do you determine whether a given character is on a string? How do you obtain a substring of a given string? What is the difference between a `String` and a `StringBuffer`?

3. How do you determine whether two strings are equal and whether one is greater than the other lexicographically? How do you turn primitive data into a string?

4. How do you determine whether a string has a given prefix or suffix? How do you reverse a string?

5. Can an instance field be declared `final`? Where, if anyplace, does the statement `xyz=value;` make sense if the variable `xyz` is `final`?

6. Can a method formal parameter be declared `final`? What does such a declaration mean? How is this useful?

7. Examine closely the method `partition` used in our quicksort (Section 2.8). Can you show that after the `while` loop the element `a[i]` is not less than `pe`? Also, is it an improvement to the `partition` code to modify the `swap` call to `swap(a, i++, j--)`?

8. If you have a method `plus` in class `Fraction` and a method `plus` in class `Complex`, is the method `plus` considered to be overloaded? Why?

9. What is a canonical representation?

10. Can you access an instance member from a static method? Can you access a static member from an instance method? How? Give examples to illustrate what is possible and what is not.

11. Access the Java API documentation at

    `http://java.sun.com/j2se/1.3/docs/api/index.html`

    and read carefully the documentation for the `String` class. It gives you all the information on how to use the class and its objects. Being able to quickly find the API information for any Java supplied type is key to writing Java programs.

Programming Assignments

1. Write a program `Expand.java` that replaces all TAB characters in its standard input by an equivalent number of spaces and sends the result to standard output. (Hint: Follow the example `Lowercase`.) You may assume that TAB stops are eight characters apart.

2. Using `switch`, write a program that counts the number of SPACE, TAB, NEWLINE, and FORMFEED characters in standard input.

3. Let words in a file be character strings or tokens, separated by one or more white space characters (SPACE, TAB, NEWLINE). Write a program that counts the number of words in the input file or standard input.

4. Write a `gcd` method that is nonrecursive and that can take any `int` arguments, not just nonnegative ones.

5. Add a private method `lcm` to the class `Fraction` that takes two `int`s and returns their *least common multiple*. (For example, `lcm(-15,12)` is 60. Hint: Use gcd.) Modify `minus` and `plus` in `Fraction` to use `lcm`.

6. Add to the class `Fraction` a method `floor` that returns the biggest integer less than or equal to the fraction. (Hint: Consider both positive and negative fractions.)

7. A proper fraction lies between −1 and 1. Add to `Fraction` a method `isProper()`.

8. Follow the `Fraction` example, and write a class `Complex` to represent complex numbers with `double` real and imaginary parts. For `Complex`, define `toString` and binary arithmetic operations.

9. Add the method `conjugate()` to the class `Complex`. Is `conjugate` useful in performing divisions of `Complex` objects?

10. Write a program that creates an array `fracArr` with `new`, initializes each element `fracArr[i]` with the `Fraction` object $\frac{1}{i+1}$, then displays the array.

11. Consider the `Matrix` class. Add the methods `plus`, `minus`, and `transpose` to it.

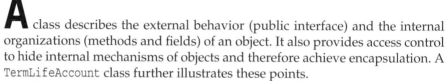

CHAPTER THREE

Object-Based Programming

A class describes the external behavior (public interface) and the internal organizations (methods and fields) of an object. It also provides access control to hide internal mechanisms of objects and therefore achieve encapsulation. A `TermLifeAccount` class further illustrates these points.

Object-based programming is a fundamental OOP technique that employs interacting objects to perform tasks or to obtain solutions. With a solid grip on object-based programming, we can move to more advanced OOP techniques (Chapter 4 and 5). As introduced in the first two chapters, object-based programming tasks are achieved by modeling interacting objects in a solution process. To do that:

1. Analyze the given problem or task to identify the objects needed, their behaviors, and their interactions.

2. Write classes as blueprints for building the desired objects.

3. Write a program that uses these objects to solve the problem or perform the desired task.

Realistic examples further illustrate the use of objects to model interacting entities in the problem domain.

To allow primitive types to behave as objects, Java supplies *wrapper classes* for each primitive type. These wrapper classes are not only useful in programming, but they also provide a model for defining classes.

Component objects can combine to form larger objects. A simulation program shows how to identify component objects and how to use them to model a pocket calculator. Study this example carefully because it is the basis of a sequence of end-of-chapter programming exercises that eventually lead to a substantial OO program.

Objects may have a recursive structure. Classes that contain references to instances of the same class are described, and a linked list example is given to illustrate recursive data structures. Our linked list also lays the foundation for later discussions on generic lists.

You may define multiple methods with the same name belonging to the same class. This *method overloading* feature can make programs easier to write. We'll see how it works in Java.

Java objects are always created at run-time and their storage locations are freed automatically when the objects are no longer needed. Not having to manage the returning of such storage removes a big concern in programming. The *automatic garbage collection* feature is explained.

3.1   A TERM LIFE INSURANCE ACCOUNT

The insurance industry is heavily computerized. Let's consider writing a term life insurance account class as a simple example of how to define this type of objects.

The TermLifeAccount constructor (line 1) takes two arguments, the account holder and the account id, as strings (line 1).

The policy holder's name, social security number (id), age, and coverage amount are kept as private members. The name and id cannot be changed (line 4), even by member methods, after a TermLifeAccount object is initialized by the constructor.

```
///////    TermLifeAccount.java    ///////

public class TermLifeAccount
{  public TermLifeAccount(String holder, String id)          // (1)
   {   name = holder;
       ss = id;
   }

 // methods later ...

 // fields
   public static double RATE = 0.00000576;                   // (2)
   public static int MINAGE=0, MAXAGE=70,
                 MINCOVERAGE=25000, MAXCOVERAGE=500000;       // (3)
   private int age=0;
   private int coverage=0;
   private final String ss;            // policy holder id    // (4)
   private final String name;          // policy holder name
}
```

Class-wide quantities quarterly rate, minimum and maximum coverage amounts, and age limits are static fields with constant initializers (lines 2–3).

A class usually will supply get and set methods for appropriate fields that are not public.

```
public int getAge()
{   return(age);    }
```

```
public boolean setAge(int i)                                    // (5)
{   if ( i >= MINAGE && i <= MAXAGE)
    {   age = i;   return true;
    }
    else return false;
}

public int getCoverage()
{   return coverage;      }

public boolean setCoverage(int amt)                             // (6)
{   if ( amt >= MINCOVERAGE && amt <= MAXCOVERAGE )
    {   coverage = amt;   return true;
    }
    else return false;
}

public String getId()
{   return ss;   }

public String getHolder()
{   return name;   }
```

Note that `setAge` and `setCoverage` both check for the validity of the setting and return `false` when the setting is incorrect.

The method `premium` computes the quarterly premium for a particular term life policy, depending on the age, coverage, and rate:

```
public double premium()                    // Quarterly premium
{   return age*coverage*RATE;   }
```

For our example, we have used an overly simplified premium computation. In practice, the premium is a table with different rates for different age brackets.

Static methods to set and get the class-wide quantities on lines 2–3 can be included in the class as well.

3.2   A TERM LIFE PREMIUM CALCULATOR

Although the purpose of the `TermLifeAccount` class is to establish term life accounts for policy holders, it can also be used simply to supply premium quotes.

Let's write a simple application that is used from the command line in the following fashion:

```
Term Life Premium Calculator
Your Age (0 to 70) = 35
```

```
Coverage (25000 to 500000) = 300000
Your Low Quarterly Premium: $60.48

Continue (Yes or No) =
```

The `TLPremium` class has no instance methods because its purpose is not to define objects, but to provide a procedure for premium quotes.

```
///////    TLPremium.java    ///////
import java.io.*;

public class TLPremium
{  public static void main(String[] args)
        throws IOException
   {   String again, age, coverage;
       TermLifeAccount tl = new TermLifeAccount();        // (A)
       do
       { System.out.println("Term Life Premium Calculator");
         age = MyUtil.getInput("Your Age (" + tl.MINAGE +   // (B)
            " to " + tl.MAXAGE + ")");
         tl.setAge(Integer.parseInt(age));                  // (C)
         coverage = MyUtil.getInput("Coverage (" +
            tl.MINCOVERAGE + " to " + tl.MAXCOVERAGE + ")"); // (D)
         tl.setCoverage(Integer.parseInt(coverage));
         double premium = tl.premium();                     // (E)
         System.out.println("Your Low Quarterly" +
                            " Premium: $" +  premium );
         again = MyUtil.getInput("\nContinue (Yes or No)");
       } while (  again.charAt(0) == 'Y' ||
                  again.charAt(0) == 'y'
              );    // end of do
   }
}
```

The `main` method creates a `TermLifeAccount` object (line A) and uses it to support the premium quote processing (lines B–E). The static method `MyUtil.getInput` can display any given prompt and retrieve a line from standard input:

```
// in class MyUtil

public static String getInput(String prompt) throws IOException
{   BufferedReader in
        = new BufferedReader(new InputStreamReader(System.in));
    System.out.print(prompt + " = ");
    System.out.flush();
    String s = in.readLine();
    if ( s != null && s.length() != 0) return s;
```

```
        return getInput(prompt);
}
```

The `main` method accesses the static age and coverage limits set in `TermLifeAccount` to formulate the user input prompts (lines B and D). The static `parseInt` method in the wrapper class `Integer` (Section 3.3) helps by turning an age/coverage string into an integer. The quotation processing runs in a loop until the user quits.

The `getInput` and other such methods can be useful in many other applications. We placed them in our own `MyUtil` class for easy code reuse.

3.3 JAVA WRAPPER CLASSES

A class attaches methods with data and forms a self-contained computation unit. This is a big advantage for OOP.

Once a class is defined, a new type is born. In Java only primitive types are not defined by classes. To be able to treat primitive types as objects and to attach related methods, Java provides a *wrapper class* for each primitive type. The wrapper classes are listed in Table 3.1.

The `Void` class is a placeholder and cannot be instantiated.

Each wrapper class provides a place for fields and methods associated with a particular primitive type. For example, each numeric type has `static final` constants `MAX_VALUE` and `MIN_VALUE`. If i and j are positive ints, you can use the code

```
if ( (Integer.MAX_VALUE - i) < j )
```

to predict whether i + j will overflow. A wrapper class also allows you to turn a primitive value into an object so it can be passed to code that requires objects.

Methods Common to All Wrapper Classes

Every wrapper class provides these methods:

- A constructor that takes a primitive value and creates a wrapper class object (for example, `Integer iobj = new Integer(175)`).

Table 3.1   PRIMITIVE TYPE WRAPPER CLASSES

Boolean	Byte	Short
Character	Integer	Long
Double	Float	Void

- A constructor that takes a string and creates a wrapper class object (for example, `new Integer("-3.75")`).
- A `toString()` method that produces a string representation (for example, `iobj.toString()`).
- An `equals` method that compares the equality of two objects in the class (for example, `iobj1.equals(iobj2)`).
- A `hashCode` method that produces a code for hashtables (for example, `iobj1.hashCode()`).
- A parse*Type* method to turn a string into a primitive value. For example, `Integer.parseInt(args[0])` obtains an int supplied on the command line (Section 1.11). Also, in Section 3.2 the `main` method of the TLPremium uses `Integer.parseInt` to get the age and coverage from user input.
- A *type*Value method that produces a primitive value of the object (for example, `iobj1.intValue()`).

Each wrapper class except `Character` also has a static `valueOf` method to decode a string and produce a wrapper class object:

```
public static Wrapper-type valueOf(String s)
```

Additionally, the `Integer` and `Long` classes provide methods for *numbers in different bases or radixes*. The `Float` and `Double` classes contain IEEE standard floating-point quantities and predicates such as `Float.POSITIVE_INFINITY`, and `isNaN()`. See the documentation for these classes for more details.

3.4 OPERATIONS ON CHARACTERS

The `Character` wrapper class provides many useful operations for characters. In addition to the common wrapper class members, `Character` also offers members related to upper- and lowercase characters and using characters as digits in numbers under different *radixes* (bases). Table 3.2 shows the set of static methods in `Character`.

We have used the `Character.toLowerCase` method in Chapter 2 (Section 2.3).

`Character` also provides the following constant fields:

`MIN_RADIX`   (minimum radix understood, usually 2)
`MAX_RADIX`   (maximum radix understood, usually 36)

Table 3.2   CHARACTER METHODS

Static Method	Tests For
boolean isUpperCase(char c)	Uppercase character
boolean isLowerCase(char c)	Lowercase character
boolean isDigit(char c)	A digit (not a letter)
boolean isSpace(char c)	SPACE, TAB, NEWLINE, RETURN, FORMFEED

Static Method	Returns
char toUpperCase(char c)	Uppercase c or c if no uppercase
char toLowerCase(char c)	Lowercase c or c if no lowercase
int digit(char c, int b)	Value of c as base-b digit or -1
char forDigit(int d, int b)	Char for d as base-b digit or -1

3.5 A URL DECODER

Information sent by a client to a Web server is usually encoded. Basically each SPACE is translated into a + sign and each nonalphanumeric character is replaced by three characters %*xx*, where *xx* is the ASCII code for the character in hex. The scheme is referred to as *URL encoding*.

Let's write a decoder for a URL-encoded string:

```
public class URLDecoder
{ public static String decode(String s)
   {   int a, b, len = s.length();
       char c, x1, x2, space = ' ';
       StringBuffer buf = new StringBuffer();     // (1)
       for (int i=0; i < len; i++)
       {  c = s.charAt(i);
          if ( c == '+' )  c = space;
          else if ( c == '%' )
          {  x1 = s.charAt(++i);                   // (2)
             x2 = s.charAt(++i);                   // (3)
             a = Character.digit(x1,16);
             b = Character.digit(x2,16);
             if ( a < 0 || b < 0 )
             {  System.err.println(
                    "Invalid code %" + x1 + x2);
```

```
            buf.append(c); buf.append(x1);
            c = x2;
        }
        else
            c = (char) (16*a+b);
    }
    buf.append(c);
    }  // end of for
    return new String(buf);                    // (4)
  }
}
```

A `StringBuffer` is used to build the decoded string (line 1). The `static`
method `digit` of the class `Character` is handy for computing the numeric
value of hex digits (lines 2–3). The returned string is constructed from the
buffer without copying the characters (line 4).

3.6 A CIRCULAR BUFFER

To demonstrate some of the key points covered so far, consider implementing
a *circular buffer*. The example builds a more complicated object further illustrating data abstraction, encapsulation, and object-based programming techniques. After being defined, the circular buffer will be applied in a program
that counts the total number of words in any given file.

A first-in/first-out (FIFO) character buffer is often useful as a mechanism
to transfer characters from a *producer* to a *consumer*. The provider of characters
for the buffer is called the *producer* and the receiver of characters from the buffer
is called the *consumer*. In sequential processing, the producer and consumer
are different parts of the same program. In concurrent (or parallel) processing,
they can be independently running processes or threads (Section 11.8). The
buffer is usually represented as a character array of an appropriate size. In the
beginning, the buffer contains nothing and is therefore empty.

Indices `head` and `tail` are used to keep track of the start of characters yet to
be consumed and the start of empty spaces available in the buffer, respectively.
The `head` advances as characters are consumed, and the `tail` advances as new
characters are put into the buffer. When an index reaches the end of the buffer,
it wraps around to the beginning of the buffer. This wrap-around property
makes the buffer *circular* (Figure 3.1). Obviously, it is an error to consume from
an empty buffer or produce into a full buffer.

A circular buffer class, `Cirbuf`, can be defined to hide the implementation
details and to supply just the right interface for producing into and consuming

Figure 3.1   CIRCULAR BUFFER

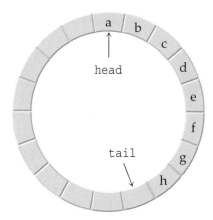

from a circular buffer object. A program can establish a `Cirbuf` object with a given buffer capacity whenever there is a need.

```
///////    Cirbuf.java    ///////

public class Cirbuf
{   public Cirbuf(int s)
    {   head = tail = length = 0;
        size = s;
        cb = new char[s];  // char array buffer
    }

    public Cirbuf() { this(SIZE); }    // null constructor

    private static final int SIZE = 16;
    private int head;      // first char in buffer
    private int tail;      // first empty slot in buffer
    private int length;    // number of characters in buffer
    private int size;      // capacity of buffer
    private char[] cb;     // character buffer
 // other members ...
}
```

The private character array cb, initialized by the `Cirbuf` constructor, provides buffering. The null constructor calls the other constructor

```
this(SIZE);     // constructor call in a constructor
```

passing to it the default buffer size, kept in the static symbolic constant SIZE. *The explicit constructor call* this(...) *is allowed only as the first statement in a constructor.*

The index head points to the first character to be consumed in cb while the index tail locates the slot for the next incoming character. The number of characters remaining in the buffer is length. The buffer is empty if length is zero. It is full if length becomes equal to size. These details are important only to the designer of the Cirbuf class. Any program that uses a circular buffer object is isolated from these details and uses a Cirbuf object only through its public interface methods:

```
public boolean isEmpty() { return length == 0; }

public boolean isFull() { return length == size; }
```

The isEmpty (isFull) test should be used before a get (put) operation. The implementations of get and put are straightforward. The get method uses a character array of length one to return a character to the caller. Note that wrap-around is handled with a call to the private method mod:

```
public boolean put(char c)      // insert c into buffer
{   if ( ! isFull() )
    {   cb[tail++] = c;
        length++;
        tail = mod(tail);       // wrap around
        return true;            // put done
    }
    return false;               // put failed
}

// array c of length 1
public boolean get(char[] c)    // extract char from buffer
{   if ( ! isEmpty() )
    {   c[0] = cb[head++];
        length--;
        head = mod(head);       // wrap around
        return true;            // get done
    }
    return false;               // get failed
}

private int mod(int n)
{ return(n >= size ?  n - size : n); }
```

In testing Cirbuf, a reasonably small size, such as 5, can be used so that wrap-around happens sooner.

Circular Buffer Usage

Putting the circular buffer to use, an example program counts the number of words, separated by SPACE, TAB, and/or NEWLINE characters, in the standard input. The main method of WordCount calls readInput and wordCount repeatedly until input is exhausted. It then makes one final call to wordCount before reporting the total word count.

```java
//////   WordCount.java   //////
import java.io.*;

public class WordCount     // a totally static class
{  public static void main(String[] args) throws IOException
    {   Cirbuf bf = new Cirbuf(128);
        wcnt = 0; word = false;
        for (;;)
            if ( readInput(bf) )                // producer
                wordCount(bf);                  // consumer
            else
            {   wordCount(bf);
                if ( word ) wcnt++;
                break;
            }
        System.out.println("total " + wcnt + " words");
    }
  // other methods ...
    private static int wcnt= 0;             // total word count
    private static boolean word= false;     // partial word indicator
    private static char[] inc= new char[1];
}
```

A producer method readInput obtains input characters and deposits them in the circular buffer until it is full:

```java
private static
boolean readInput(Cirbuf b)                 // read from standard input
        throws IOException
{   int c;
    while ( ! b.isFull() )                  // while b not full
      if ( (c = System.in.read()) != -1)
         b.put((char)c);                     // deposit into buffer
      else
         return false;                       // input closed
    return true;                             // buffer full
}
```

Then a consumer method wordCount takes characters out of the buffer and counts the number of words until the buffer is empty. These two steps are repeated until the input is finished.

The private field wcnt keeps the current total word count, inc provides a one-character array to retrieve from the circular buffer, and word indicates counting one whole word across multiple invocations of wordCount:

```
private static void wordCount(Cirbuf b)
{   while ( ! b.isEmpty() )        // while buffer not empty
    { b.get(inc);
      switch( inc[0] )              // remove char from buffer
      { case ' ' : case '\t':
        case '\r': case '\n':      // word delimiters
          if ( word )
            {   wcnt++;             // word complete
                word = false;      // partial word indicator false
            }
          break;
        default:
            word = true;           // partial word indicator true
      }
    }
}
```

Now the program is ready for some sample files. If your computer system has an independent word count program (e.g., UNIX **wc** command), it can be used to verify the output of the Java program.

3.7 POCKET CALCULATOR SIMULATION

An object-based program is more interesting when multiple objects are involved. In addition to acting as peers or agents, objects can also serve as components in other objects, and building a class with component objects can enhance encapsulation, flexibility, and modifiability. To illustrate these points, let's look at a pocket calculator simulation program.

Suppose we wish to simulate the functions and behavior of a simple handheld calculator. We can write a Java program that supports the arithmetic operations +, -, *, /, and =, as well as the C (clear), A (all clear), and N (sign change) operations.

Following is a typical session with the simulated calculator:

```
Calc:   0
32 +
Calc:   32
66 —
```

```
Calc:   98
86 =
Calc:   12
N
Calc:   -12
```

Each calculator display line has the `Calc:` prefix. User input is shown in italic. A session ends when user input ends with a ^D on UNIX or a ^Z on Windows.

Program Design

Applying object-based programming for our simulation, we employ objects found in an actual calculator:

- A *manager* object (`Calculator`) that employs a compute engine component and a user interface component to perform the simulation
- A *user interface* object (`CalcFace`) that reports user input to the `Calculator` and displays results
- A *compute engine* object (`CalcEng`) that supplies computing abilities and stores data

Figure 3.2 shows these objects and their relationships. In UML class relation diagrams (Section 13.4), a filled diamond shape indicates a *composition* relationship. `CalcEng` and `CalcFace` *compose* a `Calculator` because they are integral parts of the whole. A head is an integral part of a person and does not function separately. A hat is not like that. The object-oriented architecture isolates the arithmetic unit (`CalcEng`) from the user interface (`CalcFace`). The `Calculator` manages both components. Let's first examine the details of the calculator compute engine.

The `CalcEng` Class
Thecalculator engine object performs the computing and maintains the state for the calculator. Its *public interface* consists of four methods:

1. The method `setOperand` is used to enter numeric data into the compute engine.

Figure 3.2   CALCULATOR OBJECTS

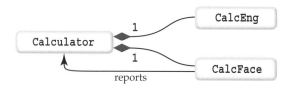

2. The method `operate` is called to enter the next opcode and trigger engine operations.

3. The method `getOpcode` is called to obtain the internally kept operator code (+, *, and so on).

4. The method `getOutput` is invoked to produce the argument currently stored.

The calculator compute engine works with three fundamental quantities:

1. The field `ans` is the answer, or result of requested computations, initialized to `0.0`.

2. The field `op` is the operation code (or opcode), one of the characters in the constant `KEYS` string, whose left operand is always `ans`.

3. The field `arg` is the right operand of `op`.

Here is the `CalcEng` class:

```
///////    CalcEng.java    ///////

class CalcEng
{  public CalcEng() {  allClear(); }        // (1)

 // returns current opcode
   public char getOpcode()
   {    return op;  }

 // returns current argument
   public double getOutput()
   {    return argcnt==2 ? arg : ans; }

 // enters an argument
   public void setOperand(double a)          // (2)
   {    if ( op == '=' ) ans = a;
        else
        {  arg = a; argcnt = 2; }
   }

   public String keys() { return KEYS; }     // operation keys
   public byte precision() { return PREC; } // precision supported

   private void allClear()                   // (3)
   {    ans = arg = 0.0;
        argcnt = 1;
        op = '=';
   }
```

```
// other methods ...

    private final String KEYS = "+-*/=NAC";
    private final byte PREC = 8;
    private double ans, arg;
    private char op;                          // operation code
    private int argcnt;                       // argument count
}
```

The `CalcEng` constructor (line 1) initializes a new engine to a pristine state by calling `allClear` (line 3), a method that also supports the `'A'` operation discussed later. Numeric (`double`) data are entered into a `CalcEng` object using the `setOperand` method (line 2). If the previous operation (still kept in `op`) is `'='`, the data is assigned to `ans` (the left operand of the next operation). Otherwise it is assigned to `arg` (the right operand) of the current `op` (one of `"+-*/"`). The private data member `argcnt` keeps track of how many operands have been entered at any given time.

When the operands are in place, an operation is triggered by a call to `operate` with the next character code from the user:

```
public void operate(char nc)              // nc is next opcode
{   switch( nc )
    {   case 'A':                         // All Clear
            allClear(); return;
        case 'C':                         // Clear
            clear(); return;
        case 'N':                         // sign change
            if ( argcnt == 1 ) ans = -ans;
            else arg = -arg;
            return;
        default :                         // +-*/=
            compute();
            op = nc;                      // new opcode
    }
}
```

The operations A, N, and C are performed immediately. Others (`"+-*/="`) trigger computations implemented by `compute` before being recorded as the new value of `op` (the next calculation to perform). The `clear` method clears the current entry:

```
private void clear()
{   if ( argcnt == 1 )
    {   ans = 0.0; op = '='; }
    else
    {   arg = 0.0; argcnt = 1; }
}
```

The `compute` method checks for the correct number of operands and actually carries out arithmetic operations. Of course, its actions are guided by the currently stored value of op:

```
private void compute()
{   if ( argcnt == 2 )
    {   switch( op )
        {   case '+':  ans += arg; break;
            case '-':  ans -= arg; break;
            case '*':  ans *= arg; break;
            case '/':  ans /= arg; break;
        }
        argcnt = 1;
    }
}
```

Testing `CalcEng`   Because a class actually defines an independent computing entity, it makes sense always to test a class and its objects independently. When combining objects into larger programs, all you have to do then is to make sure that the objects are interfaced correctly.

To test `CalcEng.java`, we use a `main` method such as the following:

```
public static void main(String[] args)
{   CalcEng cal = new CalcEng();         // instantiates object
    cal.setOperand(9.8);                 // enters operand
    cal.operate('+');                    // enters opcode
    cal.setOperand(1.2);
    cal.operate('/');
    cal.setOperand(2.0);
    cal.operate('=');
    System.out.println(cal.getOutput()); // displays answer
}
```

Of course, this simple program falls far short of a comprehensive test for the `CalcEng` class. Its purpose here is to show some typical test cases. In testing your own program, you should exercise all parts of the code and pay special attention to extreme and unusual cases. The complete `CalcEng.java` code can be found in the example package. Compile `CalcEng.java` and run

java CalcEng

to see what happens.

The `CalcEng` class is finished. Now let's consider the user interface part of the calculator.

The `CalcFace` Class   I/O to the user is the responsibility of a `CalcFace` object. This object reads user input and displays calculator output.

The `CalcFace` constructor is given a string of opcode keys and a precision setting. The `prec` field is the maximum input characters to allow by the `CalcFace`. It is the engine precision plus one to allow for the possible decimal point (line A). CalcFace initialization also creates a string buffer to hold user input (line B). CalcFace reports to a `Calculator` object that can be set by the `setCalc` method (line C).

```java
///////    CalcFace.java    ///////
import java.io.*;

class CalcFace
{  public CalcFace(String k, byte pr)
     {   keys = k;   prec = pr++;                    // (A)
         nbuf = new StringBuffer(prec);              // (B)
         reset();
     }

     public void setCalc(Calculator ca)             // (C)
     {   calc = ca; }

  // more methods later ...

     private Calculator calc;
     private String prompt="Calc:  ";
     private String keys;                 // keys recognized
     private StringBuffer nbuf;           // buffer for input number
     private byte prec;                   // max no of chars displayable
     private boolean num = false;
     private boolean before_point = true;
}
```

In addition to `setCalc`, the `CalcFace` public interface has three other methods: input, showNumber, and showOp. The method showNumber displays a given number to the user with a prompt. The showOp method can be used to display the current opcode but does not do anything at this point.

```java
public void showNumber(String s)
{   System.out.println(prompt + s);
}

public void showOp(char op) { }
```

Simulating input processing by a calculator is a bit more complicated. The strategy is to keep reading input characters and entering them into a string buffer `nbuf` (by calling enter and buildNumber()) as long as they are part of a number. As soon as an opcode character is encountered, the number is complete and both the number and the opcode are obtained. If the number part is empty, only an opcode is entered. To simulate a calculator, the input number consists of digits with one possible decimal point.

The input method runs in a continuous loop (line D), entering each input character, until the standard input is closed (inchar() returning -1). The enter method processes each input character. If the character is not an opcode, it is treated as part of an input number (line I). In case it is an opcode (line E), the enterNumber method of the calc object is called if a number has been received along with the opcode (line F). Otherwise, the enterOp method of calc is called to enter just an opcode (line G). After processing this user input, the reset method is called to set up the host CalcFace object for the next user input (line H).

```
public void input() throws IOException
{    int i;
     while ( (i= inchar()) != -1 )                        // (D)
     {    enter((char) i);    }
}

private void enter(char c)
{    if ( keys.indexOf(c) != -1 )                          // (E)
     {    showOp(c);
          if ( num )
               calc.enterNumber(extractNumber(), c);       // (F)
          else
               calc.enterOp(c);                            // (G)
          reset();                                         // (H)
     }
     else if ( nump(c) && nbuf.length() < prec )           // (I)
     {    num = true;
          buildNumber(c);
     }
}

private void reset()
{    before_point = true;
     nbuf.setLength(0);
     num = false;
}
```

When building an input number, input characters that are not recognized or are beyond the calculator's precision are ignored (line I). The private method buildNumber accumulates numeric input in the string buffer nbuf:

```
private void buildNumber(char c)
{    int i = nbuf.length();
     if ( i == 0 && c == '0') return;  // ignore leading zeros
```

```
    if ( c == '.' )                    // at most one decimal point
    {    if ( ! before_point ) return;
         else before_point = false;
    }
    nbuf.append(c);                     // to end of string buffer
}
```

The extractNumber method simply returns the string representing the input number (line J), and the inchar method obtains the next input character
from standard input:

```
private String extractNumber()                  // (J)
{   return (nbuf.length() == 0) ?  "0"
          : nbuf.toString();
}


private int inchar() throws IOException
{   return System.in.read(); }
```

Testing CalcFace   The user interface class CalcFace can be tested in-
dependently with a class that supplies a *stub implementation* of Calculator:

```
public class TestFace
{   public static void main(String[] args) throws IOException
    {   CalcEng e = new CalcEng();
        CalcFace f = new CalcFace(e.keys(), e.precision());
        f.setCalc(new Calculator());
        f.showNumber("0.0");
        f.input();
        System.out.println("Goodbye!");
    }
}

class Calculator      // a stub implementation
{   void enterNumber(String n, char c)
    {   System.out.println("number= " + n + " Op is " + c);
    }

    void enterOp(char c)
    {   System.out.println("Op is " + c);    }
}
```

Now let's see how relatively simple it is to use CalcEng and CalcFace
objects in building a Calculator object.

The Calculator Class   The `Calculator` constructor instantiates a `CalcEng` object and a `CalcFace` object (line i):

```
///////    Calculator.java    ///////

public class Calculator
{  public Calculator(CalcEng e, CalcFace f)          // (i)
   {   eng = e; cf = f;
       f.setCalc(this);
   }

   public void on() throws java.io.IOException
   {   output();
       cf.input();                                    // (ii)
   }

   public void enterNumber(String number, char op)
   {   eng.setOperand( Double.parseDouble(number) );
       enterOp(op);
   }

   public void enterOp( char op )
   {   eng.operate( op );
       output();
   }

   private void output()                              // (iii)
   {   double number = eng.getOutput();
       cf.showNumber(""+number);
   }

   private CalcEng eng = null;
   private CalcFace cf = null;
}
```

The `Calculator` class has public methods `on`, `enterOp`, and `enterNumber`. The `on` method starts the calculator by providing an initial display, then calls the looping `input()` method of the user interface (line ii). As we see from the `CalcFace` class, the `Calculator` methods `enterNumber` and `enterOp` are called by the `CalcFace` object. The private `output` method obtains the engine output for display (line iii).

Experimenting with a calculator object is now very simple indeed:

```
///////    RunCalc.java    ///////

public class RunCalc
```

```
{ public static void main(String[] args) throws java.io.IOException
    { CalcEng e = new CalcEng();
      CalcFace f = new CalcFace(e.keys(), e.precision());
      Calculator x = new Calculator(e, f);
      x.on();
      return;
    }
}
```

Compile and run the program:

javac RunCalc.java
java RunCalc

Then experiment with the program interactively to see how well it simulates a pocket calculator. To end a session with this calculator, type the input-ending character ^D (UNIX) or ^Z (Windows).

This program will evolve with chapter-end exercises to apply OO techniques. Finally it will become a program with a graphical user interface that simulates a pocket calculator in great detail (Chapter 13).

3.8 LINKED LIST

From Section 3.7 we see that a class may contain components that are instances of other classes. But is it possible or desirable for a class to contain an object that is an instance of the *same* class? Very much so. Such classes define *recursive structures*. Among recursive data structures, the linked list is one of the most well known. The class implementation of a linked list is the topic here.

A grocery list can be thought of as a structure with two members:

1. The name of a grocery item
2. A grocery list of the remaining items

In fact, this recursive structure is inherent to a list.

A *linked list* is a typical recursive structure used to store and manage data. A linked list of characters, CharList, is presented. Recursive structures are used to construct a convenient computing entity whose internal implementation is anything but simple. The example also lays the foundation for building lists of arbitrary items later.

The List Cell

A linked list is composed of *cells* that are linked. Each cell of the list contains a character and a reference to the next cell. In other words, each list cell holds a reference to the next cell, like a "chain of elephants" (Figure 3.3). Unlike a rigid array, a linked list affords great flexibility at run time—adding, deleting, and

Figure 3.3   LINKED LIST

reordering items anywhere on a list are simple. Each cell on the linked list is
an object of the class ListCell:

```
class ListCell
{    ListCell(char c, ListCell cell)
      { item=c; next=cell; }
     ListCell() { }
     char content() { return item; }
  // fields
     char item = '\0';
     ListCell next = null;
}
```

Each ListCell object stores a character in item and a reference to the next
cell in next. The following illustrates the construction of a list:

```
ListCell listX = new ListCell('C', null);   //      (C)
listX = new ListCell('B', listX);           //    (B C)
listX = new ListCell('A', listX);           // (A B C)
```

A list cell containing the character C is first created with a call to new, and listX
refers to this first cell. Another cell is created containing the character B and a
reference to the previous cell. Now listX refers to the second cell and is a list
of two characters. This can be done a number of times to create a list of any
length.

Linked List Design

Consider how the class CharList is defined. In designing any class, consideration should first be given to its public interface and external behavior. Internal
mechanisms can then be designed and implemented to support the desired
external behavior. For a linked list, what should the public interface be?

- Building a list—Establishing a new list that is empty or has one item
  (constructors); adding items to a list (putOn, append, insert).
- Accessing list cells—Retrieving list cells (first, next, last, and find,
  each returning a reference to ListCell or null if no such cell exists).
- Removing items—Deleting all cells with a certain item (remove);
  removing several cells from the front of the list (shorten).

- Substituting items—Substituting item r for the first item s on the list.
- Displaying the list—Producing a display of the entire list or a sublist starting at any given list cell (overloaded toString).

Of course many good interface designs can exist for the same class. For a list class, there are so many other possible operations that it is impossible to cover all of them here. Now examine how the public interface is implemented:

```
///////    CharList.java    ///////

public class CharList
{   public CharList() { }             // creates empty list

    public CharList(char c)           // initializes list with 1st cell
    {    head=new ListCell(c, null); }

    public ListCell first()
    {    return head; }               // gets first cell

    public boolean isEmpty()
    {    return head == null; }

 // other methods ...
    private ListCell head = null;    // 1st cell of list
}
```

The only data member, the private field head, is null (empty list) or refers to the first cell of the list, which can be accessed through the public method first.

Both access methods last and find return the list cell found (type ListCell). Note how last treats an empty list:

```
public ListCell last()                  // last cell
{   ListCell p = head;
    while( p != null && p.next != null )
        p =  p.next;
    return p;
}

public ListCell find(char c)            // first item == c
{   for( ListCell p = head; p!=null; p = p.next )
        if ( p.item == c ) return p;
    return null;                        // c not on list
}
```

The frequent idiom

```
for( ListCell p = head; p!=null; p = p.next ) // idiom
```

follows cells down a linked list efficiently. The member `find` locates the target character s, for which r will be substituted.

```
public boolean substitute(char r, char s) // substitutes r for 1st s
{   ListCell p = find(s);
    if (p == null) return false;            // s not on list
    p.item = r;
    return true;
}
```

The method `shorten` removes a number of cells from the beginning of a list. If the list can be shortened by the requested amount, n, zero is returned. Otherwise a negative integer ($listlength - n$) is returned after removing all list cells.

```
public int shorten(int n)               // removes first n cells
{   while (head != null && n-- > 0)
        head = head.next;
    return -n;
}
```

To remove all characters equal to c from the list, the method `remove(char)` first processes all list cells, starting with the second cell. Then the first cell (head) is treated separately. The total number of cells removed is returned by the method.

```
public int remove(char c)               // removes c from entire list
{   ListCell p = head;
    int count = 0;
    if ( p == null ) return count;
    while (p.next != null)              // treats all but head cell
    {   if ((p.next).item == c)
        {   count++;
            p.next = (p.next).next;
        }
        else
            p = p.next;
    }
    if( head.item == c )                // treats head cell
    {   head = head.next;
        count++;
    }
    return count;                       // number of items removed
}
```

Inserting a new item at the beginning (putOn), after a given entry e (insert), or at the end (append) is relatively simple:

```
public void putOn(char c)                 // inserts in front
{   head = new ListCell(c, head); }

public void insert(char c, ListCell e)    // inserts after cell
{   e.next = new ListCell(c, e.next); }

public void append(char c)                // inserts at end
{   insert(c, last()); }
```

Overloaded toString methods enable easy display of linked lists, either the entire list or from a particular cell to the end of the list:

```
public String toString()                  // for whole list
{   return toString(head);  }

public String toString(ListCell p)        // from p on
{   String s = "(";
    while ( p != null )
    {   s = s + p.item;
        if ( (p = p.next) != null ) s = s + " ";
    }
    return  s + ")";
}
```

The ListCell class is placed in the same file as CharList, and the code can now be tested:

```
public class TestCharList
{   public static void main(String[] args)
    {   CharList a = new CharList('B');
        a.putOn('A');
        a.append('D'); a.append('E'); a.append('F');
        System.out.println("a = " + a);
        ListCell lp = a.find('B');
        System.out.println(a.toString(lp));
        a.insert('C', lp);
        System.out.println("a = " + a);
        a.remove('E');
        a.shorten(2);
        System.out.println("a = " + a);
        a.remove('C');
        System.out.println("a = " + a);
    }
}
```

When compiled and executed, it produces the following output:

```
a = (A B D E F)
(B D E F)
a = (A B C D E F)
a = (C D F)
a = (D F)
```

A complete list class would have other methods, such as concatenating two lists, taking union or intersection, measuring the length of a list, and so on.

The advantage of using linked lists is the ability to insert and delete items anywhere on the list with ease. For instance, in a text editor program each text line can be represented by a linked list of characters to make inserting and deleting characters easy.

The preceding example dealt with characters, but the basic linked list structure and manipulations stay the same for integers, floats, strings, dates, or other types. In fact, it is easy in Java to define a list of arbitrary types (Section 4.22). Such generality brings to programs much needed flexibility and reusability.

The `ListCell` class is completely subservient to the `CharList` class. For better information hiding, `ListCell` should be encapsulated within `CharList` so that it becomes an internal mechanism. This encapsulation can be achieved through the *inner class* construct (Section 7.12).

3.9   OVERLOADING METHODS

Traditionally, a method or function performs a specific duty that is programmed for it. Java supports *method overloading*, allowing you to define multiple versions of a method with the same name in a class, as long as the versions have different *signatures*. A *signature* consists of the method name and the number, order, and types of its formal parameters. We have already used some overloaded constructors. As another simple example, consider resetting the account balance in a `BankAccount` object. The `BankAccount` class already has a method

```
public double balance();
```

that is used to retrieve the account balance. With overloading we can define a method

```
public void balance(double amt)
{    acct_bal = amt;    }
```

that sets the balance to a specified amount. The same method, depending on whether an argument is given, will either retrieve or set the balance; how convenient!

Note that overloading occurs only when the same method name is *defined multiple times within a class*. Thus, toString methods, for example, in different classes are not overloading one another. There is no practical limit on the number of different versions that can be piled on the same method name in a class.

Method Call Resolution

When a call is made to an overloaded method, Java automatically deduces, from the actual arguments, the correct version of the method to invoke. This activity is termed *call resolution*. Java performs call resolution by selecting one method from all *accessible methods that are applicable*.

A method is *applicable* if it takes the same number of parameters as the arguments given and each argument can be converted by *method invocation conversion* to the type of the parameter (Section 2.13).

The compiler performs method call resolution by matching the number and type of the actual arguments with signatures of all accessible methods and choosing an applicable method that is *most specific* or *closest*:

1. If there is an accessible method in the scope of the class that is an exact match, call that method.
2. Identify the set *CAN* of all *accessible methods that are applicable*. If *CAN* is empty, the call will fail.
3. From signatures in *CAN*, eliminate *less specific* signatures: *If arguments receivable by signature s1 can always be passed to signature s2, eliminate s2 from CAN*.
4. After all eliminations have been made, if *CAN* contains one signature, that is the one invoked. Otherwise, the call is ambiguous and invalid.

Following are example signatures that are increasingly specific:

```
methodM(long, double)     // least specific
methodM(int, double)
methodM(int, float)
methodM(short, float)     // most specific
```

On the other hand, neither of the following two signatures is more specific than the other:

```
methodN(long, float)
methodN(int, double)
```

3.10 STORAGE ALLOCATION AND MANAGEMENT

When a variable is declared, storage for it is allocated by the compiler. Thus, variables declared in a Java program have storage allocated at compile time. Primitive type variables (`int`, `double`, and so on) have just enough storage for the data; array type and class type variables have just enough storage for a reference. Static fields are created at the start of program execution and persist until the end of execution. Local variables, in a method or block, are automatically created and destroyed as control enters and leaves the block.

Object Storage Allocation with `new`

Memory space for an object is allocated at run time with the operator `new`. The Java interpreter maintains a *free store heap* from which `new` obtains storage. Memory occupied by objects no longer needed becomes *garbage* and is returned automatically to the heap to be reused.

Garbage Collection

The Java run time supports *garbage collection*, which is the automatic collection of objects no longer needed back into the heap. When storage in the heap is low and more storage is needed (by `new`), the garbage collection mechanism is activated, and unneeded objects, called *garbage*, are collected back into the heap. In your program, objects not reachable by *live references* become garbage. Consider a method with a local variable `tmp` that refers to an object allocated by `new` in the method. When the method returns, the variable (reference) is gone and, assuming that there is no other reference, the object becomes garbage. If you assign a new reference value or `null` to a variable, the old object will lose a live reference and may become garbage. Automatic garbage collection frees the programmer from having to delete objects explicitly. This simplifies programming and eliminates a frequent source of errors.

The Java run time decides when to perform garbage collection, and the time is not predictable. A program can ask for immediate garbage collection by invoking the `gc()` method of the run-time object (Section 12.3).

Even with garbage collection, it is possible for a program to deplete the heap and run out of storage by using too many objects. In this case, the operator `new` throws an `OutOfMemoryError` exception.

The Method `finalize`

When an object has been garbage-collected, the heap resource it holds is reclaimed. But what about other resources an object may hold? For example, an object may hold a temporary scratch file, a lock file, a network connection, or some other resource. It would be good, and sometimes necessary, to delete the file, close the connection, or otherwise release a resource before the object is gone.

The method `finalize` is used for this purpose. If defined, the `finalize` method is invoked automatically just before an object is garbage-collected or when the Java run time terminates. The `finalize` method supplies programmer-specified actions before an object is destroyed.

A simple `finalize` method looks something like this:

```
protected void finalize() throws Throwable
{
    // delete temporary file, for example
    ...
}
```

Section 4.9 shows how to write `finalize` for a subclass.

Because there is no guarantee of when a `finalize` will be executed, important resources requiring immediate release must not rely on `finalize` alone. Such a class should provide methods for the explicit release of such resources; `close` in `OutputStream` is an example.

3.11 SUMMARY

In object-based programming, we define classes and use their instances for problem solving. The term life insurance account example shows again how to define the the public interface of objects and also how and why to use class-wide members.

Java supplies *wrapper classes* for all primitive types (plus void). The wrapper classes provide useful fields and methods for the primitive types and a way to treat all types as objects. The `Character` class offers useful operations for Unicode-defined characters and for using characters as digits for numbers in different radixes.

The `Cirbuf` example further illustrates how to separate the external behavior of objects from their internal implementations. The calculator simulation demonstrates building objects with component objects and making them cooperate. Class diagrams from UML (*Unified Modeling Language*, Chapter 13) can clearly depict object-oriented design.

A calculator simulation program illustrates the building of larger objects with component objects and the separation of duties in an OO program. This example begins a sequence of chapter-end exercises that evolve this realistic OO program with new topics covered. A `CharList` illustrates the building of recursive structures and the designing of public interfaces. `CharList` lays the foundation for subsequent materials on generic lists.

Overloaded methods have different *signatures*. When calling an overloaded method, Java performs *method call resolution* to select a method from all *accessible* methods that are *applicable*.

In a program, all objects are allocated at run time with the operator new. Objects with no active references to them become inaccessible (garbage) and will be automatically collected to the free pool for reuse. Automatic garbage collection makes programming less error prone. Just before an object is garbage-collected, its finalize method is invoked. This can perform clean-up operations before the object is destroyed. The exact time when garbage collection takes place is not predictable.

EXERCISES

Review Questions

1. Consider method overloading. What is a method prototype? What is a method signature? What is the difference?

2. If you have a method named size in one class and another method named size in a different class, are these methods considered overloading each other? Why or why not?

3. The Character wrapper class offers what static methods and for what purposes?

4. Based on your understanding of object-based programming, explain why Java provides wrapper classes for primitive types. List as many reasons as you can.

5. Given a string representation of a primitive quantity, such as double or int, how do you convert the string into primitive data? Name two ways to do this. What happens if the string is invalid?

6. Give two examples of allocating objects where the operator new is not used explicitly.

7. The CharList class supports a list of characters. What about a list of ints, doubles, and BankAccounts?

8. The ListCell class is not declared public. Why? What is the access designation of its item and next fields? Why?

9. When the Java compiler detects an invalid call to an overloaded method, what error message is produced?

10. List all five different types of members a class may have. The difference does not involve access protection. Can you think of any code in a class that is not one of the five member types you listed?

11. Is a constructor just an instance method with a special name? Or is it a static method with a special name? If neither, what makes a constructor different? List all the reasons you can.

Programming Assignments

1. (Term Life-0) Add methods to get or set the static constants for rate and coverage for the `TermLifeAccount` class.

2. (Term Life-1) Consider the `premium` method in `TermLifeAccount` (Section 3.1). In practice, the premium is from a table with different rates for different age brackets. Find a realistic premium computation and rewrite the `premium` method.

3. (Term Life-2) Consider the `TLPremium` class in Section 3.1. When treating coverage and age input, it does not check for valid ranges. Add this check to the program.

4. Refer to Section 3.5 about URL encoding. Write a `UrlEncoder`.

5. Add a member `boolean grow(int n)` to `CirBuf`. The method increases the capacity of a `Cirbuf` object by n characters. Any unconsumed characters in the buffer remain. If `grow()` fails, `false` will be returned.

6. A *stack* is a first-in/last-out buffer. If the numbers `1.0, 2.0, 3.0` are entered into the buffer in that order, they are taken out of the stack in the sequence `3.0, 2.0, 1.0`. The operation `push` enters an item on the top of a stack, and the operation `pop` removes an item from the top of the stack. These are the only two operations that are allowed to modify a stack. Following the circular buffer example in Section 3.6, implement a class `Stack` for type `double`.

7. Use the `Stack` object in the previous exercise to implement a program **Rp** to evaluate a *reverse Polish* expression. For example

   `java Rp 3.1  -4.2 /  5.3  6.4 - 7.5 * +`

   displays the value of `3.1 / -4.2 + (5.3 - 6.4) * 7.5`. Be careful entering the command line. On UNIX or MS/DOS, you can quote wildcard characters such as * within DOUBLE-QUOTES (`"*"`). (Hint: Use `Double.parseDouble(string)`)

8.　(Calc-1) This is the first of a series of chapter-end exercises based on the pocket calculator simulation program (Section 3.7). Here we will add error treatment to the program:

(a) In `CalcEng`

- Add a constant `MAX_VALUE`, which is the largest double value within the allowed precision (currently 8 significant digits). (Hint: 99999999)
- Add a private field `String statusFlag` to `CalcEng` that can hold a status string to represent various states the engine may be in. Use the value `"E"`, for example, for arithmetic error and the value `""` for no error. Set up `final` constants for these strings.
- Add a public method `String status()` that returns the `statusFlag`.
- Add a public method `boolean isError()` that returns `true` if the engine is in an error state.
- Add a private method `isError(double n)` to determine whether a computation result n is too big (in either positive or negative directions), is infinite, or is not a number. (Hint: Wrapper class `Double`)
- Modify the `operate` method so that the clear and all-clear operations will deal with the setting of the `statusFlag`.

(b) In `CalcFace`

- Add a public method `showStatus(String e)` that changes the value of the prompt string to include or exclude an error/status indication represented by the string e. For example `"Calc [E]:　"` can be the error prompt while `"Calc:　"` is the normal prompt.
- Add a public method `errorInput(String str)` that puts the interface in *error input mode* and will disable all input characters except those specified by the argument `str`.
- Modify the `enter` method to enforce error and normal input modes.

(c) Modify `Calculator` appropriately to observe engine status, and ask the interface to show the status and to switch between error and normal input modes as appropriate.

(d) Test run the program and make sure that the error handling works correctly. Future exercises involving the calculator simulation program assume that the three classes have been modified to handle errors as suggested here.

## CHAPTER FOUR

Inheritance and Class Extension

One of the most outstanding OOP features is *inheritance*, a mechanism that defines new objects based on existing ones. Java supports inheritance with *class extension*, defining a new class based on an existing class without modifying it. Such a new class, called a *subclass* or *extended class*, *inherits* the members of an existing *superclass* and adds other members of its own. Inheriting from an extended class is also possible, giving rise to *inheritance hierarchies*.

Java supports *single inheritance* through *class extension*. In *single inheritance*, a class is *extended* from a single *superclass*. For example, a subclass JointAccount can be extended from the superclass BankAccount or a Manager from Employee. Some OOP languages, such as C++, support *multiple inheritance*, where a subclass can have multiple superclasses. By disallowing multiple inheritance, Java avoids the associated difficulties and complications that plague languages with multiple inheritance. Skillful use of inheritance through subclasses contributes significantly to a well-designed OO program.

Both conceptual understanding and experience are important to achieving proficiency in this critical area of OOP. Class extension is explained carefully, and implications of class extension are discussed comprehensively. Understanding is enhanced by the building of a vivid mental model of the extended class and objects as well as by providing good examples. Principles that guide the usage and application of class extension are given. Important topics on information hiding, member access control, and method overriding under class extension, often confusing to beginners, are made simple.

The Object root superclass and the way it enables generic programming will also be explained.

4.1 ADVANTAGES OF INHERITANCE

The inheritance mechanism brings several major advantages:

- Easy code modification—Avoid altering existing code, and use inheritance to add new features or change existing features.

- Reuse of existing code—Avoid reinventing the wheel. Simply use inheritance to employ working and tested code as a foundation.
- Adaptation of programs to work in similar, but different, situations—Avoid writing largely similar programs all over again because the application, computer system, data format, or mode of operation is slightly different. Simply use inheritance to modify existing code to suit.
- Extraction of commonality from different classes—Avoid duplicating identical or similar code and structures in different classes. Simply extract the common parts to form another class, and allow it to be inherited by the other classes.
- Organization of objects into hierarchies—Form groups of objects that have an *"is a kind of"* relationship. For example, a savings account is a kind of bank account; a checking account is a kind of account; a sedan is a kind of automobile; a sports sedan is a kind of sedan; a manager is a kind of employee; a square matrix is a kind of matrix; and so forth. Such groupings give a program better organization and, much more important, allow objects in the same hierarchy to be used as *compatible* types, as opposed to completely unrelated types.

4.2 CLASS EXTENSION BASICS

Let's look first at the class extension mechanism. Consider the BankAccount class described earlier (Section 1.6). Suppose it is now necessary to handle joint accounts. Each joint account has two owners instead of just one. This is certainly a small change from BankAccount, and you can write a JointAccount class simply by copying the source code of BankAccount and adding a joint owner and some related methods. However, there is a better approach: defining JointAccount by extending BankAccount without changing it or duplicating the code.

The existing class BankAccount, written as a suitable superclass for extension, is shown here:

```
///////   BankAccount.java     ///////

public class BankAccount
{   public BankAccount() {}
    public BankAccount(int id, String ss, double amt)
    {   acct_no = id;
        owner = ss;
        acct_bal = (amt > 0) ? amt : 0.0;
    }
```

```
        public double balance()
        {    return acct_bal;   }

        public int id()
        {    return acct_no;   }

        public void deposit(double amt)
        {    if ( amt > 0 ) acct_bal += amt; }

        public boolean withdraw(double amt)
        {    if ( amt <=0 || amt > acct_bal )
                return false;      // failure
            acct_bal -= amt;
            return true;
        }

        public String toString()
        {    return acct_no + ":" + owner + ":" + acct_bal; }

    // other members ...

        protected int  acct_no;    // protected account number
        protected String owner;    // protected owner ss

        private double  acct_bal; // account balance
}
```

Fields acct_no and owner are now declared protected, an access control designation whose meaning is explained in Section 4.4. For now, let us focus on class extension.

Joint Account

Now the new JointAccount class can be written by extending the existing Account class:

```
///////    JointAccount.java    ///////

public class JointAccount extends BankAccount               // (1)
{  public JointAccount() {}
   public
   JointAccount(int n, double b, String ss, String jss)     // (2)
   {   super(n, ss, b);                                      // (3)
      jowner= jss ;
   }
```

```
public String toString()                           // (4)
{   return acct_no + ":" + owner + ":" +
            jowner + ":" + balance();
}

protected String jowner;                           // (5)
}
```

The class header

```
class JointAccount extends BankAccount
```

specifies JointAccount as an *extended class* of BankAccount, which becomes its *superclass*. The extended class definition is given in this general form:

```
[ public ] class Name extends SuperClass
{
      extended class body
}
```

An extended class *inherits all members of its superclass*[1] and adds new members of its own. Through inheritance (line 1), members of BankAccount become *inherited members* of JointAccount. The extended class also adds a field jowner (line 5) to record the social security number of the joint owner. The owner's social security number is recorded in the member owner inherited from the superclass. Programming a joint account from scratch is avoided, and code from BankAccount is reused.

The JointAccount constructor (line 2) initializes an extended object consisting of a *superclass object* from BankAccount and an *appendant part* from class JointAccount. The superclass object is initialized by calling a superclass constructor using the Java keyword super (line 3). The toString method is again defined (line 4).

Now a joint account object can be established and used. For example:

```
JointAccount billMary =
new JointAccount(044123456, 2500, "045-22-5555",   // ss of Bill
                                  "045-33-7777");  // ss of Mary
billMary.deposit(450.75);
```

With class extension, much recoding is avoided and joint accounts are established with very little effort. Furthermore, the original BankAccount class stays unchanged, ready to establish other types of accounts. And, perhaps more important, any further refinement of BankAccount is automatically reflected in JointAccount. This is a powerful aspect of OOP, and its full implications will become clear after you become more familiar with class extension.

---

[1] except constructors and finalize

Beginners find inheritance and subclassing fascinating and are eager to learn more. Yet the subject tends to be confusing, mostly due to a vague conceptual model. The presentation in the next sections should help build a clear understanding.

4.3 CLASS SCOPE NESTING

An extended class is a composite class, with members from the superclass (*inherited members*) and additional members defined in the subclass (*appendant members*). Basically, members in a superclass are inherited by a subclass through *class scope nesting*. The extended class scope is *nested* inside the superclass scope (Figure 4.1). The nesting is similar to an inner code block nesting within an outer block.

Thus, the expression

```
billmary.deposit(54.60);
```

starts looking for the method in the scope `JointAccount` and ends up finding `deposit` in the enclosing scope `BankAccount`. Then the method `deposit` is called with the host reference `this` identifying `billmary`.

In general, when a member reference made in a subclass scope does not find the member in that subclass scope, the member is found in enclosing scopes by following the class extension chain upward. Therefore when a subclass does not introduce an appendant field (method) with the same name as an inherited field (method), the inheritance picture is clear: *All superclass members are reached via class scope nesting.*

What happens when the subclass does introduce a field or method whose name conflicts with a superclass counterpart is explained separately in Sections 4.11 and 4.13.

Figure 4.1   CLASS SCOPE NESTING

4.4 EXTENDED OBJECT COMPOSITION

An *extended object*, such as billMary, is an instance of a subclass. An extended object is made of two parts (Figure 4.2):

1. A *superclass object* consisting of the data fields and methods specified by the superclass and properly initialized by a superclass constructor. In other words, the superclass object part is built using the superclass as a blueprint. *Inherited members* are in this part.

2. An *appendant part* consisting of additional fields and methods defined in the subclass. The appendant part envelops the superclass object to form the subclass object. Members in the appendant part are referred to as *appendant members*.

Inherited members and appendant members are all considered members of a subclass object that is their host object.

If the superclass object is itself an extended object, it will contain its own superclass object in exactly the same way.

Protected Members

The members acct_no and ss have been declared protected in the class BankAccount. A protected member restricts access by code from outside the package of a class. A protected member can be accessed only by code in the same package or, as an inherited member, by code in a subclass. Thus, the protected access designation is like package except that it allows *access as inherited member* from subclasses in any package (Section 4.6). Designating certain members protected in anticipation of subclassing is an important OOP design consideration. More will be said about this later.

Figure 4.2   EXTENDED OBJECT COMPOSITION

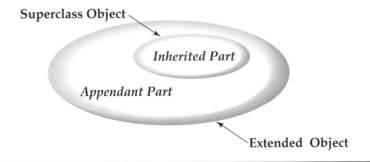

4.5   FREE CHECKING ACCOUNT

As another example of class extension, consider a free checking account that charges a monthly service fee only if the account balance drops below a preset minimum. The FreeChecking class can also be extended from the existing BankAccount class (Figure 4.3).

```java
///////    FreeChecking.java    ///////

public class FreeChecking extends BankAccount
{   public
    FreeChecking(int n, String owner, double b)    // constructor (1)
    {    super(n, owner, b);
        free = (b >= minBalance);                  // (2)
    }
    public FreeChecking() {}                        // null constructor

    public static void minbal(float m)              // set min balance
    {    minBalance = m;   }
    public static void fee(float f)                 // set fee
    {    serviceFee = f;   }
// other methods ...

    private static float minBalance = 250.0f;
    private static float serviceFee = 18.0f;
    private boolean free;
}
```

Static fields minBalance and serviceFee and static methods minbal(amt) and fee(amt) are used to record and modify the classwide quantities: minimum balance and monthly service fee. A private flag free keeps the fee-free status of the account. The constructor specifies how the superclass object and the appendant part are initialized. The flag free is initialized correctly (line 2). The flag is maintained by the appendant method withdraw and used by fee(), the method that charges a monthly fee, if required, to the account.

Figure 4.3   CLASS EXTENSIONS

```
public boolean withdraw(double amt)                      // withdraw amt
{   boolean ok = super.withdraw(amt);                     // (a)
    if (ok && balance() < minBalance) free = false; // (b)
    return ok;
}
```

The subclass FreeChecking defines a new withdraw method that monitors the account balance and sets the free flag when necessary. The method calls the withdraw method in the superclass (line a) and, after the withdrawal is made, checks the balance (line b) and sets free accordingly. A boolean return value indicates the success or failure of the withdrawal. Three important points are worth noting:

1. The appendant member withdraw has exactly the same method descriptor as its counterpart in the superclass BankAccount. This is good because the same method invocation works for withdrawing from a simple basic account or a free checking account. Any other way would be unreasonable. Imagine asking bank customers to use different messages to withdraw funds from various different types of accounts!

2. The FreeChecking withdraw completes its duty by asking the superclass withdraw to perform basic processing and by supplying additional processing itself. Thus, processing common to all types of accounts should be implemented in the superclass BankAccount. Accounts extended from BankAccount will add only their specialized processing.

3. The special keyword super has another use: It can be a reference to the host object as an instance of its superclass. In other words, super has the same value as this but has the type of the immediate superclass. Thus, it puts withdraw (line a) in the BankAccount scope. Use super to *access inherited members hidden or overridden by appendent members*. Static methods do not have the reference super.

At the end of every month, the method fee() is called to charge a service fee to the account if required:

```
public boolean fee()   // charge monthly fee
{   boolean ok;
    if ( ! free )
    {   if (ok = withdraw(serviceFee))
            free = (balance() >= minBalance);
        return ok;
    }
    return true;
}
```

The FreeChecking class is much simplified as it stands. But it can be tested right away, as follows:

```
///////     TestFreeChecking.java     ///////

class TestFreeChecking
{  public static void main(String[] args)
    {    FreeChecking susan = new
             FreeChecking(555234, "034-55-6789", 500.0);
        susan.deposit(25.50);
        susan.withdraw(250);
        susan.fee();                    // results in no charge
        System.out.println("Month 1: " + susan.balance());
        susan.withdraw(30);         // expensive move
        susan.deposit(100);         // too late
        susan.fee();
        System.out.println("Month 2: " + susan.balance());
    }
}
```

The account susan started with a balance of $500.00. At the end of the first month, the account balance should be $275.50 because there was no service charge. But the unfortunate withdrawal of $30.00 costs another $18.00 in service fees for the following month. The deposit of $100.00 is too late to avoid the service charge, and the balance becomes $327.50. The program produces the expected output:

```
Month 1: 275.5
Month 2: 327.5
```

The extended class FreeChecking is somewhat more complicated than JointAccount and is a more realistic example of class extension.

To summarize, an extended class is usually a generalization, specialization, or modification of the superclass. Often this means adding some preprocessing and/or postprocessing to existing methods in the superclass. The subclass withdraw method is a typical example: It adds some postprocessing after calling the superclass withdraw. Thus, a design technique is to collect basic operations in the superclass and allow specialized preprocessing and/or postprocessing to be added by subclasses.

4.6   ACCESS CONTROL UNDER CLASS EXTENSION

With class extension, the protected access specifier is introduced. The rules for member access control are now restated, with protected included (in order of decreasing accessibility):

- Public members—Can be accessed by any code that can access the class.

- Protected members—Can be accessed freely by code in the same package and accessed as inherited members by code in any subclass. No other access is allowed.
- Package members—Can be accessed freely by code in the same package. No other access is allowed. A member with no access specifier is a package member.
- Private members—Can be accessed only by methods in the same class. No other access is allowed.

Access to Inherited Members

The preceding rules apply to members explicitly defined in a class: all members of a nonextended class or all appendant members in an extended class. Access to inherited members—those contained in the superclass object—however, is different.

1. Access to inherited members by appendant members of a direct or indirect subclass:

   - Access is allowed to all `public` and `protected` inherited members.
   - Access to inherited `package` members is also allowed provided the subclass is in the same package as the superclass.
   - *Access is not allowed to inherited private members.* For example, an appendant method in `JointAccount` has no access to `acct_bal` in the superclass object.

2. Access to inherited members from methods outside the extended class:

   - Inherited `public` members are all accessible as public members of the subclass by methods in other classes.
   - Outside methods in the same package as the superclass of the target extended class can also access the inherited `protected` and `package` members.

The member access rules (accessibility) together with class scope nesting (visibility) give rise to some important implications. Private inherited members are not accessible to the appendant part. In a subclass hierarchy, through each subsequent extended class, the combined set of public interfaces in its superclasses is accessible. Furthermore, each subsequent extended class always has access to the combined set of public and protected members in its superclasses. Figure 4.4 and Table 4.1 summarize access control under class extension.

Figure 4.4   INHERITED MEMBER ACCESS

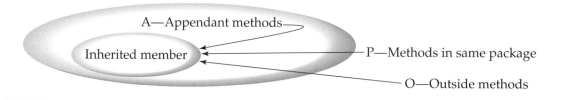

Table 4.1   ACCESS CONTROL UNDER SUBCLASSING

Access from	Member Inherited from `SuperX`			
	`public`	`protected`	`package`	`private`
A—Appendant methods in subclasses of `SuperX`	yes	yes	yes, if same package	no
P—Methods in same package as `SuperX`	yes	yes	yes	no
O—Other outside methods	yes	no	no	no

4.7 CLASS EXTENSION PRINCIPLES

A question often asked is when and how to use class extension and for what purposes. The question is central to effective object-oriented programming. The answer is not so easy. Following are a few rules of thumb:

- Use class extension when an extended object is really a certain kind of superclass object. For example, a joint account is a kind of account, and a free checking account is another kind of account. The *is-a* relation usually means that all or most of the public interface of the superclass object (a `BankAccount`) also makes sense for the subclass object (a `JointAccount`). The *is-a* relation often also means that extended and basic objects may be used together in applications as related or compatible types. For instance, a list of accounts in a banking system may include many different types of accounts.

    A class `Manager` extending the class `Employee` is another example of the *is-a* relation. A manager is a kind of employee, making subclassing appropriate.

    Thus, a superclass and a subclass have a type–subtype relationship. This is supported in Java by implicit type conversion rules allowing the automatic conversion of a subclass-type object reference to a superclass-type reference.

    It is recommended that you reserve class extension for the *is-a* relation.

- Do not use class extension when an object has no *is-a* relationship with another class, such as Xyz. If you simply wish to use the code of Xyz to make a new class easier to implement, employ a field that is an object from the class Xyz. Declare this field nonpublic so that it is part of the internal mechanism of your new class.

  For instance, a stack or a queue class may use a linked list object internally, but neither a stack nor a queue is considered a kind of linked list. The relation here is: A stack/queue is *internally implemented as* a linked list.

When considering extending a class *Sub* from a class *Sup*, make sure it is not because a *Sub* object contains a *Sup* object as a component. Consider a clock as an object. A clock has a ticker and a face as components. The correct design for such a *has-a* or *uses-a* relationship is to employ component objects rather than class extension.

Declare internal components private if they are not to be accessible from anywhere outside the class. However, if you wish to make certain components of a class available for subclasses, declare them protected. When in doubt, use protected.

To disallow the extension of a class, declare the class final.

4.8 SUBCLASS CONSTRUCTORS

The initialization of a subclass object is done by a subclass constructor, which first calls a superclass constructor to initialize the inherited object, then initializes the appendant part appropriately to complete the task.

As seen in the FreeChecking example,

```
public FreeChecking(int n, double b, String owner)
{   super(n, b, owner);
    free = (b >= minBalance);
}
```

the syntax for explicitly calling a superclass constructor is

```
super(n, b, owner);        // call superclass constructor
```

where super is a Java keyword. The very first statement in a subclass constructor should be a call to a superclass constructor. Thus, the inherited part of the object is initialized first. If the first statement is not a super call, the superclass null constructor (super()) is automatically called as the first statement. A super call cannot be placed elsewhere in a subclass constructor body.

If no constructor is specified by a subclass, a null constructor is automatically supplied, which calls the null constructor of the superclass. If the superclass does not have a null constructor, the subclass must define one or more constructors in such a way that no calls to the superclass null constructor are made.

A constructor can also call another constructor in its own class to help perform initializations. Make the call with this special notation:

```
this( ... );          // constructor call within a constructor
```

The arguments determine which constructor to call.

Object Initialization Sequence

When a basic class constructor is called, the initialization actions follow a specific order:

1. Initialize data fields, using specified or default values. Default values are zero for numeric types, \u0000 for char, false for boolean, and null for object references.
2. Execute statements in the constructor body.

When a subclass constructor is called, the superclass object part is initialized first, followed by the appendant part:

1. Call either the null constructor or an explicitly specified superclass constructor as the first statement.
2. Initialize appendant data fields, using specified or default values.
3. Execute statements in the subclass constructor body other than the call already performed in step 1.

The initialization sequence may assign one initial value and then assign another value in a later step to the same field. Because a constructor can call other member methods whose behavior may depend on the state of the object, it is important to make sure that fields needed are initialized properly before calling a member method from inside a constructor.

4.9 SUBCLASS Finalize

Just as with initialization, the superclass and subclass must also cooperate for the final cleanup before object destruction. This means that a subclass finalize method should take this form:

```
protected void finalize() throws Throwable
{   // clean-up code for appendant part
    . . .
    super.finalize();  // finalize inherited part, if defined
}
```

The notation super.*method* invokes a method in the inherited object.

4.10 TYPE RELATIONS UNDER INHERITANCE

Inheritance and class extension offer a powerful way to organize programs and group related objects. Indeed, a class hierarchy creates a set of related types that are compatible in use. The different types of bank accounts illustrate this point very well. In general, when type *SubX is-a* type *SupX*, it is logical to be able to use a *SubX* object in place of a *SupX* object. The reasoning is similar to using a char or a short value where an int is expected. In this situation, the type *SubX* becomes a *subtype* of *SupX*.

Actually such compatible use has already been applied without being explained explicitly. In Section 2.3, the method

```
public static void doio(InputStream in, OutputStream out)
```

is called either with standard I/O objects System.in and System.out or with file I/O objects:

```
doio(System.in, System.out);
doio(infile, ofile);
```

The doio parameter out can take on System.out or ofile. This works because System.out (an instance of PrintStream) and ofile (an instance of FileOutputStream) are objects extended from the same superclass OutputStream, as with System.in (an instance of InputStream) and infile (an instance of FileInputStream). Type compatibility under inheritance brought this convenience and flexibility.

Java supports object type compatibility through the conversion of reference types (mentioned but not discussed in Section 2.12). In argument passing and assignment, a subclass reference is implicitly converted to a superclass reference. This *widening reference conversion* is implicit and supports the *is-a* relationship.

It is safe to access an extended object through a superclass reference because there is always an instance of the superclass in the extended object and the public interface of the superclass object is accessible.

This implicit conversion is important for OOP because it allows the same method parameter to receive different objects in an inheritance hierarchy. For example, a method transfer should work on any account objects in a hierarchy rooted at BankAccount:

```
public static
boolean transfer(double amt, BankAccount from, BankAccount to)
```

The conversion of a superclass reference to a subclass reference, however, requires explicit casting. For example:

```
BankAccount acnt;                          // superclass reference
FreeChecking fc= new Freechecking(...);  // subclass object
```

```
anct = fc;                          // implicit conversion
fc = (FreeChecking) acnt;           // explicit conversion
```

Note that it is possible to cast a true superclass reference to a subclass reference. Through such a reference, it is even legal syntax to access an appendant member that is really not there. Of course, executing such code is disastrous:

```
BankAccount susan = new BankAccount(...); // superclass object
JointAccount jc;
jc = (JointAccount) susan;           // explicit conversion
jc.jss                               // not there !
```

But susan does not contain the member jss. Thus, be very careful with explicit casting. Java has an operator instanceof, which can be used to test whether an object is an instance of a class. If it is, the object can be safely cast into that class type.

```
if ( susan instanceof JointAccount )
    jc = (JointAccount) susan;       // safe
```

To summarize, Java supports the following implicit *widening reference conversions*:

- From a class (interface) to a superclass (superinterface)
- From a class to an interface that the class implements
- From any class, interface, or array, to Object (Section 4.19)
- From any array type to Cloneable (Section 5.13)
- From any array type $X[]$ to $Y[]$, provided that there is a widening reference conversion from X to Y

Interfaces are described in Section 5.4.

4.11 FIELD ACCESS UNDER SUBCLASSING

Consider any field *xyz* accessed through a reference of type *SubY*, an extended class. If *xyz* is an appendant field of *SubY*, it is what *xyz* refers to. Otherwise, the name *xyz* is searched in the superclass of *SubY*. If it is not found, the search will continue up the extension chain. The search ends as soon as a field with the given name is found. Then its accessibility is determined. The search will not continue even if access is denied.

Consider, for example, the reference billMary.acct_bal. It is not found in the scope JointAccount, so the search continues in the enclosing scope BankAccount, where the private member acct_bal is found. Thus, billMary.acct_bal refers to the inherited member acct_bal. The private status of acct_bal will deny such an access; the code is incorrect. A subclass field can *hide* a superclass field with the same name as described in Section 4.12.

4.12   HIDING OF FIELDS AND STATIC METHODS

If you define a field (abc) in a subclass (SubY) with the same name as a field used in a superclass (SuperX), the subclass abc *hides* the superclass abc. Thus, within SubY the identifier abc is in use and the same identifier in SuperX cannot be accessed directly. Use the notation

super.abc

to access the field abc in the superclass, where the Java keyword super is a reference to the superclass object available in instance methods.

If, for example, class SubZ extends class SubY, which extends SuperX (Figure 4.5), and each class has its own field abc (with possibly distinct type and access specification), the code

```
SuperX obj = new SubY();
System.out.println(obj.abc);
```

displays abc in SuperX, not abc in the host SubY object. Furthermore, the following instance method in class SubZ is valid as long as abc is accessible:

```
void displayAbc()
{    System.out.println(((SuperX)this).abc);  // abc in SuperX
     System.out.println(super.abc);            // abc in SubY
     System.out.println(abc);                  // this.abc
}
```

A static method in a subclass *hides* all static methods with the same signature in superclasses. Hidden methods are accessed in the same way as hidden fields. A compile-time error occurs if a subclass static method has the same signature as a superclass instance method.

In summary, hidden names (fields and static methods) are handled with the usual class scope nesting mechanism. Note also that identical field and method names in a superclass and a subclass do not conflict.

Accessing instance methods with the same name is more complicated. Sections 4.13 through 4.17 further explain method access under class extension.

Figure 4.5   CLASS EXTENSION CHAIN

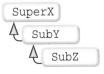

4.13   METHOD ACCESS UNDER SUBCLASSING

Class scope nesting also makes methods from superclasses available to an extended class. For example, the call `billMary.balance()` refers to `balance()` in the scope `JointAccount`; it is not defined in `JointAccount`, but rather in the enclosing scope `BankAccount`. This is how this particular call gets to the inherited member `balance()`.

A subclass method with the same name or signature as a superclass method can *overload*, *hide*, or *override* the superclass method, which would otherwise be directly accessible. *Static method hiding* has been described (Section 4.12). *Instance method overriding* (Sections 4.14–4.15) and *method overloading* (Section 4.17) under class extension are explained in the following sections.

4.14   METHOD OVERRIDING

A subclass instance method may *override* an instance method in a superclass. For example, `FreeChecking` defines a method `withdraw` that overrides the `withdraw` in `BankAccount`. Whereas inheritance allows an extended class to reuse existing code in a superclass, overriding can selectively redefine or modify certain methods to suit. The Java method overriding mechanism is important for OOP, and a good understanding is critical for the materials in later chapters.

The following rules will help you understand method overriding:

- Conflict with static methods—It is a compile-time error if a subclass instance method has the same signature as a superclass static method.

- Signature—A subclass instance method overrides any superclass instance method with the same signature. This rule tells you when method overriding will take place. The next four rules specify conditions for successful overriding. Unsuccessful overriding causes an error during compilation.

- Return type—An overriding method must have the same return type as its superclass counterpart. Thus, overriding and overridden methods have the same *method descriptor* (signature plus return type).

- Exception handling—An overriding method may have its own `throws` clause, but it cannot throw any exception not originally declared in the `throws` clause of the superclass method.

- Access control—The access specifier of an overriding method may be different from that of its superclass counterpart, provided that the access does not become more restrictive. Thus, to override a `protected` method in a superclass, the overriding method can be either `protected` or `public`, but not `package` or `private`.

- Overriding barred—A method declared `final` can't be overridden.

4.15 DYNAMIC INVOCATION OF OVERRIDING METHODS

In Java, overriding methods are *invoked dynamically at run time, depending on the true host object type*[2] as will be explained presently.

One of the primary purposes of method overriding is to allow subclasses to redefine a superclass instance method and have the new definition invoked when called through an object of the subclass. Consider the class `FreeChecking`. The usage

```
BankAccount act = new FreeChecking(555234, 500.0, "034-55-6789");
act.withdraw(30.0);    // calls withdraw in FreeChecking
```

calls `withdraw` in `FreeChecking` rather than `BankAccount`, even though the variable is of type `BankAccount`.

In general, consider a direct or indirect subclass `SubY` of a superclass `SupX`. Let `methodAbc` be a method in `SubY` overriding its counterpart in `SupX`. In the code

```
SupX var = new SubY(...);    // var references an instance of SubY
var.methodAbc(...);          // invokes methodAbc in SubY
```

the call `var.methodAbc(...)` invokes the method `methodAbc` defined in `SubY`, the class of the object referenced by `var`, not the overridden `methodAbc` in `SupX`, the type of the variable `var`. The method `methodAbc` in `SupX`, which may not be called at run time due to overriding, must nevertheless exist and be accessible for the code `var.methodAbc(...)` to be valid at compile time.

Thus, for overridden instance methods, Java checks at run time the actual class of the host object and locates a method to call in that class (Figure 4.6).

Figure 4.6   INVOKING OVERRIDING INSTANCE METHODS

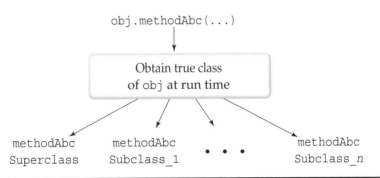

---

[2]C++ supports the same dynamic function invocation mechanism with *virtual functions.*

Note that overriding static methods do not need this dynamic invocation behavior because static members have no host objects. To further explain the effects of method overriding, let's consider a method for fund transfer from one account to another:

```
public static
boolean transfer(double amt, BankAccount from, BankAccount to)
{   boolean ok = from.withdraw(amt);        // (A)
    if ( ok ) to.deposit(amt);              // (B)
    return ok;
}
```

The `transfer` can be placed in either the `BankAccount` class or some application program. Parameters `to` and `from` can receive any accounts extended from `BankAccount`, directly or indirectly. Without the Java method overriding mechanism, the calls on lines A and B can invoke only the methods defined in the `BankAccount` class, defeating the purpose of allowing `from` and `to` to receive different account types.

The Java overriding mechanism ensures that the calls on lines A and B invoke the appropriate overriding methods. For example:

```
FreeChecking susan = new FreeChecking(555234, "034-55-6789", 500.0);
JointAccount jack_jennie = new JointAccount(
                555234, 200.0, "034-22-6666", "022-33-4567");
BankAccount.transfer(150, susan, jack_jennie);
```

Under this arrangement, one transfer method can serve many types of accounts. This is an example of *polymorphism* (Section 5.1).

4.16 EXAMPLE: NUMERIC WRAPPER CLASSES

Java uses class extension and method overriding extensively in its class libraries. For example, the classes Byte, Short, Integer, Long, Float, and Double are also subclasses of Number (Figure 4.7). Each has the static final fields MIN_VALUE and MAX_VALUE.

Each numeric type also has six methods

```
byte byteValue()      short  shortValue()      int    intValue()
long longValue()      double doubleValue()      float floatValue()
```

that override methods in Number and cast a numeric object into one of the six primitive types. The arrangement allows any numeric wrapper objects to be used as Number objects.

Figure 4.7   THE Number HIERARCHY

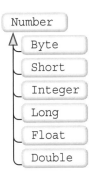

4.17   METHOD OVERLOADING IN SUBCLASSES

A subclass method overloads methods with the same name but a different signature in superclasses. Compile-time method call resolution for overloaded methods was introduced in Section 3.9. The effects of class extension on method call resolution will now be described.

The principle of first identifying accessible and applicable methods, then selecting the most specific method to invoke, still stands (Section 3.9). But with class extension, methods from all superclasses are candidates. Also, inheritance-induced implicit conversions potentially make more methods applicable. Consider a method call

name.methodAbc(...)

The expression *name*, an object or a class name, provides a type that is the class to begin a search for a *methodAbc* to call. The call resolution rules, with class extension in mind, can be restated here for clarity:

1. If there is an accessible method in the scope of the class that is an exact match, call that method.

2. Let *CAN* be the set of all *accessible signatures*, from the starting class and all its superclasses, that can receive the given arguments under method invocation conversions. If the set *CAN* is empty, the call will fail.

3. Within *CAN*, eliminate less specific signatures: If arguments receivable by signature $s1$ can always be passed to signature $s2$, eliminate $s2$ from *CAN*. *A superclass method is never more specific than a method in a subclass.*

4. After all eliminations have been made, if *CAN* contains exactly one signature, that is the one invoked. Otherwise, the call is ambiguous and invalid.

These rules determine the signature of a method to call at compile time. If the determined method is an instance method and overriding is involved, the actual method invoked will be determined at run time, as described in Section 4.14.

One implication of these rules is that an applicable method in a more distant superclass may be invoked because closer methods are either not applicable or not accessible. A second implication is call ambiguity, which can arise because several methods from different classes in the extension chain have different signatures, none more specific than another.

Method Call Ambiguity

For example, if class SubY extends SuperX

```
public int methodA(long i)    // defined in class SuperX
private int methodA(int i)     // defined in class SubY
```

and the application code

```
SubY obj = new SubY();         // outside of class SubY
obj.methodA(5);
```

invokes methodA in SuperX. This is because methodA is private in SubY. Consider another example:

```
public int methodB(int i)     // defined in class SuperX (1)
public int methodB(long i)    // defined in class SubY    (2)
```

The code

```
SubY obj = new SubY();         // outside of class SubY
obj.methodB(5);                // ambiguous call
```

results in ambiguity because both methods (lines 1 and 2) are accessible and applicable but neither is more specific than the other. Hence, be careful when you define a method with the same name in a subclass but with a less restrictive signature as its superclass counterpart.

4.18 CALCULATOR WITH SQRT

As another example of the use of class extension, let's consider adding the square-root function to the calculator simulation program from Chapter 3.

We add *SQRT* (with the s opcode) by extending CalcEng:

```
public class RootEng extends CalcEng
{  public void operate(char c)                              // (1)
   {   if ( pre_oper(c) ) return;                           // (2)
```

```
        super.operate(c);                              // (3)
    }

    public String keys() { return super.keys()+"s";}    // (4)

    protected boolean pre_oper(char c)
    {   switch( c )
        {   case 's': // sqrt
                op = '=';
                if (argcnt == 2) { ans = arg; argcnt--; }
                if ( ans < 0.0 ) statusFlag = ERROR;
                else ans = Math.sqrt(ans);             // (5)
                return true;
        }
        return false;
    }
}
```

RootEng overrides the method operate (line 1) to add the square-root processing. We again use the technique of adding some preprocessing (line 2) before calling the overridden method itself (line 3). The opcode s (for SQRT) is added to the opcode keys from the superclass (line 4).

The pre_oper method checks the opcode and performs the correct computation by calling Math.sqrt (line 5). Unlike binary operations such as + and *, square-root takes only one argument and performs the calculation immediately. We simulate this behavior of the calculator truthfully. The pre_oper method is given in a form ready to do other immediate unary operations such as %, found commonly on simple calculators.

To run a calculator with SQRT we use the simple class RunRoot:

```
///////    RunRoot.java ///////

public class RunRoot
{   public static void main(String[] args)
        throws java.io.IOException
    {   RootEng e = new RootEng();
        CalcFace f = new CalcFace(e.keys(), e.precision());
        Calculator x = new Calculator(e, f);
        x.on();
        return;
    }
}
```

The complete program, ready to compile and run, is found in the example package.

4.19 THE Object CLASS AND GENERIC CODES

In Java, a class with no declared superclass implicitly extends the built-in class Object. Therefore, all classes extend Object directly or indirectly. The two major purposes for the Object root superclass are as follows:

1. Every class inherits members from the Object class, and Object offers a set of useful members for all classes.
2. All other classes become subtypes of Object, allowing you to write *generic code* that works for all objects, independent of their types.

A set of Object methods, generic hashtables, dynamically extending arrays, as well as implementation of generic programs, will be described.

Object Methods

There are two kinds of members in Object: general utilities, described here, and thread support methods (Section 11.2). A class should override any Object-supplied method when the semantics are unsuitable.

Some of the methods supplied in Object are as follows:

- public boolean equals(Object obj)—Returns true if obj is the host object. Override this method to implement value equality for your objects. The operators == and != can only compare reference equality for objects.
- public int hashCode()—Returns a hashcode for the host object. This is useful for storing objects on hashtables.
- public String toString()—Returns a string representation of the object. The method in class Object returns a string consisting of the class name of the object, the character @, and the hexadecimal hashcode of the object.
- protected Object clone() throws CloneNotSupportedException—A convenience method for subclasses. If a subclass implements the Cloneable interface, this method will return a new copy of the host object by copying the contents of the host object. Otherwise it will throw the indicated exception. Section 5.13 discusses the copying of objects.
- public void finalize() throws Throwable—Does nothing. Override finalize to perform clean-up operations before an object is garbage-collected or when the program terminates. The call

```
System.runFinalizersOnExit(true);
```

requests the running of finalize methods as a program exits. Without the request, finalizers are not invoked when a program terminates.

• `public final Class getClass()`—Returns a unique `Class` object, which represents the class type of the host object. For example, `obj.getClass().getName()` gets you the string name of `obj`'s class.

If you override `equals` (see Section 4.22 for an example) make sure `hashcode` is modified so that equal objects have the same `hashcode`. Assuming that equal objects already have the same string representation, a simple way of defining `hashcode` is to return the `hashcode` of the string:

```
public int hashCode()
{    return toString().hashCode();   }
```

Generic Hashtable

The `java.util` package provides a generic `HashMap` class (Section 9.2) to supply hashtables that allow you to enter and retrieve objects of any type conveniently, using any valid object as the key. The capacity of the hashtable is automatically increased as needed.

For example, a hashtable of bank accounts can be established as follows:

```
HashMap accounts = new HashMap(250);        // initial capacity 250
accounts.put(jack.id(), jack);              // put(key, object)
accounts.put(susan.id(), susan);
accounts.put(billmary.id(), billmary);
```

To retrieve a bank account, use the following code:

```
BankAccount ac
    = (BankAccount)accounts.get(some_id);   // retrieval by key
if (ac != null) ...
```

Generic Array

The `java.util` package supplies a class `ArrayList` (Section 9.1). Each element in an `ArrayList` is of type `Object` and can reference any type object. Just like an array, an `ArrayList` contains items accessed by indexing. However, the size of an `ArrayList` can grow and shrink as elements are added and removed. For example:

```
ArrayList al = new ArrayList(5);  // al capacity 5
al.add(sussan);                   // first element is BankAccount sussan
al.add(jack);                     // next element is BankAccount jack
al.size()                         // value is 2
BankAccount act =
    (BankAccount) al.get(0)       // act is sussan
al.set(1, marry);                 // element at 1 is now marry
```

A HashMap or ArrayList can store only references to objects. Primitive types can be turned into *wrapper objects* (Section 3.3) before being stored.

Next, let's look at an application of ArrayList.

4.20 MANAGING TEXT LINES

It is commonplace in data processing to deal with a set of text lines and perform certain manipulations on them—sorting, editing, looking for patterns, and so on.

The TextLines class supplies basic capabilities to store and manage a set of text lines. After a TextLines object is initialized, lines can be read (input) and stored in editable string buffers within the object. After manipulations and transformations, the lines can then be written out (output).

Operations provided include adding and deleting lines, interchanging lines (swap), getting and setting lines by indexing (getLine and setLine), and reporting the number of lines stored (length).

```java
///////    TextLines.java    ///////
import java.io.*;
import java.util.ArrayList;

class TextLines
{  TextLines() { this(16); }
   TextLines(int len) { lines = new ArrayList(len); }

   StringBuffer getLine(int i)
   {  return((i>=0 && i<lines.size()) ?
         (StringBuffer)lines.get(i) : null);
   }
   public void setLine(int k, StringBuffer b) // sets line k to b
   {  lines.set(k, b); }
   public void setLine(int k, String l)     // sets line k to l
   {  lines.set(k, new StringBuffer(l)); }
   public void addLine(StringBuffer b)      // adds the given line b
   {  lines.add(b); }
   public void addLine(String l)            // adds the given line l
   {  lines.add(new StringBuffer(l));  }
   public void delLine(int i)               // delete line i
   {  if ( i > -1 && i < lines.size() ) lines.remove(i); }

   public int length() { return lines.size(); }

// other methods ...
```

```
        private ArrayList lines;
}
```

A java.util.ArrayList functions like an array but can store any Object type. Moreover, an ArrayList can automatically extend its dimensions as needed. TextLines uses an ArrayList of StringBuffers to store the text lines.

The getLine method allows the access and editing of individual lines by indexing. Thus, if tx is a TextLines object,

```
tx.getLine(n);
```

gives line n. After a TextLines object is created, lines can be added or deleted. Clearly, a TextLines object is useful whenever a program deals with lines of text from standard input or a file. This is another concrete example of building components that are reusable in many places, which is a big advantage of OOP.

The method input reads text lines from a given input source in. The class BufferedReader makes textual input efficient and provides the readLine method (line 1) to input each line conveniently. The line read is stored as a StringBuffer so that it can be edited. The input method returns the number of lines read, or -1 if an IOException occurs.

```
public int input(InputStream in)
{   String s;
    BufferedReader rdr
        = new BufferedReader(new InputStreamReader(in));
    try
    {   while ( (s = rdr.readLine() ) != null )     // (1)
            addLine(s);
    } catch ( IOException e )
      {   System.err.println("TextLines: Error reading input");
          return -1;
      }
    return lines.size();  // number of lines read
}
```

A swap method interchanges any two lines:

```
public void swap(int i, int j)       // interchange lines
{   if ( i > -1 && j > -1 && i < lines.size() && j < lines.size() )
    {   Object tmp = lines.get(i);
        lines.set(i, lines.get(j));
        lines.set(j, tmp);
    }
}
```

The `output` method sends all lines to any given output stream `out`. It uses a buffered print writer for efficient textual output. This is the recommended way to use a `PrintWriter`:

```
public void output(OutputStream out)
{   int i=0;
    PrintWriter o = new PrintWriter
        (new BufferedWriter(new OutputStreamWriter(out)));
    while(i < lines.size()) { o.println(lines.get(i++)); }
    o.flush();
}
```

The `TextLines` class can be useful in many situations. It will be applied in a number of examples later in this text.

Generic containers such as `ArrayList` are very handy. To understand how they work, let's write some generic programs of our own.

4.21 WRITING GENERIC PROGRAMS

Normally programs are written to deal with specific types. Thus, even if there is already a linked list of characters, there is still nothing for a linked list of employees. However, with the `Object` class, it is possible to write *type-independent*, or *generic*, code that works for a multitude of different types.

Consider writing a generic display method to output arbitrary types of data. The method must receive an argument of arbitrary type and display the argument correctly. Using the `Object` class, this is surprisingly simple to achieve:

```
public static void display(Object any)            // (1)
{   System.out.println(any.toString());           // (2)
}
```

The parameter `any` of type `Object` (line 1), allows you to receive any argument that is an object reference. Then the method invocation (line 2) accesses the overriding `toString` method of the object `any`, which displays the object correctly.

The `Object` superclass and its methods, such as `toString` and `equals`, are critical for writing generic programs in Java. The `java.util.ArrayList` class is an example of a generic container class that works like a extendable array. Let's build our own generic container class `ArbList`.

4.22 GENERIC LIST

`CharList` is a class presented earlier (Section 3.8). A `CharList` object represents a linked list of characters. But what about lists of integers, fractions, dates, accounts, addresses, and so on? What about lists of objects yet to be defined? Must the wheel be reinvented every time? No. A linked list containing items of type `Object` can be made to work for any target type elements you wish to put in a linked list.

Such a list is *generic* or non-type-specific. A generic list class makes the code for list manipulation *reusable* whenever and wherever a linked list of some type is required. The generic approach presented here works not only for lists but also for any *container class* such as tables, sets, trees, graphs, stacks, and queues, just to name a few. Chapter 9 describes the Java collections framework, which provides many useful generic containers (data structures). `ArrayList` is one we have seen.

Here we will explore how a generic container such as an arbitrary list is made to work. Generic list class `ArbList` can be defined by modifying the existing class `CharList`. It may be surprising how few changes are needed. To begin with, the code for `ArbCell` is simply `ListCell` with `char` replaced by `Object`:

```
class ArbCell
{   ArbCell() { }
    ArbCell(Object it, ArbCell cell)
    {   item=it; next=cell; }
    Object content()
    {   return item; }
 // fields
    Object item = null;
    ArbCell next = null;
}
```

For lists containing items of a primitive type, a wrapper class (Section 3.3) must be used, increasing memory requirements slightly. This is the price for achieving genericness.

To transform `CharList` into `ArbList`, two obvious changes are made: Replace all `ListCell` by `ArbCell` and all `char` by `Object`. Then there must be a way to check equality (for `find` and `remove`) of arbitrary items, and to display them. Thus, we require list items to have correct overriding methods `equals` and `toString`.

```
///////    ArbList.java    ///////

public class ArbList
{   public ArbList() { }                 // empty list constructor
    public ArbList(Object it)            // list with first cell
    {   head=new ArbCell(it,null); }
    public ArbCell first() { return head; }
```

```
public boolean isEmpty()
{   return head==null; }

private ArbCell head = null;    // first cell of list
// other methods ...
}
```

The methods `remove` and `find` use overriding `equals` rather than the `==` operator.

```
public ArbCell find(Object it) // 1st item equals it
{   for(ArbCell p = head; p!=null ; p = p.next)
        if(p.item.equals(it)) return p;    // calls overriding equals
    return null;                           // c not on list
}
```

Other member methods not shown are simple translations from their `CharList` counterparts.

Applying Generic Lists to Fractions

The generic linked list is a generic container class. It can contain objects from an arbitrary class that properly overrides the `equals` and `toString` methods.

Let's illustrate the usage of generic containers by applying `ArbList` to form lists of fractions. The `Fraction` class (Section 2.4) already overrides `toString` correctly. Now we have to add the required `equals` to `Fraction`:

```
public boolean equals(Object y) // overrides
{   return ( y == this ||                          // same reference or
             (this.getClass() == y.getClass()     // same class and
             && num == ((Fraction)y).num           // same num and
             && denom == ((Fraction)y).denom )     // same denom
           );
}
```

The code first checks to see that the object reference is the same. Then, if both objects are in the same class, the numerators and denominators are compared.

Following is the Java program that establishes lists of fractions from `ArbList`:

```
class TestArbList
{   static Fraction[] fra =
    {   new Fraction(1,2), new Fraction(3,4),
        new Fraction(1,3), new Fraction(3,5),
        new Fraction(1,4), new Fraction(3,7),
        new Fraction(1,5), new Fraction(3,8),
        new Fraction(3,5) };

    public static void main(String[] args)
```

```
    {     ArbList a = new ArbList(fra[0]);
          a.putOn(fra[1]);
          a.append(fra[2]); a.append(fra[3]); a.append(fra[4]);
          System.out.println("a = " + a);
          ArbCell lp = a.find(fra[8]);
          if ( lp != null )
          {    System.out.println(a.toString(lp));
               a.insert(fra[6], lp);
          }
          System.out.println("a = " + a);
          a.remove(fra[4]);
          a.shorten(2);
          System.out.println("a = " + a);
          a.remove(fra[6]);
          System.out.println("a = " + a);
    }
}
```

Running this program should produce the following output:

```
a = (3/4 1/2 1/3 3/5 1/4)
(3/5 1/4)
a = (3/4 1/2 1/3 3/5 1/5 1/4)
a = (1/3 3/5 1/5)
a = (1/3 3/5)
```

Now a generic list class has been built and can be reused in many applications.
    The wrapper classes (Section 3.3) allow you to turn primitive values into objects so they can be passed to generic code, such as our ArbList or the java.util-supplied ArrayList (Section 4.19), that requires objects of type Object.

4.23   GENERIC STACK

A stack is a common and useful object in programming. It is a last-in/first-out (LIFO) buffer, like a stack of trays in the cafeteria (Figure 4.8). A *push* operation

Figure 4.8   A STACK

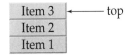

puts an item on top of the stack, while a *pop* removes the top item from the stack. Basically these are the only allowable operations on a stack.

Consider implementing a class for the stack. An array can store the items being pushed and popped. However, an array is limited because it is fixed in dimension. Consider using a linked list to store the items. Because there is a generic list class ArbList already (Section 4.22), this approach should be easier. Besides, the list is dynamic and its dimension is not fixed. Furthermore, it does not take extra effort to make the stack class generic.

```
///////    ArbStack.java    ///////

class ArbStack
{   public ArbStack() { }                         // null constructor
    public ArbStack(Object z)                     // constructor
    {    al.putOn(z);    }
    public void push(Object z)
    {    al.putOn(z);    }                         // (1)
    public Object pop()
    {    if ( al.isEmpty() ) return null;          // pop failed
         Object tmp= al.first().content();         // popped item (2)
         al.shorten(1);                            // stack popped
         return tmp;
    }
    public boolean isEmpty()
    {    return al.isEmpty(); }                    // (3)

    private ArbList al = new ArbList();     // (4)
}
```

A stack *uses-a* generic list al to store items (line 4). Operations push, pop, and isEmpty (lines 1, 2, 3) are translated into appropriate operations on the list al. This technique is often known as *forwarding*. By forwarding operations to ArbList, ArbStack is made very simple indeed. Other container classes such as queues and trees can be implemented using the same technique.

The java.util.Stack class implements a stack that can be used instead of the stack defined here.

4.24 SUMMARY

With the introduction of inheritance, we begin to move from simple object-based programming to the realm of object-oriented programming. OOP is more complicated but also much more flexible and powerful than procedural-oriented programming.

Class extension supports single inheritance and allows you to add and/or modify features from an existing class without changing its code. Repeated class extension results in class hierarchies. New concepts associated with class extension include class scope nesting, field name hiding, and method overriding. Rules for access control, method overloading, and type relations are expanded to accommodate class extension.

An extended class inherits code from its superclass. All members of the superclass except constructors and `finalize()` are inherited. An extended object is composed of a superclass object and an *appendant part* defined by the extended class. The subclass and superclass collaborate to initialize and finalize an extended object. When calling a superclass constructor explicitly, a subclass constructor must place `super(...)` as its first statement.

A subclass is nested inside the scope of its immediate superclass. A subclass field hides a superclass field under the same name, and a subclass static method hides superclass static methods with the same signature. The keyword `super`, a superclass object reference available in instance methods, can be used to access hidden fields and methods.

A subclass instance method overrides a superclass instance method with the same signature. Overriding methods are invoked dynamically, based on the host object type. A subclass method overloads superclass methods with the same name but a different signature. Resolution of calls to overloaded methods under inheritance still follow the principle of using the most specific method among accessible and applicable methods.

For class extension, the `protected` access category is introduced. Figure 4.4 summarizes access control under class extension.

Class extension captures the *is-a* relationship among objects. The Java implicit *widening reference conversion* supports the *is-a* relationship. The *has-a*, *uses-a*, and *internally-implemented-as-a* relationships should be modeled with component objects within a class.

The Java `Object` class is the superclass of all classes. It provides a set of methods useful for all objects, including object equality, string conversion, and hashcoding. As the root super type, `Object` is also critical for generic programming. Techniques for generic programming are illustrated by the `ArbList` and `ArbStack` examples.

The `HashMap` and `ArrayList` classes in `java.util` are generic containers whose capacities are extended automatically. These generic containers belong to the Java `Collections` framework presented in Chapter 9.

EXERCISES

Review Questions

1. What is the fine and important distinction between an "inherited member" and a "member in the superclass"? Consider the appendant member in `JointAccount`:

   ```
   int isIdentical (BankAccount obj)
   {    return(acct_no ==  obj.acct_no);    }
   ```

   Is there anything wrong with this method? Explain.

2. In a class, is it possible to have a static and an instance method with the same name? The same signature? How about in a superclass and a subclass?

3. Is it possible to establish a field with the same name as a field in the superclass but to make the field `static` (or nonstatic) differently in the subclass? If so, what are the implications?

4. Is it possible to define a method whose name is the same as a field name in the superclass? If so, what are the implications?

5. When a subclass overriding method is invoked through a superclass reference, which protection specifier applies? The one in the superclass or the subclass?

6. The keyword `super` is useful to access hidden or overridden members in the immediate superclass. But what if you wish to access such members in a superclass further up the class extension chain? Explain how you would access such hidden fields. Is the same technique effective for reaching overridden methods?

7. How do you reconcile the rules for method overriding and method overloading? Why is no mention made of method overriding when method resolution under class extension is discussed?

8. In a subclass constructor, a superclass constructor call must be placed at the very beginning. Is it possible to get around this restriction and have a subclass constructor do some operations before calling the superclass constructor? If so, describe your scheme.

9. Is it possible or desirable to explicitly invoke a constructor belonging to a superclass of the immediate superclass? Why?

10. Why override equals from Object if Fraction has an equals(Fraction f) method already?

11. What does it mean if a class declares all of its constructors protected?

12. What are the implications for a subclass if a superclass has no no-args constructor?

13. What is a generic program? What role does the Object class in Java play for generic programming?

14. Consider the ArbList class. What conditions, if any, are required for elements to be put on a generic list effectively? List the conditions and explain.

15. A call to super(...), if any, must be the very first statement in a subclass constructor. But a call to this(...) also must be placed first in a constructor. So where do you place a call to this(...) if you have a call to super(...)? Can this be done at all?

16. Will the notation super.super(...) or super.super.methodA(...) work? Why or why not?

17. Consider the dynamic invocation of overriding instance methods. State clearly the reason that this can be achieved only through run-time checking of the host object type and cannot be done at compile time.

18. Explain the behavior of a TextLines object. Where do you expect this class to be reusable?

Programming Assignments

1. (Match-1) Write a class MatchingLines as a subclass of TextLines. A MatchingLines can be initialized with just a string pattern (str), in which case its input methods read only matching lines from a file. Also, a MatchingLines can be initialized with a pattern and a TextLines object, in which case, only the lines containing the pattern are kept.

2. (TextLines-1) Write a class, MySort, to be used in the following form:

   java MySort [*key* [*delim*]]

   It reads all lines from standard input, sorts the lines by comparing the given *key* in the lines, and then writes the sorted lines to standard output. Each line is assumed to contain one or more fields separated by the given delimiters *delim* or by white spaces (SPACE, TAB, or RETURN). The *key* is an integer indicating which field to use for ordering the lines. If the *key* is unspecified, whole lines are compared. (Hint: Use `TextLines`, and consider a `SortKey` class that determines the relative order of two lines.)

3. (TextLines-2) Improve `MySort` in the previous exercise so that it takes several sort keys. Entries with identical primary keys are sorted by the secondary key, and so on. Can you make the program flexible enough to accommodate an unrestricted number of keys? Can you implement these improvements entirely by class extension? (Hint: Make key comparison recursive.)

4. Consider `TermLifeAccount` and object I/O. Reimplement `readAccounts` and `writeAccounts` in Section 6.4 to use object I/O instead of character I/O.

5. Follow the `ArbStack` example and write `ArbQueue` by using an `ArbList`.

6. Extend `EmpQueue`, queue of employees, from the generic queue in the previous exercise.

7. Define an `OverdraftProtection` account by extending `FreeChecking`. For over-draft protection, a checking account would have a preset "credit line" of 1000. If overdraft occurs, enough money (rounded up to the nearest 100) is trans-fered from the credit line into the account balance to cover the shortfall. Any account with a credit balance will incur the monthly fee no matter what the account balance is. The account charges interest on credit line balance with a settable rate on the *average daily balance*. Interest is charged to the account when the monthly fee is processed. Deposit into the account and repaying (part or all of) the credit line balance are two different account functions. The bank can increase/decrease the credit line for any account. (Hint: Consider a `CreditAccount` object.)

8. (Calc-2) Consider the calculator simulation program as modified through ex-ercise Calc-1 in Chapter 3. There are many `private` methods and fields. These won't make extending the classes easy. Change any that you think should be accessible or possible to override from subclasses to `protected` status. (Hint: When in doubt use `protected`.)

9. (Calc-3) Based on the revised classes from exercise Calc-2, write a `MemoryEng` class to add operations SQRT (square-root), M+ (add to memory), M- (subtract from memory), and MR (recall from memory), using the opcodes s, M, m, and R respectively. (Hint: `MemoryEng` extends `CalcEng`.)

## CHAPTER FIVE

OOP Techniques: Interfaces and Polymorphism

Classes are basic in OOP. Class extension builds new classes on existing ones, to implement improvements and refinements, without modifying existing classes.

At a higher level, OOP promotes programming and manipulating objects as "black boxes": making uniform interfaces for related objects and establishing generic programs for all *plug-compatible* objects. A combination of Java features is used to achieve these goals.

By establishing common interfaces, related objects can be treated as black boxes that are operated the same way from the outside. Thus, these black boxes become interchangeable parts, pluggable into some other program. The ability to work with different black-box objects is generally known as *polymorphism*. A *polymorphic program* is one that can use any plug-compatible objects. With polymorphism, programs can use objects from a class hierarchy as mutually interchangeable parts. Plug in improved parts and you get a better application immediately. Many examples are given to illustrate the practical use of plug compatibility.

The uniform interface of plug-compatible objects takes careful planning. Designing superclasses for inheritance is important. The Java *abstract superclass* feature makes it easy to implement common operations as well as preplan uniform interfaces. Putting the idea to use, an ordered sequence class is presented to serve as a schematic for building objects that can store, order, and retrieve arbitrary elements simply and efficiently. Then the generic ordered sequence object is applied to handle ordered lines in text files.

Although limited to extending one superclass, a Java class can *implement multiple interfaces*. An *interface* simply prescribes the public interfaces of objects without offering any implementation. Objects implementing the same interface can be used interchangeably in polymorphic programs requiring specific object behaviors.

Polymorphism and plug compatibility are central to OOP and will be explained thoroughly. Examples show their effective use in practice.

5.1 PROGRAMMING WITH PLUG-COMPATIBLE OBJECTS

One enormous advantage of OOP is the ability to treat objects as black boxes and to deal with them only through their interfaces. If a set of similar or related black boxes supports a common interface, code can be written to work on all such boxes without change.

The concept of building and operating on *plug-compatible* objects is commonplace in daily life. Consider cars. Having learned to drive one automatic car, a person can drive most other automatic cars without changing the method of driving. Many different types of cars are made interchangeable as far as the driver's interface is concerned. The fact that one car's accelerator controls the fuel injection and another the carburetor is hidden and does not affect the way they are driven.

The Java way to build plug-compatible objects (cars) and to define *polymorphic* operations (driving) on them (Figure 5.1) will be the focus here. To illustrate this important technique, bank accounts will be made plug-compatible for certain well-defined operations such as transferring funds between accounts, producing a listing of accounts, and so forth.

Compatible Types and Polymorphism

Putting all bank accounts in a class hierarchy rooted at the superclass `BankAccount` allows the different accounts to become compatible types through class extension. Because the extended types are considered a kind of `BankAccount`, there is at least a chance of making them interchangeable. The

Figure 5.1   POLYMORPHIC PROGRAM AND PLUG-COMPATIBLE OBJECTS

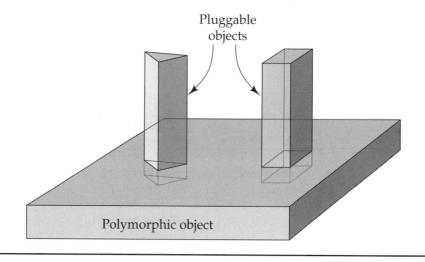

Pluggable
objects

Polymorphic object

subclasses of BankAccount we have established will help in demonstrating their polymorphic use.

To make interchangeable use meaningful, these different account objects must *support either a uniform public interface or certain critical common operations*. To a degree, this has also been done: BankAccount, FreeChecking, and JointAccount all support the same descriptors for methods balance, deposit, and withdraw. Therefore a piece of code that uses only the uniform interface has a chance to work for all of these types of account objects.

Recall the transfer method (Section 4.14):

```
public static boolean transfer
        (double amt, BankAccount from, BankAccount to)
{   boolean ok = from.withdraw(amt);
    if ( ok ) to.deposit(amt);
    return ok;
}
```

The ability for the same program to work with interchangeable objects is known as *polymorphism*. Consider transfer as an example. Each of the parameters from and to can receive multiple types of account objects (BankAccount, JointAccount, FreeChecking, and so on) instead of just one fixed type (*monomorphism*). The correct transfer procedure is performed by using the proper withdraw and deposit operations in different types of accounts.

Three conditions help the polymorphic transfer in achieving plug compatibility:

1. Use of superclass reference parameters—Here from and to are superclass object references, so accounts of any type can be passed into transfer. This is a result of the implicit widening reference conversion for arguments in method calls (Section 4.10).

2. Accessing only uniform public interface—Here withdraw and deposit are uniform, so the code makes sense for all different account types.

3. Run-time method overriding—An actual argument, of type FreeChecking, for example, referenced through the parameter from of type BankAccount causes the code from.withdraw(amt) to invoke the withdraw method in FreeChecking, not BankAccount. This is done by the Java automatic method overriding mechanism explained in Section 4.14.

Keys to Plug Compatibility

Programming with plug-compatible objects is achieved by a combination of OOP mechanisms and techniques. It represents the essence of OOP. The key ingredients are summarized as follows:

- Interchangeable objects—First of all, it must be possible to represent a collection of similar objects that are interchangeable under certain operations. Such objects usually have an *is-a* relationship and belong to a class extension hierarchy or implement the same interface.

- Uniform public interfaces—The interchangeable objects must have certain identical public interfaces to allow the same polymorphic procedure to work on all of them. This is achieved by maintaining a set of public interface methods with uniform descriptors for all plug-compatible objects.

- Polymorphic parameters—A polymorphic method that operates on the interchangeable object must declare formal parameters capable of receiving arguments of any plug-compatible type. The parameters should be base reference or interface (Section 5.4) types.

- Dynamic access of interchangeable operations—By keeping descriptors uniform for interface methods, the Java method overriding mechanism ensures type-specific method invocation at run time.

5.2   USING PLUG-COMPATIBLE COMPONENTS

The calculator simulation program (Chapter 3) has a `Calculator` that employs two components, `CalcEng` and `CalcFace`. The three objects interact and cooperate to get the job done.

Because the interface between these components has been worked out already, it is possible to develop plug-compatible compute engines (extending `CalcEng`) and plug-compatible user interfaces (extending `CalcFace`). These components are then directly pluggable into `Calculator`, resulting in new features and/or improved user I/O.

Following Section 4.18 and exercise Calc-3 of Chapter 4, we can define the subclass `MemoryEng`, adding SQRT (square-root), M+ (memory-add), M- (memory-subtract) and MR (memory-recall) operations. We can extend `MemoryEng` again to define `ScientificEng` to add *sin*, *cos*, *tan*, and *log*, for example.

```
public class ScientificEng extends MemoryEng
{   public String keys() { return super.keys()+UOPS; }

    public void operate(char c)
    {   if ( UOPS.indexOf(c) != -1 )
            computeSci(c);
        else
            super.operate(c);                           // (A)
    }

    protected final String UOPS = "SOTL";

    protected void computeSci(char c)
```

```
{   op = '=';
    if (argcnt == 2) { ans =  arg; argcnt--; }
    switch(c)
    {   case 'L':  // log
            if ( ans <= 0.0 ) statusFlag = ERROR;
            else ans = Math.log(ans);
            return;
        case 'S':  // SIN
            ans = Math.sin(ans); return;
        case 'O':  // COS
            ans = Math.cos(ans); return;
        case 'T':  // TAN
            ans = Math.tan(ans); return;
    }
  }
}
```

The opcodes in UOPS represent desired unary operations that are carried out by computeSci. Other operations are handled by calling the superclass operate (line A). Figure 5.2 shows the compatible engines. To demonstrate how the compatible engines can be dynamically plugged into Calculator and run, let's write a program to run different calculators, depending on command-line input:

```
public class Run
{   public static void main(String[] args) throws IOException
```

Figure 5.2   **PLUG-COMPATIBLE CALCULATOR ENGINES**

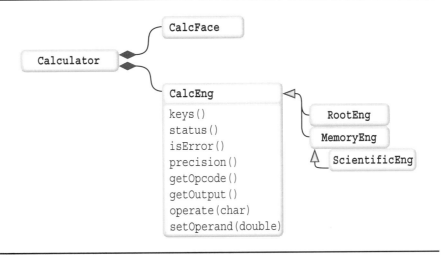

```
{   CalcEng e =null;
    String what = args[0];
    if ( what.equals("basic") )              // basic
        e = new CalcEng();
    else if ( what.equals("memory") )        // with memory
        e = new MemoryEng();
    else if ( what.equals("scientific") )    // scientific
    .   e = new ScientificEng();

    if ( e != null )
    { CalcFace f = new CalcFace(e.keys(), e.precision()); // (B)
      Calculator x = new Calculator(e, f);                // (C)
      x.on();
    }
    return;
}
}
```

Because the engines are plug-compatible, we can assign to the `CalcEng` variable a basic engine, an engine with a memory register, or a scientific engine, depending on the command-line argument. A `CalcFace` can be instantiated with the opcode keys and precision of the selected engine (line B), and both are then plugged into the polymorphic class `Calculator`, which is quite unaware of the improvements!

You can find the complete `RootEng`, `MemoryEng`, and `ScientificEng` in the example package.

5.3 PLANNING UNIFORM PUBLIC INTERFACES

Materials in the previous section showed how to write polymorphic code that works for all plug-compatible objects. One key aspect is maintaining a consistent set of public interfaces for the compatible objects, and this is the main topic here.

A uniform public interface will not happen all by itself. It takes careful analysis, planning, and skillful coding. It often involves trial and error before a final design emerges. Two Java constructs support the creation of uniform public interfaces:

1. Abstract superclass—The *abstract superclass* is used to define a uniform plug-compatible interface, to implement common mechanisms to be inherited, and to provide a schematic for implementing subclasses (Figure 5.3). An abstract class has undefined methods, whose descriptors are designated `abstract`, and it cannot instantiate objects. Once a subclass defines all abstract methods, the subclass becomes *concrete* and can create instances.

Figure 5.3   ABSTRACT SUPERCLASS

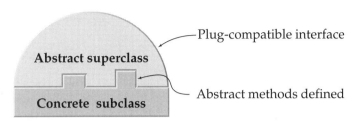

2. Interface—An *interface* is a construct that specifies method descriptors and possibly also read-only fields. No method definitions are given in an interface. Thus, an interface is like a totally abstract class. The purpose of an interface is to define the public interface of objects conforming to a certain behavior. A class can *implement an interface* by defining the methods required by that interface. A class can extend at most one superclass but can *implement multiple interfaces*.

Understanding how interfaces (Section 5.4) and abstract classes (Section 5.8) work and how to use them effectively to create public interfaces for plug-compatible objects is important for writing object-oriented programs.

In Java, achieving uniform interfaces involves several activities:

- Begin with a desire to have a certain set of common operations defined for a collection of related objects.

- Design a set of method descriptors to be followed by all compatible objects. The methods define a uniform public interface and often may involve planned interactions between the superclass and the subclass. The goal is to make the desired common operations possible on a set of plug-compatible objects.

- In the superclass, supply definitions for all or only some of the interface methods. Supply missing definitions, and redefine others in subclasses.

5.4 DEFINING INTERFACES

An interface can be considered a totally abstract class. In an interface:

- All members are public—There is no need to declare them `public`.

- All methods are abstract—Just specify the method descriptor; then there is no need to declare them `abstract` (Section 5.8).

- All fields are `static` and `final`—These can provide useful constant values.

For example the Java `Comparable` interface requires only a simple method:

```
public interface Comparable
{
    public int compareTo(Object target);
}
```

The call *host*`.compareTo(`*target*`)` returns a positive integer, zero, or a negative integer to indicate that *host* is greater than, equal to, or less than the given *target*. If the *target* cannot be compared to the host, the method throws a run-time `ClassCastException`.

A `compareTo` implementation must obey the following three rules:

1. The sign of x`.compareTo(`y`)` is the negative of the sign of y`.compareTo(`x`)` for all x and y.

2. The fact that x`.compareTo(`y`)` is negative and y`.compareTo(`z`)` is negative implies that x`.compareTo(`z`)` is negative.

3. The fact that x`.compareTo(`y`)` is zero implies that the sign of x`.compareTo(`z`)` is always the same as the sign of y`.compareTo(`z`)` for all z.

Such a `compareTo` method provides a *partial ordering* of the objects in its class. In Java we refer to this as the *natural ordering* of the objects. In other words, a class that implements the `Comparable` interface has a natural ordering.

After an interface is defined, the name of the interface becomes a type name. Any class that implements the interface becomes a subtype of it. An interface is a contract between providers and clients of a particular service. Although the method descriptors in the interface definition represent an important aspect of this contract, they by no means capture all of the contract. The detailed semantics of the methods and static fields in an interface must rely on documentation (e.g., the three rules for `compareTo`) associated with the interface.

The design of an interface affects the functionalities and capabilities on the provider side and the complexities and conveniences on the client side.

With `Comparable`, a polymorphic sorting mechanism can be created that will sort all `Comparable` objects. Java actually supplies such a sorting mechanism in its *collections framework* (Section 9.8).

In Java, all of the primitive wrapper classes as well as `String` (lexicographic), `Date` (chronological), `File` (lexicographic on pathname), `BigInteger`, and `BigDecimal` implement `Comparable` and therefore provide a natural ordering for their objects.

Java defines and uses many other interfaces, for example:

- `Runnable` for threads, `Cloneable` for copying (Section 5.13)
- `Serializable` for object serialization (Section 6.13 and Section 10.19)
- `Transferable` for copy-and-paste (drag-and-drop, Section 12.11)

- `ImageObserver`/`ImageConsumer` for decoupled image loading (Section 11.14)
- Listeners for event handling (Section 7.9)

5.5 IMPLEMENTING INTERFACES

To implement an interface in a class, we simply declare that class to implement the interface in question and define the methods required by the interface. As an example, let's implement the `Comparable` interface for the `BankAccount` class:

```
public class BankAccount implements Comparable
{  public BankAccount() {}

    // ...  other methods omitted

    public int compareTo(Object t)
    {    return acct_no.compareTo( ((BankAccount) t).acct_no);
    }

    public boolean equals(Object t)
    {    return( t == this ||
               ( this.getClass() == t.getClass() &&
                 acct_no.equals( ((BankAccount) t).acct_no) )
           );
    }

    protected String acct_no;     // account number
    protected String owner;       // owner ss
    private double   acct_bal;     // current balance
}
```

Note that the `compareTo` method casts the incoming object into a `BankAccount` object (may result in a run-time exception) and then compares the account numbers. Now `BankAccounts` have a natural ordering. Here we also show the `equals` method in the form required by the `Object` class, which is consistent with `compareTo`.

As another example, let's look at implementing `Comparable` for fractions:

```
public class Fraction implements Comparable
{    public int compareTo(Object y)
     {    Fraction tmp = (Fraction) y;
          if ( less(tmp) ) return -1;
          if ( greater(tmp) ) return 1;
```

```
            return 0;
        }

    // other members omitted ...
}
```

For `Fraction` the `compareTo` method uses the class-defined `greater` and `less` methods to help the computation. When implementing `compareTo` for a class, be sure the ordering is natural.

For objects without a natural ordering, or when the natural ordering is not applicable in a certain situation, you can use comparators that implement the `java.util.Comparator` interface and define the `compare` method:

```
public int compare(Object o1, Object o2);
```

Generic sorting programs can use supplied comparators to do their jobs. For example, the collections framework sorting algorithms allow incoming comparator parameters. Ordering text lines (Section 5.11) gives an example of comparator usage.

5.6   WHY INTERFACES?

Because Java disallows multiple inheritance, a class can extend only one superclass. The restriction makes it hard for a class to conform to more than one interface. For example, you may want a `BankAccount` object to also conform to a *help* interface for providing help information to users. With single inheritance, the class can extend either a `Help` or a `BankAccount` superclass, but not both. The need to conform to multiple interfaces is not uncommon. Consider the problem of making an object from any inheritance hierarchy runnable as a separate thread. Normally, you inherit from the `Thread` class to make something executable as a thread. This can't be done if a class is already extending another class.

The Java *interface* mechanism addresses the problem of objects conforming to two or more independent public interfaces and offers an elegant and effective solution. In Java, a class can extend at most one superclass but can *implement multiple interfaces*. Objects of such classes can be used in different ways. Thus a subclass can run as a thread by implementing the `Runnable` interface (Section 11.12), allow easy cloning by implementing the `Cloneable` interface (Section 5.13), and provide a natural ordering by implementing the `Comparable` interface.

An interface is *a direct superinterface* of a class that lists it on the class header. A class may also have indirect superinterfaces. An interface *IntF* is a superinterface of *ClassX* if:

- *IntF* is a direct superinterface of *ClassX*.

- *ClassX* has a direct superinterface that is extended from *IntF* (Section 5.7).
- *IntF* is a superinterface of a superclass of *ClassX*.

A class is said to *implement all of its superinterfaces* and is implicitly of any superinterface type. An interface can become a superinterface of a particular class in more than one way; it is all right for a class to have duplicate superinterfaces. For example, a class may have a direct Cloneable superinterface and also extend a superclass that implements Cloneable.

5.7   EXTENDING INTERFACES

It is also possible to define new interfaces based on existing ones. An interface can extend one or more other interfaces, therefore becoming a composite. The *inherited* interfaces may not have a conflict among their method specifications. A Saveable interface may require a saveAs(*file*) method. An Openable interface may require an openFile(*file*) method. A Fileable interface can extend them:

```
interface Fileable extends Saveable, Openable
{
    boolean save();   // saves back to the same file
                      // returns false for failure
}
```

and add the additional required method save() to save back to the file originally opened.

With the introduction of interfaces, the subtype–supertype relationship gets a little more complicated. Now a class or interface can be a subtype of more than one supertype. Consequently, name conflicts can occur when a method or field with the same name happens to be in two or more supertypes:

1. Method name conflict—If the inherited methods have different signatures, there is no conflict. If two methods have the same descriptor, they are the same method and there is no conflict. If two methods have the same signature but different return types, there is a conflict and the inheritance fails.
2. Field name conflict—Field names in interfaces are static, and they can always be accessed with their type-qualified names. Therefore field name conflicts can always be avoided.

5.8 ABSTRACT SUPERCLASS

In addition to interfaces, the abstract class is also a tool to plan a uniform public interface for compatible objects. An abstract class is a class with undefined or *abstract* methods. As such, an abstract class can't instantiate objects. The purpose of an abstract class is to define a public interface and to implement a subset of methods, leaving other required methods abstract, for subclasses to define. A subclass of an abstract class stays abstract until all required methods are defined.

As an example, let us consider creating a container that automatically keeps its elements sorted in a linear sequence for easy manipulation and retrieval. Such an ordered sequence container presents an external view of elements being organized into a linear sequence accessible by indexing, just like an array.

The external behavior of an ordered sequence is characterized by the public operations:

- Add an element
- Remove an element
- Find the index of an element
- Retrieve an element by indexing
- Detect the number of elements contained

These operations should be part of the public interface for any type of ordered sequence. Internally, on the other hand, an ordered sequence requires at least the following operations:

- Effective sorting of elements into order
- Efficient retrieval of elements

An ordered sequence container can be made to work if its elements have a natural order or if a way of comparing them for sorting is given.

To establish generic ordered sequences, we take a two-step approach:

1. Define an `AbstractSequence` class to capture the uniform public interface and to supply common operations.

2. Extend `AbstractSequence` to provide element storage and to define abstract methods (Figure 5.3).

5.9   ABSTRACT SEQUENCE

AbstractSequence is a superclass that defines the public interface of ordered sequences and supplies implementation for many common operations, including searching and sorting, to make subclassing easy.

```
public abstract class AbstractSequence
{  public abstract int size();            // number of elements
   public abstract Object get(int i);     // ith element, sorted
   public abstract boolean remove(int i); // removes by index
   public boolean add(Object any)         // Enters new element (A)
   {   if ( append(any) )
       {  sorted(false);
          return true;
       }
       return false;                      // add failed
   }

   protected AbstractSequence() {}           // constructor (B)
   protected AbstractSequence(Comparator c)  // constructor (C)
   {   comparator = c;   }
   protected boolean sorted()                // tests sorted status (D)
   {   return ordered;   }
   protected void sorted(boolean s)          // sets sorted flag (E)
   {   ordered = s;   }

   protected abstract
      boolean append(Object a);       // adds to end
   protected abstract
      Object getAt(int i);            // element at i, no sorting
   protected abstract
      void setAt(int i, Object t);    // element at i

 // other public and protected methods ...

   private boolean ordered = false;          // sorted flag (H)
   private Comparator comparator = null;     // (I)
}
```

The *abstractness* of AbstractSequence comes from *abstract methods* such as size, get, remove, and append that have intended semantics, prescribed descriptors, but no implementations yet. The abstract keyword is used to declare an abstract class or method. A method such as add (line A) can be coded with calls to abstract methods.

The add method asks append to put a new element at the end of the sequence and invalidates the flag ordered. Multiple elements can be entered without resorting the sequence after each add call. Sorting is deferred until the next retrieval from the sequence.

An abstract class cannot instantiate objects. A subclass of an abstract class must also be declared abstract unless it implements all of the abstract methods. Therefore an abstract method forces subclasses to supply definitions with the prescribed method descriptor. Because the constructors of an abstract class are used only by subclasses, they are normally declared protected (lines B and C).

Thus, an abstract superclass is a schematic for building subclasses rather than for establishing objects of its own. Without the proper operations supplied by a subclass, the class AbstractSequence is useless by itself. The abstract superclass is very useful in planning plug-compatible interfaces and operations required of subclasses.

The ordered flag (line H) indicates the sorted state of the sequence. Methods for examining and setting the sorted flag are provided (lines D and E). The Comparator object (line I) supplies an element ordering. If no Comparator is present, the natural ordering of the elements will be used in sorting the sequence.

There is no field for a sequence of elements. No assumption is made on how the sequence of elements will eventually be stored. It is designed to work together with all properly extended classes.

Note that an abstract class may have static members; however, abstract methods cannot be static, because they need to be overridden by subclass-defined methods.

Implementing Common Operations

In addition to defining uniform interfaces for subclasses, an abstract superclass can supply implementation of useful operations common to all subclasses, thus simplifying subclass implementation and increasing code reuse.

What common operations can be defined in AbstractSequence where neither the elements of the sequence nor their type is known? Well, quite a few. In fact it is surprising how many nontrivial operations can be supplied, given the right interface design between the superclass and the subclass. To begin with, consider searching:

```
public int index(Object el)
{   if ( ! sorted() ) sort();
    int low = 0, high = size()-1, mid, test;
    while (low <= high)
    {   mid = (high + low)/2;
        test = cmp(el, mid);                    // (J)
        if ( test == 0 ) return mid;
        else if ( test > 0 ) low = mid + 1;
```

```
            else high = mid - 1;
    }
    return -1;    // entry not found
}
```

If the sequence is not already in sorted order, it is sorted first. Then an efficient binary search algorithm is employed to locate the desired element, calling upon the cmp method to compare elements (line J). Element comparison uses the natural ordering of elements if no Comparator is present. A Comparator object implements the Comparator interface and provides the compare(Object, Object) method:

```
private int cmp(Object el, int j)
{    if ( comparator != null )
        return comparator.compare(el, getAt(j));
    Comparable a = (Comparable) el;
    return a.compareTo( getAt(j) );           // (K)
}
```

AbstractSequence implements sorting, using the now familiar quicksort algorithm:

```
protected void sort()
{    if ( sorted() ) return;
    quicksort(0, size()-1);
    sorted(true);
}


private void quicksort(int l, int r)
{    if ( l >= r || l < 0 ) return;
    int k = partition(l, r);
    quicksort(l, k-1);
    quicksort(k+1, r);
}
```

The abstract size(), to be defined by a subclass, gives the length of the sequence. The method partition(), where all of the actual sorting work is done, relies on properly defined element comparison (cmp(i,j)) and interchange (swap(i,j)) methods:

```
private int partition(int l, int r)
{    int i=l, j=r;
    swap((i+j)/2, r);                          // pivot moved to r
    while (i < j)
    {   while (cmp(i, r) <= 0 && i < j) i++;   // cmp
        while (j > i && cmp(j, r) >= 0) j--;   // cmp
        if (i < j) swap(i++,j);                // swap
    }
```

```
      if (i != r) swap(i,r);                    // swap
      return i;
}
```

The swap and overloaded cmp methods are also defined:

```
private void swap(int i, int j)
{   Object tmp = getAt(i);
    setAt(i, getAt(j));
    setAt(j, tmp);
}

private int cmp(int i, int j)
{   if ( comparator != null )
        return comparator.compare(getAt(i), getAt(j));
    Comparable a = (Comparable) getAt(i);
    return a.compareTo( getAt(j) );
}
```

The abstract getAt and setAt methods are defined by the subclass and perform get and set of elements in the sequence without paying attention to the sorted status of the sequence. They are used only internally for sorting the sequence.

Some abstract methods are not part of the public interface but part of the internal operations required by methods. These are declared protected.

Subclass: ArraySequence

The class ArraySequence realizes an ordered sequence by extending AbstractSequence, using an Object array to store the elements and defining all required methods.

```
///////    ArraySequence.java    ///////
import java.util.Comparator;

public class ArraySequence extends AbstractSequence
{   public ArraySequence() { this(256); }        // (1)

    public ArraySequence(int m)                   // capacity = m (2)
    {   MAX = m; obj = new Object[m]; }

    public ArraySequence(Comparator c, int cap)  // (3)
    {   super(c); MAX = cap;
        obj = new Object[cap];
    }

// other methods ...
```

```
        private Object[] obj;                   // Object array
        private int len = 0;                    // no. of elements
        private int MAX;
}
```

You can create a new ArraySequence with a default (line 1) or specified (line 2) maximum capacity. If a Comparator is not given (line 3), the natural ordering of the elements will be used for sorting the sequence.

The public methods as required by AbstractSequence are as follows:

```
public int size() { return len; }              // current length of seq

public Object get(int i)                        // returns ith element
{   if ( i >= len || i <= 0 ) return null;
    if ( ! sorted() ) sort();                   // (4)
    return obj[i];
}

public boolean remove(int i)                    // remove element i
{   if ( i < len && i > -1 )
    {   if ( ! sorted() ) sort();
        for ( int j=i ; j < len ; j++ )         // (5)
            obj[j] = obj[j+1];
        len--;
        return true;
    }
    return false;
}
```

The get method returns null if the index i is invalid. It makes sure that the sequence is already sorted (line 4) before retrieving the element at position i. An element is removed by moving all elements after it in the array up one slot (line 5).

Critical protected methods that are required by methods defined in AbstractSequence are as follows:

```
protected Object getAt(int i)                   // get element at i
{   return obj[i];   }

protected void setAt(int i, Object t)           // set element at i
{   obj[i] = t;   }

protected boolean append(Object t)              // add element at end
{   if ( len < MAX )
    {   obj[len++] = t;
        return true;
    }
}
```

```
        return false;                      // array full
}
```

As you can see, it is relatively simple to write a concrete ordered sequence class by following the plan set forth by AbstractSequence. The capacity of an ArraySequence is fixed at instantiation time. One can certainly consider another subclass of AbstractSequence that removes this restriction.

5.10 A SEQUENCE OF DATES

ArraySequence is a generic container that can hold any type of Comparable objects or objects with a given Comparator. Let's illustrate this by using ArraySequence to organize a list of dates.

In java.util, the classes Date and GregorianCalendar support sophisticated date and time computations. In the following example, SimpleDate class, simple objects to represent dates are sufficient:

```
///////    SimpleDate.java    ///////

public class SimpleDate implements Comparable
{   public SimpleDate() {}
    public SimpleDate(int m, int d, int y)
    {   month=m; day=d; year=y; }

    public int compareTo(Object t)
    {   SimpleDate d = (SimpleDate) t;
        if ( year != d.year )
            return year-d.year;
        else if ( month != d.month )
            return month-d.month;
        else
            return day-d.day;
    }

    public String toString()
    {   return month + "/" + day + "/" + year;  }

    private int month, day, year;
}
```

Note that SimpleDate is a Comparable type and the compareTo method defines a natural ordering for these dates.

Following is a program that sets up an ordered sequence of dates and performs a few operations on it:

```
///////    TestDates.java    ///////

public class TestDates
{  public static void main(String[] args)
   {   SimpleDate[] d =
        {new SimpleDate(2,12,1949), new SimpleDate(4,20,1949),
          new SimpleDate(3,15,1949), new SimpleDate(11,6,1986),
          new SimpleDate(7, 4,1996), new SimpleDate(2,12,1959),
          new SimpleDate(4,20,1959), new SimpleDate(3,15,1959),
          new SimpleDate(11,7,1998), new SimpleDate(7, 23,1997)};
       ArraySequence mydates = new ArraySequence();      // (I)
       int i;
   // enter 10 dates
       for ( i=0; i < 10; i++) mydates.add(d[i]);          // (II)
       for ( i=0; i < mydates.size(); i++)                 // (III)
       {
            System.out.println((SimpleDate) mydates.get(i));
       }
       i = mydates.index(d[6]);
       mydates.remove(i);
       System.out.println("\nEntry " + i + " removed");
       i = mydates.index(d[6]);     // access should fail
       System.out.print(d[6]);
       if ( i == -1 )
            System.out.println(" entry not found");
   }
}
```

After the 10 dates (line II) are added into the ordered sequence (line I), the sorted result is displayed (line III). Running this example produces the following output:

```
2/12/1949
3/15/1949
4/20/1949
2/12/1959
3/15/1959
4/20/1959
11/6/1986
7/4/1996
7/23/1997
11/7/1998
```

```
Entry 5 removed
4/20/1959 entry not found
```

In summary, an abstract superclass can enforce a preplanned uniform interface and can also provide partial (or default) implementations. Interfaces and abstract classes form a powerful tool for building plug-compatible objects and writing polymorphic codes for them.

5.11 ORDERING TEXT LINES

Now let's apply `ArraySequence` to a more realistic problem, sorting text lines. Because we already have the `TextLines` class (Section 4.20), our job is made simpler. Here is the strategy:

1. Define a `SortKey` class that is a `Comparator` (Section 5.4).
2. Use a `TextLines` object to read a text file.
3. Enter the lines (`StringBuffer` objects) into an `ArraySequence` with a supplied `SortKey` comparator.

Ordering textlines is different from ordering names or dates because textlines don't have a natural order. The purpose of a `SortKey` is to compare text lines based on specified keys within the lines. If `SortKey` implements the `Comparator` interface, we can use this comparator in an ordered sequence for sorting the lines.

Comparing Keys

To compare two lines for sorting, we have to extract the keys and compare them. A `SortKey` object supplies the capability to identify and compare specific key positions.

When initialized, a `SortKey` object holds the key position and the delimiter string, quantities used by the private member function key to extract a substring sort key in a text line. An established `SortKey` object is then used to compare two text lines.

Letting the application specify the key and delimiter fields for the initialization of a `SortKey` object provides the kind of flexibility that characterizes good programs. By default, white space are used as delimiters.

```java
///////    SortKey.java    ///////
import java.util.StringTokenizer;

public class SortKey implements Comparator
{   public SortKey(int pos, String dlm)
    {   delim = dlm;
        position = pos;
    }
```

```
    public SortKey(int pos) { position = pos; }
    public SortKey() { }

    public int compare(Object a, Object b)
    {   return cmp( ((StringBuffer) a).toString(),
                     ((StringBuffer) b).toString()
                   );
    }
// other methods ...

    private String delim = "\t \r";  // delimiter string
    private int    position = 0;     // key position
}
```

The method key extracts a substring in the text line, based on the key position and the delimiters. If the key position is zero (line 1) the whole line will be returned. Otherwise a tokenizer is used to extract the correct token (line 2).

```
public String key(String s)
{   if ( position == 0 ) return s;                          // (1)
    StringTokenizer st = new StringTokenizer(s, delim);
    String key = null;
    int j = st.countTokens();
    if ( position <= j )                                    // (2)
    {   for (j=0; j < position; j++)
            key = st.nextToken();
    }
    return key;
}
```

The compare method required by the Comparator interface calls cmp, which compares two text lines, a and b. Basically, cmp performs a string compareTo on the keys extracted by key. The condition (line 3) takes care of missing keys from lines.

```
public int cmp(String a, String b)
{   String ka = key(a);
    String kb = key(b);
    if ( ka == null )                                       // (3)
    {   if ( kb == null )
            return 0;
        else
            return -1;
    }
    if ( kb == null ) return 1;
```

```
        return ka.compareTo(kb);
}
```

ArraySequence of Text Lines

With a Comparator defined for text lines, we now can put lines of text in the generic ArraySequence and perform ordering:

```
///////    SortLines.java    ///////
import java.io.*;
import java.util.Comparator;

public class SortLines
{ public static void main(String[] args) throws IOException
  {   if (args.length > 2 || args.length < 1 )
      {   System.err.println("Usage: SortLines [ key ] file");
          System.exit(1);
      }
      int keypos=0;
      if (args.length == 2)
      {   keypos=Integer.parseInt(args[0]);
          args[0] = args[1];
      }
      FileInputStream myin = new FileInputStream(args[0]);
      TextLines txtobj = new TextLines();
      txtobj.input(myin);                                  // (A)
      Comparator k = new SortKey(keypos);                  // (B)
      System.out.println("Original lines:");
      txtobj.output(System.out);                           // (C)
      ArraySequence lines = new ArraySequence(
                            k, txtobj.length());           // (D)
      for (int i = 0; i < txtobj.length(); i++)            // (E)
      {   lines.add(txtobj.getLine(i));
      }

      System.out.println();
      System.out.println("Sorted result:");                // (F)
      for (int i = 0; i < lines.size(); i++)
      {   System.out.println((StringBuffer) lines.get(i));
      }
  }
}
```

Based on command-line arguments, we read the specified text file into a TextLines object (line A) and set up a SortKey comparator based on the given key position (line B). The text lines are displayed as-is (line C) and entered into an `ArraySequence` with the `SortKey` comparator (lines D and E). The sorted result is displayed simply by use of the `ArraySequence get` method (line F). The complete program, ready to compile and execute, is in the example package.

We have seen how to define an abstract class, to extend it into a concrete class, and to apply the class in sorting elements with a natural or comparator-defined ordering. The way interfaces and abstract classes combine to enable polymorphism is made clear.

5.12 INTERFACES VS. ABSTRACT CLASSES

Both the interface and the abstract superclass can define a uniform public interface for plug-compatible objects. However, a class can implement multiple interfaces but can extend only one superclass. A class can conform to many interfaces by simply implementing them. This is the main advantage of an interface over an abstract class (Section 5.8). However, an abstract class can supply default implementations for methods whereas an interface must remain completely abstract. Providing default or convenience definitions for common methods for subclasses is the main advantage of the abstract superclass. Because of the single-class extension restriction, public interfaces defined by classes (abstract or not) cannot be easily combined in a subclass.

For certain interfaces, implementation afresh by each different class makes sense, and there is no problem. The question is how to provide a base implementation for an interface if there is such a need.

A creative solution is as follows:

1. For an interface *Abc*, create a class *AbcAdapter*

```
class AbcAdapter implements Abc
{   ...
}
```

that supplies a base implementation for all or a subset of the required methods. The Java event listening adapters such as `MouseAdapter` and `KeyAdapter` are examples (Section 7.9).

2. Interface adapters allow three possibilities for implementing an interface-conforming class:

   • The class can implement the interface `Abc` directly.
   • The class can can extend `AbcAdapter` and define or override methods to suit.

- The class can implement Abc by employing an AbcAdapter object internally and forward method calls to it:

```
class ClassX implements Abc
{   AbcAdapter impObj = new AbcAdapter();
    type interfaceMethod( ... )
    {   return impObj.interfaceMethod( ... );
    }
    ...
}
```

This way, you can have your interface and supply implementation, too.

5.13 CLONING OBJECTS

In Java, objects are accessed through variables that reference them. New objects are created by the operator new that returns a reference. Object references are assigned, passed as arguments, and returned by methods. There is not an immediate need for copying objects. However, it is not possible to avoid object copying entirely. Consider an occasion in which you need to pass an object by value. You must first create a copy and then pass a reference to the copy. A class designer can include a constructor that takes an object from the same class to make a copy. But that solution does not work well when classes are extended. Java offers an arrangement involving

- The Object.clone method
- The Cloneable interface[1]
- The CloneNotSupportedException

to help the systematic management of object copying.

Copying Using Object.clone

The Java defined interface Cloneable is interesting. It is an interface with no content, but it provides a way for any class to allow/disallow the

obj.clone()

call.

In many situations, you may enable the cloning of objects in a class by simply declaring that a class *implements the* Cloneable *interface* and writing a simple clone method. For example:

```
public class Fraction implements Cloneable
{   public Object clone()
```

------

[1]The name is different from the correctly spelled English word "clonable."

```
    {   try
        {   return super.clone();     // call protected method
        }   catch (CloneNotSupportedException e)
            { return null; }
    }
    // other methods ...
}
```

Let `obj` be an instance of `Fraction`. Then the call

```
(Fraction) obj.clone();
```

makes a copy of `obj` and returns a reference to it.

The protected `clone` method inherited from `Object` first checks to see whether the class of the host object (`obj`) implements the `Cloneable` interface. If not, it throws a

```
CloneNotSupportedException
```

Otherwise, it creates a new object of the same type as `obj` and initializes its fields with the values stored in `obj`. It then returns a reference (of type `Object`) to the newly created object.

When a class implements `Cloneable`, any subclass also inherits the interface. The subclass may implement `clone` as appropriate. For a subclass to bar cloning, it must override `clone` to throw the `CloneNotSupportedException` and document this clearly.

The `Object`-supplied `clone` works in many situations. For example, the `Vector2D`, `Fraction`, and `BankAccount` classes may implement `Cloneable` to enable object copying.

Copying of array objects is explained a little later in this section.

Overriding `Object.clone`

The copying semantics of `Object.clone` usually work, but there are situations in which a class must modify it. Consider copying a `Cirbuf` object that contains the following field:

```
private char[] cb;   // character buffer
```

Figure 5.4 shows what happens when copying a `Cirbuf` object `obj1`. The clone refers to the same buffer as `obj1`. This is totally unacceptable because the put and get operations in both objects now use the same buffer. Such coupling of objects as a side effect of copying (Figure 5.5) is almost always unexpected and unwanted. Similar copying difficulties arise when an object uses a file, a socket, or some other operating system resource. The situation is even worse if the class releases such resources via a `finalize` method. To allow copying in

Figure 5.4   INCORRECT CLONING OF `Cirbuf`

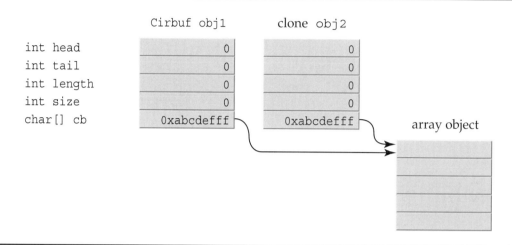

Figure 5.5   EFFECT OF DEFAULT CLONING

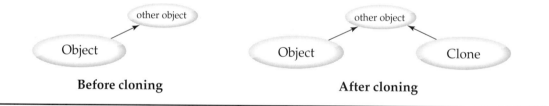

such situations, a class can implement `Cloneable` and override `clone` with the correct copying semantics.

```
///  add in class Cirbuf  ///
public Object clone()
{   try
    {   Cirbuf copy = (Cirbuf) super.clone();       // (1)
        copy.cb = (char[]) cb.clone();              // (2)
        return copy;
    } catch (CloneNotSupportedException e)          // (3)
        {   throw new InternalError(e.toString());
        }
}
```

The revised copying action first calls `super.clone()` (line 1), then assigns to the field `cb` a copy of the character array (line 2). It is important that the `super.clone()` call be the first action. The call can pick up an overriding `clone` method in a superclass, which in turn calls super.clone(); this eventually leads to the Object-supplied clone. The try and catch (line 3) setup is mandatory, but in this case no exception is expected. Because of the call to clone() in Object, remember to add "implements Cloneable" to the class header of Cirbuf.

If a class wants to forbid cloning, it does not implement Cloneable or it overrides clone to throw CloneNotSupportedException. If a class does not implement Cloneable and passes on a protected version of clone, the class does not support copying itself but makes it possible for subclasses to do so. The Object class is an example.

Next, let's consider the copying of arrays.

Array Copying

Arrays are objects and are passed in reference form in method calls. Passing an array by reference is fine in these situations:

- The receiving method does not modify the array.
- The calling method does not care whether the array is modified.
- The calling method wants the modified result in the array.

Otherwise, a copy of the array object should be passed in a method call. The copying of an array arrObj can be done simply by calling arrObj.clone(). The clone method makes an exact copy of the array. The copy consists of new array cells containing values, primitive data, or references from the original array. The array copy is then cast to its correct type:

(type[]) arrObj.clone();

The System.arraycopy method provides an efficient way to copy a number of elements from one array to another. The call

System.arraycopy(source, i, target, j, len)

copies len elements from the source array starting with element i to the target array starting at target[j].

5.14   INHERITANCE PLANNING

For a class, the public members represent an interface to the outside. This interface is well understood by now. In addition, the combined public and protected members present another interface to a subclass. When writing a superclass for further extension, this second interface and certain other factors must be considered carefully. Without proper planning, the extension of a class may run into problems quickly. Often these problems can be solved by revising the superclass in question, assuming that the programmer has access to the source code and is allowed to make modifications to it. The situation can be quite different if modifying the superclass is not possible. It is best to plan ahead and take possible extensions into account while designing a superclass.

The key principle of planning for inheritance is a well-formed model of the overall behavior of the superclass object in relation to extended objects. This model will help you make decisions in the following critical areas:

- Protected or private—Consider whether a private or package member should be designated protected instead for access by a subclass. When in doubt, use `protected`.

- Return type of overriding methods—Realize that if the method signature overrides a superclass method, the return type must be the same.

- Hooks for method overriding—Include do-nothing methods that subclasses can override to add or supply proper functions. Event listeners are good examples.

- Abstract methods—Use these to preplan subclass interfaces.

- Interface or abstract superclass—Use abstract superclasses to supply partial or default implementations. Use interfaces to prescribe well-defined but auxiliary behaviors to be *mixed in* with a wide variety of object types.

- Constructors versus initialization methods—Subclass and superclass constructors are subject to strict calling orders and can be inflexible. Initialization methods, such as `init()` used in applets, can be more flexible. Such initialization methods can be called anywhere from a constructor or other methods. If a superclass `init` checks to see that a field is `null` before initializing it, a subclass can selectively replace fields with plug-compatibles, then call superclass `init`s to do the rest of the initializations.

- Constants—Consider using `final` instance variables to store constants that may have different values in subclasses. Supply access methods for the constant values if they are part of the public interface. The methods can be overridden to supply new constant values in subclasses. Unless a constant stays the same for all subclasses, don't use a `public static final` field for it.

Sometimes the behavior of objects from a certain class must be fixed, and deviations are not expected or permitted. Such classes should be declared `final` to avoid being extended.

Method Composition

An extended class often overrides a superclass method to augment its capabilities. For example, the `FreeChecking` method

```
public boolean withdraw(double amt)
{   boolean ok = super.withdraw(amt);    // call inherited withdraw
```

```
      if ( ok && balance() < min_bal )    // added processing
         free = false;
      return ok;
}
```

first calls its superclass counterpart, then performs some additional processing. In general, a subclass may add either *preprocessing*, *postprocessing*, or both to a superclass method to achieve more complicated behavior. This way of composing methods is an important inheritance technique. However, a certain amount of planning is needed to make such method composition possible.

5.15 SUMMARY

A major advantage of OOP is the ability to have programs use interchangeable objects that are *plug-compatible*. Such *polymorphic* programs are powerful, flexible, and easy to maintain, modify, improve, and reuse. Critical conditions for polymorphism include *type compatibility*, *uniform API*, and *run-time method selection*. Abstract superclasses and interfaces help create uniform APIs, and the Java method overriding mechanism handles dynamic method selection.

An abstract class contains undefined abstract methods and serves as a starting point for class extension. It defines a uniform API and may also implement certain methods common to all subclasses.

An interface represents a totally abstract class with all members public, all methods abstract, and all fields static and final. A class can extend one superclass but implement multiple interfaces. By implementing interfaces, a Java subclass can support different external interfaces and produce objects that are plug-compatible in different ways. Java built-in interfaces help object cloning, threads, image loading, and so on. Adaptor classes can provide default implementations for interfaces, providing an alternative to writing all the required methods from scratch. Interfaces can also be extended. The creative use of interfaces is important to OOP.

A class that implements the Comparable interface is said to *define a natural ordering*. A polymorphic sorting program can be written to order any sequence of comparable objects. For objects without a natural ordering, a Comparator object can be supplied to compare and order them.

The Cloneable interface and the protected clone method in the root Object class provide a means to copy objects and arrays. Care must be taken when copying objects that use or modify other objects.

If a class is placed inside another class as a member, it is an inner class. Inner classes can enhance encapsulation and provide instantiation control.

A class presents one interface to the public and another to its subclasses. Careful planning can facilitate future class extension.

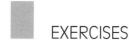 EXERCISES

Review Questions

1. Name and explain the four key conditions for plug compatibility.

2. Consider the uniform interface the Java `Object` superclass enforces. List the methods in this uniform interface, and explain the purpose of each.

3. Consider the following interface:

```
public interface HasMain
{   public static void main(String[] args);
}
```

Is there anything wrong with it?

4. Explain in detail how the `ImageObserver` and `ImageConsumer` interfaces in Java work.

5. Consider the generic `ArbList` (Section 4.22). Establish an interface `Listable`, and modify `ArbList` to contain `Listable` items rather than any `Object`. Explain the advantages and disadvantages of this approach.

6. What does the `clone()` method in `Object` do? In what situations is cloning by simply calling the `clone()` supplied by `Object` not enough?

7. Can a subclass implement `Cloneable` if its superclass does not? Can a class prevent the cloning of its objects? The cloning of objects of all its subclasses?

8. When you copy an array using `arrObj.clone()`, do objects that are array elements also get copied, or is only the array copied?

9. Explain in detail how the `Cloneable` interface and the `clone` method in `Object` help in the cloning of objects.

Programming Assignments

1. `Number` is the superclass of numeric wrapper types. Discover the common public interface of these compatible types. Write a polymorphic program that demonstrates their compatibility.

2. Apply the `ArraySequence` class and establish an ordered sequence of `BankAccounts`.

3.   The `ArraySequence` class has a fixed capacity. Create `DynamicSequence`, by extending `AbstractSequence`, that is similar but has dynamically expanding capacity. (Hint: Use the Java-supplied `ArrayList`.)

4.   Improve the sorting of lines by enabling the use of *secondary keys*. A secondary key is used when two lines compare equal under the primary key for sorting. (Hint: Extend `SortKey`.)

5.   Define a `Sortable` interface and a `SortAlgorithm` interface. The purpose is for any `SortAlgorithm` object to receive any `Sortable` object and sort it into order. Demonstrate your interface with implementations.

6.   How do you get a sequence to order the elements in reverse of their natural ordering? Write a program to demonstrate your technique.

7.   Add cloning to `TermLifeAccount`.

## CHAPTER SIX

Packages and Core Classes

Java comes with many built-in classes. The classes are organized into *packages*, which are designated name spaces, for easy usage, management, and maintenance.

The java.lang package is most basic to the Java language. Classes and interfaces under java.lang can be used directly without importing. They include string classes (Section 2.9), primitive-type wrapper classes (Section 3.3), mathematical computation classes (Section 6.18), and error and exception handling classes (Section 6.15).

Other packages constitute the *standard Java class library* (packages with java. prefix) and the *standard Java extension library* (packages with javax. prefix). The standard java.awt and the extension javax.swing packages support *graphical user interface* (GUI) programming and will be covered in Chapters 7 and 8. The *collections framework* of generic containers from java.util is the topic of Chapter 9.

Although several library facilities are covered in this chapter, I/O remains the main focus. Many types of I/O streams are supported by the java.io package, including byte-oriented and character-oriented streams. Moreover, I/O streams can be interconnected to achieve a variety of functionalities. Useful I/O operations are described and illustrated with examples.

Often data are formatted before output. The java.text package provides *locale-sensitive* formatting of numbers and dates. The capabilities are handy for practical applications.

I/O often is the source of run-time errors. The java *exception mechanism* deals with errors encountered by programs at run time. The throwing, catching, and declaring of exceptions are explained carefully. You'll learn how to apply the *catch or specify* principle of exception handling.

We begin by describing the Java package mechanism. The information also enables you to organize your own Java code into packages.

6.1   PACKAGES

In Java, names of types (classes and interfaces) are in the same name space and must be kept distinct in a program to avoid conflicts. Without a systematic scheme, this is not entirely easy to achieve, especially for a large program involving code from many different sources. In practice, related source files usually form a separate *package* that affords a distinct name space. Type names in different packages will not conflict with one another. Generally, the *package* mechanism helps achieve several purposes:

- To organize related source code files
- To avoid type name conflicts
- To provide package-level encapsulation and access control

Putting the declaration

```
package somePackage;
```

at the very beginning of a source code file makes the file part of *somePackage*. All types (classes and interfaces) defined in this file join the specified package. Only one `package` declaration is allowed in each file, but multiple files on the local file system can belong to the same package. The package declaration simply causes every type name defined in the file to be implicitly prefixed with the package name:

```
somePackage.TypeName
```

Thus, type names cannot conflict among different packages because they are actually different. A source code file without a `package` declaration becomes part of the `unnamed` package. Types in the `unnamed` package do not need a package specifier. When creating a new package, use a name not likely to conflict with other package names. Note that a package name may contain the period (`.`) character.

Importing from Packages

You may use `import` declarations to tell the Java compiler to include certain class and interface names from specified packages. After it is imported, a type name can be used directly without the package-name prefix.

There are two forms of `import`:

```
import someTargetPackage.SomeType     (import the class or interface)
import someTargetPackage.*;           (import all classes and interfaces
                                       in the package)
```

It is not possible to import types contained in the unnamed package into another package. Thus, packageless types are useful for experimentation, testing, and brevity in providing examples. Place code intended as a class library in a named package.

Package Access Control

Java provides two levels of access control: class level and package level. Class-level access rules have been described (Section 4.6) and summarized here in Figure 6.1. A package consists of types (classes and interfaces) defined in all its files and nothing else. Package-level access for a type is either `public` or `package`. Only public types are accessible from other packages (Figure 6.2). Thus, the collection of all public types forms the external interface of a package to all other packages. In other words, a class can access public types and their public members in another package. A subclass can access the public and protected members of its superclass in another package.

Codes inside a package can access all type names, and all methods/fields not declared `private`, in the same package.

In Java, an identifier not otherwise declared has access protection `package`. There is one exception: interface members are public by default.

Figure 6.1   CLASS-LEVEL ACCESS CONTROL

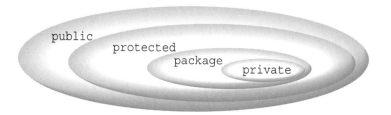

Figure 6.2   PACKAGE-LEVEL ACCESS CONTROL

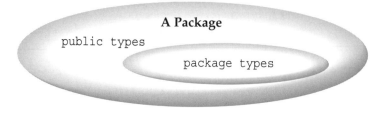

Package Name Conventions

The worldwide use of Java makes it advisable to follow certain conventions to avoid package name conflicts. One idea is to use the Internet domain name of your institution to form a prefix to your package name. For example,

```
package EDU.kent.cs.factor;
```

names a `factor` package under the domain name `cs.kent.edu`. The all-caps leading component further reduces the chance of a name conflict with packages not following this naming convention.

Managing Packages

Most Java compilers and interpreters assume that package names are reflected in the file organization of your Java code:

- Files for different packages are stored in different directories. Files belonging to a package *abc* are put in a directory *abc*. Files in a package *abc.xyz* are stored a directory *xyz* under the directory *abc*. Let's call the top directory of a package its *package directory*. For a file in the unnamed package, its package directory is the directory containing the file.
- To put a package on the the class search path, you simply include its package directory in CLASSPATH.
- When executing a Java program, you must specify the fully qualified class name containing the target `main` method and issue the **java** command from the directory that contains the package directory. Run a class in the unnamed package from the directory where the class file is located. Thus, run

  java EDU.kent.cs.factor.FactorPolynomial *arg1* ...

  from the directory that contains

  ```
  EDU/kent/cs/factor/FactorPolynomial.class
  ```

The easiest way to compile code in a package *abc.xyz* is to go to the parent of the package directory and issue this command:

javac abc/xyz/*.java

Run the code from the same package directory with something like:

java abc.xyz.*SomeClass arg1* ...

A simple `matrix` package (Section 6.16) shows the handling of a package.

6.2 JAVA-SUPPLIED PACKAGES

The Java class library consists of many useful packages. Part of learning Java is getting to know the available packages and their uses:

- Package `java.io`—Supports Java input and output streams.
- Package `java.lang`—Contains essential classes for the Java language:
  - For programming—`String`, `Object`, `Math`, `Class`, `Thread`, `System`, type wrapper classes, and the `Cloneable`, `Runnable` interfaces
  - For language operations—`Compiler`, `Runtime`, and `SecurityManager`
  - For error and exceptions—`Exception`, `throwable`, and many other classes

  The `java.lang` package is the only one that is automatically imported into every Java program.
- Package `java.math`—Supplies *big integer* and *big decimal* calculations.
- Package `java.net`—Supports networking facilities: URLs, TCP sockets, UDP sockets, IP addresses, and binary-to-text conversion.
- Package `java.rmi`—Supports *remote method invocation* (Section 10.19) for Java programs.
- Package `java.util`—Contains various utility classes: bit sets, enumeration, generic containers (`ArrayList` and `HashtMap`), time, date, token separation, random number generation, and system properties.
- Package `java.text` —Provides classes and interfaces for handling text, dates, numbers, and messages in a manner independent of natural languages.
- Package `javax.swing` —Supports graphical user interface programming with new features and capabilities to supersede the Java AWT in many situations.

The Java library contains many other packages. All packages and classes in Java are listed and explained in the Java documentation.

6.3 ACCESSING JAVA DOCUMENTATION

SJDK software and documentation can be downloaded from the official Java Web site,

```
http://java.sun.com/jzse
```

where you can find the most recent release. The documentation can be accessed via a Web browser remotely from Sun. For *Java 2 Platform*, use something like the following:

```
http://java.sun.com/jzse/1.4/docs/
```

Or you can download the documentation for local use on your computer.

Demos, tutorials, guides to topics, description of Java tools, and *Application Programming Interface* (API) documentation are included. The Java API, available at

`http://java.sun.com/jzse/version/docs/api/index.html`

is organized into three levels:

1. All packages
2. All classes, interfaces, and exceptions within a package
3. All member constructors, methods, and fields within a class

To use the API, access a target class to find how a method or a field in that class works. For example, you would visit the `String` class API for information on its `charAt` method. If you do not know which class you are looking for, use the index of all methods in the API documentation.

The Web site for this textbook has many useful resources for learning Java, including a search facility for classes and interfaces in the Java documentation.

6.4 INPUT AND OUTPUT

The `java.io` package provides byte-oriented and character-oriented I/O streams to support many useful input/output operations and to isolate programs from operating-system-specific I/O details. A stream is an object representing an ordered sequence of data, bytes or characters, with an input *source* or an output *destination* (Figure 6.3).

Three standard I/O streams, `System.in`, `System.out`, and `System.err` (Section 1.10), are available for every Java program. These are static fields in the `System` class for receiving bytes from and sending bytes to the terminal. Among other things, they support I/O for ASCII characters, as you have seen. `System.in` is an instance of the `InputStream` class, whereas `System.out` and `System.err` are instances of the `PrintStream` class. Byte-oriented I/O is supported by `InputStream`, `OutputStream`, and their subclasses. Unicode-character

Figure 6.3   I/O SOURCE AND DESTINATION

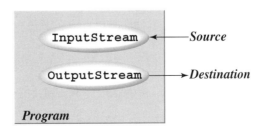

(16-bit) oriented I/O is supported by Reader, Writer, and their subclasses. Use the latter for reading and writing text and the former for ASCII and binary I/O.

To perform I/O in a Java program, create appropriate I/O stream objects to do the job.

I/O Stream Hierarchies

Input (Output) streams form an inheritance hierarchy based on the InputStream (OutputStream) *abstract superclass*. Figure 6.4 shows common input streams and Figure 6.5 shows common output streams. Appendix G provides a complete listing of Java I/O streams.

The purpose of an *abstract* class is to define a common interface for its subclasses, not to create instances (Section 5.8). For each *SomeInputStream* subclass, there is usually a corresponding *SomeOutputStream* subclass. Table 6.1 lists methods defined in InputStream that are available in all subclasses; Table 6.2 lists methods defined in OutputStream. The methods throw IOException for I/O errors, return −1 for end-of-input, and block to complete the requested I/O.

The Java I/O Model

Java offers a variety of I/O classes to create I/O stream objects. Some allow you to create stream objects by specifying input sources or output destinations. For example, you use FileInputStream and FileOutputStream to open streams

Figure 6.4   COMMON INPUT STREAMS

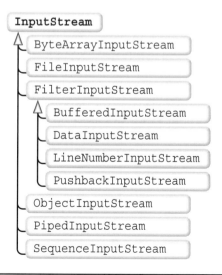

Figure 6.5   COMMON OUTPUT STREAMS

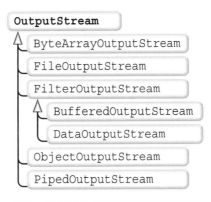

to files, and the URL, URLConnection, and socket classes to obtain streams for networking (Chapter 10).

Other classes allow you to add functionalities to an existing stream. This is done by connecting an existing stream with another stream to form a pipeline for well-defined I/O purposes. For example, you may connect System.in to an InputStreamReader to make reading text lines easy or connect a file output stream to a DataOutputStream to store binary data in a file. Keep this model in mind as you read the following sections.

Table 6.1   InputStream METHODS

Method	Description
abstract int read()	Returns byte read or −1
int read(byte[] b)	Returns number of bytes read into b or −1
int read(byte[] b, int i, int n)	Reads from byte i for at most n bytes into b; returns number of bytes read or −1
long skip(long n)	Skips n bytes of input; returns number of bytes skipped
int available()	Returns the number of bytes that can be read without blocking
synchronized void mark(int k)	Marks the current position in the input stream; k bytes can be read before the mark is erased
synchronized void reset()	Repositions the stream to the last marked position
boolean markSupported()	Returns true if the stream supports mark and reset
void close()	Closes the input stream

Table 6.2   `OutputStream` **METHODS**

Method	Description
`void write(int b)`	Writes one byte b
`void write(byte[] b)`	Writes an array of bytes
`void write(byte[] b, int i, int n)`	Writes from b[i] n bytes
`void flush()`	Outputs any buffered bytes
`void close()`	Closes the stream

6.5 FILE I/O

Use `FileInputStream` (`FileOutputStream`), a direct subclass of `InputStream` (`OutputStream`), for file input (output):

- new `FileInputStream`(*name*)—Opens an input stream connected to the file name, `File` object, or `FileDescriptor` object, specified by *name*.
- new `FileOutputStream`(*name*)—Opens an output stream connected to the file name, `File` object, or `FileDescriptor` object, specified by *name*.
- `streamObj.getFD()`—Returns the file descriptor associated with the I/O stream object.

The `Lowercase` example (Section 2.3) illustrates character I/O to files.

The `File` class of `java.io` provides methods to examine and manipulate file names, files, and directories on a host platform. You can determine the existence and read permission of a file before opening an input file stream, for example. A `File` object is created with

```
new File(name)
new File(dir, name)
```

where *name* is a string and *dir* is a string or a `File` object representing a directory. Note that instantiating a `File` object does not automatically result in a file on the host system. A file is created only when it is opened for reading or writing. After creating a file object, the methods listed in Table 6.3 can be used:

```
File fobj = new File("xyz");
if ( fobj.canRead() )
   FileInputStream in = new FileInputStream(fobj);

// now read the file ...

in.close();
```

Table 6.3   File METHODS

Method	Description
`String getName()`	Returns the simple file name
`String getPath()`	Returns the path name
`String getParent()`	Returns the name of the parent directory
`boolean exists()`	Returns `true` if file exists
`boolean canWrite()`	Returns `true` if file is writable
`boolean canRead()`	Returns `true` if file is readable
`boolean isFile()`	Returns `true` if file is ordinary file
`boolean isDirectory()`	Returns `true` if file is a directory
`long lastModified()`	Returns the last modification time (relative to an unknown past point in time)
`long length()`	Returns the number of bytes in the file
`boolean mkdir()`	Creates a directory and returns `true` if successful
`boolean renameTo(File dest)`	Renames a file and returns `true` if successful
`String[] list()`	Returns a list of files in a directory
`boolean delete()`	Deletes the specified file and returns `true` if successful

A file name string can be given relative to the current working directory or as an absolute pathname. Be sure to escape the \ separator in a string:

```
File fobj = new File("c:\\abc\\xyz");
```

6.6 BUFFERED I/O

The classes `BufferedInputStream` (`BufferedReader`) and `BufferedOutput-Stream` (`BufferedWriter`) add a byte (character) buffer to significantly reduce the actual I/O operations performed. You may specify the buffer capacity or use the default value. For example,

```
BufferedOutputStream out = new BufferedOutputStream
                (new FileOutputStream("outfile"));
```

or the code used in the `input` method of the `TextLines` class (Section 4.20):

```
BufferedReader rdr = new BufferedReader
                (new InputStreamReader(in));
```

Note that if you close a stream, attached streams in the same pipeline will also be closed.

6.7 PRINT WRITERS

Use a `PrintWriter` to output the character string representations of primitive types and objects. The `PrintWriter` print method converts primitive data types, strings, and objects with overriding `toString` methods to a sequence of characters and outputs the sequence. The method `println` is the same except that it also outputs appropriate system-dependent line termination.

To create a `PrintWriter` use:

```
new PrintWriter(OutputStream destination)
new PrintWriter(OutputStream destination, true)  // auto flushing
```

Auto flushing means that a \n produced by a `println` method will cause an automatic `flush()`.

For better efficiency, you may use an output buffer:

```
PrintWriter out = new PrintWriter(new BufferedWriter(
                new OutputStreamWriter(System.out)));
```

Use `out.flush()` to send any remaining output on its way. If you close a stream, it will be flushed and streams connected also closed. If you still need `System.out`, don't execute `out.close()`; use `out.flush()` instead. It is important to make sure that a buffered stream is flushed before a stream downstream is closed.

6.8 TERM LIFE ACCOUNT FILES

As an example, let's add the capability of reading and writing account files to the `TermLifeAccount` class. To be placed in a data file, each term life account is serialized into a string in the form

name:*ss*:*age*:*coverage*

and stored as a single line.

First we add a `toString` method and a constructor to make things easier:

```
public class TermLifeAccount
{ // add new constructor
    public TermLifeAccount(String str)
    {  StringTokenizer tk = new
                StringTokenizer(str, ":");
        if ( tk.countTokens() == 4 )  // need 4 tokens
        {  name = tk.nextToken();
           ss = tk.nextToken();
           setAge(Integer.parseInt( tk.nextToken() ));
           setCoverage(Integer.parseInt( tk.nextToken() ));
        }
```

```
                else System.err.println("Ill-formed data: " + str);
        }

    // add new method
      public String toString()
      {    return name + ":" + ss + ":"
              +  age  + ":" +  coverage;
      }

    // ...

}
```

To read accounts from a data file, we can use the static method readAccounts, which is called with any input stream and returns an ArrayList of term life accounts read from the file. The java.util.StringTokenizer (Section 2.9) helps parse input lines.

```
// method in TermLifeAccount
public static ArrayList readAccounts(InputStream in)
        throws IOException
{    ArrayList account= new ArrayList(16);
     String s;
     BufferedReader rdr = new BufferedReader                    // (1)
                  (new InputStreamReader(in));
     while ( (s = rdr.readLine() ) != null )                    // (2)
     {    account.add(new TermLifeAccount(s));
     }
     return account;
}
```

A buffered input stream reader is created (line 1) to read each line (line 2) from the given input source. The line read is used to instantiate a new TermLifeAccount, which is added to an ArrayList.

To output a list of term life accounts to any given output stream, a method that uses a PrintWriter can be added to TermLifeAccount:

```
public static void writeAccounts(OutputStream out, List act)
        throws IOException
{    PrintWriter w = new PrintWriter(new BufferedWriter(
                  new OutputStreamWriter(out)));
     for (int i = 0; i < act.size(); i++)
     {    w.println(act.get(i));    }
     w.flush();                          // sends buffered output
}
```

To test file I/O for term life accounts, a simple program like the following can be used:

```
public class TLAccounts
{   public static void main(String[] args) throws IOException
    {   if ( args.length != 1 )
        {   System.err.println("Usage: java TLAccounts filename");
            System.exit(1);
        }
    // read file
        FileInputStream infile = new FileInputStream(args[0]);
        TermLifeAccount a;
        ArrayList act = TermLifeAccount.readAccounts(infile);
        infile.close();
        for (int i = 0; i < act.size(); i++)
        {   a = (TermLifeAccount)(act.get(i));
            System.out.println(a.toString());
        }
    // write file
        FileOutputStream outfile =
            new FileOutputStream(args[0] + ".copy");
        TermLifeAccount.writeAccounts(outfile, act);
        outfile.close();
    }
}
```

6.9 FILE UPDATING

The same file can be opened for both reading and writing, using the class RandomAccessFile

```
new RandomAccessFile(name, mode)
```

where *name* is a String or File object and *mode* is either "r" or "rw".

The RandomAccessFile uses a *file pointer*, a byte count from the beginning of the file (first byte is 0) to keep track of the location for the next I/O byte in a file. The pointer is advanced by each I/O operation. The getFilePointer method returns the current pointer value, seek(*index*) sets the file pointer to the given *index*, and skipBytes(*n*) advances the file pointer forward *n* bytes. Use

```
void write(int i);          (outputs low byte of i)
void write(byte[] b);       (outputs b.length bytes)
```

to output one or more bytes.

Use the "rw" mode to update a file in place. Under this mode, file contents stay the same if not explicitly modified. Modification is done by positioning and writing the revised bytes over the existing bytes. LowerIO implements the lowercase program (Section 2.3) with in-place file updating:

1. Open the given file with RandomAccessFile under "rw" mode.

2. Read characters until an uppercase letter is encountered.

3. Overwrite the uppercase letter with the lowercase letter.

4. Repeat steps 2 and 3 until finished.

```
public static void doio(RandomAccessFile iofile)
{   int i; char c;
    try
    {   while ( (i = iofile.read()) >= 0 )
        {   c = (char) i;
            if ( Character.isUpperCase( c ) )
            {   iofile.seek(iofile.getFilePointer()-1);      // (1)
                iofile.write(Character.toLowerCase(c));       // (2)
            }
        }
    } catch( IOException e )
        {   JavaSystem.error(e);                              // (3)
            System.exit(1);
        }
}
```

After detecting an uppercase character, the file position is on the next byte to read. Thus, the file pointer should be moved to the previous byte (line 1) in order to overwrite it (line 2). Clearly, this program works for ASCII characters but not Unicode characters. JavaSystem (line 3) is a convenient class we defined for error reporting (Section 6.17).

The main method establishes a RandomAccessFile object after checking the given file with File methods, calls doio to do the work, and then closes the file.

```
public class LowerIO
{ public static void main (String[] args)
    {   if ( args.length != 1 )     // takes one arg
        { JavaSystem.err.println( "Usage: LowerIO file");
          System.exit(1);
        }
        File file = new File(args[0]);
        if ( file.isFile() && file.canRead() && file.canWrite() )
        { try
            { RandomAccessFile iofile = new RandomAccessFile(file, "rw");
              doio(iofile);
```

```
            iofile.close();
        }  catch ( IOException e )
            {  JavaSystem.error(e);
               System.exit(1);
            }
     }
     else
     { JavaSystem.err.println("Can't open file for I/O " + args[0]);
       System.exit(1);
     }
  }
  // doio shown earlier
}
```

Adding to End of File

When there is a new term life account, it needs to be added to an account data file. For this, we write the instance method appendToFile for TermLifeAccount:

```
public void appendToFile(String file) throws IOException
{   RandomAccessFile afile =
        new RandomAccessFile(file,"rw");              // (A)
    if ( afile != null )
        afile.seek(afile.length());                   // (B)
    else
        throw(new IOException());
    afile.writeBytes(toString() + MyUtil.EOL);        // (C)
    afile.close();
}
```

The given file is opened as a random access file (line A). The file pointer is moved to the end of the file (line B), and the string form of the host object is written out with a platform-dependent end-of-line marker (line C).

The static EOL in the MyUtil class is set as follows:

```
public static
String EOL = System.getProperties().getProperty("line.separator");
```

The EOL is a *system property* (Section 6.20) that is also used by println methods.

6.10 OTHER I/O STREAMS

In-Memory I/O

The source or destination of I/O is usually the terminal or a file. However, it is sometimes useful to use an in-memory array or buffer as the source/destination. The classes

```
ByteArrayInputStream        ByteArrayOutputStream
StringReader                StringWriter
```

fill this need. Also `PipedInputStream` and `PipedOutputStream` perform in-memory I/O between two threads in the program through a FIFO pipe (Section 11.9).

Additional I/O

A number of other I/O streams are not covered here, including:

- `FilterInputStream` and `FilterOutputStream`—to connect to I/O streams to add intermediate processing
- `LineNumberInputStream`—to keep track of line numbers while reading input
- `PushBackInputStream`—to provide easy look-ahead
- `SequenceInputStream`—to read multiple input streams in sequence
- `StreamTokenizer`—to help break input into tokens

6.11 TEXTUAL AND UNICODE CHARACTER I/O

As mentioned, Java character I/O is done with subclasses of the abstract `Reader` and `Writer` (Figure 6.6). For example, the classes `InputStreamReader` and `OutputStreamWriter` provide basically the same operations as `InputStream` and `OutputStream`, except that the operations now work on characters rather than bytes.

Concrete `Reader` and `Writer` objects connect to a byte I/O stream by converting Java `char` encoding to and from bytes based on an *encoding used for character I/O* (Figure 6.7). The character encoding can be specified explicitly or defaults to the system property `file.encoding` (Section 6.20). Depending on the encoding, I/O for a single character may read/write one or more bytes, in big- or little-endian. For example, you have `FileReader`, `FileWriter`, `CharArrayReader`, `CharArrayWriter`, and so on. You can also turn

Figure 6.6   CHARACTER READERS AND WRITERS

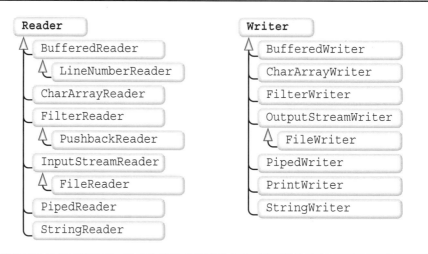

any I/O stream into a character reader/writer with `InputStreamReader` and `OutputStreamWriter`. For example:

```
new OutputStreamWriter(outStream, "Unicode")
new InputStreamReader(inStream, "Unicode")
```

An `InputStreamReader` turns byte input streams into character input streams: It reads bytes and translates them into characters, according to the specified *character encoding*. The `InputStreamReader`'s read methods may consume one or more input bytes. Similarly, `OutputStreamWriter` turns byte output streams into character output streams. For example, the code

```
int i;  char c;
InputStreamReader cin = new InputStreamReader(System.in);
while ( (i = cin.read()) != -1 )
{    c = (char) i;
    ...
}
```

Figure 6.7   JAVA CHARACTER I/O

will work for any text I/O encoding (including Unicode) that is specified by `file.encoding`. To read a line of characters, use:

```
BufferedReader rdr = new BufferedReader (new InputStreamReader(in));
String line = rdr.readLine();
```

The method `readLine()` returns the next line read. A line is terminated by a `'\n'`, a `'\r'`, or a `'\r''\n'` pair. The value `null` is returned if end-of-stream has been reached.

Here is an example of character I/O where the program specifies `Unicode` encoding:

```
import java.io.*;

class UnicodeIO
{ public static void main(String[] args) throws IOException
  {  char pi = '\u03C0';
     FileOutputStream f = new FileOutputStream("datafile");
     OutputStreamWriter out = new OutputStreamWriter(f, "Unicode");
     out.write((int) pi);        // output a single char
     out.close();
     FileInputStream g = new FileInputStream("datafile");
     InputStreamReader in = new InputStreamReader(g, "Unicode");
     int b1 = in.read();
     if (pi == (char)b1) System.out.println("Written and read pi.");
  }
}
```

Java also has security, compression and decompression, and other I/O facilities. Appendix G lists all Java I/O classes.

6.12   NONCHARACTER I/O

Most I/O covered so far deals with ASCII (1-byte) or Unicode (2-byte) characters. We convert `double`, `float`, and other noncharacter data to their character representations for output and read these character representations on input. The strings read are then parsed to produce the desired input data.

It is possible to perform I/O without converting to characters. The

```
DataInputStream
DataOutputStream
```

classes provide methods for reading and writing all primitive Java data types directly. The methods are in the form:

`readType()`—Returns the primitive type read. For example, `readFloat()` returns a `float`.

write*Type*(d)—Writes the argument d as the indicated primitive type. For example, writeShort(5). The return type is void.

Note that the methods readChar and writeChar deal with 16-bit Unicode characters. These methods are final, and they implement the DataInput and DataOutput interfaces respectively. The RandomAccessFile class also implements both interfaces.

When using data streams, you are reading/writing the binary representation of the data items. Usually a DataInputStream is used to read data produced by a DataOutputStream.

To create a data I/O stream use

```
new DataInputStream(InputStream source)
new DataOutputStream(OutputStream destination)
```

where source and destination can be any stream object in the appropriate class extension hierarchy. For example, the code

```
public class DataIO
{ public static void main(String[] args)
        throws IOException
  {   double r = Math.sqrt(2.0d);                       // (A)
      DataOutputStream out = new DataOutputStream(
              new FileOutputStream("double.data"));
      out.writeDouble(r);                                // (B)
      out.close();
      DataInputStream in = new DataInputStream(
              new FileInputStream("double.data"));
      r = in.readDouble();                               // (C)
      System.out.println("sqrt(2.0)=" + r);
  }
}
```

writes $sqrt(2.0)$ (line A) an 8-byte quantity to a file (line B) and reads it back with readDouble() (line C).

The methods writeUTF and readUTF are also useful for performing I/O in UTF (*Unicode Transmission Format*). They allow you to write Java strings in UTF and read UTF-coded files into Java strings.

6.13 OBJECT I/O

Data streams perform direct binary I/O of primitive types and strings. You still need a general way to read and write objects directly. The

```
ObjectInputStream
ObjectOutputStream
```

answer this need by supplying, in addition to `readFloat`, `writeDouble`, and so on for primitive types, the `readObject` and `writeObject` methods for direct I/O of objects (Figure 6.8).

To use direct object I/O, the object must belong to a class that *implements the* `Serializable` *interface* (Section 5.4). To implement `Serializable`, simply add

```
implements Serializable
```

to the class header. There are no methods to implement. For example:

```
public class Fraction implements Serializable
public class BankAccount implements Serializable
```

After a class implements `Serializable`, all of its subclasses do the same. Direct I/O of `FreeChecking` objects can then be performed easily:

```
public class FreeIO
{  public static void main(String[] args) throws IOException
    {    FreeChecking susan = new
            FreeChecking(555234, 500.0, "034-55-6789");
        ObjectOutputStream out = new ObjectOutputStream(
            new FileOutputStream("checking.data"));
        out.writeObject(susan);                                      // (1)
        out.close();
        try
        {  ObjectInputStream in = new ObjectInputStream(
                new FileInputStream("checking.data"));
            susan = (FreeChecking) in.readObject();                  // (2)
        }  catch (ClassNotFoundException e) { }

        System.out.println("Balance: " + susan.balance());
    }
}
```

The `FreeChecking` object susan is written to a file (line 1) and read back in again (line 2).

Figure 6.8   SERIALIZABLE OBJECT I/O

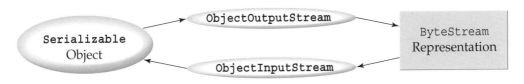

It is a good idea to make a class serializable if direct I/O or remote use of its objects is a possibility.

6.14 NUMBER AND DATE FORMATTING

The `java.text` package provides support for the language-independent processing of numbers, dates, and other textual messages. Capabilities include formatting, parsing, sorting, and iteration. We will focus on formatting of numbers and dates here.

You instantiate a formatter object for the default locale (or a given locale) supported by the Java platform, then use that formatter to format numbers or dates. A `Locale` (`java.util`) specifies a language and a country plus an optional variant. For example:

```
new Locale("en", "US");        // English-USA
new Locale("fr", "FR");        // French-France
new Locale("es", "MX");        // Spanish-Mexico
new Locale("zh", "CN");        // Chinese-China
```

The two-letter language and country codes follow the ISO (International Standards Organization) standards. Automatic locale-dependent formatting can make applet and other widely accessed codes more locale-friendly. Setting specific locales is normally not necessary in your formatting code because you use the default locale of the Java platform executing your code.

The abstract class `NumberFormat` is the superclass of all number formats. `NumberFormat` helps format and parse numbers for any locale so that your code can be independent of the local conventions for decimal points, thousands-separators, or even the digit symbols. Use these static methods to obtain number, currency, and percentage formatters:

```
import java.text.*;

NumberFormat nf = NumberFormat.getNumberInstance();
NumberFormat cf = NumberFormat.getCurrencyInstance();
NumberFormat pf = NumberFormat.getPercentInstance();
```

The `getxxxInstance` methods can also be given a locale argument. Such methods are sometimes called *factory methods* because they make objects to suit when called. The object returned makes it easy to format numbers into desired strings for display. For example, if `double n = 1234.567;`,

```
                                   // English-USA   French-France
System.out.println(nf.format(n));  // 1,234.567     1 234,567
System.out.println(cf.format(n));  // $1,234.57     1 234,57 F
System.out.println(pf.format(n));  // 123,457%      123 457%
```

produce the indicated displays for the locale English-USA and French-France, respectively. This is very handy indeed.

With any of the formatters, you can also control the number of digits displayed before and after the decimal point. For example:

```
nf.setMaxmumIntegerDigits(6);
nf.setMinimumIntegerDigits(2);
nf.setMaxmumFractionDigits(4);
nf.setMinimumFractionDigits(2);
```

With these settings also for cf and pf, the output becomes:

```
1,234.567        1 234,567
$1,234.567       1 234,567 F
123,456.70%      123 456,70%
```

For finer control over the formatting, you can cast a NumberFormat object to a DecimalFormat object and specify *format patterns*. Following is a simple static method that we placed in our MyUtil class:

```
public static String doubleFormat(double p, String fs)
{   NumberFormat nf = NumberFormat.getNumberInstance();
    DecimalFormat df = (DecimalFormat)nf;
    df.applyPattern(fs);                    // pattern
    return df.format(p);
}
```

Table 6.4 shows some sample patterns.

With a formatter, you can also parse strings into numbers. The method

```
Number x = nf.parse(str);
```

returns a Long, if possible, or a Double.

Table 6.4   SAMPLE FORMAT PATTERNS

Number	Pattern	String
123456.789	###,###.###	123,456.789
123456.789	###.##	123456.79
123.78	000000.000	000123.780
12345.67	$###,###.###	$12,345.67
12345.67	\u00a5###,###.###	¥12,345.67

The `DateFormat` class is handy for turning `Date` objects (Section 6.19) into locale-appropriate strings. Use these factory methods to obtain date-time formatters for the default locale:

```
DateFormat pf = DateFormat.getTimeInstance();
DateFormat cf = DateFormat.getDateInstance();
DateFormat nf = DateFormat.getDateTimeInstance();
```

Then use the `format(Date)` method to obtain a formatted string. These factory methods also take a *style* parameter:

- `DateFormat.SHORT`—completely numeric, such as 12.13.52 or 3:30pm
- `DateFormat.MEDIUM`—somewhat longer, such as Jan 12, 1952 (the default style)
- `DateFormat.LONG`—longer yet, such as January 12, 1952 or 3:30:32pm
- `DateFormat.FULL`—completely specified, such as Tuesday, April 12, 1952 AD or 3:30:42pm PST

After the style parameter, a `Locale` parameter can also be given. You can find an example in Section 6.19.

For more information, see the documentation for `DateFormat`. Section 6.19 tells you how to create `Date` objects.

6.15 ERROR AND EXCEPTION HANDLING

An important aspect of robust software is the proper handling of errors during program execution. Possible sources for run-time errors include division by zero, argument not within legal domain, results out of allowable range (too large or too small), unexpected arguments, illegal references, array index out of range, nonexistent or inaccessible file, and I/O error.

If a method encounters an error during execution, it may return a predefined error value that a calling method can check. The `read()` method of an input stream is an example. It returns −1 when end-of-stream is reached. The `indexOf(char c)` method of a string is another example. It returns −1 if the character is not in the string. Methods returning a reference normally can return `null` as an error value. Methods returning nonzero normally can return zero as an error value.

In addition to simple error values, Java supports *exceptions*, a systematic way of representing, transmitting, capturing, and handling well-defined errors during program execution. Exceptions in Java are represented as objects of classes extending, directly or indirectly, the `java.lang.Exception` class. A number of Java-defined exception classes exist, and you may define your own exceptions. For example, I/O stream methods use exceptions belonging to the

`IOException` class. The Java keywords `try`, `catch`, `throw`, `throws`, and `finally` are used for exception handling and allow you to:

- Capture and handle exceptions
- Specify exceptions that a method throws
- Detect and throw exceptions

In addition to dealing with existing exceptions, you can also create new exceptions for specific error handling needs in your programs.

Catching Exceptions

The keyword `try` controls a code block (compound statement) whose exceptions can be caught and handled by code supplied with the keyword `catch`. A *try block* has the general form:

```
try
{    statements
}    catch(e-type₁ e)
     {    statements    }
     catch(e-type₂ e)
     {    statements    }

     . . .

     finally
     {    statements    }
```

An exception caused by any statement in the `try` part results in a certain exception object being thrown by a method reached through a chain of method calls. This exception object is passed up directly to the nearest `try` in the call chain, which captures it (Figure 6.9) and matches it with the declared exception types listed by the *catch clauses* sequentially. Each catch clause is in the form of a method definition with a parameter list and a body of statements. The exception object is passed to the parameter `e` of the first matching clause and the statements executed. Only matching exceptions are caught. Uncaught exceptions are passed further up the call chain.

Recall that the `Lowercase` program has a `doio` method, which uses a try block to handle I/O exceptions:

```
public static void doio(InputStream in, OutputStream out)
{    int c;
     try {  while ( (c = in.read()) >= 0 )
            {  c = Character.toLowerCase( (char) c);
               out.write(c);
            }
     } catch( IOException e )
```

Figure 6.9   THROWING AND CATCHING AN EXCEPTION

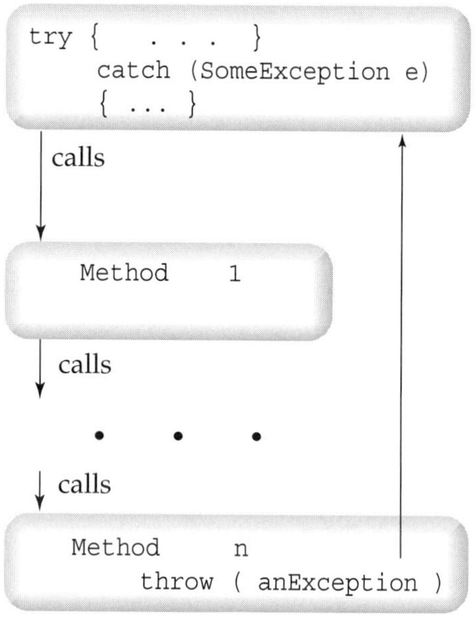

```
                                { System.err.println("doio: I/O Problem");
                                  System.exit(1);
                                }
}
```

Note that execution will continue normally after the catch clause if the program does not call System.exit.

The finally clause is always executed, whether or not any exceptions occur in the try block. Use the finally clause to supply clean-up actions needed, in any case. For example, if the try part opens file streams and you want to make sure that these streams are properly closed, use code such as:

```
try
{   FileInputStream infile = new FileInputStream(args[0]);
    File tmp_file = new File(tmp_name);
    // ...
}   catch ( FileNotFoundException e )
      { System.err.println("Can't open input file " + args[0]);
        error = true;
      }
    catch ( IOException e )
      { System.err.println("Can't open temporary file" + tmp_name);
```

```
    error = true;
}
finally
{ if ( infile != null ) infile.close();
  if ( tmp_file != null ) tmp_file.delete();
  if ( error ) System.exit(1);
}
```

Code supplied by `finally` is executed at the end no matter how the try block completes: normally by exception, by `return`, or by `break`.

Types of Exceptions

The `Throwable` class in the `java.lang` package is the ultimate superclass of any Java exception object. There are two types of exceptions:

1. Java interpreter exceptions—The Java run-time system interprets bytecode and can detect many kinds of errors and exceptions during program execution. Such exceptions include referencing a null pointer, dividing by zero, and illegal array indexing. Exceptions under the `RuntimeException` and `Error` classes are reserved for the Java interpreter, and the Java interpreter throws only these exceptions.

2. Checked exceptions—All exceptions not for the Java interpreter are checked exceptions. Checked exceptions are used by user code and are part of the method call interface. A method specifies checked exceptions that it may cause with the `throws` clause in the method header. The `throws` specification is *checked for correctness by the compiler*. Thus, when you call any Java method, you know what checked exceptions you should treat. Checked exceptions are under the `Exception` superclass.

Specifying Exceptions

The preceding `doio` method can be recoded as follows:

```
public static void doio(InputStream in, OutputStream out)
        throws IOException                    // (1)
{   int c;
    while ( (c = in.read()) >= 0 )
    {  c = Character.toLowerCase( (char) c);
       out.write(c);
    }
}
```

Instead of catching the `IOException` as before, it now simply specifies it (line 1). The general form of the `throws` clause is:

```
throws Exception_1, ..., Exception_i
```

Catch or Specify Principle

For Java programs, the *catch or specify* principle states that each checked exception that may result from inside a method call must either be caught in the method or specified in the `throws` clause.

The `throws` clause of an overriding method does not have to match that of its superclass counterpart exactly. However, the subclass method can specify only exceptions covered by the `throws` clause of the superclass method. In particular, the overriding method may specify no exceptions.

Java interpreter errors and exceptions can be caught if you wish. However, your methods are not required to catch or specify such exceptions.

Throwing Exceptions

A method can detect an error and initiate or throw an exception. To throw an exception, simply create an exception object and use the `throw` operator. For example,

```
throw new IOException();
```

or, if you have a short string message,

```
throw new IOException("File not found");
```

Messages in Exceptions

The `Throwable` superclass provides several useful methods for exception handling. The message string in an exception object can be retrieved by calling `getMessage()`. A `Throwable` also records the status of the execution stack when the exception object is created. The execution stack can be displayed with `printStackTrace()` to provide a backtrace for debugging. The `doio` method, for example, can be refined (lines a–b) as follows:

```
public static void doio(InputStream in, OutputStream out)
{   int c;
    try
    {   while ( (c = in.read()) >= 0 )
        {   c = Character.toLowerCase( (char) c);
            out.write(c);
        }
    }   catch( IOException e )
        {   System.err.println("doio: I/O Problem "
                        + e.getMessage());                  // (a)
```

```
                    e.printStackTrace();                              // (b)
                    System.exit(1);
              }
      }
}
```

Creating Your Own Exceptions

For certain errors detected in your own code, you may also want to throw exceptions. If an existing exception is appropriate to throw, that is the easiest thing to do. Otherwise you may create your own exception classes. One such error is *creating a fraction with a zero denominator*. Recall the Fraction constructor (Section 2.4):

```
public Fraction(int n, int d)    // d is not zero
{    int g;
     if ( d == 0 )
     {  System.err.println("Fraction: fraction with 0 denominator?");
        System.exit(1);
     }
     . . .
}
```

Instead of exiting, the constructor may elect to throw an exception. To do this, first define a new exception class

```
public class ZeroDenominatorException extends Exception
{   public ZeroDenominatorException () {}

    public ZeroDenominatorException (String s)
    {    super(s);    }    // msg string
}
```

and then modify the constructor code to throw the exception:

```
public Fraction(int n, int d) throws ZeroDenominatorException
{    if ( d == 0 )
     {  throw(new ZeroDenominatorException(
            "Fraction: fraction with 0 denominator?"));
     }
     init(n,d);
}
```

After verifying d != 0, the initialization is performed by a separate private method, which can be used by member methods to create fractions when d is not zero.

```
private void init(int n, int d)
{    int g;
     if (n == 0)
```

```
      {  num = 0; denom = 1; return; }
      if (d < 0) { n = -n; d = -d; }
      if ( (g = gcd(n,d)) != 1 )   // remove gcd
      { n /= g; d /= g; }
      num = n;
      denom = d;
}
```

Following is a method that creates a new fraction:

```
public Fraction divide(Fraction y) throws ZeroDenominatorException
{    return new Fraction(num * y.denom, denom * y.num );
}
```

6.16 MATRIX WITH EXCEPTIONS: AN EXAMPLE

Let's take the simple `Matrix` class from Section 2.11, put it into its own package (matrix), and add exception handling. This example further illustrates:

- Creating and managing your own packages
- Defining and treating related exceptions

To create the `matrix` package, first make a subdirectory `matrix` in a directory listed on CLASSPATH. Put all source code files of the `matrix` package in the `matrix` directory. Files in the package include:

`Matrix.java`	(Matrix class)
`TestMatrix.java`	(Test program)
`MatrixException.java`	(Exception superclass)
`SingularException.java`	(Exception subclass)
`InvalidIndexException.java`	(Exception subclass)
`IncompatibleDimException.java`	(Exception subclass)

All exceptions used by the `matrix` package will be subclasses of `MatrixException` defined as:

```
package matrix;

public class MatrixException extends Exception
{    public MatrixException() {}

     public MatrixException(String s)
     {    super(s);    }    // msg string
}
```

Using this superclass, the matrix package can then subclass a variety of related exceptions:

- `SingularException`

- IncompatibleDimException
- InvalidIndexException

The getElement and setElement methods in the Matrix class now throw InvalidIndexException:

```
public double getElement(int i, int j)
      throws InvalidIndexException
{  if ( i < 0 || j < 0 || i >= nr || j >= nc )
      throw new InvalidIndexException(
         "getElement(" + i + "," + j + ")" +
         "in " + nr + "X" + nc + " Matrix");
   return mat[i][j];
}
```

The times method is also revised to handle exceptions. The exception specified covers incompatible dimensions and invalid indices:

```
public Matrix times(Matrix b) throws MatrixException
{  if ( nc != b.nr ) throw new
      IncompatibleDimException("Matrix times: "+
              nr+"X"+nc + " and " + b.nr+"X"+b.nc);
   Matrix p = new Matrix(nr,b.nc);
   for (int i=0 ; i < nr ; i++)
   {  for (int j=0 ; j < b.nc; j++)
        p.setElement(i,j,  // InvalidIndexException
           rowTimesCol(i, b.mat, j));
   }
   return p;
}
```

The test program TestMatrix.java can use a single catch clause

```
catch(MatrixException e) { handle(e);  System.exit(1); }
```

to catch and treat all of these matrix exceptions. The exception handler handle can be coded as:

```
private static void handle(MatrixException e)
      throws ClassNotFoundException
{  if ( e instanceof SingularException )
   {  System.err.println("S:" + e.getMessage()); }
   else if ( e instanceof IncompatibleDimException )
   {  System.err.println("D:"+ e.getMessage()); }
   else if ( e instanceof InvalidIndexException )
   {  System.err.println("I:"+ e.getMessage()); }
}
```

To compile code for the `matrix` package, go to the parent directory of the `matrix` package directory and enter the command:

```
javac matrix/*.java
```

To run, give the command

```
java matrix.TestMatrix
```

from the same parent directory.

6.17 CHARACTER-BASED STANDARD I/O AND ERROR REPORTING

Standard I/O provided by the Java class `System` is byte- or ASCII-based. We now define the `JavaSystem` class that makes character-based I/O and error reporting easy:

```
///////    JavaSystem.java    ///////
import java.io.*;

//  System-wide utility.

public final class JavaSystem
{   //  convenient error display method.
    //  outputs to standard error
    public static void error(Exception e)
    {   err.println(e.getMessage());
        e.printStackTrace(err);
    }

    //  character-based standard in, out, and err.
    public final static BufferedReader in = new
        BufferedReader(new InputStreamReader(System.in));
    public final static PrintWriter out = new PrintWriter(
        new BufferedWriter (new
            OutputStreamWriter(System.out)), true);
    public final static PrintWriter err = new PrintWriter(
        new OutputStreamWriter(System.err), true);
}
```

With this class, you can use code such as

```
catch( IOException e ) { JavaSystem.error(e); }
```

to handle exceptions and

```
JavaSystem.err.println(msg);
```

to display error messages. Such code will work under any character code. Henceforth, we can use `JavaSystem` for error reporting.

6.18 MATHEMATICAL COMPUTATIONS

The core `java.lang.Math` class supplies constants and methods for numeric computing to perform elementary exponential, logarithm, square root, and trigonometric calculations. The methods conform to standard published algorithms as available from the well-known numeric library `netlib`[1] and compliant to the "IEEE 754 core function" standard. The computations are executed with all floating-point operations following the rules of Java floating-point arithmetic.

In addition the `java.math` package includes `BigInteger` and `BigDecimal` classes:

- Arbitrary-precision big integers come with a full complement of operators, making their use comparable to primitive integers. In addition, big integers provide operations for modular arithmetic, greatest common divisor, primality test, prime generation, single-bit manipulation, and so on.
- Arbitrary-precision big decimals are signed decimal numbers suitable for numerical calculations. Big decimals provide operations for basic arithmetic, scaling, comparison, format conversion, and hashing.

The `java.util` package supplies the class `Random` to generate random numbers. The calls

```
Random rg = new Random();
Random rg = new Random(Long seed);
```

give a new random number generator with possibly a *seed*.

Then a call such as `nextInt()`, `nextLong()`, or `nextDouble()` returns a uniformly distributed number of the indicated variety.

---

[1] http://cm.bell-labs.com/netlib/master/readme.html

6.19 DATE AND CALENDAR

Date represents a specific time with millisecond precision. For example,

```
import java.util.*;
```

```
Date d = new Date();
```

creates a Date object representing the instant of its creation, in milliseconds, from the base time January 1, 1970, 00:00:00 GMT, known as *the epoch*. This long field is retrieved and set by the following:

```
long mill = d.getTime();
d.setTime(mill+60*1000);     // an hour later
```

To obtain the Date for a past or future time, use the Calendar class. For example,

```
Calendar now = Calendar.getInstance();
```

gets a Gregorian calendar for the default locale set to the current time. And

```
Date t = now.getTime();
```

is a date object corresponding to the time set in the calendar now.

For most parts of the world, the GregorianCalendar, a subclass of Calendar, is useful in setting a calendar to a specified date. For example:

```
Calendar cal
    = new GregorianCalendar(year, month, day);
Calendar cal
    = new GregorianCalendar(year, month, day, hrs, min);
Calendar cal
    = new GregorianCalendar(year, month, day, hrs, min, sec);
```

Then cal.getTime() returns a Date set in cal. As mentioned in Section 6.14, the DateFormat class is useful for displaying dates. For example, the following program displays dates given on the command line (line A) in the FULL style (Section 6.14) for the default locale (line B) and the French locale (line C):

```
///////    DisplayDate.java    ///////

import java.util.*;
import java.text.DateFormat;

public class DisplayDate
{  public static void main(String[] args)
   {  int month = Integer.parseInt(args[0])-1;
      int day = Integer.parseInt(args[1]);
      int year = Integer.parseInt(args[2]);
```

```
        Calendar cal = new GregorianCalendar(year, month, day); // (A)
        Date t = cal.getTime();
        DateFormat cf
            = DateFormat.getDateInstance(DateFormat.FULL);        // (B)
        String ds = cf.format(t);
        System.out.println(ds);
        cf = DateFormat.getDateInstance(DateFormat.FULL,
                                     Locale.FRANCE);              // (C)
        System.out.println(cf.format(t));
    }
}
```

Note that the `month` parameter is zero-based (line A).

Run this, for example, with

java DisplayDate 3 29 1998

and get the following display:

```
Sunday, March 29, 1998
dimanche 29 mars 1998
```

The `java.util` package provides many other useful classes. A large part of `java.util` is the `collections` generic container framework discussed in Chapter 9. We have seen the classes `StringTokenizer` (Section 2.9) and `Locale` (Section 6.14) already. The `Properties` class is discussed in (Section 6.20).

6.20 SYSTEM AND ENVIRONMENT PROPERTIES

To run a program, any program, you must specify the program name and arguments. For Java programs, you also specify the interpreter:

java *ClassX arg1 arg2 ...*

Any command-line arguments *arg1, arg2* are accessed as an array of strings (`String[] args`) in the `main` method of `ClassX` (Section 1.11).

Much less obvious than the command-line arguments, *environment settings* representing *system attributes* and *user choices* are also made available to a program as it starts to run. Environment settings usually describe hardware and software configurations (for example, modem speed and operating system name), executing environment values (for example, user name and current directory), and user preferences (for example, window size and CLASSPATH[2]). Each environment setting is represented by a name-value pair:

name=value

---

[2]See Appendix A.

For example:

```
PWD=/usr/pwang
DISPLAY=monkey:0.0
CLASSPATH=.:$HOME/javaproj.1/classes:$HOME/javaproj2/classes
```

When the Java interpreter starts, a complete set of environment settings is transmitted to it by its parent process. The Java interpreter makes a select subset of these, other useful settings, and any settings given by the -D option on the command line in the form

```
-Dname=value
```

available to your Java program as *system properties*. In your program, system properties are obtained through this call:

```
Properties sysProps = System.getProperties();
```

Whereas System is a core class, Properties is in the java.util package and a Properties object maintains a property list. Each property is represented by a name-value pair. Standard system properties have prescribed names such as java.class.path (CLASSPATH), and user.home (home directory). The API documentation for System describes all Java system properties.

When a program starts, it often uses the following sequence to load and set properties:

```
// obtain system properties first
  Properties sysProps = System.getProperties()

// add basic properties
  Properties baseProps = new Properties(sysProps);
  FileInputStream in =
        new FileInputStream("baseProperties");
  baseProps.load(in);
  in.close();

// add application-specific properties
  Properties myProps = new Properties(baseProps);
  in = new FileInputStream("appProperties");
  myProps.load(in);
  in.close();
```

Now the desired properties are in the object myProps. Install it as the systemwide property list by

```
// set system properties
  System.setProperties(myProps);
```

and you are finished. The method System.getProperty(name); will now get values from the new system property list.

You may work with multiple property lists. To get the value of a particular property *name* from a specific property list, use the instance method

```
public String getProperty(String name, [ String default ])
```

which returns the property value, if found, or the optional default value, or null for failure. For example,

```
String user = myProps.getProperty("user.name");
String dir = myProps.getProperty("user.dir");
```

get the userid and current working directory, respectively. The instance method `propertyNames` returns an `Enumeration` of all names contained in the `Properties` object.

To display a property list *pl*, simply call `pl.list()`. To save it into a file, use:

```
FileOutputStream out = new FileOutputStream("filename.txt");
pl.save(out, comment);
out.close();
```

The string *comment* will be included at the beginning of the file.

Java Property-File Format

In addition to system-defined properties, a Java program can also access user-defined properties. Such a program documents its dependence on such properties, their meanings, and possible values. User-defined properties are stored in text files (use the conventional .txt suffix) prepared in a simple format using a text editor.

The following lines in a Java program

```
FileOutputStream o = new FileOutputStream("prop.txt");
System.getProperties().save(o, "Here it is");
```

produce a listing of properties in the property file prop.txt. Following are some sample properties:

```
user.language=en
java.home=/usr/java/j2sdk1.4.0/jre
java.version=1.4.0
file.separator=/
line.separator=\n
user.region=US
file.encoding=ISO-8859-1
user.timezone=EST
user.name=pwang
user.dir=/user/pwang/java   (the current working directory)
java.class.path= ...
java.class.version=48.0
```

```
os.version=2.2.14-5.0
path.separator=:
user.home=/users/research/wang/pwang
```

Do not put extra white space anywhere in the file. Comments begin with a #
character.

To load user-defined properties into your Java program, use the `load`
method of a `Properties` object:

```
Properties mypl = new Properties();
InputStream in = InputStream("myProperties.txt");
mypl.load(in);    // throws IOException
```

Then individual property values can be obtained, using the `getProperty`
method.

It is often useful for a user-defined property list to draw default values
from the system-defined property list. This is easily achieved with these calls:

```
Properties mypl = new Properties(System.getProperties());
mypl.load(someStream);
```

Thus a user-defined property file should revise system properties and add new
properties only as needed.

Certain platforms, such as the Mac OS, do not allow a command line. In
such cases, the property list is the way to transmit command-line arguments.

6.21 SUMMARY

A package provides a user-designated namespace to organize related files and
to provide package-level access control. Java provides a rich set of class libraries
organized into packages. The `java.lang` package contains language essentials
and is automatically imported. Application programmers can establish their
own packages and follow a package naming convention to avoid class name
conflicts. The `package` declaration puts a file in a specified package. Without it,
a file belongs to the unnamed package.

Java provides low-level byte-oriented I/O, higher-level character I/O,
primitive-type I/O, and object I/O. Input (output) streams can be connected
into pipelines to add power and functionality:

- `InputStream` (`System.in`), `OutputStream`, `FileInputStream`,
  `FileOutputStream`—Support byte-oriented I/O (8-bit).
- `InputStreamReader`, `OutputStreamWriter`—Provide character I/O
  (16-bit Unicode), built on top of byte-oriented I/O through a
  char-to-byte conversion dependent on the I/O character encoding.

- `BufferedInputStream, BufferedOutputStream, BufferedReader, BufferedWriter`—Buffer byte and character I/O. The `BufferedReader` `readLine()` method is convenient for reading text lines.
- `PrintStream (System.out), PrintWriter`—Output ASCII and string representation of primitive and object types. `PrintWriter` should be used to produce character (Unicode) output. The `println` method is convenient to output a text line.
- `RandomAccessFile`—Performs byte-oriented file updating and appending.
- `DataInputStream, DataOutputStream`—Perform binary I/O for primitive types.
- `ObjectInputStream, ObjectOutputStream`—Perform binary I/O for serializable objects.

The `NumberFormat` and `DateFormat` classes from the `java.text` package supply static factory methods that return locale-sensitive formatting objects for numbers, currencies, percentages, and dates.

Java programs treat run-time exceptions systematically. A method either catches a *checked exception* (with `try` and `catch`) or specifies the exception with a `throws` clause. Checked exceptions are organized under the `Exception` class. The `throws` clause is part of the API of each method. Application programs may define their own exceptions.

Library methods for mathematical computations are found in the class `java.lang.Math`. Extended precision integer and floating-point computations are supplied in the `java.math` package.

Use `System.getProperties()` to obtain system default properties. Open an input stream to a `.txt` file containing user-defined properties to load and add such properties into your Java program.

EXERCISES

Review Questions

1. From a Java program, how do you determine whether a file exists, or is readable or writable?

2. From a Java program, how do you rename files and create new file directories?

3. Can `System.out` be used directly to produce output in Unicode? If not, what output object should be used? Construct an example.

4. Consider file updating with RandomAccessFile. Can the example shown in Section 6.9 be made to work for Unicode files? For files with the default platform character encoding?

5. What are *checked exceptions*? Are there other kinds of exceptions?

6. When parsing a string representation of a primitive quantity, what exception should you expect in case the string representation is invalid? Can you catch such exceptions?

7. In the java.math package, what mathematical operations are supported? What exceptions are used?

8. Java I/O Readers and Writers can use different *character encodings* to perform Unicode I/O. What is the default encoding used on your Java platform? What encodings are supported by Java? (Hint: See API documentation.)

9. What happens if you call the close() method on System.in, System.out, or System.err? Once these are closed, do you have a way of performing standard I/O?

10. Different computer platforms use different *line separators*, which are used in text files to separate two lines of text. On UNIX systems, the line separator is usually the NEWLINE (\n); on PC/Windows it is the RETURN followed by NEWLINE (\r\n). In Java, what quantity gives you the platform-dependent line separator?

11. In a Java program, how do you obtain the current working directory?

Programming Assignments

1. Consider the Lowercase example (Section 2.3). Rewrite it so it works for Unicode characters. (Hint: Use OutputStreamWriter and InputStreamReader.)

2. Revise the doio(RandomAccessFile iofile) method for file updating so that it works for Unicode characters.

3. Write a program that displays three dates: yesterday, today, and tomorrow.

4. Write a program that will read lines in the form

    name:ss:age:coverage

    from a file using a StreamTokenizer object.

5. Write a program that displays the current time and date.

6. Consider the formatting of numbers. Write a static method that formats doubles always with two digits after the decimal point. A negative number -*n* is formatted as (n) instead of - n.

7. Write a program that displays a list of prices represented by double in the usual notation for prices in your locale.

8. (Bookmark-1) Consider creating a simple Web bookmark database with a text file containing lines in the form

    some-URL (*notes about the URL*)

    Following is a sample file:

    ```
    http://www.son.com/jzse    (Java SDK releases)
    http://icm.mcs.kent.edu/ (ICM, Kent State University)
    http://www.unicode.org/charts   (Charts for UNICODE Characters)
    http://www.SymbolicNet.org/ (Center for Symbolic Computation)
    http://www.son.com/jzse/1.4/docs/ (Java JDK documentation)
    ```

    (a) Refer to the class MatchingLines (Exercise Match-1, Chapter 4).
    (b) Write a Bookmark class that receives a string *str* on the command line and displays only the URLs from lines in your bookmark database that contain the given *str*.

9. (Term Life-3) Consider the term life premium calculator example given in Section 3.2. The program displays the premium by converting a double to a string. This can produce funny-looking displays such as $24.3333333. Improve this program by using a currency formatter, as explained in Section 6.14.

10. Consider Serializable objects. What if we declare FreeChecking or Joint-Account to implement Serializable without declaring the superclass BankAccount to be serializable?

11. Make the TextLines class (Section 4.20) and the Matrix class (Section 6.16) serializable, and try object I/O on these objects.

12. (Calc-4) Take the calculator with memory and add a square root and a percent operation to it, using the opcodes S and % respectively. (Hint: Find out how a percent key works on a real pocket calculator. Percent usually only works with a previous multiply or divide opcode.)

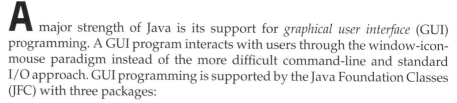

## CHAPTER SEVEN

Applets and Event-Driven Programming

A major strength of Java is its support for *graphical user interface* (GUI) programming. A GUI program interacts with users through the window-icon-mouse paradigm instead of the more difficult command-line and standard I/O approach. GUI programming is supported by the Java Foundation Classes (JFC) with three packages:

1. `java.awt` (Abstract Windowing Toolkit)—provides for basic windowing, events, font, color, graphics, and images
2. `javax.swing` (Swing)—supplies a set of components for building GUIs with settable *look and feel*
3. `java.applet`—supports *applets* for Web pages

Applets are special Java programs that can be included in Web documents to add graphics, interactions, and dynamism. Applets involve GUI and event-driven programming. After compilation, an applet is placed in a Web page, an HTML document, to be used by anyone on the Web. The Java browser plug-in utility makes it easy for end users to add applet-processing capabilities to popular Web browsers.

Besides applets, regular Java applications can also benefit from GUIs. The topic is covered comprehensively in this and the next chapter.

After a brief introduction to networking, the Web, and HTML documents, we proceed to build example applets. The introduction of GUI and event-driven programming concepts is reinforced by practical usage of applets. Materials are based on swing components and lay a good foundation for Chapter 8, GUI Programming.

7.1 ABOUT NETWORKING

A *computer network* is a high-speed communications medium connecting many, possibly dissimilar, computers or *hosts*. A network is a combination of computer and telecommunication hardware and software. The purpose is to provide fast and reliable information exchange among the hosts and between

Figure 7.1   CLIENT AND SERVER

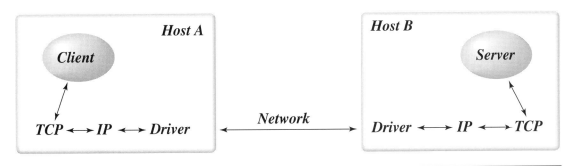

processes (executing programs) on different hosts. The Web is one of the most widely used Internet services. Others include electronic mail, file transfer, remote job entry, and remote login, just to name a few.

Basically, networking involves one program talking to another on a different host. Programs follow established *protocols* to communicate over the network. Different networking services use different protocols. Among common networking protocols, the *Internet Protocol* (IP) suite[1] is the most widely used. IP is the basic protocol for the *Internet*, which is by far the most predominant worldwide network. The World Wide Web is a service that uses HTTP (the Hypertext Transfer Protocol), which is based on Internet protocols.

Client and Server

Most commonly, a network application involves a *server* and a *client* (Figure 7.1):

- A *server* process provides a specific service on a host machine that offers such a service. Example services are remote host access (`telnet`), file transfer (`ftp`), and the Web (`http`). Each standard Internet service has its own unique *port number*, which is identical across all hosts. The port number, together with the Internet address of a host, identifies a particular server anywhere on the network. For example, `ftp` has port number 21 and `http` has 80.

- A *client* process on a host connects with a server on another host to obtain its service. Thus a client program is the agent through which a particular network service can be obtained. Different agents are usually required for different services.

---

[1]Including TCP, UDP, and others.

A Web browser, such as Netscape Navigator or Internet Explorer, is a Web client. It runs on your computer and helps you retrieve information from Web servers on other computers on the Internet.

7.2 THE WEB

The *World Wide Web*, alternatively known simply as the Web, is a very successful distributed information dissemination and retrieval system initiated in Europe (CERN, in Switzerland). There is no central control or administration for the Web. Anyone can potentially put material on the Web and retrieve information from it. The Web consists of a vast collection of *documents* located on computers throughout the world. These documents are created by academic, professional, governmental, and commercial organizations as well as by individuals. The documents are prepared in special formats and retrieved through *server programs* on each computer that provides Web service. Each Web document can contain many links to other documents served by different servers in other locations, and therefore become part of a "web" that spans the entire globe. New materials are being put on the Web continuously, and instant access to this collection of information can be enormously advantageous. As the Web grows explosively, MIT of the USA and INRIA of France have agreed to become joint hosts of the *W3 Consortium*, which will further develop Web-related protocol specifications and reference software.

A *browser* program helps a user obtain information from the Web (Figure 7.2). Given the location of a target document, a browser client connects to the correct Web server and allows you to select information for retrieval or to follow links for visiting other documents. Using a browser, you can retrieve information and access *Web servers* anywhere on the Internet.

Figure 7.2 WEB BROWSING

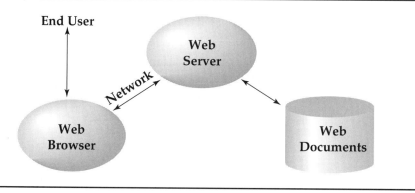

Many different Web browsers are available. *Mosaic*, developed at the U.S. National Center for Supercomputing Applications (NCSA), is the original browser. Today widely used Web browsers include Netscape's *Navigator*, Microsoft's *Internet Explorer*, IBM's *WebExplorer*, JavaSun's *HotJava*, and America Online's AOL browser. Web browsers compete to offer speed and convenience for users and are evolving at a rapid pace. New features include overlapping information display with file retrieval, and message encoding for privacy and security.

Java adds increased dynamism and interactivity to Web documents. An HTML document can contain a special Java program called an *applet*. A browser can retrieve the bytecode of an applet from a Web server and run the applet within the browser. With applets, a Web page comes alive with moving images, sound effects, and dynamic user interactions. The Sun Java plug-in enables Netscape and Internet Explorer to run applets.

Hypertext

A Web browser communicates with a Web server (Figure 7.3) through an efficient *Hypertext Transfer Protocol* (HTTP) designed to work with *hypertext* and *hypermedia* documents that may contain regular text, images, audio, and video. Parts of the document may also represent links to other documents. Each server handles its local documents. A Web browser can follow the links to contact various servers to retrieve information. On the Web, documents can take on many different formats for text, images, video, and sound. Native Web documents are set in the *Hypertext Markup Language* (HTML). The Web employs

Figure 7.3   TEXTBOOK WEB SITE

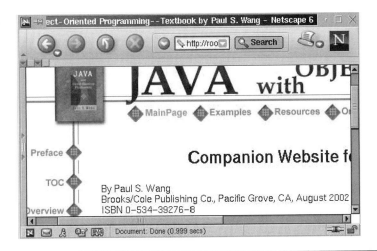

an open addressing scheme, allowing links to many kinds of documents and services. Consequently, a Web browser provides the ability to access a wide variety of information on the Internet. After a piece of information is retrieved, the browser can also display the information for viewing. Web browsers have built-in programs to display and present many common types of files and use *plug-ins* to handle additional information formats.

URL

To retrieve information, you give your Web browser a *Uniform Resource Locator*, or URL. The URL enables browsers to perform a specified function or to locate a particular document, contacting an appropriate network server if necessary.

A full URL usually has this form:

scheme://*server*[:*port*]/[*pathname*]

The *scheme* part indicates the information service type and therefore the protocol to be used. Following is a list of some common schemes:

- http—Service is Web. The file located is retrieved by the Web-defined Hypertext Transfer Protocol (HTTP).
- ftp—Service is FTP. The URL locates a file, a directory, or an FTP server; for example,

  ftp://ftp.java.sun.com

- telnet—Service is Telnet for remote login to another host. No file name is needed; for example,

  telnet://monkey.cs.kent.edu

- mailto—Service is email. The user is allowed to send email to a specified address. The form is mailto:*email-address*.
- news—Service is NEWS. The URL locates a USENET newsgroup.
- file—Service is loading a file on the local host. The server part is omitted; for example,

  file:///usr/local/file

The *server* is a domain name or IP number that identifies a host and a server program. The optional port number is needed only if the server does not use the default port (80 for HTTP). The remainder of the URL, when given, is a file pathname. If this pathname has a trailing / character, it represents a directory, rather than a data file. The suffix (.html, .txt, .ps, etc.) of a data file indicates the type of file. The pathname can also lead to an executable file that produces a valid HTML document as its standard output. Such a program is a *gateway*; for security reasons, gateways are located only in controlled directories.

Within an HTML document, you can link to another document served by the same Web server by giving only the *pathname* part of the URL. Such URLs are *partially specified*. A partial URL with a / prefix (e.g., /file_xyz.html) refers to a file under the *document root*, the beginning of the document space controlled by a Web server. A URL leading to a directory usually displays the index page in that directory. Failing to find an index page, a listing of the directory is usually displayed. A partial URL without a leading / points to a file relative to the location of the document that contains the URL in question. Thus a simple file_abc.html refers to that file in the same directory as the current document. It is also possible to include an in-document reference location at the end of the URL.

The java.net package of Java provides networking tools. Among other things, it provides a URL class for creating and using URLs. For example, the Java code

```
URL loc = new URL(String str);
```

creates a URL object from the *str* specification. A URL object supplies methods to parse the URL, to open network connections, and to retrieve information conveniently (Section 10.1).

7.3   WEB PAGES AND HTML

Documents for the Web (or Web pages) are set in the *Hypertext Markup Language* (HTML). A hypertext document can link, with URLs, to documents in almost any other format and to executable programs on the server side. A Web page can also include *executable contents* such as Java applets. A basic understanding of HTML will help you place Java applets in Web pages.

A document written in HTML contains ordinary text interspersed with *markup tags* and uses the .html file name extension. The tags mark portions of the text as title, section header, paragraph, reference to other documents, and so on. Because the page will be formatted by a browser, line breaks and extra white space between words in the text are generally ignored. In addition to structure, HTML tags are used to include graphics, link to other documents, mark reference points, generate forms or questionnaires, and invoke certain programs. Various visual editors or *page makers* provide a GUI environment for creating and designing HTML documents. The *Netscape Composer* is an example. If you don't have ready access to such tools, a regular text editor can be used to create HTML documents. An HTML tag takes the form <tag>. A *begin tag* such as <h1> (level-one section header) is paired with an *end tag*, </h1> in this case, to mark text in between.

Table 7.1 lists some frequently used tags. Following is a sample HTML file:

```
<html><head><title>A Sample HTML File</title>
</head><body>
```

Table 7.1   SOME HTML TAGS

Marked as	HTML Tags
Document Title	`<title>...</title>`
Level *n* Heading	`<hn>...</hn>`
Paragraphs	`<p>...</p>`
Line Break	`... `
List Item	`<li> ... </li>`
Unnumbered List	`<ul>...</ul>`
Numbered List	`<ol>...</ol>`
Comment	`<!-- ... -->`
Anchor	`<a href="URL">...</a>`
Picture or Image	`<img src="imageURL">`
Applet	`<applet ...> ... </applet>`

```
<h1>Introduction</h1>
<p> Here is the first paragraph.</p>
<p> The second paragraph and a list of things.</p>
<ol>
<li> Apples</li> <li> Oranges</li>
<li> Bananas</li>
</ol>
</body></html>
```

Pictures can be included in-line with text by the tag

```
<img src="URL">
```

where the URL points to an image file.

7.4 APPLETS

Most HTML tags present fixed content. It is also possible to embed executable programs in HTML documents. Such *executable content* is downloaded from the *server side* by a browser (client) and executed on the *client side*. The Java applet is one way to supply executable content.

An *applet* is a special Java program placed in a Web page that can be loaded and executed by a Web browser. On a *server* computer, an applet is written, compiled, and put into a Web page. When a *Java-enabled* Web browser (Figure 7.4) on a client computer retrieves the Web page, it displays the document and runs the applet program in it. Applets can add moving images,

Figure 7.4   APPLET IN WEB PAGE

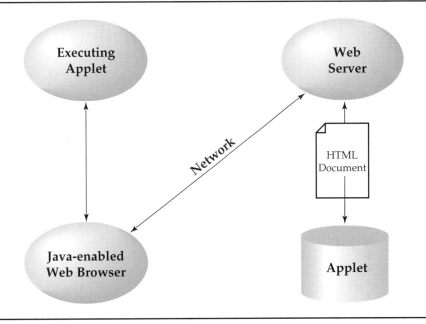

sound effects, and responsive user interactions to a Web page, making it more interesting, exciting, and effective.

A Java-enabled browser either contains a Java Virtual Machine (JVM) or has a Java plug-in that provides the ability to run applets. The popular Netscape and Internet Explorer browsers, and many others, are already Java-enabled. Because the JVM in browsers does not keep pace with Java development, it is a good idea for a Web surfer to install the Sun Microsystems Java plug-in for consistent support of all applets.

When installed for a browser, the Java plug-in runs applets with its own JVM instead of the one in the browser, which may not be up to date. Go to the free plug-in download page

```
http://java.sun.com/products/plugin
```

and follow the instructions to download and install the plug-in.

The `applet` Tag

To include an applet *AppletName*.`java` in an HTML document, first compile it into *AppletName*.`class`. Then use an HTML tag to introduce the bytecode file into a Web page.

At various times in the recent past, Java applets have been included in Web pages with the `<object>` tag, the `<embed>` tag, or the `<applet>` tag. It is still not clear whether `<object>` or `<applet>` will be the standard. The Sun Java plug-in supports both tags. The example package deploys applets with both `<applet>` and `<object>` tags. Because `<applet>` is simpler, we use it here in the book.

```
<applet code="MyApplet.class" width=200 height=50>
If you see this line, your browser is not Java-enabled.
</applet>
```

The `<applet>` tag is given in the basic form:

```
<applet code="ClassName.class" width=wd height=ht>
</applet>
```

The `code`, `width`, and `height` attributes are mandatory. The width *wd* and height *ht* values are given in pixels and define the size of the *display area* reserved for the applet in the Web page. A Web browser treats the applet display area just like an image from an `<img>` tag. The bottom of the display area is aligned with the surrounding text by default. You control the positioning of an applet exactly the same way as you control an image.

A Java-enabled browser loads the applet by loading the bytecode file given by the `code` attribute, which is usually a simple file name located in the same directory as the enclosing Web page. The file must be Web accessible. If multiple `.class` files are involved, they must all be located in the same directory.

If the applet `.class` files are located in a different directory, the directory location can be specified by the optional `codebase` attribute of the `<applet>` tag:

```
<applet codebase="url"  ... >
```

Between the `<applet>` and the `</applet>` tags can be other HTML constructs, which are meant to be displayed by browsers that do not support applets. Between these tags, you can also supply *named arguments and values* for the Java applet program. These are given with the `<param>` tag. Section 7.13 gives details.

Applet vs. Regular Application

An *applet* is distinguished from a *regular Java application* program in several important aspects:

- An applet is not a stand-alone program. It does not need a `main` method and is structured to run inside another application, usually a Web browser.

- A regular application is a stand-alone program that has a starting `main` method and usually cannot be executed inside a Web browser.

- The Java Virtual Machine (**java**) runs applications but not applets. Use the **appletviewer** tool or a Web browser to run applet code.

- For speedy loading by a browser, an applet is usually small in size (hence the name).

- Most likely an applet is an *event-driven* program.

- An applet does I/O through the graphical user interface (GUI) and uses standard output/error only to send error messages.

- The main class of an applet is a subclass of the Applet (an AWT applet) or JApplet (a Swing applet). New applet code should extend the JApplet class in order to use classes supplied by the Swing package.

- To run an applet, the execution context instantiates the applet's main class to create an applet object and calls prescribed methods in this applet object (Section 7.7).

- For security, an applet is barred from certain operations such as reading and writing files on the client machine.

7.5 A FIRST APPLET

Consider an applet that counts mouse clicks. To introduce applets, the example is kept simple but not overly so. It shows a clear framework for applets and demonstrates the interactivity Java can bring to a Web page.

The applet class is Click, and its source code is contained in the file Click.java. The Click applet displays the number of mouse clicks a user makes in the applet display area.

Now let's see how the applet is written. In this text, we will focus on Swing applets and not cover the old-style AWT (Abstract Windowing Toolkit) applets. The source code file begins by importing symbols from the java.awt package, which provides many basic classes, methods, and constants. Classes in the java.awt.event package provide definitions for keyboard, mouse, and other types of events. Also needed is the Swing package (javax.swing) providing JApplet and other classes. These import declarations are typical for applet code.

```
///////   Click.java   ///////
import java.awt.*;
import java.awt.event.*;
import javax.swing.*;

public class Click extends JApplet                          // (1)
{   public void init()                                      // (2)
    {    lb = new JLabel(cl + n, JLabel.CENTER);             // (3)
         getContentPane().add(lb, BorderLayout.CENTER);     // (4)
```

```
        lb.addMouseListener(new ClickHandler(this));      // (5)
    }

    public void doClick()
    {   n++;  lb.setText(cl+n);   }                        // (6)

    private String cl = "CLICK ME:   ";
    private JLabel lb;
    private int n = 0;
}
```

To write an applet, you extend the `JApplet` class (line 1). An applet does not need a `main` method because its execution is controlled by a Web browser (or the **appletviewer**) in a prescribed manner (Section 7.9). Initialization of an applet object is done with an `init` method (line 2) instead of a constructor. A label to display a string (centered in the label) is created (line 3) and added to the center of the content pane of the applet (line 4). Hence, this applet basically displays a string in the center of its display area.

Registering *event handlers* (or *event listeners*) is a common task within `init()`. The `Click` applet registers an *event handler object*, which listens and responds to mouse click events on the label (line 5). Mouse clicks not on the label are not events for the label. The `doClick` method is called by the event handler to increment the click count n and to cause display updating with the `setText` call (line 6).

The `ClickHandler` defines the event handler needed by the `Click` applet:

```
class ClickHandler extends MouseAdapter
{   ClickHandler(Click ap) {  app = ap;  }                // (7)

    public void mouseClicked(MouseEvent e)
    {   app.doClick();   }                                 // (8)

    private Click app;
}
```

A call to `mouseClicked` is triggered every time the user clicks the mouse over the applet area. Event handlers must conform to well-defined interfaces. The AWT provides a number of *adapters* (Section 5.12) to make event handlers easy to write. Simply extend the appropriate adapter (`MouseAdapter`, in this case) and override one or more methods (`mouseClicked`, in this case). A detailed description of event handling is given later in Section 7.9.

One technique worth noting here is how a `ClickHandler` is instantiated with a reference to the applet (lines 5 and 7) and how it calls an applet method to handle the click event (line 8).

The method get ContentPane is inherited from JApplet and its superclasses. Thus there are many ready-made methods that help applet coding. Knowing the inherited methods is part of learning Java applets.

7.6 TESTING AND DEPLOYING APPLETS

After an applet is written, you have to test and debug it. Then you can put it to use on the Web. A simple page Click.html can be used:

```
<html><head><title>JApplet Test Page</title></head>
<body><h1>Testing JApplet</h1>
A Swing applet
<applet width=200 height=50 code="Click.class">
<p>Applet not supported by this browser.</p>
</applet>
being tested.
</body></html>
```

The simplest way of testing and debugging your applet is to use the **appletviewer** supplied by the SDK. Simply invoke the viewer on the .html file containing the applet

appletviewer Click.html

and it displays the applet without the surrounding material on the page. Any error messages are sent to standard output. You can also resize and iconize the display window of the viewer dynamically to see how the applet reacts to these events. Fix the code if necessary, and run it again. You can discover and fix most problems with this approach. For harder bugs you may need the Java debugger (Appendix I).

Having passed the **appletviewer** test, you are ready to try the new applet on the Web. But first test it using a browser with the Java plug-in installed. Open the test page through the Open Page option on the browser's File menu. Figure 7.5 shows the appearance of the Click applet after several mouse clicks. If something goes wrong with the applet, the browser sends error messages to the *Java Console* window. To view the Java Console:

- For Netscape 6, the Java Console is a Tools option on the Tasks menu.
- For Internet Explorer 5 and above, the Java Console is on the View menu after you have enabled it from the

  Tools->Internet Options->Advanced

  menu.

To deploy a working applet, insert the HTML code into the target Web page and place all .class and other files needed by the applet along with it. Make sure that permissions for all files are set for Web access.

Figure 7.5   TESTING THE Click APPLET

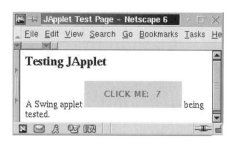

7.7 BROWSER CONTROL OF APPLETS

An applet is a special Java program that is contained in a Web page. The applet is loaded and executed by a Web browser to add interactivity and dynamism to a Web page. As such, an applet executes under the control of a Web browser or the `appletviewer` tool, which is convenient for testing applets. Under such *execution contexts*, an applet usually runs under a GUI in an *event-driven* mode. An event could be a key press, a mouse move, a mouse button press, a mouse button release, and so on.

A good mental model of how an applet is instantiated, controlled, and executed by a Java-enabled browser is important. Understanding clearly the context within which an applet functions helps in writing effective applet code.

When a browser (or `appletviewer`) encounters the `<applet>` tag, it locates the specified code

`AppletName.class`

and loads it across the network into the browser. When the loading is complete, an object (an instance of class *AppletName* that extends `Applet` or `JApplet`) is instantiated and initialized (by calling `init()`). For instantiation, the null constructor for *AppletName* must exist. The resulting object is often referred to simply as the *applet*. Then the method `start()` of the applet is invoked, and the appearance of the applet is drawn (by calling `paint`). Basically, the browser is in control. It also monitors mouse clicks, key presses, and other *events* and calls registered *event listeners* to handle the events. For example, the `ClickHandler` is a listener used in the `Click` applet. The `mouseClicked` method in the listener is invoked every time the user clicks a mouse button.

The browser manages the graphical user interface (GUI) and monitors events continuously. A browser usually sets up a separate *applet-control thread* for each applet to execute concurrently. Figure 7.6 illustrates browser control of an applet.

Figure 7.6   BROWSER CONTROL OF APPLET

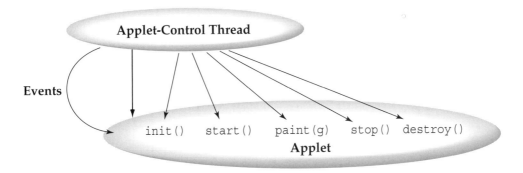

Applet Life Cycle

In addition to delivering events, the browser manages an applet's *life cycle* by invoking the appropriate *milestone methods* inherited from the `Applet` class. The `Applet` class defines do-nothing versions of the milestone methods that can be overridden for the following purposes:

- `init()`—Called to initialize the new applet object after the applet code is loaded or reloaded. The `init` method performs initializations but should perform tasks that do not take very long. Longer running initializations, such as loading files across a network, should be done in a separate thread.

- `start()`—Called to set up the applet to run. This method must finish its job quickly and may create independently running threads to perform time-consuming or repetitive tasks. The method is called when an applet is loaded and initialized for the first time, when the applet is resized, and when a user revisits after leaving the Web page containing the applet. The `paint()` method (Section 8.9) is called automatically to display the applet after `start()` is called.

- `stop()`—Called to stop the applet. This usually means stopping the execution of any threads launched in `start()`. The method may be invoked when a user leaves the Web page containing the applet, resizes or iconifies the browser window, or quits the browser.

- `destroy()`—Called to perform final clean-up before the applet is *unloaded*. Unloading happens before the applet is reloaded and before the browser terminates. In a sense, `destroy()` is an applet's special finalize method.

The applet control call sequence is: `init()`, `start()`, `paint()`, then `stop()`, and `destroy()` as appropriate (Figure 7.6). An applet can transit between the *started* and *stopped* states many times before finishing. An applet may define none, one, several, or all of the milestone methods. When writing an applet, define only the life-cycle methods you need. Many applets, like the Click example, need only the init() method.

Ordinary programs follow a predetermined sequence of steps. Applets and GUI applications, however, are *event-driven programs* that are always ready to respond to a set of external events whose sequencing cannot be predicted. To keep event-driven programs responsive, event-handling code must not take too long to execute. For applets, this means that the milestone methods and event handlers must return quickly. Certain time-consuming tasks such as display drawing and data file loading are usually done with separate threads to avoid taking over the applet control thread.

To further illustrate the milestone methods, let's improve the Click example. The Click2 applet displays status strings and reacts to both mousePressed and mouseReleased events.

```
///////    Click2.java    ///////
import java.awt.*;
import java.awt.event.*;
import javax.swing.*;

public class Click2 extends JApplet
{  public void init()
     {    lb = new JLabel(msg, JLabel.CENTER);
          lb.addMouseListener(new MouseHandler(this));
          getContentPane().add(lb, BorderLayout.CENTER);
     }

   public void start()
     {    showStatus("Click2: started"); }

   public void stop()
     {    showStatus("Click2: stopped"); }

   public void doDown()
     {    msg = "Ups = " + u + "  and  Downs = " + ++d;
          lb.setText(msg);
     }

   public void doUp()
     {    msg = "Ups = " + ++u + "  and  Downs = " + d;
          lb.setText(msg);
     }

   private JLabel lb;
```

Figure 7.7 **COUNTING UPS AND DOWNS**

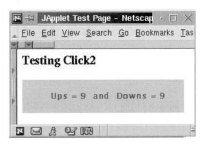

```
    private int u=0, d=0;
    private String msg = "Counting Ups and Downs";
}
```

The method showStatus, inherited from Applet, displays a string in the Web browser *status window*. The MouseHandler object handles mousePressed and mouseReleased events. This is arranged by overriding the particular event methods inherited from MouseAdapter. The doDown and doUp methods in the applet are called in response to these events.

```
class MouseHandler extends MouseAdapter
{   MouseHandler(Click2 ap) { app = ap; }

    public void mousePressed(MouseEvent e) { app.doDown(); }

    public void mouseReleased(MouseEvent e) { app.doUp(); }

    private Click2 app;
}
```

Figure 7.7 shows the appearance of the Click2 applet after several mouse clicks.

7.8 GUI PROGRAMMING BASICS

A *graphical user interface* (GUI) allows end users to control and interact with a program easily and effectively. The GUI program reacts to *events*, such as keystrokes and mouse clicks, and performs tasks depending on the event. Think of a GUI as a receptionist. Instead of pursuing a set course of action, the receptionist handles whatever comes along, be it a visitor or a phone call. The degree to which a GUI is easy, effective, and user-friendly depends on its design, which is an area of study all by itself.

A GUI is built from *GUI components*. A GUI component is an object that contains appropriate fields and methods to support a specific user-interface feature such as a button, a menu, or a text area. In GUI literature, such windowing objects are frequently referred to as *widgets*. The on-screen display area associated with a component is its *window*. In Java, a GUI program can be an applet or a stand-alone GUI application.

Java provides two types of GUI components, or widgets:

1. The original AWT (Abstract Windowing Toolkit) widgets in the `java.awt` package—AWT widgets have a *native*, or platform-dependent, look and feel. AWT components are superseded by Swing components.

2. The new Swing widgets in the `javax.swing` package—Swing widgets are completely disassociated with native codes, more capable, and support user-specified look and feel.

Generally, a program should use either AWT or Swing widgets but not a mixture. For new GUI programs, it is highly recommended that you use Swing widgets.

A GUI makes a program more intuitive by displaying visual controls for applying and managing a program. The keyboard and mouse actions from the user are *events* that the GUI monitors and handles with preprogrammed responses. This activity is called *event handling* and is an important part of GUI programming.

An applet is a special kind of GUI program. Important aspects of applet programming include:

1. Interacting with the execution context (Section 7.7)
2. Drawing graphics
3. Handling events
4. Dealing with GUI components (widgets)

Learning GUI programming involves handling events, drawing graphics, and making use of widgets such as labels, buttons, text fields, windows, and menus. Thus the preceding items 2, 3, and 4 are common between applets and stand-alone GUI applications. The GUI programming materials to come are useful for writing stand-alone GUI applications as well as applets.

7.9 EVENT HANDLING

GUI programs, whether applets or stand-alone applications, are event driven to allow easy user interactions. An event-driven program normally does nothing until an event triggers some preprogrammed action. The Click and Click2 applets are examples. You'll see many stand-alone, event-driven GUI applications in Chapter 8.

A GUI program usually does nothing after being initialized. Part of the initialization sets up the monitoring and handling of certain events. When such an event occurs, the GUI program reacts to the event, handles it quickly, and goes back to doing nothing—being ready for the next event.

Basically an event-driven program indicates which events are monitored by which widgets (components) and specifies actions in response to these events when they occur. Handling events is not difficult when you understand the Java event-handling model.

Java provides a systematic framework to represent, report, and handle events, and it supports event processing in its GUI widget hierarchy. An applet is a widget and employs the same system to handle events.

The execution context (a JVM or browser) of a GUI program runs an independent *thread* (Chapter 11) to monitor user events. When an event takes place, the *event monitoring thread* calls an appropriate *event handler*, a method defined by your program, to respond to the particular event. When the event handler returns, the event thread goes back to monitor events. Hence an event handler ought to return quickly to preserve the responsiveness of the GUI. Because another thread is monitoring events, the main method of a GUI program usually can exit after having registered event handlers.

When the *event thread* gets an event, it performs these actions:

1. Determines which widget is to process the event. This widget is the *event source*. For example, the JLabel in the Click example is an event source.

2. Creates an event object, a subclass of java.util.EventObject, to represent the event. In the Click example, the event object involved is a MouseEvent.

3. Reports the event to the source widget by invoking its processEvent method (Figure 7.8); reporting is done only if the source widget is monitoring this event, and monitoring is done only for events with registered listeners. In the Click example, a MouseListener is registered.

4. The event source processEvent method leads to *firing of the event*—calling an appropriate event-handling *callback* method in each registered event listener object. In the Click example, the callback is the mouseClicked method in the ClickHandler object registered with the JLabel.

The event-handling model, representation, reporting, and handling of events are described in the following subsections.

The Delegation Model

Event handling with the delegation model is simple when you understand the model. Events are organized into an *event hierarchy*, delivered (or *fired*) by

Figure 7.8 EVENT-HANDLING MODEL

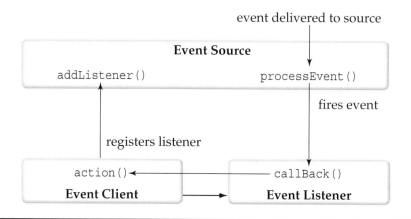

event sources, and handled by *event listeners* (Figure 7.8). The same object may be both a source and a listener or a source and a client.

- Event hierarchy—The EventObject class (java.util package) is the superclass of all event types in the delegation model. Java provides a set of event types including KeyEvent, MouseEvent, ActionEvent, and so on, in the java.awt.event package, each a subclass of java.awt.AWTEvent. You may define your own event types by subclassing EventObject or an existing event class.

- Event sources—An *event source* is an object that originates or delivers events. GUI widgets are event sources. A source may emit *component-level* or *semantic* events, as will be explained. An *event listener* is an object that is interested in receiving and handling certain types of events when they occur. A listener must first be registered with an event source in order to receive event notification from that source.

- Event listeners—A GUI program defines *event listeners* to handle the events it wishes to process. An *event listener* is any object that implements an *event listener interface* by coding required methods. All listener interfaces[2] are extended from the class java.util.EventListener.

    Java provides an event listener interface for each available event class and *adapters* that provide default implementations for the event listener interfaces (Figure 7.9).

---

[2]See Section 5.4 for more details on Java interfaces.

Figure 7.9   WRITING EVENT HANDLERS

An application establishes one or more concrete listeners (or handlers) to handle events and registers the listeners with appropriate sources. The listeners usually do not contain application-specific logic for handling the events received; instead they invoke appropriate methods in application objects (client objects) to handle the events. A widget, in addition to being a source, can also be a listener and/or a client, so widgets can cooperate in event handling.

Event Types and Representation

An event is represented by an event object that stores attributes and provides methods to deal with the event. The majority of event objects used in both AWT and Swing are subclasses of `java.awt.AWTEvent`. Additional event objects for Swing are in the `javax.swing.event` package (Section 8.14). The delegation model categorizes events into a hierarchy of event classes. An event class may represent one or more types of event. For example, `MouseEvent` includes such events as `mousePressed`, `mouseReleased`, `mouseClicked`, `mouseMoved`, and so on. Data in an event object are retrieved and set (if settable) by

```
getAttr()
setAttr()
```

methods. For example, `MouseEvent` provides:

```
int getX()       (x position of mouse)
int getY()       (y position of mouse)
```

These will be applied by `ClickHandler` in the Tic Tac Toe example (Section 7.10). `KeyEvent` provides:

```
int getKeyCode()                  (gets integer keycode)
void setKeyCode(int keyCode)      (sets keycode)
```

Table 7.2   **COMPONENT-LEVEL EVENTS**

Event Class	Events
ComponentEvent	Component resized, moved, . . .
FocusEvent	Component got focus, lost focus
InputEvent	Component got any input event
KeyEvent	Component got key press, key release, . . .
MouseEvent	Component got mouse down, mouse move, . . .
ContainerEvent	Container added or removed a child
WindowEvent	Top-level window status changed

Java distinguishes between *component-level* and *semantic* events, as follows:

- Component-level events—Represent user or window-system actions such as a mouse click, a key press, and so on. All component-level events are subtypes of the class java.awt.event.ComponentEvent. The Component class defines processing and listener registration methods for component-level events. Table 7.2 lists component-level events.

- Semantic events—Represent higher-level functions or meanings of events. Pushing a button or double-clicking a text line are examples. Processing and listener registration methods for semantic events are defined in their respective widget classes. Table 7.3 lists semantic events.

The getSource method of an event object returns the object (usually a widget) that is the source of the event.

Table 7.3   **SEMANTIC EVENTS**

Event Class	Events
ActionEvent	An action is requested.
AdjustmentEvent	The value has been adjusted.
ItemEvent	An item state has changed.
TextEvent	The value of the text object has changed.

Event Listeners

Event handling, in an applet or a regular application, is done by establishing listener objects and registering them with event sources. An event source delivers events by calling fixed *call-back* methods in registered listener objects. You implement actions triggered by events in call-back methods.

Register and unregister a listener with methods add*Xyz*Listener and remove*Xyz*Listener, provided by widgets. Listener registration is usually done when widgets are set up: in constructors or applet init methods. But registering and unregistering can be done dynamically anywhere. By requiring registration, Java can filter events so that unmonitored events are not reported at all, making event processing much more efficient.

You establish an event listener class by implementing an event listener interface. For each event class, there is at least one event listener interface (all subinterfaces of java.util.EventListener): KeyListener, MouseListener, MouseMotionListener, ActionListener, ListSelectionListener, and so on. An EventListener interface typically has one call-back method for each distinct event type contained in the event class. The effect of a particular event is accomplished by sending an EventObject instance to a specific method in an EventListener. For example, a FocusListener has two methods:

```
void focusGained(FocusEvent)
void focusLost(FocusEvent)
```

You can write a listener class by implementing one of the listener interfaces. To implement an interface, you code all of the methods required by the interface and declare that the class implements the interface. For example:

```
import java.awt.event.*;

class ActionHandler implements ActionListener
{   ActionHandler(ClientClass  cl)
    {   client = cl;   }

    private ClientClass client;

    public void actionPerformed(ActionEvent e)
    {   // event handling code here
        // such as client.doAction(...);
    }
}
```

A method such as actionPerformed is a *call-back method* that will be called by an event source to deliver a particular type of event. To receive the event, a listener object must first be registered with the source. See Section 8.5 for an example that implements ActionListener.

Event Sources

Each widget is an event source and can deliver (fire) component events and, depending on the widget, additional semantic events. As an event source, a widget provides registration methods for listeners. In the simple `Click` example (Section 7.5), the `Click` widget is a `JApplet` and it is both the event source and the event client (Figure 7.10).

Generally, you use the

```
addEventTypeListener(EventTypeListener el)
removeEventTypeListener(EventTypeListener el)
```

methods to register and unregister the specified listener el. Event sources support *event multicasting*: sending an event to multiple listeners.

Extending `Component`, the `JComponent` class, the superclass of all Swing widgets, provides listener registration methods for events:

```
addComponentListener(ComponentListener)
addFocusListener(FocusListener)
addKeyListener(KeyListener)
addMouseListener(MouseListener)
addMouseMotionListener(MouseMotionListener)
```

Higher-level widgets, such as `JButton` and `JList`, also fire semantic events by invoking call-back methods such as

```
actionPerformed
itemStateChanged
```

in listeners registered with:

```
addActionListener(ActionListener)
addItemListener(ItemListener)
```

Table 7.4 shows semantic event sources.

Figure 7.10 `Click` **APPLET: EVENT SOURCE AND CLIENT**

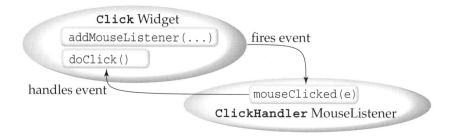

Table 7.4   **SWING SEMANTIC EVENT SOURCES**

Source Widget	Registration
JButton	addActionListener
JRadioButton	addActionListener
JCheckbox	addItemListener
JList	addActionListener
	addItemListener
JMenuItem	addActionListener
JScrollbar	addAdjustmentListener
JTextArea	addTextListener
JTextField	addActionListener
	addTextListener

Note that Java makes no promises on the order in which events are delivered to a set of registered listeners. However, it is safe for a listener to modify the state of an event object received without interfering with other listeners receiving the same event.

Sequenced event delivery can be achieved by registering one listener and then propagating the event under program control.

Writing Listeners with Adapters

Many component-level event listener interfaces treat multiple event subtypes. To make implementing listeners easier, Java provides a set of *adapter* classes in the java.awt.event package:

```
ComponentAdapter
FocusAdapter
KeyAdapter
MouseAdapter
MouseMotionAdapter
WindowAdapter
```

Each adapter implements a corresponding listener interface by supplying do-nothing routines for the required methods. The scheme allows you to subclass an adapter and override only the methods you need. The Click, Click2, and TicTacToe examples demonstrate the use of adapters, listener registration, call-back methods, and event treatment.

Event Handling Summary

For event handling, follow these simple steps:

1. Decide on the exact events from the event sources you wish to handle. For each event, perform the following steps.

2. For a component-level event, write a listener by extending an `adapter`. For a semantic event, write a listener by implementing a semantic listener interface.

3. Program the call-back method in the listener to handle the desired event.

4. Register an instance of the listener with the appropriate event source.

Important pieces of information for performing these steps include which call-back method handles the target event, which adapter or listener interface contains this call-back method, which type of event object is passed to the call-back method, and which fields and methods are available in the event object. The Java API documentation contains all of this information.

7.10 TIC TAC TOE

An applet that plays Tic Tac Toe interactively with a user is now described. The computer plays **0** and the user **X**. They take turns going first. The user enters moves conveniently with mouse clicks on a displayed game board. The applet generates counter moves, using a simple strategy. The game pieces are graphical images.

This is a realistic example involving the object-oriented implementation of an applet. The UML (Section 13.4) class diagram shows the object-oriented design of the Tic Tac Toe applet (Figure 7.11). Many techniques discussed earlier are put to use. The program involves the following classes:

- `TicTacToe`—A `JPanel` that provides user control and game display. It initializes (reinitializes) a new game, decides when to display (redisplay) the game board, receives user moves by mouse clicks, and controls move sequencing. It uses a `TicBoard` object for the board display aspect of the game and a `TicGame` object for the rules, moves, and state of the game.

- `TicApplet`—A `JApplet` (top-level widget) that creates a `TicTacToe` object and uses it as the content pane.

- `TicBoard`—A `JPanel` that serves as the game board that draws the board and displays individual tokens in specific locations on the board.

- `TicGame`—A *game player* object that checks moves, records player positions, generates moves, and determines game status. This is the model, or game engine, in the MVC design pattern (Section 13.7).

- `ClickHandler`—An event handler that receives user moves.

Figure 7.11   OO DESIGN OF TIC TAC TOE APPLET

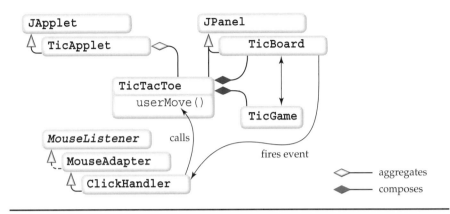

The TicTacToe panel contains all key elements of the game. It is placed in a JApplet to run as an applet. It can just as easily be placed in a top-level JFrame to run as a stand-alone application.

The program demonstrates OO design, illustrates event handling, shows nontrivial custom drawing, and introduces (briefly) image display. The realistic example also provides a starting point for later enhancements. Figure 7.12 shows the applet on a Web page. Each class is described separately.

The Swing Applet TicApplet

The applet itself is very simple. The init method first obtains the code base of the applet (line 1) as a URL object (Section 10.1). The codebase is a URL pointing to the directory containing the class and other files for the applet. It

Figure 7.12   TIC TAC TOE APPLET

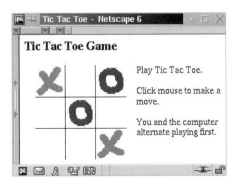

is by default the same directory as that of the page containing the applet but can be set by the codebase parameter (Section 7.13) to a different directory. The image (.gif) files are retrieved from a subdirectory images at the applet codebase (lines 2–3).

A TicTacToe panel is then created (line 4) and set as the applet's content pane (line 5). As a top-level Swing widget, a JApplet has a content pane where child widgets are added, or the content pane can be replaced by a suitable container, such as a JPanel, that holds the desired child widgets.

```
///////    TicApplet.java     ///////
import java.awt.*;
import javax.swing.*;
import java.net.URL;

public class TicApplet extends JApplet
{  public void init()
   {   URL codeBase = getCodeBase();                      // (1)
       Image o = getImage(codeBase, "images/o.gif");      // (2)
       Image x = getImage(codeBase, "images/x.gif");      // (3)
       TicTacToe tic = new TicTacToe(o, x);               // (4)
       setContentPane(tic);                               // (5)
   }
}
```

The TicTacToe Panel

Let's look at the TicTacToe class, which performs the following major functions:

- Initially sets up a TicBoard object with the images of the game pieces and a background color (line 6)
- Initially creates a game object to play the game on this board (line 7)
- Sets up a new game on demand
- Executes user moves (via mouse events) and generates countermoves
- Asks the board to update the game display as needed

```
///////    TicTacToe.java    ///////
import java.awt.*;
import java.awt.event.*;
import javax.swing.*;

public class TicTacToe extends JPanel
{  public TicTacToe(Image o, Image x)
   {   init(o, x);  }
```

```
    protected void init(Image o, Image x)
    {   if (board == null)
        {   board = new TicBoard(o, x, Color.white);    // (6)
            game = new TicGame(board);                  // (7)
        }
        setLayout(new BorderLayout());                  // (8)
        add(board, BorderLayout.CENTER);                // (9)
        board.setGame(game);
        board.addMouseListener(new ClickHandler(this)); // (10)
        newGame();                                      // (11)
    }

    protected TicTacToe() {}

 // other methods ...

    protected TicBoard board = null;
    protected TicGame game = null;
    protected boolean first = false; // user moves first
}
```

The init method adds the board at the center of the panel (lines 8–9), registers a click handler (line 10), and initializes a new game (line 11). The field first keeps track of who goes first.

The newGame method sets up a new game.

```
protected void newGame()
{   game.reset();
    if (first)                              // computer goes first
    {   game.move(game.genMove(TicGame.PLAYER_O),
                TicGame.PLAYER_O);
    }
    first = !first;                         // opponent first next time
    board.repaint();                        // redisplays board
    gameBegin();                            // starts game
}
```

The user and the computer alternate going first. In newGame, after the game object is reset, a move is generated if the computer goes first. The repaint call requests the redrawing of a widget. Later an independent running drawing thread will call the paintComponent method of a Swing widget to redisplay it. We'll look at the paintComponent method of TicBoard shortly. Other chores at the start of a new game are specified in gameBegin. Now let's consider handling user moves in the applet. The userMove method processes a user move at pixel location (x, y):

```
public void userMove(int x, int y)
{   if ( game.ended() )                    // game ended
    {   newGame();                         // sets up new game (a)
        return;
    }
    // determine mouse position on board
    int c = board.col(x);                                   // (b)
    int r = board.row(y);                                   // (c)
    if ( ! move(c+r*3, TicGame.PLAYER_X) )  // X moves (d)
        invalidMove();                     // X move incorrect (e)
    else if ( ! game.ended() )
    {   c = game.genMove(TicGame.PLAYER_O); // generates move
        if ( c != TicGame.NOMOVE )
            move(c, TicGame.PLAYER_O);             // O moves (f)
    }
}
```

The userMove method is called by the ClickHandler, which listens for a mouse click in the board display area (from the TicBoard). Figure 7.13 shows the event source, listener, and client relationship in this example.

If the game has already ended, a new game is set up (line a). Otherwise, the row-column position of the mouse is determined from its (x, y) coordinates (lines b and c). The indicated move is made for the user (user plays X, line d). If the move is not valid, invalidMove is called (line e). If the move is valid and a reply is needed, move is called with a generated move for the computer (computer plays O, line f).

The method move makes the indicated move m for the given player. It returns true if the move is made successfully:

```
protected boolean move(int m, boolean player)
{   int status = game.move(m, player);
    if ( status == TicGame.NOMOVE )
        return false;
    board.repaint();
```

Figure 7.13   EVENT HANDLING

Source	Listener	Client

```
      if ( status == TicGame.WIN_X || status == TicGame.WIN_O )
         winner();
      return true;
 }
```

The call to game.move makes the indicated move for the specified player and returns an integer status. If m is not a valid move, the method returns false. Otherwise, the new move is displayed. The status is checked for a possible win, and winner() is called no matter who wins.

The TicTacToe class defines several no-op methods:

```
protected void invalidMove() {}
protected void winner() {}
protected void gameBegin() {}
```

These are hooks for subclass improvements to the game. Planning ahead for class extension is an important aspect of OOP.

The ClickHandler Class

This is the event handler (listener) registered with the TicBoard. It responds to the mouseClicked event and calls userMove in the TicTacToe object with the (x, y) coordinates of the mouse pointer:

```
class ClickHandler extends MouseAdapter
{   ClickHandler(TicTacToe ap) { app = ap; }

    public void mouseClicked(MouseEvent evt)
    {   app.userMove(evt.getX(), evt.getY()); }

    private TicTacToe app=null;
}
```

See MouseEvent API documentation for more information on mouse events.

The TicBoard Class

A TicBoard object is initialized with the coordinates of its upper-left corner, the overall width and height of the board, and the graphical images for the game tokens. It determines the game token display area dimensions (tw and th) and supplies methods to draw the board, draw a specified game piece in a designated board position, and determine the row and column position of a mouse location.

```
///////   TicBoard.java   ///////
import java.awt.*;
import javax.swing.JPanel;
```

```
public class TicBoard extends JPanel
{  public TicBoard(Image o, Image x, Color bg)
   {   this.x = x; this.o = o;
       setBackground(bg);
   }

   public void setGame(TicGame g)
   {   game = g;   }

   protected TicBoard() { }   // for class extension

// paintComponent and other methods ...

   protected TicGame game;
   protected Graphics g;        // graphics context
   protected Image x, o;        // graphical images for pieces
   protected int  x0=0, y0=0;   // upper-left corner of board
   protected int width, height; // of board
   protected int tw, th;        // token area width and height
   protected int lw = 1;        // thickness of line

}
```

TicBoard extends JPanel to override the paintComponent method for custom drawing. Before drawing, super.paintComponent is called to clear the drawing area (line A). Drawing must be done within the dimensions of the display area assigned by the parent widget to the drawing widget (line B). It asks the game object, where the move record is kept, to request the drawing of individual game pieces (line C).

```
public void paintComponent(Graphics g)
{   this.g = g;
    super.paintComponent(g);        // paint background    (A)
    size(getWidth(), getHeight());  // display area         (B)
    g.setColor(Color.black);        // foreground color
    drawBoard();
    game.draw();                    // draws pieces played (C)
}

public void size(int w, int h)
{   width = w; height = h;
    tw = (width-2*lw)/3;
    th = (height-2*lw)/3;
}
```

Two drawing methods are supplied. One draws the game board and the other a token at a designated position. According to the width and height of the drawing area, the drawBoard method simply draws four straight lines, using the given graphics context object g. A subclass can override this method and draw thicker or more artistic lines.

```
protected void drawBoard()
{    g.drawLine(tw, y0, tw, height);
     g.drawLine(2*tw+lw, y0, 2*tw+lw, height);
     g.drawLine(x0, th, width, th);
     g.drawLine(x0, 2*th+lw, width, 2*th+lw);
}
```

The drawPiece method simply draws the desired game token image in the designated board square i:

```
public void drawPiece(boolean player, int i)
{    int r= i/3, c = i%3;  // row and column
     g.drawImage( (player==TicGame.PLAYER_X) ? x : o,
          c*(tw+lw)+1, r*(th+lw)+1, tw-1, th-1, this);
}
```

The drawImage method in Graphics draws the given image inside the specified rectangle. The image is scaled to fit when necessary. The last argument is an *image observer* object used in decoupling image drawing from image loading (Section 11.15).

The TicBoard class supplies two more public methods to determine the row and column position on the board, given a y/x coordinate relative to the upper-left corner of the board:

```
public int col(int x)
{    return( (x * 3) / width ); }
```

```
public int row(int y)
{    return( (y * 3) / height ); }
```

These are used to determine where a user is placing a game piece (in the userMove method of the TicTacToe class).

The TicGame Class

The TicGame class has knowledge of the Tic Tac Toe game and supplies methods and mechanisms for making moves, determining game status, and checking game-ending positions. It can also generate moves for either player and draw the game display, given a board object and a graphics context object.

The nine board positions are indexed from 0 to 8 (Figure 7.14). Bit positions in the integers circle and cross record the squares occupied by players 0 and X, respectively. For example, the code

```
cross |= 1 << 5
```

Figure 7.14   TIC TAC TOE BOARD POSITIONS

registers an **X** in square 5. A running move count keeps track of the total number of moves made by the players, and an end-of-game flag indicates a completed game.

```
///////    TicGame.java    ///////
import java.applet.Applet;
import java.awt.Graphics;

public class TicGame
{   public TicGame(TicBoard b)
    {   reset(); board = b;}

    public void reset()
    {   moveCount = circle = cross = 0;
        end = false;
    }

    public boolean ended() { return end; }

    protected TicBoard board;
    protected int circle, cross;      // current position for O and X
    protected int moveCount = 0;      // total number of moves made
    private boolean end;              // end-of-game flag

 // other members ...
}
```

The draw method paints the game board and the pieces played. Bit-pattern manipulations make this method efficient.

```
public void draw()
{   int mv = moveCount;
    int o = circle, x = cross;
    int i = 0;
    while ( mv > 0 )
    {   if ( (o & 1) != 0 )
        {   board.drawPiece(PLAYER_O, i);
```

```
            mv--;
        }
        else if ( (x & 1) != 0 )
        {   board.drawPiece(PLAYER_X, i);
            mv--;
        }
        i++; o >>= 1; x >>= 1;
    }
}
```

Playing a specified move m for a specific player is the function of the move method. In any case, the proposed move is checked for validity (line i). NOMOVE is returned if the move is invalid (line ii). For a valid move, the move count is incremented and the move recorded (line iii). The method returns the game status after a successful move.

The class also has a do-nothing unMove method that can be defined by a subclass.

```
public int move(int m, boolean player)
{   if ( (m < 0) || (m > 8)                     // no such square (i)
          || end ||                             // game ended
          (((cross | circle) & (1 << m)) != 0)  // square taken
        )
        return NOMOVE;                          // (ii)
    moveCount++;
    if ( player == PLAYER_X ) cross |= 1 << m; // (iii)
    else circle |= 1 << m;
    return (status());
}


// for subclassing
public boolean unMove() { return false; }
```

The status method examines the game status and returns WIN_O, WIN_X, TIE, or PLAY if the game is not over yet. It also sets the end-of-game flag as appropriate.

```
public int status()
{   if ( moveCount < 5 ) return PLAY;
    if ( isWin(circle) )                // O has won
    {   end = true; return WIN_O; }
    if ( isWin(cross) )                 // X has won
    {   end = true; return WIN_X; }
    if (moveCount >= 9)
    {   end = true; return TIE; }
    return PLAY;
}
```

```
public static final int NOMOVE = -1;
public static final int PLAY = 0;
public static final int WIN_O = 1;
public static final int WIN_X = 2;
public static final int TIE = 3;
public static final boolean PLAYER_X = true;
public static final boolean PLAYER_O = false;
```

To determine whether a position represents a win, the method isWin compares it to an array of eight preset winning positions stored in win[]:

```
public static boolean isWin(int pos)
{   for (int i=0; i < 8; i++)
      if ( (pos & win[i]) == win[i] )
          return true;
      return false;
}
// The winning bit pattern
static int win[] =                      // 8 winning positions
{    (1 << 0) | (1 << 1) | (1 << 2),
     (1 << 3) | (1 << 4) | (1 << 5),
     (1 << 6) | (1 << 7) | (1 << 8),
     (1 << 0) | (1 << 3) | (1 << 6),
     (1 << 1) | (1 << 4) | (1 << 7),
     (1 << 2) | (1 << 5) | (1 << 8),
     (1 << 0) | (1 << 4) | (1 << 8),
     (1 << 2) | (1 << 4) | (1 << 6)
};
```

The quality of any interactive game depends, to a large extent, on how well the computer can generate the moves it plays. A simple move generator uses a preset array (moves) of moves ordered by the importance of the squares on the Tic Tac Toe board. The genMove method generates a move for the indicated player by the priority list:

1. Finding a winning move
2. Blocking a winning move by the opponent
3. Making any valid move

```
// The squares in order of importance
protected static int moves[] = {4, 0, 2, 6, 8, 1, 3, 5, 7};

public int genMove(boolean player)
{   int amove = NOMOVE, self, opponent;
    if ( end ) return NOMOVE;
    if ( (cross|circle) == 0 )                 // opening move
       return((int)(Math.random()*9));         // random placement
```

```
    if (player == PLAYER_X)
    {  self = cross; opponent = circle; }
    else
    {  self = circle; opponent = cross; }
    for (int i = 0 ; i < 9 ; i++)
    {  int m = moves[i], mv = (1 << m);
       if ( ((self|opponent) & mv) == 0)         // open square
       {  if (isWin(self | mv)) return m;        // self wins
          if (isWin(opponent | mv)) amove = m;   // blocks opponent
          else if (amove == NOMOVE) amove = m;
       }
    }
    return amove;  // move found
}
```

This completes the description of the TicGame class. Compile all of these files

```
ClickHandler.java  TicBoard.java  TicTacToe.java
TicApplet.java     TicGame.java
```

and test the applet for yourself. The image and class files are also available in the example package.

HTML File for TicTacToe

To deploy the Tic Tac Toe applet, use an HTML file similar to this:

```
<html><head><title>Tic Tac Toe</title></head>
<body><h1>Tic Tac Toe Game</h1>
<applet width=140 height=140 code="TicApplet.class"
  archive="TicApplet.jar">
<p>Applet not supported by this browser.</p>
</applet>
<p>Play Tic Tac Toe.<br>Click mouse to make a move.
<br>You and the computer alternate playing first.</p>
</body></html>
```

Figure 7.12 shows the Web page with the applet.

A browser loading the Web page of an applet also downloads all of the necessary .class, .gif, and other media files, either from the same directory or a directory indicated by the codebase parameter. The optional archive parameter specifies a *Java Archive file* that packs all .class files to make an applet much faster to load across a network (Section 7.13).

Example Summary

The Tic Tac Toe applet consists of five classes, two images, a `.jar` file, and a simple HTML file:

1. `TicApplet.java`—Swing applet.
2. `TicTacToe.java`—`TicTacToe` panel serves as game control, and `ClickHandler` listens to mouse clicks.
3. `TicBoard.java`—Game board object draws the board and game pieces and records on-screen locations of board squares.
4. `TicGame.java`—Game object has knowledge of game, keeps track of game status, generates moves, and uses supplied game board.
5. `ClickHandler.java`—Event handler.
6. `images/o.gif`—Image for **0** token.
7. `images/x.gif`—Image for **X** token.
8. `TicApplet.html`—HTML test file.
9. `TicApplet.jar`—Java archive file that packs five `.class` files produced by the command (on one line):

```
jar cvf TicApplet.jar TicApplet.class TicBoard.class
      TicTacToe.class TicGame.class ClickHandler.class
```

The Tic Tac Toe applet example begins to demonstrate the writing of realistic GUI programs with OOP techniques. The complete code is available in the example package.

7.11 SOUND EFFECTS

The Java sound engine provides support for audio in applets as well as applications. Audio file formats supported are AIFF, AU, WAV, MIDI (type 0 and type 1), and RMF. Both 8- and 16-bit audio data, in mono or stereo, with sample rates from 8KHz to 48KHz, can be played.

Programs can easily produce sound effects. The `Applet` methods

```
play(URL url)
play(URL dir, String filename)
```

play a sound file located by the given `url` and the sound file `filename` located in the directory `dir`, respectively. For security reasons, the URL normally leads back to the applet's host computer.

An applet uses one of these methods

```
getAudioClip(URL url)
getAudioClip(URL dir, String filename)
```

to load the given sound file and create an `AudioClip` object, conforming to the `java.applet.AudioClip` interface, for playing the sound. An `AudioClip` object offers three methods:

```
play()      // plays the sound clip once
loop()      // plays the sound clip repeatedly
stop()      // stops the looping
```

It is usually appropriate to place the `loop()` call in the applet `start` method and the `stop` call in the applet `stop` method.

As an example, let's add sound effects to the Tic Tac Toe game from Section 7.10. Because hooks for just this kind of improvement have been left in the `TicTacToe` class, the task of adding sound effects is easy. The `invalidMove`, `gameBegin`, and `winner` methods are now defined to play appropriate sounds when invoked:

```
///////    TicSoundApplet.java    ///////
import java.awt.Image;
import javax.swing.JApplet;
import java.net.URL;
import java.applet.AudioClip;

public class TicSoundApplet extends JApplet
{  public void init()
   {   URL codeBase = getCodeBase();
       Image o = getImage(codeBase, "images/o.gif");
       Image x = getImage(codeBase, "images/x.gif");
       TicSound tic = new TicSound(o, x,                    // (A)
          getAudioClip(codeBase, "audio/return.au"),
          getAudioClip(codeBase, "audio/joy.au"),
          getAudioClip(codeBase, "audio/beep.au") );
       setContentPane(tic);
   }
}
```

The `TicSoundApplet` creates a `TicSound` object, passing it three audio clips obtained from the applet codebase (line A). The sound effects are added by class extension. The `TicSound` class extends `TicTacToe` and adds sound effects:

```
///////    TicSound.java    ///////
import java.awt.Image;
import java.applet.AudioClip;

public class TicSound extends TicTacToe
{  public TicSound(Image o, Image x,
        AudioClip rc, AudioClip jc, AudioClip bc)
   {   super(o,x);
```

```
            returnClip= rc;
            joyClip= jc;
            beepClip= bc;
        }

        protected void invalidMove()                    // (B)
        {   if (beepClip != null) beepClip.play(); }

        protected void winner()                         // (C)
        {   if (joyClip != null) joyClip.play(); }

        protected void gameBegin()                      // (D)
        {   if (returnClip != null) returnClip.play(); }

        protected AudioClip returnClip;
        protected AudioClip joyClip;
        protected AudioClip beepClip;
    }
```

The three methods (lines B–D) override their do-nothing counterparts in the super class. The sound files can be found in the example package.

The preceding example shows sound playing in applets. Java applications can use the static method

```
public static final AudioClip newAudioClip(URL r)
```

from the class `java.applet.Applet` to create `AudioClips`. For an audio file on the local host, the URL is in the form `file:path-to-file`.

7.12   INNER CLASSES

An *inner class* is one placed within another class or a method. Thus one class may have another as a member. Event handlers are often written as inner classes.

The principle purposes of class nesting are:

- To enhance encapsulation—*Slave classes* intended only for the use of a *master class* can be enclosed within the master to prevent outside access.
- To control instantiation—If instances of a `ClassB` should be obtained only through `ClassA`, `ClassB` can be hidden in `ClassA`.
- To grant member access—A class has access to all members of its enclosing class.

With class nesting, we distinguish between two kinds of classes:

1. Top-level class—A top-level class is either a member of a package or a `static` member class of a top-level class. Instance methods in a top-level class have a unique host object reference `this`.

2. Inner class—Any class that is not a top-level class is an inner class. Codes in an inner class can refer to an immediate host object as well as enclosing host objects. Members of an inner class cannot be `static`.

For example, if class *Abc* is a member of class *Xyz*, code in *Abc* can use `this` (the host) as well as *Xyz*.`this` (the *enclosing host*). The inner *Abc* can access members of *Xyz* directly. The Java compiler generates an internal name for the inner class

Xyz$Abc

which is used to name its `.class` file, for example.

Multilevel class nesting is allowed. Enclosing a class inside a method or block is also possible but seldom useful.

Inner Class Examples

Instead of having both `ArbCell` and `ArbList` as top-level classes (Section 4.22), we can:

- Enclose `ArbCell` inside `ArbList` and call it `Cell` instead.
- Make `Cell` a public member so that the type `ArbList.Cell` can be used anywhere.
- Make the constructor of `Cell` private so that only `ArbList` can create `Cell`s.
- Make the `content()` method in `Cell` public.

```
// member of ArbList
   public static final class Cell
   {  public Object content() { return item; }

      private Cell(Object c, Cell cell) { item=c; next=cell; }
      private Cell() { }
      private Object item = null;
      private Cell next = null;
   }
```

```
// Usage
ArbList.Cell cell_a = alist.find(item);
```

Similarly, the `ClickHandler` event handler class can be placed inside the `Click` applet as a `static` member:

```
private static final class
ClickHandler extends MouseAdapter
```

```
{  MouseHandler(Click ap) { app = ap; }
   public void mousePressed (MouseEvent e) { app.doDown(); }
   public void mouseReleased (MouseEvent e) { app.doUp(); }
   private Click app;
}
```

And the applet init method will add the mouse listener with this code:

```
addMouseListener(new ClickHandler(this));
```

In the preceding example, ClickHander is a static inner class. You can also elect to code it as an instance inner class:

```
private final
class ClickHandler extends MouseAdapter
{   public void mousePressed(MouseEvent e) { doDown(); }   // (a)

    public void mouseReleased(MouseEvent e) { doUp(); }    // (b)
}
```

Now, the applet init method will add the mouse listener with this code:

```
addMouseListener(new ClickHandler());
```

Note the direct use of doUp and doDown (lines a and b) from the instance inner class.

The .class file produced by the compiler for an inner class has a compound name generated by the compiler:

```
EnclosingClass$InnerClass.class
```

For example, the file name generated for the preceding inner ClickHandler is:

```
Click$ClickHandler.class
```

An inner class that is used only once to establish an object does not really need a name. Anonymous classes are often used to define event handlers.

Anonymous Event Handlers

You may have noticed a regular pattern for coding event handlers: *registering an instance of a class that either extends an adapter or implements a listener.* The classes are given names such as ClickHandler, KeyHandler, and so on, and they are not used in any way other than providing one instance to register as a listener.

Such event-handling classes and their associated code can be improved and simplified through the use of *anonymous classes.* An anonymous class has no name and is used to create only one object. It is a type of *inner class.*

Typically, you create an instance of an anonymous class with the special notation:

```
new SupertypeName() {   class body   };
```

The object created is an instance of a class with the given *class body* that extends (implements) the specified superclass (interface) *SupertypeName*.

Using an anonymous class, the `Click` applet can be simplified:

```
public class Click extends Applet
{  public void init()
   {    addMouseListener                                         // (1)
        (  new MouseAdapter()                                    // (2)
           {  public void mouseClicked(MouseEvent e)
              {  n++;  repaint(); }                              // (3)
           }
        );                                                       // (4)
   }

   public void paint(Graphics g)
   {   g.drawRect(0, 0, getSize().width-1, getSize().height-1);
       g.drawString("  CLICK IN THIS BOX : " + n, 5, 30);
   }

   private int n = 0;
}
```

The anonymous class here (line 2) extends `MouseAdapter` and contains one method, `MouseClicked`. Because the class is enclosed within `Click`, its methods (line 3) have direct access to all members in `Click` .

One drawback of this style is the complexity of the listener registration code (lines 1–4). The instance or static inner class are alternative approaches.

When packing a `.jar` file for an applet, be sure to include any `.class` files for inner classes.

7.13 APPLET PARAMETERS

Section 7.4 introduced the `<applet>` tag for including an applet in an HTML document. Each applet has a display area defined by a `width` and a `height` attribute. In the applet code, the width and height values are accessed by

```
getWidth()      (returns applet width)
getHeight()     (returns applet height)
```

respectively.

The applet bytecode resides in the same directory as the enclosing Web page or a different location given as a URL by the `codebase` attribute. Normally codebase is a directory on the computer where the Web page resides. However, codebase can be a full URL indicating a directory served by another HTTP server. In an applet, the call

```
getCodeBase();    (returns codebase URL)
```

returns a URL object that can be used readily to access information on the Internet (Section 10.1). Similar to codebase, a name=*id* attribute gives the applet an identifying name.

User-Defined Applet Parameters

We already know that applets are deployed in Web pages with the <applet> tag. In the <applet> tag, certain attributes can be given such as code and height. You can also place <param> tags inside <applet> and </applet> to add parameters of your own. Thus you can supply parameters to an applet just as you can command-line arguments to an application. For example,

```
<applet    . . . >
   <param name="soundFile"  value="beep.au">
   <param name="oImageFile" value="o.gif">
   <param name="xImageFile" value="x.gif">
   <param name="name"       value="tictactoe">
</applet>
```

defines four parameters with values. Because they are specified by name-value pairs, parameters can be given in any order. Parameters are always passed to an applet as strings. *Parameter values are case sensitive, but names are not.* The name="name" parameter has the same meaning as the name attribute of the <applet> tag.

An applet uses, for example, the call

```
getParameter("oImageFile");      (returns parameter value as string)
```

to obtain the string "o.gif".

Applets that take <param> parameters are more flexible. The user can configure various aspects of the applet by specifying <param> parameters. A parameter name should be chosen to give a clear idea of its meaning. In addition, you should document the parameters by defining the

```
public String[][] getParameterInfo()
```

method to return an array of String[], each consisting of three strings—name, value type, and description of a parameter. This way, an applet documents its parameters within itself and supplies this information to any caller of getParameterInfo().

See Section 8.8 for an example of getParameterInfo().

JAR and the archive Attribute

Frequently an applet involves multiple files for bytecode, images, and sound.[3] JAR (Java ARchive) is a file format based on the popular Zip file format for

---

[3]Sometimes images or sounds don't work inside a JAR. It is safer to archive only .class files.

combining several files into one. Use the Java tool **jar** to combine specific files and directories into a .jar file:

```
jar cvf TicTacToe.jar
    TicTacToe.class TicBoard.class TicGame.class
    ClickHandler.class TicApplet.class images
```

The `TicTacToe.jar` created bundles five bytecode files and the `images` directory for easy loading across a network. The **jar** tool is used almost exactly like the UNIX **tar** command. Consult your SDK documentation for more usage information.

After `TicTacToe.jar` is made, the `TicTacToe` applet (Section 7.10) can be introduced into a Web page with an additional `archive` attribute in the `<applet>` tag:

```
<applet archive="TicTacToe.jar" ... >
```

Web browsers can use the `archive` information to download the bundled and compressed .jar file with one HTTP transaction, making it much faster. The `code` attribute is still needed because it indicates the applet class where execution begins. The `archive` string may contain multiple .jar files separated by commas.

For security reasons, a .jar file can also be signed by the applet author so that its origin can be authenticated (Section 12.13).

7.14 APPLET SECURITY RESTRICTIONS

Because an applet is loaded across the network from a remote host (*applet host*) and run by a Web browser on a *local host*, it is important for the local host to be sure that the incoming applet program will do no harm. This is critically important for the wide acceptance of applets in Web pages.

Security is maintained in the Java run-time environment by a *Security-Manager* object that provides *security check* methods. Security-sensitive methods related to file system, network access, system commands and properties, top-level windows, and so on will use specific security checks provided by the security manager. Any security violation detected causes a `SecurityException` error and a warning message to standard output.

Existing applet viewers and Web browsers impose the following security restrictions on applets loaded from remote hosts:

- An applet usually cannot read or write files on the local machine. It can read files, local or remote, specified by full URLs because that is reading data from a Web server. It can also pass data back to a program running on the applet host. That program can use the data in any way, including saving it in a file on the applet host.

- An applet cannot make network connections except back to the applet host.

- An applet cannot start other programs on the local host.
- An applet cannot read certain system properties (Section 6.20).
- An applet cannot load libraries or use functions written in another language. It relies on only the Java API.
- An applet does not have access to the system clipboard.
- Top-level windows established by an applet look different from those established by a regular Java application. Visual cues are provided to identify top-level windows by applets clearly.

An applet is said to run in a restricted *sandbox* contained in a browser. If an applet is loaded from a local host (on the `CLASSPATH`), it should not be restricted to the sandbox as a remote applet. *Signed applets* (via the `javakey` and `jar` tools) contain the creator's encrypted signature so that a browser may allow *trusted applets* to go beyond the sandbox (Section 12.13).

Browsers can offer users the option of relaxing security restrictions, depending on whether an applet carries an authenticated signature of its creator and whether the creator is trusted. For example, a browser may allow *trusted applets* to read or write to local storage or to access a URL other than their own.

Java security measures have evolved and improved through time. Applets and applications now offer users more versatile security policies based on digital signatures, point of origin of programs, and operation types. Chapter 12 has more coverage on Java security.

7.15 SUMMARY

Web servers and clients use the HTTP protocol. Web pages are written in HTML and can link to other documents of many types. Resources on the Web are located by URLs, which can indicate the service scheme, host address, and file location of a resource.

An applet is a special Java program, different from a regular Java application, that can be included in an HTML document to make Web pages more versatile, interactive, and exciting. The `applet` tag introduces applets into Web pages. The Java plug-in utility enables Web browsers to retrieve and execute applets embedded in HTML documents. The Java plug-in keeps pace with the latest Java development and is a better choice than native browser support for applets.

An applet supports *milestone* methods `init()`, `start()`, `stop()`, and `destroy()`. An applet has convenient methods for loading images and playing sounds.

Applets are event-driven programs with a GUI composed of widgets supplied by the JFC. Widgets are useful for applets and regular applications alike. They provide useful elements for constructing graphical user interfaces, event handling, building a containment hierarchy of widgets, and performing custom graphics drawing.

It is advisable to write Swing-based applets by extending the superclass `javax.swing.JApplet` instead of the old-style AWT applets. JApplet is a top-level widget that can hold other widgets in its content pane. The Tic Tac Toe example shows an object-oriented applet with many features. The Java tool **appletviewer** is convenient for testing applets.

The JFC provides an effective event-handling mechanism based on the *delegation model*. Events are fired by event sources (widgets) and handled by event listeners. JFC-defined events are represented by different event objects. Events fall into two broad categories: component-level events and semantic events. A Java program registers listeners with appropriate sources to treat desired events. Java also provides event *adapters* to make many listeners easier to write. Often event listeners can be implemented as either *anonymous* or *inner* classes.

Parameters can be supplied to an applet through the <param> tag. The **jar** tool packs multiple files into one. An applet involving multiple files can be packaged with **jar** into a single .jar file, which is specified by the archive attribute of the <applet> tag.

Security restrictions, known as the *sandbox*, apply to applets to safeguard the host system from potential damage from applets coming from anywhere on the Web.

EXERCISES

Review Questions

1. Do you have access to a computer connected to a network? If so, find the domain name and IP address for your workstation. Is there anything obviously wrong with the IP address `131.123.5.366`?

2. What is the difference between the partial URLs /xyz.html and xyz.html? Is an empty string a valid URL?

3. To identify a particular server on the Internet, why do you need both the IP address and the port number?

4. How do you pack and unpack file hierarchies with **jar**? Compare it to the UNIX **tar** command.

5. What are the differences between an applet and a regular Java application? List as many as you can.

6. Can an applet use `System.out`, `System.in`, or `System.err`? If so, how, and for what purposes?

7. Use the tool **jar** to pack all files for the Tic Tac Toe applet, and modify its Web page to use the `.jar` file instead of the `.class` file. (Hint: Use the `archive` attribute.)

8. Consider event-driven programming. What is the major difference between a main-line program and an event-driven program?

9. In the delegation model, what is an event source? An event listener? An event client? An event object?

10. What is the difference between a *component-level event* and a *semantic event*?

11. In treating mouse events, how do you know which mouse button is involved in the event?

12. In treating keyboard events, how do you detect modifier keys such as SHIFT, CONTROL, and ALT?

13. Find the `demo/applets` directory of the Java SDK and experiment with the applets there. Are these Swing applets or AWT applets?

14. The `demo/applets/TicTacToe` directory of the Java SDK also contains an applet that plays Tic Tac Toe. Examine its source code, and compare that with the OOP approach taken in this chapter.

15. Is it possible to register a listener to an event source that does not deliver that particular event type? Why or why not?

16. What is an *event adapter*? Why is it useful?

17. Consider inner classes. What is the difference between a static and an instance inner class? Why declare an inner class `private` or `public`? Does it make sense to have a `public` inner class with a `private` constructor or a `private` inner class with a `public` constructor?

18. Why must an applet have many security restrictions not applied to regular Java programs? What are these restrictions?

Programming Assignments

1. Follow the `Click` example (Section 7.5) to write an applet that changes color when the mouse is over its display area and returns to its original color when the mouse leaves the area.

2. Modify the `TicApplet` example so that the human player always goes first.

3. Look at the move generation algorithm used by the Tic Tac Toe program. It is only slightly more effective than generating moves randomly. How would you modify the programming to use the random-move strategy?

4. The `TicApplet` class uses a `ClickHandler` (Section 7.10). Rewrite the code so that `ClickHandler` becomes (a) an inner class (b) an anonymous class.

5. Add to the `TicApplet` example so that it displays the tokens, and let the user pick the token to use (this also determines who goes first). Use class extension to add the feature.

6. Again using class extension, add the feature of keeping score to the TicTacToe game.

7. Add an "unmove" feature to the Tic Tac Toe applet. The player can type upper-case U, for example, to undo a move. Do not modify any of the existing classes. Use class extension to build a new applet.

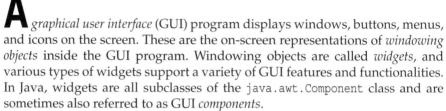

## CHAPTER EIGHT

GUI Programming

A *graphical user interface* (GUI) program displays windows, buttons, menus, and icons on the screen. These are the on-screen representations of *windowing objects* inside the GUI program. Windowing objects are called *widgets*, and various types of widgets support a variety of GUI features and functionalities. In Java, widgets are all subclasses of the `java.awt.Component` class and are sometimes also referred to as GUI *components*.

Java provides excellent support for GUI development:

- The AWT (Abstract Windowing Toolkit) supplies a set of platform-independent widgets and supports event handling, colors, fonts, and simple graphics. AWT widgets have native code support and are known as *heavyweight components* in Java.

- Improving on the AWT, the Swing package supplies a larger and richer set of widgets with additional functionalities and customizable *look and feel*. Swing widgets contain no native code and are known as *lightweight components* in Java.

- The `Java2D` and `Java3D` classes supply powerful 2D and 3D drawing capabilities.

- The `JApplet` class, replacing the older `Applet`, supports applet writing for Web pages.

We recommend that you use Swing widgets to write applets as well as stand-alone GUI applications. Applets are discussed in some detail in Chapter 7. In this chapter, we will focus on stand-alone GUI applications. It is a simple matter to turn a GUI application into an applet and vice versa.

Effective GUI programming in Java requires knowledge of the following:

- Types of widgets available
- Purposes, characteristics, and functionalities of different widgets
- How widgets combine and cooperate
- Arranging the layout of widget windows
- Event handling (Section 7.9)
- Drawing graphics, displaying images, and playing sounds
- Applying widgets in realistic situations

Section 7.9 describes event handling in depth. Other topics are covered here comprehensively so that you can begin to write sophisticated GUI programs with relative ease. Well-designed examples show practical applications of Swing widgets and object orientation. Materials covered apply to stand-alone GUI applications as well as to applets.

8.1 GUI PROGRAMMING OVERVIEW

A GUI program employs and displays various widgets to provide visual control and operation for a program. An *atomic widget* is one that corresponds to a basic GUI feature such as a button or label. A *container widget* is a GUI component that can contain and manage other widgets. A GUI application usually has a top-level widget (the root window) that contains and manages other widgets in the program.

A GUI program works by responding to specific events from the user. Reactions to an event are written into the GUI program. The GUI program execution environment usually supplies event monitoring, input focusing, window rendering, graphics drawing, and parent-child window coordination. The programming environment typically provides a collection of widgets (called "GUI components" or just "components" in Java) for constructing effective GUIs. The Java Swing package provides many useful widgets.

8.2 WIDGET CONCEPTS

A *widget* or *GUI component* is an object that supports a specific user-interface feature such as a display label, a button, or a text input box. The on-screen display area associated with a widget is its *window*.

Java supplies a rich set of useful widgets. Many are *standard widgets* that are completely pre-made and have a well-defined appearance. Standard widgets know how to paint their windows and require or allow little programmer control over their drawing. A *custom widget*, on the other hand, lets the program define how it is drawn. The most used custom widget in Swing is JPanel.

A *container* is a widget that can hold and manage other widgets placed in it. Widgets in a GUI program are organized in a hierarchy, with a root widget (root window) at the top. Only subclasses of java.awt.Window can be top-level widgets. A container holds *child widgets*, which can be atomic or container widgets themselves. A *child window*, the display area of a child widget, is always within the bounds of its parent window. A parent widget manages the size and position of its children to achieve a desired layout. This is done dynamically in response to resizing of the parent window. Usually child windows cannot overlap one another. Thus a child widget must normally fit within the width and height prescribed by its parent widget and therefore won't be able to set its own dimensions arbitrarily.

With a GUI, users control multiple windows, each of which can be affected by a user action (an *event*), but not all windows are interested in all events. A *mouse event* (moving the mouse cursor or using a mouse button) is reported to the windows containing the mouse cursor. A keyboard event (pressing and releasing a key) is reported only to the widget that has the *input focus*. Normally only one component has input focus at any time. You switch input focus by moving the mouse cursor to a different window (and clicking if necessary). Often a window changes appearance when it gains or loses input focus to provide a visual cue. Be sure that the intended window has input focus before you type on the keyboard; otherwise the keyboard events may go to a different widget or get lost altogether.

A variety of useful widgets are supplied by the AWT and by Swing to help you construct a GUI for an applet or a regular application. Swing widgets are designed to replace AWT widgets, and this textbook focuses only on Swing widgets.

8.3   SWING BASICS

Swing is part of the *Java Foundation Classes* (JFC) for GUI programming. Swing provides a large set of widgets that are more powerful and flexible than AWT widgets. Unlike AWT, Swing widgets do not depend on any native code and are therefore completely platform independent. Swing widgets can have borders as well as support settable *look and feel* and *drag and drop*. It is recommended that new GUI applications use Swing widgets and older programs convert to Swing. It is also best to avoid mixing AWT and Swing widgets in the same program.

Swing widgets use names in the form J*Xyz*. Most AWT widgets have Swing counterparts named by prefixing the letter J to their names (e.g., JComponent, JPanel, JFrame, JButton, etc.). This makes converting old AWT programs to Swing easier. There are three broad types of Swing widgets: *atomic widgets, intermediate containers,* and *top-level containers.* A top-level container holds intermediate containers and atomic widgets. An intermediate container groups other widgets to form a composite widget.

GUI Program Outline

In a typical GUI application, the main method performs these steps:

1. Create a top-level container, usually a JFrame.
2. Compose the GUI by adding widgets to containers in a desired layout.
3. Set up and register event handlers (listeners) to respond to user interaction.
4. Display the GUI and return.

Except for menu bars, widgets are added to a `JFrame` not directly but to its *content pane* (of type `Container`):

```
JFrame frame = new JFrame("Frame Name");
frame.getContentPane().add(label, BorderLayout.CENTER);
```

We have seen several applets. Now let's look at our first GUI application, `Hello.java`, which produces the display shown in Figure 8.1. This example shows the necessary steps in setting up a Swing-based GUI application:

```
///////    Hello.java    ///////
import java.awt.*;
import java.awt.event.*;
import javax.swing.*;                                        // (1)

public class Hello
{  public static void main(String[] args)
   {    JFrame win = new JFrame("Hello");                    // (2)
        win.setSize(154, 84);                                // (3)
        JLabel l = new JLabel("Hello there!", JLabel.CENTER); // (4)
        win.getContentPane().add(l, BorderLayout.CENTER);    // (5)
        win.addWindowListener(new WindowHandler(win));       // (6)
        win.setVisible(true);                                // (7)
   }
}
```

The three `import` declarations are usually required for Swing applications (line 1) because you need AWT defined symbols for events, layouts, and so on, in addition to Swing defined symbols. Note that the `swing` package is part of `javax`, the Java *standard extension libraries*.

The first step is to create a top-level container and give it an appropriate title (line 2) and size (line 3). Then you create widgets that go into the GUI. This simple example needs only a label with centered text (line 4). As mentioned, widgets are not added to a `JFrame` directly. Instead they are added into the `JFrame`'s *content pane*. The content pane uses *border layout* by default (Section 8.11). Here the label `l` is centered in the content pane (line 5). The main

Figure 8.1   HELLO IN SWING

method proceeds to register a window listener (line 6) to make the GUI visible (line 7), and then to return.

A `WindowListener` that responds to the window closing event is usually needed by a stand-alone GUI application. The `windowClosing` method in this `WindowHandler` hides the frame being closed (line 8), disposes of the frame (line 9), and then terminates program execution (line 10). This `WindowHandler` provides the basic close-window function triggered when the user clicks on the × button at the upper-right corner of the top-level window:

```
///////    WindowHandler.java    ///////
import java.awt.event.*;
import javax.swing.JFrame;

public class WindowHandler extends WindowAdapter
{  public WindowHandler(JFrame f)  { fr = f; }

   public void windowClosing(WindowEvent e)
   {    fr.setVisible(false);                    // (8)
        fr.dispose();                            // (9)
        System.exit(0);                          // (10)
   }

   private JFrame fr;
}
```

The `WindowAdapter` class implements the `WindowListener` interface with do-nothing methods. Our `WindowHandler` extends `WindowAdapter` and overrides only the `windowClosing` method. This basic `WindowHandler` is good enough for most Swing-based GUI applications.

Powerful GUI programs with many widgets follow the same program outline explained here.

8.4 OVERVIEW OF SWING WIDGETS

Most Swing widget classes are subclasses of `JComponent`. `JComponent`, in turn, is a subclass of the AWT `Container`, which extends the base AWT `Component`, the reason widgets are also known as *components* in Java documentation.

Through inheritance, `JComponent` supplies Swing widgets with important operations including:

- Event handling—listener registration (add*Xyz*Listener(*handler*), remove*Xyz*Listener(*handler*)), event processing, event dispatching, and enabling and disabling the handling of some or all events
- Basic drawing support—repaint, update, paint, and paintComponent for custom graphics as well as image drawing support

- Child component layout and management—adding (`add(c)`) and removing (`remove(c)`) child widgets, automatic layout, validating dimensions, and painting for child widgets
- Setting and getting attributes—dimensions (`getHeight()`, `getWidth()`, `getSize()`, `setSize(w, h)`), position (`getX()`, `getY()`), visibility (`setVisible(boolean)`), viability (`setEnabled(boolean)`), child widget supplied layout hints (`getMinimumSize()`, `getPreferredSize()`)

Swing Widget Features

Swing widget features, above and beyond those of AWT widgets, include:

- Tool tips—`setToolTipText(`*string*`)` defines *string* to be the cursor-tip advice for the widget.
- Borders—`setBorder()` specifies the border that a widget displays around its edges.
- Keyboard-generated actions—`registerKeyboardAction()` enables users also to use the keyboard to operate the GUI. The `setMnemonic()` method in certain Swing widgets can also be used for this purpose.
- Application-wide pluggable look and feel—In Swing, each `JComponent` has an associated `ComponentUI` object that performs all drawing, event handling, size determination, and so on for that `JComponent`. In other words, the look and feel of each Swing widget is provided by its associated `ComponentUI`. Associating a different `ComponentUI` dynamically, a widget takes on a different look and feel. The static method `UIManager.setLookAndFeel()` is used to change the `ComponentUIs` of all Swing widgets to another look and feel.
- Application-defined widget properties—*Properties* (name/object pairs) may be associated with any `JComponent` (`putClientProperty`, `getClientProperty`).
- Support for layout—The `JComponent` class adds setter methods for layout hints: `setPreferredSize`, `setMinimumSize`, `setMaximumSize`, `setAlignmentX`, and `setAlignmentY`.
- Image drawing—Built-in double buffering results in smooth image drawing.
- Efficient methods—Methods `getX`, `getY` (coordinates of upper-left corner of the widget), `getWidth`, and `getHeight` do not involve object instantiation and are less expensive and faster than `getBounds` and `getSize`.

8.5 SWING WIDGETS

Swing provides a large number of widgets. Container widgets can hold and manage child widgets. Atomic widgets perform well-defined functions and cannot hold other widgets. Some important Swing widgets are described briefly here to get you started.

Top-Level Containers

Swing has three root-window containers: JFrame for general use, JDialog for creating pop-up dialog boxes (Section 8.12), and JApplet for writing Swing-based applets. Each top-level container has a *content pane* that manages all child widgets and controls their layout. The getContentPane() method gives you the content pane (a Container). We have seen how widgets are added to the content pane.

Each top-level container may also have an optional menu bar (JMenuBar). The setJMenuBar(*menu_bar*) method adds the menu bar, which is outside the content pane. In practice, only JFrame and JApplet use a menu bar (Section 8.13).

Intermediate Containers

You often use intermediate containers to control and lay out integral parts of your GUI. These intermediate containers are then added to the content pane of a top-level container. Containers use *layout managers* (Section 8.11) to control the layout of child windows. Each intermediate container has a default layout manager, which, in some cases, can be replaced by the explicit setting of a different layout manager.

Intermediate containers include:

- JPanel—Offers the most flexible intermediate container used to group related widgets or to make layout easier. With the setBorder method, you can easily add borders to a JPanel. Although FlowLayout is the default layout manager, JPanel can use any layout manager. The content pane of a JFrame is a special intermediate container that uses a BorderLayout.

- JScrollPane—Provides scroll bars around a large or growable widget.

- JSplitPane—Displays two widgets in a fixed amount of space, letting users adjust the amount of space devoted to each widget.

- JTabbedPane—Contains multiple widgets but shows only one at a time. Users can easily switch from one child widget to another.

- JToolBar—Holds a group of widgets (usually buttons) in a row or column, optionally allowing users to drag the tool bar to different locations.

- JLayeredPane—Allows windows of child widgets to overlap. Each child widget is given a *depth* (an integer) setting. A child with a higher depth can cover another with a lower depth when necessary.

Other intermediate containers include JDesktopPane, JInternalFrame, and JRootPane (Section 8.13).

A container, top-level or intermediate, has methods for setting the layout manager (setLayout) and adding (add) and removing (remove) child widgets. After adding or removing child widgets, a container needs validating (validate) to compute the sizes and locations of child widgets. The validate() call also recursively validates any child that is a container. By calling pack() you validate a top-level container and set its size to be just enough to accomodate the child widgets. Alternatively, you can call setSize(w,h) first to set the size of a top-level container and then call validate() explicitly.

A Toy GUI

As an example of adding widgets into containers and having them interact, let's build a GUI for a pocket calculator. It is a toy GUI (Figure 8.2) because it has only these elements:

- Numeric keys 1, 2, and 3
- A clear-display key C
- A display window

To further simplify the example, we will not interface this GUI to the pocket calculator simulation discussed in Section 3.7. Completing the GUI and integrating it with the calculator program is left as a programming exercise.

The design of this toy GUI (Figure 8.3) calls for three classes:

1. The Keypad widget to supply the keys for operating the calculator

Figure 8.2   A TOY GUI

Figure 8.3   TOY GUI DESIGN

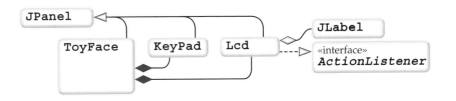

   2. The Lcd widget to display input and results

   3. The ToyFace class that puts items 1 and 2 together

```
class Keypad extends JPanel
{  Keypad(ActionListener f)
   {  c = new JButton("C");                                      // (1)
      c.setVerticalTextPosition(JButton.CENTER);                 // (2)
      c.setHorizontalTextPosition(JButton.CENTER);               // (3)
      c.setActionCommand("clear");                               // (4)
      c.addActionListener(f);                                    // (5)
      add(c);                                                    // (6)

      for (int i=3; i > 0; i--)
      {  b[i-1] = new JButton(""+i);                             // (7)
         b[i-1].setVerticalTextPosition(JButton.CENTER);         // (8)
         b[i-1].setHorizontalTextPosition(JButton.CENTER);       // (9)
         b[i-1].setActionCommand(""+i);                          // (10)
         b[i-1].addActionListener(f);                            // (11)
         add(b[i-1]);                                            // (12)
      }
   }

   protected JButton c;
   protected JButton[] b = new JButton[3];
}
```

The Keypad is a JPanel whose constructor adds a clear button c (lines 1 and 6) and three numeric buttons b[0] through b[2] (lines 7 and 12). A JPanel uses the *flow layout* (Section 8.11) in which child widgets are placed left to right in a row as they are added.

   The JButton constructor is given the text to appear on the button (lines 1 and 7). The text on each button is centered horizontally and vertically (lines 2, 3, 8, and 9).

   Inherited from the SwingConstants interface, the static constants CENTER, TOP, and BOTTOM indicate vertical text positioning and the constants RIGHT, CENTER, and LEFT indicate horizontal positioning. By default, text on a JButton centers vertically and right-adjusts horizontally. Thus lines 2 and 8 are not necessary.

   Clicking a button sends an action event, carrying its *action command* (lines 4 and 10), to the registered action listener (lines 5 and 11).

   In this example, the action listener is an Lcd widget that can display user input and computed results.

```
class Lcd extends JPanel implements ActionListener
{  Lcd(int size)
   {  MAX = size;
```

```
        setBorder(BorderFactory.createCompoundBorder        // (A)
        ( BorderFactory.createLoweredBevelBorder(),
          BorderFactory.createEmptyBorder(5,10,5,10))));
        d = new JLabel(in, JLabel.RIGHT);                    // (B)
        setLayout(new BorderLayout());
        add(d, BorderLayout.CENTER);
        clear();
    }

// methods later ...

    protected String in = "0";      // initial display
    protected int count=0;          // number of digits
    protected static int MAX;       // max digits
    protected JLabel d;

// HTML coded strings
    protected String hl= "<html><p align=right>" +          // (C)
            "<font color=blue size=+1><tt><b>";
    protected String ht="</font></b></tt></p></html>";      // (D)
}
```

Lcd is a JPanel with a *compound border* (line A) made of an outside border beveled to appear lowered and an inside border for margins on the four sides. Within the compound border sits a lone child, JLabel (line B), used to display calculator input and results.

The clear() method sets the input digit count to zero, and the display to the initial HTML text (lines C, D, and E):

```
protected void clear()
{   count=0;  in = "0";
    d.setText(hl+in+ht);     // (E)
}
```

Lcd is also an ActionListener and implements the actionPerformed method to handle incoming events. Depending on the button clicked, the action is either clearing or constructing the display. Overflow of the display window is avoided by checking the maximum number of digits allowable (line F):

```
public void actionPerformed(ActionEvent e)
{   String cmd = e.getActionCommand();
    if ( cmd.equals("clear") )
        clear();
    else if ( count < MAX )   // (F)
    {   if ( count == 0 )
            in = cmd;
```

```
        else
            in += cmd;
        d.setText(hl+in+ht);
        count++;
    }
}
```

ToyFace stacks a Keypad and an Lcd in a single-column grid layout (line G), giving them the same width, and the main method displays a ToyFace in the usual manner:

```
public class ToyFace extends JPanel
{   public ToyFace()
    {   lcd = new Lcd(13);
        keypad = new Keypad(lcd);
        setLayout(new GridLayout(0, 1));        // (G)
        add(lcd);
        add(keypad);
    }

    protected Lcd lcd;
    protected Keypad keypad;

    public static void main(String[] args)
    {   JFrame win = new JFrame("ToyFace");
        win.addWindowListener(new WindowHandler(win));
        ToyFace cf = new ToyFace();
        win.setContentPane(cf);
        win.pack();                             // (H)
        win.setVisible(true);
    }
}
```

The pack() method (line H) sets the size of the top-level window (win) based on the layout and the sizes of child widgets.

In summary, the ToyFace example illustrates the following:

- Creating a GUI by organizing widgets into intermediate containers

- Putting borders on windows

- Implementing the ActionListener interface for a widget

- Nontrivial layout of widgets

- Usage of the classes JButton, JPanel, JLabel, JFrame, and BorderFactory

8.6 ATOMIC WIDGETS

Swing offers a collection of widgets to perform various user interface functions. These widgets are *atomic* because they are self-sufficient and cannot contain other widgets. Part of learning Swing and GUI programming is to get to know these widgets and how to put them to use. Some widgets are displayed in Figure 8.4. For a complete visual index of Swing widgets visit:

`java.sun.com/docs/books/tutorial/uiswing/components/components.html`

A set of frequently used atomic widgets is introduced here. Widgets for user input with the mouse include the following:

- Buttons—JButton creates a simulated *pushbutton*. The button label is a string (plain text or HTML) and/or image icon. The button has an *action command string* set by setActionCommand. Clicking the button invokes the actionPerformed call-back method of any listeners registered with the button by addActionListener. The ActionEvent passed to actionPerformed contains the action command string.

- Checkboxes—A JCheckBox object displays a label with a checkbox in front. You check or uncheck the box by clicking it with the mouse. Each checkbox in a group is checked and unchecked independently. Users may check all boxes that apply in a given situation. For example, you can ask people to check all sports they like. A Checkbox invokes the itemStateChanged call-back method of listeners registered by addItemListener.

- Pop-up choices—A JComboBox presents choices in a space-saving format. An uneditable combo box looks like a button. When the user presses or clicks it, a menu of choices appears. An editable JComboBox allows the user to choose or enter a value.

- Radio buttons—A JRadioButton object displays a label with a selection circle in front. You create several radio buttons and add them to the

Figure 8.4   SOME SWING WIDGETS

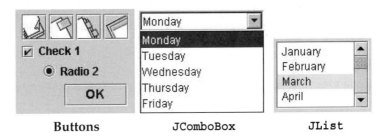

Buttons   JComboBox   JList

same `ButtonGroup` object. Only one button in the group can be selected. Selecting one radio button automatically deselects all others in the group. Clicking a radio button invokes the `actionPerformed` call-back method of any listeners registered by `addActionListener`.

- Selection lists—A `JList` presents users with a group of items, displayed in a column, from which to choose. Lists can have many items, so they are often put in scroll panes. Because of this, `JList` is a scrolling-savvy class. You can set up a list to allow the user to choose multiple items or only one item. An item is selected or unselected by clicking the mouse over it. Selecting an item invokes the `valueChanged` call-back method, passing a `ListSelectionEvent` object, of any listeners registered by `addListSelectionListener`. The `getSelectedIndex` and `getSelectedValue` (`getSelectedIndexes` and `getSelectedValues`) methods of `JList` return the selected index and value object (indices and value objects).

- Sliders—A `JSlider` lets users choose one of a continuous range of values.

- Trees—A `JTree` displays hierarchical data, such as files and folders, for users to choose.

Widgets for displaying information include the following:

- Labels—A `JLabel` presents text, an icon, or both. An `ImageIcon` is created from a `GIF` or `JPEG` file identified by a local file name or a URL.

- Progress bars—`JProgressBar` and `JProgressMonitor` display progress toward a goal to give users feedback while waiting for a task to complete.

- Tables—A `JTable` displays data in a flexible grid format.

- Tool tips—The `JComponent` method `setToolTipText("string")` sets up a small text label that appears briefly, to inform the user, when the mouse cursor lingers over a widget's window.

A Radio Button Group

A group of radio buttons allows users to select one, and only one, of several choices given. As a simple example, let's write a `RadioGroup` class that makes the choice, smoker or nonsmoker, available (Figure 8.5).

Figure 8.5   GROUP OF RADIO BUTTONS

RadioGroup is a panel that contains two RadioButton widgets (lines 1 and 2) in a flow layout (line 5). The buttons are independent until they are added to the same ButtonGroup object (lines 3 and 4). The button j1 is marked as initially selected (line 1). The selection field is updated when a radio button is clicked (line 6).

```java
///////    RadioGroup.java    ///////
import java.awt.*;
import java.awt.event.*;
import javax.swing.*;

public class RadioGroup extends JPanel
{  public RadioGroup()
   {    selection="Nonsmoker";
        j1= new JRadioButton(selection, true);          // (1)
        j2= new JRadioButton("Smoker");                 // (2)
        Font f = new Font("TimesRoman", Font.BOLD, 16);
        j1.setFont(f);    // font for radio button
        j2.setFont(f);
        j1.addActionListener( new ActionHandler() );
        j2.addActionListener( new ActionHandler() );
        bgp.add(j2);                                    // (3)
        bgp.add(j1);                                    // (4)

        this.setLayout(manager);                        // (5)
        this.add(j1);
        this.add(j2);
   }

   private final class ActionHandler
         implements ActionListener
   {    public void actionPerformed(ActionEvent e)      // (6)
        {    registerSelection(e); }
   }

   private void registerSelection(ActionEvent e)
   {    selection = e.getActionCommand();
   }

   public String getSelection()
   {    return selection; }

   private String selection;
   private JRadioButton j1, j2;
   private ButtonGroup bgp = new ButtonGroup();
```

```
        private LayoutManager manager = new FlowLayout();
}
```

Clicking a radio button sends the default action command that is the string label of the button. The getSelection method of RadioGroup returns the current selection kept in the selection field.

We will use RadioGroup in the GUI for a term life premium calculator presently. The RadioGroup class also serves as a template for writing radio button groups. An exercise (RadioGroup) shows how RadioGroup can be generalized to supply an arbitrary set of radio buttons.

Fonts for Widgets

The RadioGroup class sets the font for the buttons. In general, you can use the setFont method to set the font used for a widget. Java supports various fonts, depending on the implementation, but the following fonts should be available:

```
Default     Dialog      Symbol        Courier
Serif       SansSerif   Monospaced
```

The constructor

```
Font(String name, int style, int pt)
```

creates a font with the indicated name, style, and point size (pt). Bit constants

```
Font.BOLD      Font.ITALIC      Font.PLAIN
```

are used alone or in combination to indicate a desired style. The deriveFont method of a Font object returns a new font by changing various font attributes such as size and sytle. The available font names can be obtained from your local graphics environment:

```
String[] names = GraphicsEnvironment.getLocalGraphicsEnvironment()
                                 .getAvailableFontFamilyNames();
Font[] fonts = GraphicsEnvironment.getLocalGraphicsEnvironment()
                                 .getAllFonts();
```

The method getAllFonts() returns an instance for every available font of one size.

8.7 TEXT INPUT WIDGETS

In addition to input with the mouse, textual input via the keyboard is often needed. Several widgets help with keyboard input:

- Single-line text fields—JTextField extends JTextComponent and supports the entering and editing of a single line of plain text (Figure 8.6). The code

  ```
  new JTextField(str, col)
  ```

  creates a TextField object with the initial text *str* and a window width of *col* columns. Both arguments are optional. After entering and editing the text, a user types RETURN (ENTER) in the text field window to trigger call-backs to ActionPerformed methods in registered action listeners. The JTextComponent method getText() retrieves the text.

- Text areas—JTextArea extends JTextComponent and offers a multiline area for entering, displaying, and editing text. Editing can be barred. The code

  ```
  new JTextArea(str, row, col)
  ```

  creates a *row* by *col* text area with an initial text *str*. Usually an external event, from a button, for example, is used to trigger an action on the text area. The JTextComponent method getText() retrieves the text. The append(*str*) method appends the given string to the end of the text in the text area.

Let's see how text input combines with other widgets to form an integrated GUI.

GUI for a Term Life Premium Calculator

As shown in Figure 8.7, our premium calculator GUI is composed of these widgets:

- Text labels: the title, the instructions, and the computed premium
- Text input fields: the age, the coverage amount
- Radio buttons: smoker or nonsmoker

Figure 8.6 `JTextField` **FOR USER INPUT**

Enter Coverage (25000 to 500000):

Figure 8.7   TERM LIFE CALCULATOR

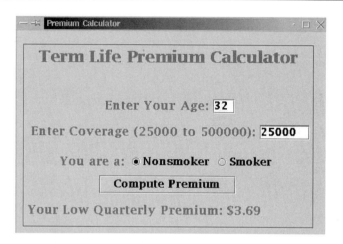

TermLife is a panel with a border (line 1) that arranges child widgets in a single-column grid layout (line 2). The title label (line 3) is on top, followed by a vertical spacer[1] (line 4), a sequence of input panels (line 5), and the computed premium (line 6) at the bottom.

```
public class TermLife extends JPanel
{   public TermLife()
    {   myBorder();                                      // (1)
        setLayout(new GridLayout(0,1));                  // (2)
        JLabel t = new JLabel(title, JLabel.CENTER);     // (3)
        add(t);
        add(Box.createRigidArea(new Dimension(0,10)));   // (4)
        setInputPanels();                                // (5)
        pl = new JLabel(resultStr);                      // (6)
        add(pl);
        nf=NumberFormat.getCurrencyInstance();
        nf.setMaximumFractionDigits(2);
    }

    private void myBorder()
    {   setBorder(BorderFactory.createCompoundBorder
        (   BorderFactory.createEmptyBorder(20, 10, 10, 20),
            BorderFactory.createLineBorder(Color.blue)
        ));
    }
```

---

[1]See Section 8.11.

```
// other members ...
}
```

For user input, a sequence of panels containing input widgets and instructions are used. These are set up by the setInputPanels method. The input
text fields for coverage (line 7) and age (line 8) display using 16-point boldface Courier font and are connected with appropriate event handlers (lines 9
and 10).

```
private void setInputPanels()
{ // age
    JPanel ip = new JPanel();
    ip.add(new JLabel(ageStr));
    ip.add(age_in = new JTextField(""+age, 3));
    add(ip);

  // coverage
    ip = new JPanel();
    ip.add(pl = new JLabel(coverageStr));
    ip.add(cov_in = new JTextField(""+coverage, 7));
    add(ip);
    Font g = new Font("Courier", Font.BOLD, 16);
    cov_in.setFont(g);                                       // (7)
    age_in.setFont(g);                                       // (8)
    cov_in.addActionListener(new CovHandler());              // (9)
    age_in.addActionListener(new AgeHandler());              // (10)

  // smoking status
    ip = new JPanel();
    Label label = new JLabel();
    label.setText(pickStr);
    ip.add(label);
    ip.add(rb = new RadioGroup());                           // (11)
    add(ip);

  // compute button
    ip = new JPanel();
    JButton comp = new JButton(" Compute Premium ");
    Font f = new Font("TimesRoman", Font.BOLD, 16);
    comp.addActionListener(new ButtonHandler());
    comp.setFont(f);
    ip.add(comp);
    add(ip);
}
```

The term life premium is lower for nonsmokers. The smoking status is
selected via a radio button group (line 11) already discussed in Section 8.6. A

button, with a 16-point bold Times Roman button label, triggers the premium computation through the `ButtonHandler`:

```
private final class ButtonHandler implements ActionListener
{  public void actionPerformed(ActionEvent e)
   {    if ( setAge(age_in.getText())  &&                    // (12)
              setCoverage(cov_in.getText()) )                // (13)
          displayPremium();
        else
          displayNoPremium();
   }
}

protected boolean setAge(String a)
{   age = Integer.parseInt(a);
    return (age > 0 && age < 71);
}

protected boolean setCoverage(String a)
{   coverage = Integer.parseInt(a);
    return (coverage >= 25000 && coverage <= 500000);
}

protected void displayPremium()                              // (14)
{    pl.setText(resultStr + " <font size=+1 color=green><b>" +
             nf.format(computePremium()) + "</b></font></html>");
}

protected String resultStr = "<html><font size=+1>" +
        "<b>Your Low Quarterly Premium:</b></font>";
protected String pickStr
   = "<html><font size=+1><b>You are a:</b></font></html>";
```

Note that the current text from the two text fields (lines 12 and 13) are obtained before the premium is computed and displayed in the locale-specific currency format (line 14) discussed already in Section 6.14.

The `setAge` and `setCoverage` methods are the *application event logic* called by event handlers. Later we'll see how these methods are improved to display error messages (Section 8.12).

The `main` method simply instantiates a `TermLife` object and calls the `go` method, which is reusable in many GUI programs:

```
public static void main(String[] args)
{   JFrame win = new JFrame("Premium Calculator");
    TermLife tml = new TermLife();
    tml.go(win);
}
```

```
protected void go(JFrame win)
{   win.setResizable(true);
    win.setContentPane(this);
    win.addWindowListener(new WindowHandler(win));
    win.pack();
    win.setVisible(true);
}
```

This example combines many atomic widgets and uses several intermediate containers to form the GUI. It also shows how text input, label, and button widgets cooperate to perform the task. The complete TermLife code can be found in the example package.

8.8 DRAWING CUSTOM GRAPHICS

To draw custom graphics or display images, you can extend a JPanel where you override the method

```
public void paintComponent(Graphics g)
```

to define how the window is drawn. In a paintComponent method, call super.paintComponent(g) (in JPanel) first to clear the background. The paintComponent() method is called automatically to draw a widget's window. A graphics window calls repaint() to register a redrawing request.

Let's look at an example of custom graphics.

A Parameterized Pie Chart

Consider displaying a pie chart. Based on input parameters specifying the title and percentage of each item, the chart displays the circular sections and corresponding labels with specified colors. This example demonstrates custom graphics with JPanel.

Figure 8.8 shows a simple pie chart. The object-oriented design (Figure 8.9) of the program is:

1. A PiePlot, subclass of JPanel, to draw the pie

2. A ColLabel vertical panel containing color-coded labels, each identifying a pie section

3. A PieChart (subclass of JPanel) to initialize and contain the previous two widgets

Figure 8.8   SIMPLE PIE CHART

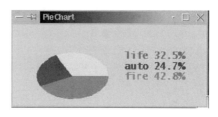

Figure 8.9   OO DESIGN OF PIE CHART

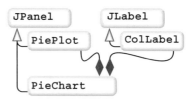

Class PiePlot

PiePlot is responsible for the actual drawing of the pie diagram. An object is initialized with the number of items n, an array of percentages perc, and a corresponding array of colors to use:

```
///////    PiePlot.java    ///////
import java.awt.*;
import javax.swing.*;

public class PiePlot extends JPanel
{ public PiePlot(int n, double[] perc, Color[] c)
   {   items = n; color = c;
       ang0 = new int[n];
       ang1 = new int[n];
       int start=0;
       for (int i=0; i < items; i++)
       {  if ( start >= 360 ) break;
          ang0[i] = start;
          ang1[i] = Math.max(2, (int)(360*perc[i]+0.5)); // (A)
          if ( start + ang1[i] > 360 )                   // (B)
             ang1[i] = 360 - start;
          start += ang1[i];
       }
   }
}
```

```
// other members ...
}
```

The constructor sets up two int arrays: starting angles in ang0 and section angles in ang1. Angles are in degrees. The angle of each pie section is converted from a percentage and rounded to the nearest degree (line A), but with a minimum of two degrees. The last pie section is treated properly (line B). The following fields are initialized:

```
protected int items;        // no. of sections
protected Color[] color;    // section colors
protected int[] ang0;       // starting angles
protected int[] ang1;       // section angles
```

The overriding paintComponent method computes the location (x0, y0), width (w), and height (h) of a rectangle that fits in the given display area. An elliptical pie diagram will be inscribed in this rectangle whose h/w equals the golden ratio (lines 1–3), by default. The pie diagram is centered horizontally but lowered vertically to leave some head room.

```
public void paintComponent(Graphics g) // override
{   super.paintComponent(g);    // paints background
    int wd = getWidth();
    int ht = getHeight();
    w = wd*4/5; h = (int)(w*ratio);                   // (1)
    if ( h > ht - 12 )                                // (2)
    {   h = ht - 12;
        w = (int)(h/ratio);                           // (3)
    }
    x0 = ( wd - w )/4;                        // left margin
    y0 = ht - h;                              // headroom
    for (int i=0; i < items; i++)
    {   g.setColor(color[i]);                         // (4)
        g.fillArc(x0, y0, w, h, ang0[i], ang1[i]);    // (5)
    }
}
```

```
protected double ratio = 0.62;      // golden ratio
protected int x0=0, y0=0, w=0, h=0; // area for oval pie
```

The method then draws each section of the pie in a for loop. The fillArc method (line 5) in the graphics context g draws a pie section of ang1[i] degrees, starting at ang0[i]. The positive X-axis is degree zero. The specified plot color is set in the graphics context (line 4).

Note that paintComponent calls super.paintComponent(g) (of JPanel) to clear the background. It also recomputes the location and size of the oval each time it is called. This is a good idea because the graphics must fit in the bounding window, whose size may change.

Class `ColLabel`

The `ColLabel` class is simply a `JLabel` with several lines of text, arranged in a vertical column and set in HTML (line 6). The constructor takes title strings (name) and background colors (`clr`) for the labels:

```
public class ColLabel extends JLabel
{  ColLabel(String[] name, String[] c)
   {  StringBuffer s = new StringBuffer(64);
      s.append("<html>");
      int items = name.length;
      for (int i=0; i < items; i++)
      {  s.append("<font face=courier color="          // (6)
            +c[i]+"><b>"+name[i]+"</b></font><br>");
      }
      s.append("</html>");
      this.setText(s.toString());
   }
}
```

Class `PieChart`

The application `PieChart` is parameterized and completely configurable with command-line arguments

java PieChart *item1 percent1 color1 . . .*

where each percentage is given as a floating-point number. For example:

java PieChart Life 0.3 green Auto 0.25 blue Fire 0.45 red

The percentages must add up to 100%. The `PieChart` constructor calls `treatArgs` to process the arguments (line A) and initialize the percentage, color, color name, and item name arrays. Then a `PiePlot` object (line B) and a `ColLabel` object (line C) are created. These are added in the `PieChart` panel under `BorderLayout` (line D), with the plot in the center (line E), and the labels to the right (line F). We also specify the `PieChart` margins on all four sides for a better layout (line G).

```
public class PieChart extends JPanel
{   public PieChart(String[] args)
    {   treatArgs(args);                                // (A)
        PiePlot p = new PiePlot(items, perc, clr);      // (B)
        ColLabel l = new ColLabel(name, cstr);          // (C)
        setLayout(new BorderLayout());                  // (D)
        add(p, BorderLayout.CENTER);                    // (E)
        add(l, BorderLayout.EAST);                      // (F)
        setBorder(BorderFactory.createEmptyBorder       // (G)
```

```
        (   30 /*top*/, 30 /*left*/,
            10 /*bottom*/, 30 /*right*/));
    }

    protected PieChart() {}

// other members ...
}
```

The `treatArgs` method takes the `args` array and initializes the number of items (`items`), the colors (`clr`), the percentages (`perc`), and the item names (`name`). The percentages are formatted (line H) correctly using `NumberFormat` (Section 6.14).

```
protected boolean treatArgs(String[] args)
{   items = args.length/3;
    clr = new Color[items];
    cstr = new String[items];
    perc = new double[items];
    name = new String[items];
    NumberFormat nf= NumberFormat.getPercentInstance();
    nf.setMaximumFractionDigits(2);
    int j=0;
    for (int i=0; i < items; i++)
    {   perc[i] = Double.parseDouble(args[++j]);
        name[i] = args[j-1] + " " + nf.format(perc[i]);   // (H)
        cstr[i]=arg[++j];
        clr[i] = whichColor(cstr[i],                       // (I)
            (i%2==0)?Color.gray:Color.white);
        j++;
    }
    return true;
}
```

The method `whichColor` (line I) takes a color name and a default color as arguments. It returns a color constant (e.g., `Color.red`) for the named color (e.g., `"red"`) if the color is found in class `Color`. Otherwise the default color is returned. The complete program can be found in the example package. Consult Appendix F for more information on colors in Java.

The `main` method in `PieChart` checks the command-line arguments, creates a `PieChart`, and runs it in the usual manner:

```
public static void main(String[] args)
{   if ( args.length == 0 || args.length%3 != 0 )
    {   System.err.println("Usage: PieChart " +
            "Life 0.3 green Fire 0.45 red ...");
        return;
    }
```

```
        PieChart chart = new PieChart(args);
        chart.go(new JFrame("PieChart"));
    }

    void go(JFrame win)
    {   win.setContentPane(this);
        win.addWindowListener(new
                WindowHandler(win));
        win.setSize(450, 200);          // (J)
        win.validate();                 // (K)
        win.setVisible(true);
    }
```

Note how we set the size of the top-level JFrame (line J) and then lay out the container[2] (line K). If pack() is used instead of setSize, the size of the container is set according to the layout and the preferred sizes of child widgets.

This program demonstrated a number of additional points:

- Overriding paintComponent
- Drawing custom graphics and using the graphics context
- Using HTML and setting fonts and colors in HTML
- Setting colors and applying the Color class

8.9 DRAWING SUPPORT

Widget Painting

A Swing GUI renders itself on the screen when the need arises to reflect a change in the display. For example, calling the setText method of a widget causes it to request repainting automatically. A widget can request painting by calling its repaint method. Painting starts from the top-level container, proceeds down the widget containment hierarchy, and is performed by the event handling thread. Swing uses double buffering—first painting to a memory buffer before showing the result on the screen. The size and location of widgets are determined automatically. A widget can call revalidate() explicitly to recompute widget sizes and locations for the next repaint.

A Swing widget can be opaque or transparent. If a widget is not opaque, then it paints only a subset of pixels in its display area, typically the foreground. Hence, the parent window shows through the background of a transparent child. Most Swing widgets under standard look and feel are opaque by default. You can check the opaqueness by calling the isOpaque() method and set it using the setOpaque(boolean) method.

---

[2]See Section 8.11.

When a JComponent is painted, this sequence is followed:

1. If the widget is opaque, its background is painted.
2. Any custom painting, defined by its overriding paintComponent method, is done.
3. Borders, if any, are painted.
4. Child widgets, if any, are painted.

Custom Painting

Standard atomic widgets know how to render themselves according to the look and feel in force at the time. If you subclass a widget and override its paintComponent method, you can give it a custom look. For displaying application-specific graphics or multiple images, use JPanel and define the rendering by overriding its paintComponent method.

The drawing of Swing widgets is controlled by the Java GUI environment, which sequences and executes all drawing requests (Figure 8.10). Three member methods are involved in the drawing of a Swing widget:

1. paintComponent—This method draws the widget. Standard widgets, such as buttons and menus, have well-defined paintComponent methods. Custom widgets, such as panels and applets, override

   ```
   public void paintComponent(Graphics g)
   ```

   to custom draw themselves.
2. repaint—A widget calls repaint to register a drawing request to update the appearance of the widget:

   - repaint()—requests the redrawing of the whole component.
   - repaint(long *tm*)—requests the redrawing of the whole component within *tm* milliseconds.

Figure 8.10   GUI DRAWING CONTROL MECHANISM

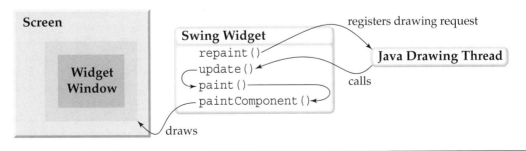

- repaint(int x, int y, int w, int h)—requests the redrawing of the specified rectangle in the component.
- repaint(long *tm*, int x, int y, int w, int h)—request the redrawing of the specified rectangle within *tm* milliseconds.

Certain methods such as setText for a label will invoke repaint() automatically.

3. update—Java calls a widget's update(Graphics g) method in response to a repaint request. The update method is called with a *graphics context* object, an instance of Graphics, which defines the environment within which drawing takes place. The graphics context object carries important attributes such as foreground color, background color, font, and display area on the screen. The built-in JComponent update calls paint(g) without clearing the display area first.

The paint method of a Swing widget delegates the painting job to three protected methods: paintComponent, paintBorder, and paintChildren. If the *look and feel delegate* is set, paintComponent calls the delegate's paint method to perform the rendering. In a JPanel, for example, you can override paintComponent to perform custom painting, as demonstrated in Section 8.8.

The paintComponent method draws in its *display area*. The location and dimensions of the display area are usually determined dynamically by its *parent container*, using well-defined layout policies (Section 8.11). Hence the parent can set the location and size of its child widgets to realize certain layouts. The upper-left corner of a widget's drawing area (Figure 8.11) always has coordinate $(0, 0)$. The current display area dimensions are obtained by calling the JComponent methods:

```
getWidth()      // display area width in pixels
getHeight()     // display area height in pixels
```

Figure 8.11   WINDOW DRAWING AREAS

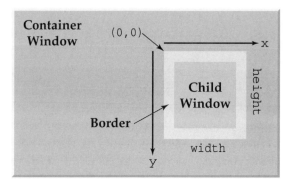

Because a Swing widget may have a border, the actual painting area is reduced by the size of the border. Make sure a widget paints only within its drawing area. Use the following code in paintComponent to determine the drawing area:

```
Insets insets = getInsets();
int width = getWidth() - insets.left - insets.right;
int height = getHeight() - insets.top - insets.bottom;
```

A drawing method, such as paintComponent, receives a Graphics argument, which supplies the graphics context. Actual drawing is performed with the given graphics context object. A Graphics object:

- Stores a graphics context as part of its state
- Provides methods to set and examine the current graphics context
- Supplies methods to perform drawing within the graphics context

The class Graphics provides many useful drawing methods: drawString, drawArc, drawLine, drawRect, draw3DRect, drawRoundRect, drawOval, drawPolygon, drawImage, and more. See the Graphics API documentation for details.

As usual with computer graphics, coordinates in drawing requests use pixel counts. The origin (0, 0) is the upper-left corner of the current drawing area. *X* increases to the right, and *Y* increases downward (Figure 8.11).

Java 2D is a flexible and full-featured rendering package. For example, the Graphics2D class can render virtually any two-dimensional geometric shape. With Java 2D, you can also draw styled lines of any width and fill geometric shapes with desired texture. For Swing code, the graphics context reference g passed into update, paint, and paintComponent is actually of type Graphics2D, a subclass of the basic Graphics class. When overriding paintComponent, for example, you can simply cast the reference into type Graphics2D immediately after receiving it

```
Graphics2D g2 = (Graphics2D) g;
```

and then use g2 to access Java 2D features.

Displaying Images

JFC supports images in GIF, JPEG, and PNG formats. To display images follow these steps:

1. Instantiate an Image object. This can be done in a number of ways including:

```
Image pic = Toolkit.getDefaultToolkit()
                .createImage(filename or URL);   (in an application)
Image pic = getImage(URL);                        (in an applet)
```

2. Draw an image inside the paintComponent method with a Graphics (or Graph2D) object g:

```
g.drawImage(Image img, int x, int y, int width, int height,
            ImageObserver observer);
```

The call draws the given image img inside the specified rectangle, scaling the image to fit if necessary. The ImageObserver parameter indicates the widget that draws the image.

Because image files tend to be large, Java decouples image loading and image drawing by loading the file in a separate thread (See Section 11.15).

In Swing, labels and buttons, for example, can include images as well as text. For such purposes, you use ImageIcon objects instantiated, among other ways, by giving the ImageIcon constructor a file name or a URL.

8.10   RAISED PIE CHART

Let's improve the simple pie chart (Section 8.8) by allowing users to select an item and identify the corresponding pie section (Figure 8.12). Here is the object-oriented design (Figure 8.13):

Figure 8.12   INTERACTIVE PIE CHART

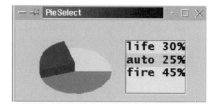

Figure 8.13   OO DESIGN OF INTERACTIVE PIE CHART

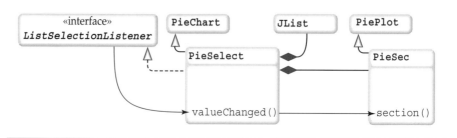

1. Use a selection list (JList), instead of a label, to allow the selection of one item at a time. Do this by writing PieSelect as a subclass of the PieChart.

2. *Raise* the identified pie section by increasing its thickness in response to an *item-selected* event. Do this by writing PieSec as a subclass of PiePlot.

Figure 8.12 shows the improved pie chart. The example demonstrates:

- Setting up JList objects
- Handling the list selection event
- Implementing a ListSelectionListener
- Animating the raising of a pie section
- Adding features to a program through class extension

Class PieSec

The PieSec class extends PiePlot and records the *selected pie section* (indexed by sec). The selected section stands out because a number of pixels are added in the negative-*Y* direction. The pie is redrawn every time the raised section changes (method section).

```
public class PieSec extends PiePlot
{    public PieSec(int n, double[] perc, Color[] c, int r)
     {    super(n, perc, c);
          if (r>0) rise = r;    // raise r pixels
     }

     protected PieSec() { }

     public void section(int i)
     {    if ( sec != i && i >= 0 && i < items )
          {    sec = i;
               repaint();
          }
     }

 // other methods ...

     int sec=0, rise = 12;
}
```

The paintComponent method first calls

```
super.paintComponent(g)
```

of PiePlot to draw the base pie chart (line 1). Then it computes a *shaded color* (line 2) for the target section, indexed by sec. The target section is raised by drawing repeatedly, with the shaded color, in consecutive *y* positions (lines 3–4). Finally, the top surface of the raised section is drawn in the original color, giving the intended visual effect (lines 5–6).

```
public void paintComponent(Graphics g)   // override
{   super.paintComponent(g);                                  // (1)
    Color t = color[sec];
    color[sec] = shaded(t, 0.8);                              // (2)
    int j = Math.min(y0, rise);
    g.setColor(color[sec]);                                   // (3)
    for (int i=1; i < j; i++)                                 // (4)
    {   g.fillArc(x0, y0-i, w, h, ang0[sec], ang1[sec]); }
    g.setColor(color[sec]=t);                                 // (5)
    g.fillArc(x0, y0-j, w, h, ang0[sec], ang1[sec]);          // (6)
}
```

The method shaded darkens a given color c by a percentage s:

```
public Color shaded(Color c, double s)
{   return new Color( (int)(s*c.getRed()), (int)(s*c.getGreen()),
                      (int)(s*c.getBlue()) );
}
```

Class PieSelect

PieSelect extends the existing PieChart and also performs as a list selection event listener. After the argument strings are processed (line a), a PieSec object is created. Section 0 is raised in the beginning (line b). A single-selection JList (lines c and d) is created, listing all items for the pie chart. The selection list font and background are given (line e), and the initial selection is set to the first item (line f). The JList is placed as the *view* in a scroll pane just in case it is a long list (line g). The view of a scroll pane (lp) can be changed by this call:

```
lp.getViewport().setView(wid);
```

The host object is registered as a selection listener on the JList (line h).

```
public class PieSelect extends PieChart
            implements ListSelectionListener
{ public PieSelect(String[] args)
   {  treatArgs(args);                                        // (a)
      p = new PieSec(items, perc, clr, 0);
      p.section(0);                                           // (b)
      setBorder(BorderFactory.createEmptyBorder
      ( 30 /*top*/, 30 /*left*/, 10 /*bottom*/, 30 /*right*/));
      setLayout(new BorderLayout());
```

```
    l = new JList(name);                                        // (c)
    l.setSelectionMode(ListSelectionModel.SINGLE_SELECTION); // (d)
    l.setFont(new Font("Courier", Font.BOLD, 16));
    l.setBackground(Color.cyan);                               // (e)
    l.setSelectedIndex(0);                                     // (f)
    JScrollPane lp = new JScrollPane(l);                       // (g)
    l.addListSelectionListener(this);                          // (h)
    add(p, BorderLayout.CENTER);
    add(lp, BorderLayout.EAST);
  }

 // other methods ...

  protected JList l;
  protected PieSec p;
}
```

A JList allows the selection of a single item by default. To allow multiple items, use:

```
// to allow one contiguous section
list.setSelectionMode(ListSelectionModel.SINGLE_INTERVAL_SELECTION);
// to place no restrictions on selection
list.setSelectionMode(ListSelectionModel.MULTIPLE_INTERVAL_SELECTION);
```

When selecting items, a left-click starts a new selection; a control-left-click adds an item to the selection.

The JList fires a ListSelectionEvent event if an item is clicked. To implement the ListSelectionListener interface, define the valueChanged method as follows:

```
public void valueChanged(ListSelectionEvent e)
{   if (e.getValueIsAdjusting()) return;  // ignore transient events
    if ( ! l.isSelectionEmpty())                    // (i)
    {   p.section(l.getSelectedIndex()); }      // (j)
}
```

For a finalized selection, make sure something is selected (line i) and then call the section method of PieSec with the selected index (line j).

The main method is as expected:

```
public static void main(String[] args)
{   if ( args.length == 0 || args.length%3 != 0 )
    {   System.err.println("Usage: PieSelect Life 0.3 green " +
                        "Fire 0.45 red ...");
        return;
    }
    PieSelect sel = new PieSelect(args);
```

```
        sel.go(new JFrame("PieSelect"));
}
```

This example also shows how to retrieve a selected item from a `JList`, create custom `Color` objects, and use class extension to make the improving of code easy and straightforward.

8.11 LAYOUT MANAGEMENT

An important aspect of GUI programming is achieving a desired appearance for the user interface. *Layout* refers to the positioning and sizing of child windows inside a containing window. *Layout management* is the process of determining the layout. Java allows you to take either of these two approaches:

1. Automatic layout—Use a *layout manager* to determine the layout automatically.
2. Manual layout—Use no layout manager; specify the position and size of each widget window explicitly.

Each container widget comes with a default layout manager. For example, `JPanel` uses `FlowLayout`, and the content pane of a `JFrame` uses `BorderLayout`, by default. These are likely the containers most often used. The command

```
container.setLayout(layout-manager);
```

sets the layout manager for a `container` to one that is *acceptable*. For example, `JScrollPane` accepts only `ScrollPaneLayout`. If the `layout-manager` given is `null`, automatic layout is disabled.

Manual Layout

A container with a `null` layout manager will not manage the location or size of its child widgets. To perform manual layout (or absolute positioning) you take the following steps:

1. Set the layout manager to `null` for the container.
2. Add child widgets to the container.
3. Use the `setSize(width, height)` (`setBounds(x0, y0, w, h)`) method of each widget to specify its size (location and size).

Manual layout is usually not recommended, because it responds poorly to the resizing of top-level windows and system differences.

Automatic Layout

In automatic layout, a layout manager enforces a particular layout policy. You have to take the layout manager into account when adding child widgets to a container. For example, the order in which widgets are added is important for FlowLayout and GridLayout. For BorderLayout, an additional position argument to add is needed. Child widgets can provide size and alignment hints to layout managers, but layout managers decide the actual size and position of each child widget in the final layout.

With automatic layout, a child widget cannot directly specify its size or location. Thus, methods such as setSize and setBounds don't work. Instead a widget can specify its preferred, minimum, and maximum size to help the layout manager achieve a better layout. You can either use setPreferredSize, setMinimumSize, and setMaximumSize to set these sizes or override the methods getPreferredSize, getMinimumSize, and getMaximumSize in a subclass. If a size hint is not provided by a widget, the look and feel in effect can supply that information.

Java supplies five common layout managers: BorderLayout, BoxLayout, FlowLayout, GridLayout, and GridBagLayout. The special CardLayout is for multiple views of the same window. Appendix E describes these layout managers in some detail.

Currently, only BoxLayout pays attention to the maximum size information. BoxLayout is also the only layout manager that uses the alignment hints provided by the

```
setAlignmentX      setAlignmentY
getAlignmentX      getAlignmentY
```

methods of widgets. For example,

```
JLabel lb = new JLabel("Example", JLabel.CENTER);
lb.setAlignmentX(Component.CENTER_ALIGNMENT);
```

tells BoxLayout to center the label lb horizontally when placing it with other widgets in a vertical column.

Computing Layout

Let's describe how automatic layout is done with layout managers. The size of a top-level window (e.g., JFrame) is either *set explicitly* (with setSize) or *computed automatically* (with pack()) through the preferred sizes of its child widgets.

After adding all child widgets, setting borders, and setsize(...) for the top-level window (top), call top.validate() to compute the size and location of child widgets (i.e., to recursively lay out child widgets). At any time, a widget is either *validated* (layout computed) or *invalidated* (layout needs to be computed). A validated widget can become invalidated if its size changes, a child widget it contains is invalidated, or its invalidate() method is called.

If you do not want to set top to some fixed size, you may call top.pack() instead of top.validate(). Packing a window means setting the window size depending on its layout manager and the preferred sizes of its child widgets.

The position of a top-level window can be set independently with the setLocation method. A JFrame is by default resizable. In any case, resizing can be enabled and disabled with setResizable(*boolean*).

Based on the understanding of layout management presented here, we can review the instance method go again as a template for starting a Swing application. The method go uses instance variables such as packing and sizing to perform correctly.

```
void go(JFrame win)     // main calls go to start GUI
{   win.setContentPane(this);
    win.addWindowListener(new WindowHandler(win));
    win.setResizable( resize );
    if ( location ) win.setLocation(x0, y0);

    if ( packing ) win.pack();        // packing or
    else if ( sizing )                // set explicit size
    {   win.setSize(width, height);
        win.validate();
    }
    win.setVisible(true);
}
```

Spacing between Widgets

For a visually pleasing layout, it is often important to add spacing between displayed windows. Three factors affect the amount of space between windows:

1. The layout manager—Some, but not all, layout managers put space automatically between widgets.
2. Empty borders—You can affect the space between windows by adding empty borders to widgets. This works best for widgets such as panels and labels, which normally have no borders.
3. Invisible components—You can create lightweight components that perform no painting but can take up space in the GUI. Often you use invisible components in containers controlled by BoxLayout.

The class Box has a nested Box.Filler class that supplies invisible components used to provide spacing for layouts. Convenience methods in the Box class help create common fillers:

- Box.createRigidArea(*dimension*)—An invisible widget with the given size.
- Box.createHorizontalGlue()—A *horizontally stretchable* widget to take up any excess horizontal spacing in the layout. Put one of these at the beginning of a row of widgets, for example, and the visible widgets will be right-adjusted. Put one between two widgets and they will be pushed to the left and right as far as possible.
- Box.createVerticalGlue()—A *vertically stretchable* widget that takes up any excess vertical spacing in the layout.
- Box.Filler(*minSize*, *prefSize*, *maxSize*)—A custom-specified filler widget.

Figure 13.8 shows an example of BoxLayout and spacing control.

8.12 USING DIALOGS

A *dialog* is a widget with a *pop-up* window for displaying dynamically generated information for user acknowledgement, confirmation, or approval. In addition, a dialog can also obtain more complicated user input. In Swing the JOptionPane class provides easy-to-use static methods for displaying common dialogs.

Supported by a special top-level container, a dialog is attached to a *parent frame*. When displayed, the dialog window pops up over the frame. If a frame is iconified, its dependent dialogs also disappear from the screen. They reappear automatically as the frame is deiconified. A *modal dialog*, when displayed, blocks input to all other widgets in the same application. Hence the user must deal with the dialog before the application will proceed. Dialogs created by JOptionPane methods are modal. Nonmodal dialogs can be created by using JDialog directly.

A GUI program normally uses dialogs, instead of standard I/O, to display error, alert, and other informational messages to users. The errorDialog method, placed in our MyUtil class, is convenient for displaying error messages.

```
public static void errorDialog(JFrame f, String msg)
{    JOptionPane.showMessageDialog(
        f,                          // attached frame
        msg,                        // message to display
        "Error Message",            // dialog title
        JOptionPane.ERROR_MESSAGE); // icon to display
}
```

The showMessageDialog method creates and displays a modal dialog attached to the given frame f, with the dialog window title set to Error Message. The dialog displays an error message icon, the specified string msg, and a default OK button. The pop-up dialog window disappears after the user clicks the OK button, and the showMessageDialog method returns a JOptionPane defined static integer value corresponding to the button clicked on the dialog. If the parent frame is given as null, a default frame is used as the parent, and the dialog is usually centered on the screen (depending on the look and feel).

Let's put MyUtil.errorDialog to use.

Premium Calculator with Error Dialog

In Section 8.7 we discussed a term life premium calculator (TermLife). The GUI collects the age and coverage amount with JTextField widgets. The setAge and setCoverage methods can be improved to better check the input and to display an appropriate error dialog when needed. Figure 8.14 shows an error dialog with a title, a message, an error icon, and an OK button. We can extend TermLife to make the improvement. The TermLifeDialog class shows how easily well-designed OO programs can be improved through class extension, as well as how to use error dialogs.

```
public class TermLifeDialog extends TermLife
{   public TermLifeDialog(JFrame f)
    {   super();   frame=f;   }

    protected JFrame frame = null;

    public static void main(String[] args)
    {   JFrame win = new JFrame("Premium Calculator");
        TermLifeDialog tml = new TermLifeDialog(win);   // (1)
        tml.go(win);
    }
}
```

Figure 8.14   ERROR DIALOG

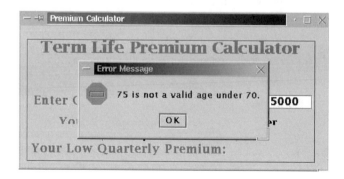

```
protected boolean setAge(String a)
{   try
    {   age = Integer.parseInt(a);
        if ( 0 < = age && age < 70 ) return true;    // (2)
    }   catch (NumberFormatException e) { }
    MyUtil.errorDialog(frame,                         // (3)
        a + " is not a valid age under 70.");
    return false;
}

protected boolean setCoverage(String a)
{   try
    {   coverage = Integer.parseInt(a);
        if ( coverage >= 25000 &&
             coverage <= 500000 ) return true;
    }   catch (NumberFormatException e) { }
    MyUtil.errorDialog(frame,
        a + " is not a valid coverage \n" +
        "between 25000 and 500000.");
    return false;
}
}
```

The `TermLifeDialog` is instantiated with a reference to its top-level frame (line 1). This reference is needed when attaching dialogs to it.

The `setAge` method is overridden to return `true` only when the input is a valid age 70 or under (line 2); otherwise it displays an error dialog (line 3) and returns false.

The `setCoverage` is done the same way. Because all event handlers in `TermLife` use the application event logic, namely the `setAge` and `setCoverage` methods, everything works.

Common Dialogs

`JOptionPane` provides these useful methods:

- Asking the user to confirm an operation:

```
showConfirmDialog(frame,        // parent frame or null
  message,                      // string
  title,                        // string
  JOptionPane.YES_NO_OPTION); // buttons
```

- Displaying an error or other message:

```
showMessageDialog(frame,        // parent frame or null
  message,
```

```
      title,
      JOptionPane.ERROR_MESSAGE); // error icon
```

- Showing a flexible dialog with customizable icons and texts for standard buttons:

```
Object[] options = { "OK", "CANCEL"};
showOptionDialog(frame,
  message,
  title,
  JOptionPane.DEFAULT_OPTION,    // buttons
  JOptionPane.WARNING_MESSAGE,   // warning icon
  null,                          // custom icon, if given
  options,                       // button text array
  options[0]);                   // default button designation
```

The option dialog is flexible enough to give you any confirm or message dialog.

- Displaying a dialog of items for user choice:

```
Object[] item = { "First", "Second", "Third" };
Object selectedValue =
  JOptionPane.showInputDialog(frame,
    message,
    title,
    JOptionPane.INFORMATION_MESSAGE,    // info icon
    null,                               // no custom icon
    item,                               // to choose from
    item[0]);                           // default choice
```

- Displaying a dialog to obtain an input string:

```
String inputValue =
  JOptionPane.showInputDialog("Please type your input");
```

The integer returned by these methods is one of YES_OPTION, NO_OPTION, CANCEL_OPTION, OK_OPTION, or CLOSED_OPTION. The last one indicates that the dialog window was closed without an option button being clicked.

Use an instance of JOptionPane to configure and manage other custom-designed dialogs, including nonmodal ones (see the API documentation for JOptionPane for details). In addition to JOptionPane, JFileChooser (for choosing a file interactively by browsing directories) and JColorChooser (for choosing a color from a palette) also supply standard dialogs.

8.13 USING MENUS

Menus are familiar GUI features that provide program controls and options for users. A menu is a widget that contains one or more *menu items*. Each menu item is either a selectable item (such as a button) or a submenu. A JMenu is usually added to a menu bar (JMenuBar) and is displayed when the menu title in the menu bar is clicked.

A popup menu (JPopupMenu) is independent of the menu bar and shows up when the mouse is right-clicked over a pop-up enabled widget. The right mouse click triggers an event-handling method that invokes the show method of a pop-up menu.

In Swing, a JFrame contains a JRootPane that has four parts:

1. The *layered pane*—Positions the content pane and the optional menu bar. (A JLayeredPane can hold overlapping child widgets in layers with different depths in the Z *direction*.)

2. The *content pane*—Holds and displays the frame's visible widgets, except the menu bar.

3. The *menu bar*—Holds menus. The menu bar is optional.

4. The *glass pane*—Is normally not visible and serves to monitor events for the frame.

When a menu bar (JMenuBar) is added to a JFrame, it usually appears just above the content pane. A JMenuBar may contain one or more menus:

```
JMenuBar bar = new JMenuBar();        // menu bar
frame.setMenuBar(bar);                // attaches menu bar to frame
JMenu opt = new JMenu("Options");     // menu title
bar.add(opt);                         // adds menu opt to menu bar
```

A menu may contain items and submenus for user selection. The method add puts an item (JMenuItem) or submenu (JMenu) into a menu. For example:

```
JMenuItem it = new JMenuItem("New Game");
                                      // menu item with string label
opt.add(it);                          // puts it on menu opt
```

Register an action listener, in the usual manner, to each menu item to respond to the user selection. Keyboard *mnemonics* and *accelerators* can be established to help access and speed menu operations.

Let's add a menu to control the Tic Tac Toe game (Figure 8.15):

• Add an Options menu in a menu bar.

• Provide an Unmove option.

• Provide a New Game option.

• Provide a choice among User First, Computer First, and User & Computer Alternate.

Figure 8.15   A MENU

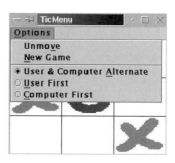

We'll do this by extending the the `TicUnMain` class, an application version of the Tic Tac Toe game (Section 7.10) with an additional *unmove* feature:

```
public class TicMenu extends TicUnMain
{  public TicMenu() { }

   protected void init()
   {   tic = new TicOption(o, x); }                        // (1)


   public static void main(String[] args)
   {   TicMenu tm = new TicMenu();
       tm.go(new JFrame("TicMenu"));                       // (2)
   }

// other methods ...

   protected static String u1 ="User First";
   protected static String c1 ="Computer First";
   protected static String uc ="User & Computer Alternate";
   protected ActionListener ah;
}
```

We override the `init` method to use a `TicOption` object (line 1), which extends `TicTacUn`, a `TicTacToe` object with an added unmove feature. The method `go` (line 2) sets up a `JFrame` to display the `TicOption` and a menu bar, as we desired.

The method `go` creates a menu bar (line 3), attaches it to a frame (line 4), instantiates the `Options` menu, with the ALT-o mnemonic and cyan background, and adds it to the menu bar (line 5). It then proceeds to create items in the menu (line 6), Unmove (mnemonic v) and New Game (mnemonic n), and associate the same action listener to each menu item.

```
public void go(JFrame win)
{ //Creates menu bar
    JMenuBar bar = new JMenuBar();                                // (3)
    win.setJMenuBar(bar);                                         // (4)

  //Creats menu                                                   // (5)
    JMenu opt = new JMenu("Options");
    opt.setMnemonic(KeyEvent.VK_O);
    opt.setBackground(Color.cyan);
    bar.add(opt);

  //Creates menu items                                            // (6)
    JMenuItem menuItem =new JMenuItem("Unmove", KeyEvent.VK_V);
    opt.add(menuItem);
    ah = new ActionHandler((TicOption)tic);
    menuItem.addActionListener(ah);

    menuItem = new JMenuItem("New Game", KeyEvent.VK_N);
    opt.add(menuItem);
    menuItem.addActionListener(ah);

    chooseFirst(opt);
    super.go(win);
}
```

The chooseFirst methods helps create a group of three radio button menu items to let users choose who goes first in the game:

```
protected void chooseFirst(JMenu menu)
{   menu.addSeparator();                                          // (7)
    ButtonGroup group = new ButtonGroup();

    JRadioButtonMenuItem rb = new JRadioButtonMenuItem(uc); // (8)
    group.add(rb);
    rb.setSelected(true);
    rb.setMnemonic(KeyEvent.VK_A);
    rb.addActionListener(ah);
    menu.add(rb);

    rb = new JRadioButtonMenuItem(u1);                            // (9)
    group.add(rb);
    rb.setMnemonic(KeyEvent.VK_U);
    rb.addActionListener(ah);
```

```
      menu.add(rb);

      rb = new JRadioButtonMenuItem(c1);                   // (10)
      group.add(rb);
      rb.setMnemonic(KeyEvent.VK_C);
      rb.addActionListener(ah);
      menu.add(rb);
}
```

A line separator is added to the menu (line 7). Then three radio button menu items (lines 8–10) are added, each with its keyboard mnemonic. These items all use the same action listener ah established earlier.

The inner class action handler implements the actionPerformed method, which checks the action command received and reacts by calling the appropriate event logic in TicMenu:

```
private final static class ActionHandler implements ActionListener
{  ActionHandler(TicOption p)
   {    op = p;   }

   public void actionPerformed(ActionEvent e)
   {    String cmd = e.getActionCommand();
        if      ( cmd.equals("Unmove") )   op.unMove();
        else if ( cmd.equals("New Game") ) op.newGame();
        else if ( cmd.equals(uc) ) op.setWhoFirst(op.ALTERNATE);
        else if ( cmd.equals(u1) ) op.setWhoFirst(op.USER);
        else if ( cmd.equals(c1) ) op.setWhoFirst(op.COMPUTER);
   }
   private TicOption op;
}
```

The TicOption class extends TicTacUn to add user control of who goes first. We add an instance field whoFirst and static fields for the options. The newGame() method is overridden to enforce who goes first for the next game:

```
/////// TicOption.java  ///////
import java.awt.Image;

public class TicOption extends TicTacUn
{  public TicOption(Image o, Image x)
   {    super(o, x);   }

   protected TicOption() {}

   protected void newGame()
   {    switch ( whoFirst )
        {    case USER:    first=false; break;
```

```
            case COMPUTER: first=true;
        }
        super.newGame();
    }

    public void setWhoFirst(int w)
    {   whoFirst = w;
        newGame();
    }

    protected int whoFirst=ALTERNATE;
    protected static final int ALTERNATE=0;
    protected static final int USER =1;
    protected static final int COMPUTER=2;
}
```

Again, sound OO programming with class extension allows us to add the menu feature to the Tic Tac Toe game simply and easily. The complete example, ready to compile and run, can be found in the example package.

Although keyboard mnemonics allow you to use the keyboard instead of the mouse to access a menu, they still involve displaying the menu and selecting the item. A keyboard accelerator, on the other hand, invokes the desired event of a menu item directly, with no menu display involved. We have seen mnemonics defined in the TicMenu example. Accelerators can be defined only for leave menu items. For example, to make ALT-n an accelerator for starting a new game, use

```
menuItem.setAccelerator(KeyStroke.getKeyStroke(
        KeyEvent.VK_N, ActionEvent.ALT_MASK));
```

where the KeyStroke object combines a key, given by a KeyEvent constant, and a modifier-key mask, specified by an ActionEvent constant.

8.14   EVENT-HANDLING NOTES

The event-handling code must return quickly to preserve the responsiveness of the GUI event-handling thread. Sometimes an event-handling method may need to run for a long time. In such situations, it ought to spawn another thread to take care of business and return itself quickly so that event handling can continue to function normally. Examples of such GUI applications can be found in Chapter 11.

As you may have noticed, event handling in Swing follows the delegation model presented in Section 7.9. Swing does introduce more event and event listener types to serve the variety of new widgets in the package.

Swing-introduced event types are in the `javax.swing.event` package. For example, the

```
ListSelectionEvent
```

used with `JList` in Section 8.10 is introduced by Swing. Other Swing events include `MenuEvent`, `PopupMenuEvent`, and `TreeSelectionEvent`.

Along with new event types come additional event listener interfaces. For example,

```
ListSelectionListener
```

which is used in Section 8.10. Currently there are few event adapters, and you handle events by implementing the methods required by a particular event listener. Each Swing widget type provides add-listener methods for the events it supports.

When handling keyboard events in Swing, be sure that the widget has keyboard focus. Otherwise the key events may not be delivered to your listeners. If you run into such a problem, these steps can usually help:

- Override the `isFocusTraversable` method of the event source widget to return `true`.
- Make the widget request keyboard focus explicitly when appropriate. For custom widgets, you can implement a mouse listener that calls `requestFocus` when the mouse is clicked over the widget.

8.15 APPLET-APPLICATION DUAL-PURPOSE PROGRAMS

There are differences between a GUI application and an applet, but the two are very similar. Many programs can run as either and can actually be programmed as one dual-purpose program.

To write an applet-application dual-purpose program, follow these ideas:

- Organize all of the widgets in the GUI with a `JPanel` (the *top panel*), which will serve as the `contentPane` of a top-level container.
- In the class that extends `JApplet`, place a `main` method for setting up the program to run as an application and an `init` method to initialize the program to run as an applet.
  The init method will:

  1. Execute applet-only operations such as `getCodebase` and `loadImage`
  2. Create an instance of *top panel* (TP), passing to a constructor any quantities from step 1 as arguments
  3. `setContentPane(TP);`

The `main` method will:

1. Execute application-only operations for initialization
2. Create an instance of *top panel* (TP), passing to a constructor any quantities from step 1 as arguments
3. Create a `JFrame` and set its content pane by `frame.setContentPane(TP);`
4. Pack and make the frame visible

If you don't organize all widgets in a panel, you can always add them all to the content pane of the top-level container (`JApplet` or `JFrame`) directly.

Applet-specific methods that require an applet context (a browser or an applet viewer) include:

```
getCodeBase
getParameter
getImage
getAudioClip
play
getDocumentBase
getAppletContext
```

GUI applications can use the code

```
Toolkit.getDefaultToolkit().createImage(file or URL);
```

to create images. Applications can also create `AudioClip`s by calling the static method

```
public static final AudioClip newAudioClip(URL r)
```

without requiring an `AppletContext`.

An application may have command-line arguments whereas an applet may have <param>-supplied arguments. Argument processing in a dual-purpose program can be simplified if a single <param> parameter supplies all necessary arguments in the same form as command-line arguments:

```
<param name="args"  value="arg1 arg2 ...">
```

As a concrete example, let's write a `TicDual` class that is an applet but also has a `main` and other methods to enable it to run as a stand-alone GUI application:

```
///////    TicDual.java    ///////
import java.awt.*;
import javax.swing.*;
import java.net.URL;

public class TicDual extends JApplet
```

```
{ public void init()           // for applet
  {   URL codeBase = getCodeBase();
      o = getImage(codeBase, "images/o.gif");
      x = getImage(codeBase, "images/x.gif");
      tic = new TicTacToe(o, x);
      setContentPane(tic);
  }

  protected void mainInit()  // for main
  {   tk = Toolkit.getDefaultToolkit();
      o = tk.createImage("images/o.gif");
      x = tk.createImage("images/x.gif");
      tic = new TicTacToe(o, x);
  }

  void go(JFrame win)           // for main
  {   win.addWindowListener(new WindowHandler(win));
      win.setContentPane(tic);
      win.setSize(300, 320);   // width, height
      win.validate();
      win.setVisible(true);
  }

  public static void main(String[] args)
  {   TicDual tm = new TicDual();
      tm.mainInit();
      tm.go(new JFrame("TicTacToe"));
  }

  protected Image x, o;
  protected TicTacToe tic = null;
  protected Toolkit tk = null;   // for main
}
```

8.16 SUMMARY

To write a GUI program, you set up a top-level container, add child widgets, arrange them in a desired layout, register listeners to connect events with handling logic, and go. With Swing, the top-level container is typically a JApplet for an applet or a JFrame for a stand-alone application. Using a JPanel to organize all widgets makes it simple to write applet-application dual-purpose programs.

Major artifacts in GUI programming are widgets, events, event handlers, layout managers, and graphics contexts.

Many types of widgets (components) supply well-defined UI functions. Swing widgets have additional features and important advantages over older AWT widgets and are recommended for writing new programs. Swing widgets include top-level containers (e.g., `JApplet` and `JFrame`), intermediate containers (e.g., `JPanel` and `JScrollPane`), and atomic widgets (e.g., `JLabel` and `JButton`). Additional event and listener types introduced by Swing are in the `javax.swing.event` package.

A container component can manage child components and enforce a designated layout policy. With automatic layout, child widgets can provide maximum, minimum, and preferred size information to guide the layout computation. Ultimately, the parent container decides the location and size of each child widget. The size of an intermediate container depends on the size and layout of its child widgets. The size of top-level windows can be set with `setSize` or determined by `pack()` to wrap tightly around child widgets.

To perform custom drawing, you use `JPanel` and override the `paintComponent` method and request redisplay by calling the `repaint()` method. The `Graphics` and `Graphics2D` classes provide many useful drawing and image-displaying methods.

Dialog boxes make special interactions with the user easy to handle. Menus on the menu bar enable easy user control of complicated applications. Swing and JFC have much more to offer. Chapter 7 and 8 get you started.

Materials on multithreaded GUI programming, image loading, and animation can be found in Chapter 11. The pluggable look and feel and the model-view-controller architecture of Swing are discussed in Chapter 13. For further information see the Java API documentation.

EXERCISES

Review Questions

1. What is a widget? An `AWT` widget? A Swing widget? In Java API documentation, what is the term used for widgets? What are the notable features of Swing widgets that make them more desirable than AWT widgets?

2. What is a top-level container? An intermediate container? An atomic widget? Explain the widget containment hierarchy.

3. What are the major differences, from an application viewpoint, between the AWT `Label` and the Swing `JLabel`?

4. What are the container widgets of Swing? Which containers can be at the top level? What default layout policies do they use?

5. What is the concept *keyboard focus*?

6. What Swing widget supports displaying data or images that do not easily fit in a window? What layout manager does JScrollPane use?

7. What are manual layout and automatic layout? What is the purpose of a layout manager? List and explain the available layout policies.

8. Why does the method setSize not work for a child widget? How does one provide layout hints for the size of a child widget? In what situation does setSize work?

9. How is the size of a top-level window determined? What is the difference between pack() and setSize?

10. How does one draw text in different fonts? What fonts does Java support?

11. What is the purpose of a JTextPane?

12. How does the PieChart application deal with unknown colors specified by command-line parameters?

13. What colors are available for Java GUI? How are colors named, represented, and manipulated? Explain the facilities offered in the class Color (see Appendix F).

Programming Assignments

1. (Bookmark-2) Refer to exercise *Bookmark-1* in Chapter 6. Use the MatchingLines class and add a GUI front end (a regular application) to the Bookmark program. A *str* pattern is entered interactively through a JTextField, and the matching URLs are displayed in a JList window.

2. (Bookmark-3) Improve the GUI Bookmark application of exercise *Bookmark-2* (above) and implement an additional Edit feature: (A) All lines from the bookmark file are displayed in an editable JTextArea window. (B) The user may edit existing lines, enter new lines, and save them back to the bookmark database.

3. (Tic-5) Write a new Tic Tac Toe program that displays a single TicTacToe button. Clicking the button displays a top-level window to play the game. Be sure to reuse as much code from the existing Tic Tac Toe as you can.

4. Add a tool tip "70 max" to the label and text field for age in the term life premium calculator program (Section 8.7).

5. (Term Life-4) Refer to exercise Term Life-3 in Chapter 6. Connect the premium calculator GUI (Section 8.7) to the term life calculator.

6. Improve the program in exercise Term Life-4, and add a `JSlider` to make it easier to see premiums for different insurance coverages.

7. (RadioGroup) Write a class `RadioGroup` where:
    - The constructor takes an array of strings as radio button titles and an optional layout manager.
    - The constructor initializes a group of `JRadioButtons`, using the given layout manager (default `FlowLayout`).
    - The first button is initially selected.
    - Each button click records the selection, using the button title.
    - The `public String selected()` method returns the current selection.

    How do you suppose this class is useful? Use `RadioGroup` to add selections to the premium calculator.

8. (Tic-A) Turn the Tic Tac Toe applet in Chapter 7 into an applet-application dual-purpose program.

9. (Tic-B) Take the program in exercise Tic-A and add an unmove button to it. (Hint: Use class extension.)

10. (Tic-C) Add different levels of difficulty to the program in exercise Tic-B, and present a menu that lets users set and change the level dynamically.

11. Write an application to play the game *Othello*. The program opens its own top-level window. Use an object-oriented approach so that similar board games can reuse much of the code.

12. Write an electronic puzzle. Use a picture image and tear it into a number of vertical strips, destroying two or three pixels along the irregular tear. Randomly order the vertical strips, and display them. The picture provides clues as to how to reorder the strips correctly. Add difficulty levels by increasing the number of strips, by reorienting some strips upside down, and by using two-sided pictures in which some of the strips can be flipped. Players use mouse operations to rearrange the displayed strips and solve the puzzle. A timer that enforces a deadline can add to the challenge. The program stops the timer as soon as the puzzle is solved.

13. Write a three-dimensional Tic Tac Toe game using a $3 \times 3 \times 3$ cubic space as its playing space.

## CHAPTER NINE

Generic Containers

A recurring task in programming involves building appropriate data structures to hold the items that are being manipulated. The design and efficient implementation of data structures have been the subject of computer science, and many data structures have emerged as being flexible and efficient in practice.

In OOP, a data structure that contains and organizes a collection of objects is known as a *container*. Arrays, lists, stacks, sets, trees, and hash tables are common containers. A container groups elements into a single unit for easy manipulation and transmission in method calls. Natural data units such as a guest registry, a telephone directory, a checkbook, and a grade sheet are examples of containers. A *generic container* can store data of any type, instead of only a fixed type, and is reusable in many different applications.

By supplying well-defined generic containers, Java makes many programming tasks much simpler. A container is characterized by its:

- Application programming interface (API)
- Internal data structuring and operations implementation

In Java, generic containers are called *collections* and are part of the *Java Collections Framework* in the `java.util` package. The collections framework provides a well-designed architecture to support the representation, manipulation, and interoperability of collections (generic containers). Two broad types of generic containers are available:

1. `Collection`—a container of data elements
2. `Map`—a container of key-value pairs

Five major components make up the Java Collections Framework:

1. Interfaces—The API definitions for the `Collection` (Figure 9.4) and `Map` (Figure 9.5) hierarchies. Containers conforming to the same interface are plug-compatible (Chapter 5) and therefore interchangeable in use.
2. Container Classes—Concrete classes defining sequenced (`List`), unsequenced (`Set`), and access-by-key (`Map`) containers that implement the interfaces. Different implementations for the same interface can provide containers efficient in different applications.
3. Conversions—Automatic conversions between compatible container types making it easy to send/receive containers within a program.

4. Iterators—Container-supplied *functors* (Section 9.7) allowing systematic visits to the stored elements.

5. Algorithms—Static methods implementing common operations such as searching and sorting to work with all compliant containers

General-purpose container classes defined in the collections framework include `ArrayList`, `LinkedList`, `HashSet`, `TreeSet`, `HashMap`, and `TreeMap`. A list represents elements in a linear sequence and allows duplicate elements. A set represents a group of distinct elements. A map is a collection of key-value pairs.

The collections framework, together with its classes and interfaces, is described and illustrated with practical examples. The material helps you understand the Java supplied containers and how to use them effectively in practice. You'll also be able to define your own containers that fit particular purposes while conforming to the collections framework. The framework architecture, design features, and implementation strategy give a concrete example of OO design and programming.

9.1   LISTS

Both `ArrayList` and `LinkedList` implement the `List` interface and represent a linear sequence of elements accessible by indexing. Elements can be of any type, can be duplicated, and can be `null`. An `ArrayList` uses a resizable array to hold the elements and is fast and efficient. It is a good choice in most applications in which a list or sequence is needed. Applications requiring frequent insert and delete operations at the beginning or in the middle of a very long list and, in the meantime, performing very few random-access (indexing) operations into the list may want to use a `LinkedList`, which stores elements in list cells. Because the `ArrayList` is so fast and efficient, it is advisable to measure program performance with both list types before deciding to go with a `LinkedList`.

An `ArrayList` is roughly equivalent to the legacy `java.util.Vector` class, which does not conform to the collections framework. For programming, it is recommended that you avoid `Vector` and use `ArrayList` instead.

To create a new `ArrayList`, use one of the following constructors:

`ArrayList ([int capacity])`—Constructs an empty list with the given initial capacity. The optional argument is non-negative or will cause an `IllegalArgumentException`.

`ArrayList (Collection c)`—Constructs a list containing the elements of the given container c, in the order induced by the iterator of c. The initial capacity of the list created is 1.1 × size of c.

Following is the set of basic operations for `ArrayList`:

• `int size()`—returns the number of elements in the list

- `boolean isEmpty()`—tests whether the list has no elements
- `boolean contains(Object e)`—tests whether e is in the list
- `int indexOf(Object e), int lastIndexOf(Object e)`—returns the index of the first (last) occurrence of e or −1
- `Object get(int i)`—returns the element at index i
- `Object set(int i, Object e)`—replaces the element i by e and returns the displaced element i
- `boolean add(Object e)`—appends e to the end of the list
- `void add(int i, Object e)`—inserts e at position i
- `Object remove(int i), void clear()`—removes the element at the specified position in this list; removes all elements

The `contains` and `indexOf` operations rely on the `equals` method of the list elements for equality testing. An invalid index `i < 0 || i >= size()` causes an `IndexOutOfBoundsException`.

Also provided are operations that iterate over a given container:

- `boolean containsAll(Collection c)`—tests whether the list contains all elements in c
- `boolean removeAll(Collection c)`—removes from the list all elements that are also in c
- `boolean retainAll(Collection c)`—removes all elements from the list that are not in c, therefore retaining only the elements in the list that are also in c
- `boolean addAll(Collection c), boolean addAll(int i, Collection c)`—adds all of the elements in c, in the order induced by the iterator of c, to the list at the end or at position i

Except for `containsAll`, the preceding operations return `true` to indicate that the list has been modified. You can also turn an `ArrayList` into an array or make a copy easily with the following:

- `Object[] toArray()`—returns an array containing references to all elements in the list, in the same order
- `Object[] toArray(Object[] arr)`—returns an array containing references to all elements in the list, in the same order. The run-time type of the returned array is that of arr. If arr is big enough, the list is put in it, setting any extra cells at the end to `null`. Otherwise a new array is allocated with the given run-time type
- `Object clone()`—returns a copy `ArrayList` containing references to the elements in this list

Two methods help you manage the capacity of a list:

1. `void trimToSize()`—trims the capacity of the `ArrayList` to match its current size.

2. void ensureCapacity(int n)—sets the capacity of the ArrayList to at least n.

Applying ArrayList

A stack is a *last-in first-out* container. The java.util.Stack class implements a stack using a Vector. Let us implement our own ArrayStack, using an internal ArrayList.

You can give the ArrayStack constructor no argument or an initial capacity (lines A and B). The first element can be pushed onto the stack at instance creation time as well (lines C and D).

```
///////    ArrayStack.java    ///////
import java.io.*;
import java.util.*;

public class ArrayStack
{   public ArrayStack()
    {   list = new ArrayList(); }                    // (A)

    public ArrayStack(int capacity)
    {   list = new ArrayList(capacity); }            // (B)

    public ArrayStack(Object element)               // (C)
    {   this(); push(element); }

    public ArrayStack(int capacity, Object e)       // (D)
    {   this(capacity); push(e); }

    public Object pop()
    {   return  list.isEmpty() ? null
            : list.remove(list.size()-1);
    }

    public void push(Object element) { list.add(element); }

    public Object top()                      //top element
    {   return  list.isEmpty() ? null
            : list.get(list.size()-1);
    }

    public boolean isEmpty() { return list.isEmpty(); }

    public int length() { return list.size(); }

    public void clear() { list.clear(); }
```

```
      protected ArrayList list;
}
```

Stack inspection methods are top (returns element on top), isEmpty, and length (number of elements). State changing methods are push, pop, and clear. All methods call methods of the internal ArrayList to perform simple tasks.

We'll put ArrayStack to use next.

Using ArrayStack

Consider the problem of detecting whether all parentheses are properly balanced within a textual document or a sequence of characters. For our example, let's assume that round, square, curly, and angle brackets are present:

```
( [ ] { } ) < >        balanced
()}                    not balanced
(<)>                   not balanced
><                     not balanced
```

Intervening text between brackets is ignored.

We will write a Bracket class that checks nested brackets, using our ArrayStack:

```
///////   Bracket.java   ///////
import java.io.*;

public class Bracket
{  public Bracket(String open, String close)      // (1)
   {  this.open = open;
      this.close = close;
   }

   public boolean isBalanced(InputStream in)
         throws IOException
   {  int c;
      char ch;
      Character cobj;
      ArrayStack stk = new ArrayStack();           // stack
      while ( (c=in.read()) > -1 )
      {  ch = (char) c;
         cobj = new Character(ch);
         if ( isOpen(ch) ) stk.push(cobj);         // push open bracket
         else if ( (ch=getOpenChar(ch)) != '\0' ) // close bracket
         {  if ( stk.isEmpty() )                   // (2)
               return false;                       // imbalance
            cobj = (Character)stk.top();           // (3)
            if ( ch == cobj.charValue() )          // if matching
```

```
              stk.pop();                        // pop matching open bracket
          else
              return false;                     // bracket mismatch
        }
      }
    return stk.isEmpty();                        // balanced if empty
  }

  protected boolean isOpen(char c)
  {    return (open.indexOf(c) > -1);   }

  protected char getOpenChar(char c)
  {    int i = close.indexOf(c);
       if ( i > -1 ) return open.charAt(i);
       return '\0';
  }

  private String open, close;
}
```

You instantiate a `Bracket` object with the desired open and close brackets, in the form of two strings (line 1). The `isBalanced` method checks to see whether the brackets in the given `InputStream` are balanced. The method pushes open brackets onto a stack `stk` and pops off the matching open bracket when a closing bracket is read. It is important to make sure that a stack is not empty before popping (line 2) and to cast the object popped off the generic container to the correct type (line 3) before using it.

To test run `Bracket`, a simple `main` method such as the following can be added to the class:

```
public static void main(String[] args) throws IOException
{   Bracket br = new Bracket("(<{[", ")>}]");
    if ( br.isBalanced(System.in) )
        System.out.println("Balanced.");
    else
        System.out.println("Not balanced.");
}
```

Other Lists

For efficiency, `ArrayList` is not always synchronized. For thread-safety, use the static method

```
List sl = Collections.synchronizedList(List l);
```

to get a synchronized version of the given list `l`.

Similar to, but different from `ArrayList` is the `List` returned by the static method `java.util.Arrays.asList`:

```
static List asList(Object[] arr)
```

It returns a fixed-size list supported by the given array `arr`. Such a list disallows add and remove operations. Setting an element in such a list sets the corresponding array cell.

A `LinkedList` uses list cells to store elements. It provides the same methods as in `ArrayList` plus operations to add, get, and remove elements at the beginning or end of the list (`addFirst`, `getFirst`, `removeFirst`, `addLast`, `getLast`, `removeLast`).

9.2 MAPS

A map is an *associative container* that couples stored *values* with symbolic names, or even objects, that serve as *keys* to retrieve the stored values. Think of it as an array with *noninteger indices* called *keys* (Figure 9.1). For example, capitals can be stored and retrieved by names of countries, bank accounts by customer IDs, stock quotes by ticker symbols, and so on. Naturally, the key (e.g., customer ID) is often part of the value (e.g., bank account).

The collections framework provides two associative containers, the `HashMap` and the `TreeMap`. The `HashMap` can store arbitrary keys and values, including `null`. The keys must be distinct. `HashMap` implements the `Map` interface and employs an internal hash table to store the key-value pairs. If you need an associative container, most likely a `HashMap` will do the job nicely. If you need to keep the keys in a map in order, consider using the `TreeMap`. Let's focus on the `HashMap` for now.

HashMap

Consistent with `ArrayList`, a `HashMap` constructor can also take no argument, a `Collection`, or an initial capacity. To keep a hash table working efficiently, it is advisable always to leave some room for new elements. The *load factor* is

Figure 9.1   MAP AS ASSOCIATIVE CONTAINER

key ⟶ **Map** ⟶ value

the maximum for the ratio *size/capacity* and defaults to 0.75, which is a good setting in most situations. The constructor

```
HashMap(int capacity, float loadFactor)
```

sets the load factor to the specified value. For example,

```
import java.util.HashMap;
```

```
Map nyse_stock = new HashMap(12000);
```

establishes `nyse_stock` as a new `HashMap` with an initial capacity of 12000 and a default load factor of 0.75. If you need a map for more than tens of elements, instead of using the default values, it is more efficient to set the initial capacity to the anticipated total number of elements divided by the load factor.

Now we enter some entries into `nyse_stock`:

```
nyse_stock.put("IBM", quote1);
nyse_stock.put("SUNW", quote2);
```

Later the notation

```
Quote q = (Quote) nyse_stock.get("IBM");   // returns quote1
```

can be used to retrieve quotes in `nyse_stock`.

`HashMap` implements the `Map` interface and provides these basic operations:

- `int size()` (`boolean isEmpty()`)—Tells you the number of elements in the map.
- `Object get(Object` *key)*—Returns the value for the given *key* or null if there is no such key. Because values can be `null` , a null returned may also be a stored value. You can use the `containsKey` method to make sure.
- `Object put(Object` *key,* `Object` *value)*—Enters the given key-value pair element into the map. Any previous value for *key* is replaced.
- `Object remove(Object` *key)*—Removes the element for this key from the map and returns the value part of the element or null if the map contains no such key.
- `void clear()`—Removes all elements from the map.
- `boolean containsKey(Object` *key)* (`boolean containsValue(Object` *val)*)—Returns true if the map contains an element with the given key (value).

Other useful `Map` operations include the following:

- `void putAll(Map` *ac)*—Enters a copy of each map entry (key-value pair) from the given *ac* into the map.
- `Set keySet()`—Returns a set view of the map keys. The set is backed by the map, so changes to the set are reflected in the map, and vice

versa. The set supports element removal, which removes the corresponding entry from the map, but it does not support any element addition operations.

- `Collection values()`—Returns a collection view of the map values. The collection is backed by the map, so changes to the collection are reflected in the map, and vice versa. The collection supports element removal, which removes the corresponding entry in the map. It does not support any element addition operations.
- `Set entrySet()`—Returns a set view of the map entries (`Map.Entry`). The set is backed by the map, so changes to the set are reflected in the map, and vice versa. The set supports element removal, which removes the corresponding entry from the map. It does not support any element addition operations. A `Map.Entry` provides three methods: `getKey`, `getValue`, and `setValue`.

The following subsection puts `HashMap` to use in an application.

Example: URL Decoding

Forms on the Web are filled out by a remote user and sent to a program on the Web server side for processing (Section 10.7). Data collected by a form is in *URL-encoded* format,

```
name=Paul+S%2E+Wang&address=Math%2fCS%2C+Kent+State+U%2E%2C+OH&
email=pwang%40cs%2Emcs%2Ekent%2Eedu
```

as one continuous sequence of characters. Form data contain *key=value* pairs separated by & characters. A space is encoded as a + sign. Other nonalphanumeric characters are represented by three-character codes

```
%XY
```

where *XY* is the ASCII code in hexadecimal for the character. For example:

```
%2f  is  /
%2C  is  ,
%2E  is  .
%40  is  @
```

A program receiving the encoded form data must first decode it. The `FormData` class has an `unpack()` method to URL-decode the incoming form data string kept in the field `input` and to store the resulting key-value pairs in the member associative container `data`:

```
public class FormData
{   public FormData(String in)
    {   input = in;
        data = new HashMap();
```

```
        unpack();
    }

 // methods ...

    protected String input;          // the form input
    protected Map data;              // associative container
}
```

The StringTokenizer (Section 2.9) makes it easy to split tokens delimited by & (line 1) or = (line 2):

```
void unpack()
{   String s1;
    StringTokenizer tk = new StringTokenizer(input, "&");   // (1)
    while ( tk.hasMoreTokens() )
    {   s1 = tk.nextToken();
        if ( s1.charAt(0) == '=' ) continue;
        StringTokenizer nv =
            new StringTokenizer(s1, "=");                    // (2)
        int count = nv.countTokens();
        if ( count < 1 || count > 2 ) continue;
        String key = nv.nextToken();
        if ( count == 2 )
        {   StringBuffer value =
                new StringBuffer(nv.nextToken());
            urlDecode(value);                                // (3)
            data.put(key, value.toString());                // (4)
        }
        else // count == 1
            data.put(key, "");                               // (5)
    }
}
```

Having obtained the key and value, we then decode the value part by calling urlDecode (line 3) and enter the result into the map data (line 4). The member function get helps retrieve form data by key:

```
public String get(String key)
{   return (String) data.get(key);
}
```

Unspecified values are entered as empty strings (line 5).

The urlDecode method modifies the incoming string buffer s by replacing any + character by a space (line 6), and any three-character combination %*XY* by the correct ASCII character (lines 7–9). The static parseInt method of Integer (Section 3.3) is very helpful in converting the two-character hex string x to an integer value ch (line 8). The value ch is then cast into the desired character (line 9). If the *XY* is not a valid hex number, the conversion is not performed (line 10).

```
void urlDecode(StringBuffer s)
{   int len = s.length(), pos=0;
    char c, space = ' ';
    for (int i=0; i < len; i++)
    {   c = s.charAt(i);
        if ( c == '+' )
            s.setCharAt(pos++, space);             // (6)
        else if ( c == '%' )                       // (7)
        {   String x =   s.substring(i+1,i+3);
            try
            {   int ch = Integer.parseInt(x, 16);  // (8)
                s.setCharAt(pos++, (char) ch);     // (9)
                i += 2;
            } catch( NumberFormatException e )     // (10)
                {  s.setCharAt(pos++,c);   };
        }
        else if ( pos == i )
            pos++;
        else
            s.setCharAt(pos++,c);
    }
    s.setLength(pos);  // shorten string           // (11)
}
```

Note that urlDecode performs the decoding in place and shortens the string buffer when necessary (line 11).

TreeMap

As an associative container, HashMap, presented earlier in this section, suits most applications. However, HashMap does not keep the keys in any particular order. If that is what you need, you can use TreeMap, which is a *red-black tree* (data structure) implementation of the SortedMap interface. A TreeMap keeps the keys in ascending order and provides $log(n)$ time operations for size n maps.

To create a new TreeMap use one of these constructors:

```
TreeMap()               // natural key ordering
TreeMap(Map m)          // copy m in natural key ordering
TreeMap(TreeMap tm)     // copy tm, same key ordering
Treemap(Comparator comp)  // comparator-defined key ordering
```

A TreeMap also supports methods for obtaining the first key, the comparator, or a view on a submap of consecutive keys.

9.3 ITERATORS

In OOP, objects hide their internal workings and therefore reduce software complexity. But is there a down side to this approach? Specifically, are there operations made harder or impossible to perform without knowledge of the internal structures? One operation that comes to mind is visiting every item contained in a container. Consider, for example, the circular buffer class. Suppose there is a need to inspect each character still in a Cirbuf object without consuming any characters. One solution is adding another public method next() to return characters in succession. The approach does not work well because it can keep track of only one iteration at a time.

A better solution involves defining a separate *iterator class* to create iterator objects that provide systematic and independent access to internal elements of a target object. An iterator class can implement two methods:

```
hasNext()     // tests whether there is a next item to visit
next()        // returns the next item
```

To provide an iterator, a class usually implements:

- A public inner class (Section 7.12) Iterator as an instance member with private constructors
- A public method iterator() to return an instance of the inner Iterator

Consider an inner Iterator for the Cirbuf class.

```
// in class Cirbuf
  public final class Iterator
  {   private Iterator()                                    // (1)
      {    i0 = head;   i1 = tail; }

      public char next()
      {    if ( i0 == i1 )
              throw new java.util.NoSuchElementException();
           char c =  cb[i0++];
           i0 = mod(i0);
           return c;
      }

      public boolean hasNext()
      {    return ( i0 != i1);  }

      private int i0, i1;   // head, tail indices
      }
```

With this `Iterator` inner class, the method `iterator` of `Cirbuf` can return an instance of the `Iterator`:

```
// in class Cirbuf
    public Iterator iterator()
    {    return new Iterator();
    }
```

The constructor (line 1) is `private` so that the `iterator` method is the only way to obtain an iterator. The iterator returned can be used in the following way:

```
public class TestCirbuf
{   public static void main(String[] args)
    {    Cirbuf cb = new Cirbuf();
         char[] r = new char[1];
         cb.put('a'); cb.put('b'); cb.put('c');
         cb.put('d'); cb.put('e');
         cb.get(r);
         Cirbuf.Iterator cb_itr = cb.iterator(); // creates iterator
         char c;
         while ( cb_itr.hasNext() )              // performs iteration
         {    c = cb_itr.next();
              System.out.println("Next character = " + c);
         }
    }
}
```

Multiple iterations can be ongoing without mutual interference. The preceding code assumes that the circular buffer under iteration does not change during an iteration. To safeguard against potential problems, an iterator can be instantiated with a complete copy of the target object.

The `Iterator` Interface

The iterator is an important technique for hiding internal structures of objects while still providing necessary access from the outside. The ideas behind the `Cirbuf Iterator` can be generalized to build iterators for any containers such as sets, lists, trees, buffers, hashtables, and so on. The way to build such a generic iterator is to define an interface that governs how iterators work. The `Iterator` interface from the `java.util` package does exactly that. The java `Iterator` interface specifies these methods:

```
public boolean hasNext()        (tests whether there is a next item to visit)
public Object next()            (returns the next item as Object)
public void remove()            (deletes the last item returned (optional))
```

Implementing java.util.Iterator, the inner class Iterator of Cirbuf is now written as follows.

```
// in Cirbuf
    private final class Iterator
            implements java.util.Iterator              // (a)
    {  private Iterator()
       {  i0 = head;  i1 = tail; }

       public Object next()
       {  if ( i0 == i1 )
             throw new java.util.NoSuchElementException();
          char c =  cb[i0++];
          i0 = mod(i0);
          return new Character(c);                     // (b)
       }

       public boolean hasNext()
       {  return ( i0 != i1);  }

       public void remove()        // read-only iteration  // (c)
          throws UnsupportedOperationException
       {  throw new UnsupportedOperationException
             ("remove not allowed by Cirbuf iterator");
       }

       private int i0, i1;  // head, tail indices
    }
```

Making Iterator private (line a) enhances encapsulation. Returning an Object makes next generic (line b). We also elect not to support the optional remove operation (line c), which is not needed in a read-only iterator.

Application code that uses this new Iterator looks as follows:

```
Cirbuf cb = new Cirbuf();
...
java.util.Iterator it = cb.iterator();
Character c;
while ( it.hasNext() )
{  c = (Character) it.next();
   System.out.println("Next character = " + c);
}
```

The Iterator interface is used extensively in the Java *collections framework* to support many useful generic containers.

9.4 SETS

A Set is a group of distinct elements. The class HashSet implements the Set interface with a hash table (actually a HashMap) whereas the class TreeSet implements SortedSet, a subinterface of Set, with an internal TreeMap. In most set applications, element order is not important, and HashSet should be used because it is fast and efficient. If the order of elements in a set is important, use TreeSet instead.

To create a HashSet, consistent with HashMap, you can give no argument, or an initial capacity and an optional load factor (defaults to 0.75).

Commonly used methods for HashSet include the following:

- boolean contains(Object el)—tests whether the given element is in the set (Figure 9.2)
- boolean isEmpty()—tests whether the set has no elements
- int size()—returns the number of elements in this set
- boolean add(Object el)—adds the given element to the set and returns true if the element is not already present
- void clear()—removes all elements from the set
- boolean remove(Object el)—removes the given element from the set and returns true if the element is present

For example, we can add a method names() to the FormData class

```
public Set names()
{    return data.keySet();
}
```

and use the following code fragment to access all names in a submitted Web form:

```
FormData form = new FormData(form_string);
Set names = form.names();
Iterator it = names.iterator();
while ( it.hasNext() )
{    System.out.println( (String) it.next() );
}
```

The iterator() method returns an Iterator (java.util) that allows you to visit each element stored in a HashSet.

Figure 9.2   SET MEMBERSHIP

element————?————▶   Set   ————————▶ true/false

A `TreeSet` is best understood as a `TreeMap` where the keys are associated with no values. The same sets of constructors and operations are supported.

9.5 COLLECTIONS FRAMEWORK INTERFACE HIERARCHIES

Containers in the *collections framework* support uniform public interfaces so that they become interchangeable or plug-compatible in usage. Figures 9.3, 9.4, and 9.5 show the interfaces defined in the collections framework and the implementation hierarchies. Looking at the interface hierarchies, we see that the collections framework offers two kinds of containers: `Collection` and `Map`. Concrete containers are implemented by extending abstract classes that make different concrete containers easy to implement (Section 9.12).

A `Set` container is just a collection of distinct elements. A `List` container organizes its elements in a linear sequence (e.g., a waiting list). A `Map` container stores key-value pairs so that the values are easily retrieved through the keys (e.g., a phone book). A sorted map allows the elements (keys) to be sequenced in any desired order.

Figure 9.3   COLLECTIONS FRAMEWORK INTERFACES

Figure 9.4   COLLECTION IMPLEMENTATIONS

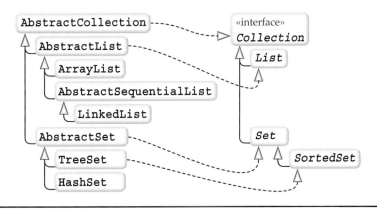

Figure 9.5   MAP IMPLEMENTATIONS

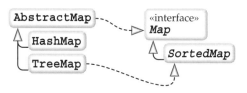

The concrete classes `ArrayList`, `LinkedList`, `HashMap`, `TreeMap`, `HashSet`, and `TreeSet` implement these interfaces. The `Collection` superinterface extracts the common parts of `List` and `Set`. Methods receiving `Collection` or `Map` parameters can be polymorphic over different containers.

Let's take a closer look at the `Collection` interface, which specifies required and optional methods for any `Collection` (`List` or `Set`):

```
public interface Collection
{// Basic Operations
    int size();
    boolean isEmpty();
    boolean contains(Object element);
    Iterator iterator();
    boolean add(Object element);        // optional
    boolean remove(Object element);     // optional

  // Array Operations
    Object[] toArray();
    Object[] toArray(Object a[]);

  // Multi-element Operations
    boolean containsAll(Collection c);
    boolean addAll(Collection c);       // optional
    boolean removeAll(Collection c);    // optional
    boolean retainAll(Collection c);    // optional
    void clear();
}
```

As we have seen, each of `ArrayList`, `LinkedList`, `HashSet`, and `TreeSet` implements all required and optional methods. These collection objects are *read-write* containers and are totally plug-compatible. A *read-only* collection will implement the `Collection` interface but refuses to support any of the modification methods, which are designated *optional* for this very reason. To *not support an optional method* means you define the method to throw an `UnsupportedOperationException`.

By convention, a container implementation should always support a *copying constructor* that initializes a new container by copying all the elements from the given container. Specifically, any Collection or Map type must supply a copying constructor taking a Collection or Map argument, respectively.

Now we have described all methods in the Collection interface except one, the iterator method, which is our next topic.

9.6 FRAMEWORK ITERATORS

Each Collection container must provide an iterator method that returns an iterator object for *traversing*, or systematically visiting, the elements in the container. An iterator object implements the

java.util.Iterator

interface:

```
public interface Iterator
{   boolean hasNext(); // tests whether there is a next item to visit
    Object next();     // returns next element
    void remove();     // removes last element returned (optional)
}
```

The next() method returns the next element in the collection according to the element ordering used by the Collection. A Collection can use either the natural ordering of the elements (compareTo, Section 5.4) or an order given by a Comparator specified at instance creation time. Make sure that there is a next element to visit before calling next(). Examples in Section 9.3 show how to implement iterators.

Lists and Sets provided by the collection framework all support iterators with well-defined remove operations. The remove() method may be called only once per call to next(); otherwise an exception will be thrown. Other than through remove(), a Collection must not be modified while an iteration is in progress. Otherwise the behavior of the iterator is undefined.

The following snippet uses an Iterator to go through a Collection and remove every element satisfying some *test*:

```
for (Iterator i = c.iterator(); i.hasNext(); )
{   if ( test(i.next()) )
        i.remove();
}
```

Note that this code fragment works for any Collection c that supports the Iterator interface. It is polymorphic, and the collections framework makes such polymorphism possible. Bulk operations such as containsAll depend on the collection iterator to work.

Because elements in a list form a linear sequence, a more powerful ListIterator, extending Iterator, that can go up and down the sequence and allows both adding and removing elements, is available. For any List *al*, the call

```
ListIterator lit = al.listIterator( );
ListIterator lit = al.listIterator( i );
```

returns a `ListIterator` object `lit` for the entire sequence or the subsequence starting at given index i. Then you can use

```
lit.hasNext()          // boolean
lit.next()             // element forward
lit.hasPrevious()      // boolean
lit.previous()         // element backward
```

for either forward or backward traversal. You can also obtain the index of the next or previous element.

```
lit.nextIndex()        // returns size of list if no next element
lit.previousIndex()    // returns -1 if no previous element
```

Normally, you iterate either forward or backward, but you may also mix calls to next() and previous(). When you change traversal direction, the first element you get is the very element you got just before changing direction. Thus alternating next() and previous() will give you the same element all the time.

9.7 FUNCTORS

A *functor* is an object representing a function or action. A `Comparator` (Section 5.4) performs comparisons, and an `Iterator` (Section 9.3) traverses a container. They are examples of functors.

You may wonder why we use functors when static methods can already perform actions. But functors have advantages over static methods in several important ways:

- A static method usually does not retain information across invocations. In other words, one method call has nothing to do with the next call. A functor, being an object, can easily keep *state information* across invocations. For example, an iterator remembers its current traversal position, so its next() method can return a new element for each call.

- A static method may try to use `static` fields to retain information from one call to the next. However, one sequence of calls (e.g., an iteration) must be finished before another unrelated sequence of calls (e.g., another iteration) begins. Otherwise the two call sequences interfere with each other through the static fields. On the other hand, distinct functors can take care of different call sequences at the same time without mutual interference.

- A functor can also have auxiliary methods, such as remove() in Iterator, to help achieve certain purposes. A functor can be initialized differently to perform in different operating modes (e.g., iterating a tree in different traversal orders).

- Functors can be passed as arguments to methods. Writing methods that work with supplied functors has advantages. The sort, min, and max methods of the Collections class (Section 9.8) are examples. These generic algorithms depend on the supplied functors to work.
- Functors, as objects, can be organized in class hierarchies and can employ polymorphism.

9.8 GENERIC ALGORITHMS FOR CONTAINERS

Using generic containers provided by the collections framework has major advantages:

- With each container, you get many basic operations that are effective and efficient.
- These containers are plug-compatible with polymorphic codes written for the Collection or the Map interface.
- For Collection containers, you also get many useful algorithms in the form of static methods from the Collections class.

The java.util.Collections class provides a number of static methods that supply good implementations of well-selected algorithms for common operations on containers:

- void sort(List *list* [, Comparator c])—Sorts the given list, using the natural ordering of the elements or the supplied comparator if given. The algorithm is a modified *mergesort* that does not reorder equal elements and guarantees $nlog(n)$ performance.
- int binarySearch(List *list*, Object *el* [, Comparator c]))—Looks in *list* for the element *el*, using the binary search algorithm. The list must be in ascending order already. The natural or comparator-defined ordering is used to determine equality. If the list contains multiple elements equal to *el*, one of them is found. The index of the element found is returned.
- void shuffle(List *list* [, Random rnd])—Permutes *list*, using a default or specified source of random numbers. If the numbers are truly random, all permutations are equally likely. The algorithm goes from the end of the list to the beginning, swapping each current element with a randomly selected element in the unprocessed portion of the list. The algorithm is linear for ArrayLists and costly for linked lists.
- void reverse(List *list*)—Reverses the order of the elements in *list*.
- void fill(List *list*, Object *el*)—Sets all elements in *list* to *el*.

- void copy(List *destination*, List *source*)—Copies all elements from the *source* list to the *destination* list, which must be big enough to receive all the elements. If *destination* is longer, elements at the end are not affected.
- Object min(Collection *c* [, Comparator *cp*]))—Returns the minimum element in the given collection *c*, under the natural or the *cp*-induced element ordering. The method max works the same way.

In the preceding static methods, only max and min can take any suitable Collection. All other methods take only lists.

As an example, let's apply the Collections.sort method to sort an array of integers. The array of ints (line 1) is first placed into an Integer array ia (line 2), so we'll be dealing with objects rather than primitive ints. The method Arrays.asList conveniently turns ia into an ArrayList (line 3) on which Collections.sort can operate.

```
///////    SortTest.java    ///////
import java.util.*;

public class SortTest
{ public static void main(String[] args)
    { int[] a = {5,3,-1, 79, 32, 96, 63, 32, 98};        // (1)
      int len = a.length;
      Integer[] ia = new Integer[len];                   // (2)
      for (int i=0; i < len; i++)
          ia[i] = new Integer(a[i]);
      List l = Arrays.asList(ia);                        // (3)

  // sort into ascending order
      Collections.sort(l);                               // (4)
      System.out.println("Ascending order:");
      for (int i=0; i < len; i++)
          System.out.println(ia[i]);

  // sort into descending order
      Comparator b = new ReverseCompare();               // (5)
      Collections.sort(l, b);                            // (6)
      System.out.println();
      System.out.println("Descending order:");
      for (int i=0; i < len; i++)
          System.out.println(ia[i]);
    }

    static class ReverseCompare implements Comparator
    { public int compare(Object i, Object j)
        { Integer b = (Integer) j;
          return b.compareTo(i);  // reversing the comparison
```

```
          }
      }
}
```

Applying Collections.sort using natural ordering on integers, we achieve ascending ordering (line 4). Using a Comparator we define, we achieve descending order (lines 5 and 6). The inner class ReverseCompare supplies the required comparator for descending order.

Let's implement a generic algorithm of our own, sum, as a static method in the TestSum class. The sum method computes the sum of all elements in any given Collection of numbers and returns a Number object. It visits each element, using the Iterator of the collection.

```
public static Number sum(Collection c)
        throws NonNumericException
{   if ( c.isEmpty() )
        return new Integer(0);                              // (A)

    double ans = 0.0;
    Class num = null; Object el;

    try { num = Class.forName("java.lang.Number"); }  // (B)
        catch (ClassNotFoundException e) { }

    Iterator it = c.iterator();                         // (C)
    while ( it.hasNext() )
    {   el = it.next();
        if ( num.isInstance(el) )                       // (D)
            ans += ((Number) el).doubleValue();         // (E)
        else
            throw new NonNumericException();            // (F)
    }
    return new Double(ans);                             // (G)
}
```

If the given collection is empty, zero is returned (line A). Otherwise the element returned by the collection's iterator (line C) is examined to see whether it is a numeric type (lines B and D). If not, an exception is thrown (line F). The sum is computed by adding double values of the collection elements. The returned object is a Number represented by a Double object (lines E and G).

NonNumericException is defined separately:

```
public class NonNumericException extends Exception
{   public NonNumericException() {}

    public NonNumericException(String s)
    {   super(s);    }    // msg string
}
```

Following is a simple main method that puts sum to use:

```
///////    TestSum.java    ///////
import java.io.*;
import java.util.*;

public class TestSum
{  public static void main(String[] args)
        throws IOException, NonNumericException
   {   int[] a = {5,3,-1, 79, 32, 96, 63, 32, 98};
       int len = a.length;
       Integer[] ia = new Integer[len];
       for (int i=0; i < len; i++)
           ia[i] = new Integer(a[i]);
       List l = Arrays.asList(ia);
       Number s = sum(l);              // the call
       System.out.println("Sum = " + s.intValue());
   }

   // put static method sum here
}
```

9.9 SYNCHRONIZED CONTAINERS

The collections framework containers covered so far are not *thread-safe* (Section 11.2). This means that you don't want to use such a container in a multithreaded program in which multiple threads can access the same container. Creating and managing multiple threads in a program is the subject of Chapter 11. You may want to return to this section while reading Section 11.6.

It is simple to turn a container into a thread-safe one. Just call one of these static methods in the Collections class:

```
Map Collections.synchronizedMap(Map m)
Set Collections.synchronizedSet(Set s)
List Collections.synchronizedList(List list)
SortedSet Collections.synchronizedSortedSet(SortedSet s)
SortedMap Collections.synchronizedSortedMap(SortedMap m)
Collection Collections.synchronizedCollection(Collection c)
```

Each of these methods creates a new container that wraps around the given container and adds the thread-safety feature to it. This means all methods of a container thus created are safe to use by threads concurrently. Methods that manufacture an object for a certain purpose are sometimes called *factory methods*. For example, to get a synchronized list you can use:

```
List sl = Collections.synchronizedList(new ArrayList());
```

Now operations supported by sl are thread-safe.

You must be careful if you use an iterator returned by a synchronized container such as sl and begin to loop over the elements. You have to use a synchronized block like this one

```
synchronized(sl)
{  Iterator i = sl.iterator(); // Must be in synchronized block!
   while (i.hasNext())
       do-something-to(i.next());
}
```

to avoid thread safety problems.

9.10 READ-ONLY CONTAINERS

It is sometimes useful to make a container read-only after it is constructed. You can achieve this by calling one of these factory methods in the Collections class:

```
Map Collections.unmodifiableMap(Map m)
Set Collections.unmodifiableSet(Set s)
List Collections.unmodifiableList(List list)
SortedSet Collections.unmodifiableSortedSet(SortedSet s)
SortedMap Collections.unmodifiableSortedMap(SortedMap m)
Collection Collections.unmodifiableCollection(Collection c)
```

For example, to get a read-only list based on another list you can use:

```
List r_list = Collections.unmodifiableList(list);
```

The object r_list wraps around list and bars all state-changing operations, but modifications are still possible through list. To eliminate all possibility of modification, you can lose the reference to the original list.

The Collections class also offers methods for the convenient creation of certain special collections:

- List Collections.nCopies(n, Object el)—Gives you a read-only list containing n copies of the element el. Here is a way to quickly initialize a list:

```
Integer zero = new Integer(0);
List age_list = new ArrayList(Collections.nCopies(150, zero));
```

- Set Collections.singleton(Object el)—Gives you a read-only set with the given element in it. Here is an example:

```
Integer bad = new Integer(13);
n_list.removeAll(Collections.singleton(bad));
```

This removes all integers 13 from a list.

9.11 CONTAINER COMPATIBILITY

The collections framework provides interfaces and implementations to make containers highly plug-compatible and interoperable. It is advisable to stay with the framework containers for developing new code.

However, there are other containers in Java:

- Legacy containers—Vector, HashTable, and Enumeration, which predate the collections framework
- The ordinary array—a basic Java language feature

Legacy containers may return Enumerations for iteration purposes. New code should use Iterators instead.

Java has also retrofit the Vector class to implement the List interface and the HashTable class to implement the Map interface. If an older program returns a Vector (HashTable), you can pass it to a collections framework program as a List (Map) directly.

We already know that a List view of an array arr can be obtained by:

```
List l = Arrays.asList(arr);
```

For backward compatibility, the toArray method can turn any Collection into an array, and static method Collections.enumeration(c) can turn any collection c into an Enumeration. An added constructor now takes a Map and creates a HashTable.

The collections framework provides an environment for designing and implementing polymorphic and reusable programs. Follow these rules to design your API (*Application Programming Interface*):

- Declare formal parameters for methods with the most general framework interface type. Then write the methods to be polymorphic over their parameter types.
- Declare a method return type to reflect the most specific object type being returned.

9.12 DEFINING CUSTOM CONTAINERS

For most occasions, the Java supplied general-purpose containers in the collections framework will be enough. Still there are situations that call for specially designed containers to satisfy requirements of the application at hand. For example, you may need a container that knows how to save and restore itself from disk. Or you may want to use a different internal data structure to store the elements for increased efficiency. Or you may need to add functionalities to or eliminate features from existing containers.

It is not difficult to write custom containers conforming to the collections framework, because you can do it by extending a framework-supplied abstract or concrete class. A set of abstract classes is provided for just this purpose. The concrete containers (Figures 9.4 and 9.5) supplied by Java are extensions of these classes.

- `AbstractList`—Extend this abstract class to define a linear sequence (a list) based on an indexed data store for constant time access to any element. For a read-only list, you only have to implement the `get` and `size` methods. To allow modification, you then have to override the `set`, `add`, and `remove` as appropriate. `AbstractList` defines these methods to throw `UnsupportedOperationException`. The `iterator` and `listIterator` methods defined in `AbstractList` works because they call member methods `get`, `set`, `add`, and `remove`.

- `AbstractSequentialList`—Extend this abstract class to define a container based on a linked-cells data store. To implement a linked list, implement the `listIterator` and `size` methods. For a read-only list, you only have to implement the list iterator's `hasNext`, `next`, `hasPrevious`, `previous`, and `index` methods. To allow modification, you may define the `set`, `add`, and/or `remove` method in the list iterator as appropriate. The `get`, `set`, `add`, and `remove` methods supplied by `AbstractSequentialList` work because they use the list iterator you define.

- `AbstractMap`—Extend this abstract class to define a map. For a read-only map, you need only implement the `entrySet` method to return a set-view of the map entries (key-value pairs). Usually the returned set is a read-only extension of `AbstractSet`. For a modifiable map, you must override the `put` method and also make sure that the iterator of `entrySet()` implements its `remove` method, which is used by the `AbstractMap` remove method to delete map entries. Note that the `AbstractMap`-defined operations work by iterating over the entry set (linear time). This can be very inefficient, especially for the `get` and `containsKey` operations. It is advisable to override these methods also with more efficient operations in your implementation.

- `AbstractSet`—Extend this abstract class to define a set in which all elements are distinct. For a read-only set, you need only implement the `iterator` (to return a read-only `Iterator`) and the `size` methods. For a modifiable set, you must also override the `add` method and make sure that the iterator has a `remove` method.

- `AbstractCollection`—Extend this abstract class to define a set whose elements are not necessarily all distinct. Usage is the same as `AbstractSet`.

In every case, it is assumed that the extended class will provide the store for the elements, a no-args constructor, and a copying constructor (Section 9.5) that takes a `Collection` (Map). It is rarely beneficial in practice to start from something like an `AbstractMap`. Extending `HashMap` usually will do the job.

9.13 SUMMARY

The Java collections framework, in the `java.util` package, provides a well-designed infrastructure for using and building generic containers. `Collection` containers store data elements, whereas `Map` containers store key-value pairs.

Five major components make up the Java Collections Framework: interfaces, container classes, automatic conversions among compatible containers, iterators, and algorithms. The containers are easy to apply, and they are compatible and interchangeable in use to a large degree.

A list implies a linear ordering of elements. A set is a group of distinct elements in which membership is the main concern. A map is a way to associate keys with values. Among the general-purpose containers (`ArrayList`, `LinkedList`, `HashSet`, `TreeSet`, `HashMap`, and `TreeMap`) `ArrayList`, `HashMap`, and `HashSet` are the most useful.

The `toArray()` method of a collection container and the static `asArray()` method of the `java.util.Arrays` class make converting between collection containers and arrays easy.

The `java.util.Collections` class provides static methods implementing useful algorithms usable on collection containers. Operations include searching, sorting, and shuffling.

For efficiency, operations on the collections containers are normally not thread-safe (Chapter 11). The `Collections` class has static factory methods to return thread-safe, or synchronized, versions of the containers.

By following the abstract classes and interfaces in the collections framework, defining new collection containers is made systematic.

EXERCISES

Review Questions

1. What is a container? A generic container?

2. What types of containers are available in the collections framework? What differentiates these types of containers from one another?

3. When should you use a `LinkedList` rather than an `ArrayList`?

4. List the advantages of a functor over a static method.

5. Consider iterators for `Collection` containers. Why is it that a container under iteration must not be modified, other than through the `remove` method of the iterator?

6. Consider the "no disallowed modifications" restriction in the previous exercise. What if the iteration is on a copy of a container? Then the original container can be modified independently of the iteration. Even if we iterate over the same container without making a copy, can you identify modifications that can be allowed without affecting an ongoing iteration? Explain.

7. In what sense is a Set a degenerate Map?

8. How do you convert an array to a List and vice versa?

9. Is it correct to view a set as a map, where the keys are the values? Explain.

10. In what ways are the collections containers interoperable? List as many aspects as you can find.

11. What is a functor? Give some examples.

Programming Assignments

1. Consider the TextLines class (Section 4.20). Implement it as a collections framework compatible container.

2. The Swing JList (Chapter 8) uses a plug-compatible *model* to store the list that it displays. Find out how this works, and define an ArrayListModel class that extends ArrayList and implements ListModel. Make sure your model works with JList by writing a GUI test program to demonstrate it.

3. Define a class DistanceChart, where the distance between two points (cities for example) is retrieved by a method call such as:

   ```
   chart.get("Boston", "New York");
   ```

4. Apply generic containers to write a program that lists the distinct words used in a text file together with their frequencies.

## CHAPTER TEN

Networking

One of the reasons for Java's popularity is its suitability for Internet and Web applications. We've already seen how Java applets can make Web pages more dynamic.

In the `java.net` package, Java further provides easy-to-use mechanisms for obtaining and supplying services on the Internet:

- Creating and parsing URLs
- Obtaining resources identified by URLs
- Connecting to Web servers
- Encoding messages in standard Web format (URL encoding)
- Conversion between domain names and IP addresses
- Establishing Internet clients and servers
- Invoking methods in objects running on remote hosts (RMI)

At the application program level, *networking* means interprocess communication, where the processes are running on different computers connected by a network. With these facilities, you can write Java programs for many different network applications including:

- Downloading and uploading files
- Posting queries to and obtaining responses from server-side programs on the Web
- Processing queries from Web clients and constructing replies
- Accessing standard Internet services
- Implementing custom client-server applications

Key network concepts are presented in more detail. Examples illustrate how to apply and combine networking tools to achieve specific goals in practice.

10.1 NETWORKING BY URL

A *Uniform Resource Locator* (*URL*) (Section 7.2) is a standard way to identify and locate resources (files and services) on the Internet. A URL can specify the following information:

- Scheme—The type of service (protocol), for example `http` for a Web server.
- Host—The domain name or IP number of a host computer, for example `www.javasoft.com`.
- Port number—The integer port number of the server, normally specified only when a nonstandard port is used.
- File name—The pathname of a file, for example `index.html`. This name is relative to the *document root*, a location configured by the server.
- Query string—A string of name-value pairs as arguments to server-side services.

The components are given in a well-defined format. Here is a sample URL:

```
http://www.javasoft.com:80/index.html
```

The URL is developed for the Web but is useful in general. The amount of information needed in a URL depends on the scheme and the server-side resource.

Java programs can access resources on the Internet through URLs with ease. You may have noticed that Java applets can load image and sound files.

- The `Applet` method `getCodeBase` obtains the URL of the document containing the applet.
- The `Applet` method `getImage` loads an image file across the Internet. For example:

```
getImage(URL, "images/x.gif");
```

- The `Applet` methods `getAudioClip` and `newAudioClip` load a sound file across the Internet. For example:

```
getAudioClip(URL, "audio/laughter.au");   (from an applet)
Applet.newAudioClip(URL);                  (from an application)
```

- The `Applet` method `play` plays a sound file directly. For example:

```
play(URL, "audio/laughter.au");
```

For security reasons, the *URL* is usually restricted to the host machine that supplied the applet. Most commonly, the *URL* argument is the codebase of the Web document containing the applet. The second argument in these methods supplies a file name relative to the URL's first argument. The two arguments are combined into a URL for the desired file and then used to retrieve it.

There are versions of the preceding methods that take a single URL argument (Section 7.11).

10.2 CREATING AND MANIPULATING URLS

You create and manipulate URLs with the class URL. URL constructors provide convenient ways to initialize a URL object:

```
URL(url-string)
URL(URL, relative-url)
URL(scheme, host, filename)
URL(scheme, host, port, filename)
```

A MalformedURLException is thrown if the URL cannot be formed. For example,

```
URL symbolicNet = new URL("http", "SymbolicNet.org", "index.html");
```

accesses a Web server for SymbolicNet, an information center for *Symbolic Mathematical Computation*. And

```
URL icmFactor = new URL("http://icm.mcs.kent.edu",
                        "/cgi-bin/icm.demo?factor=x^4-y^4");
```

sends the query string factor=x^4-y^4 to a demo program.

Given any URL object urlobj, its constituent parts can be retrieved with:

```
urlobj.getProtocol()        // returns scheme string
urlobj.getHost()            // returns host string
urlobj.getPort()            // returns port int
urlobj.getFile()            // returns file name string
urlobj.getRef()             // returns reference anchor string
```

10.3 READING FROM A URL

To read the resource located by a urlobj, obtain its InputStream with:

```
InputStream in = urlobj.openStream()
```

The stream thus opened can be used, just like any other input stream, to obtain data from the URL (Figure 10.1). An IOException results if the URL cannot be opened for some reason.

For writing to a URL, you must create a URLConnection that allows both reading and writing (Section 10.4).

Figure 10.1   READING A URL

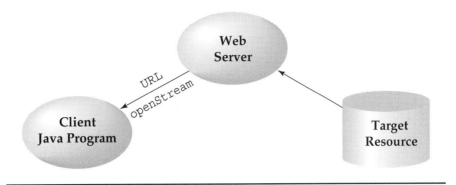

For reading textual input, it is convenient to make a BufferedReader and use its readLine method:

```
BufferedReader sn = new BufferedReader
        (new InputStreamReader(symbolicNet.openStream());
String line = sn.readLine();
```

Let's write a class ReadUrl to read bytes from a given URL and to output the data:

```
///////    ReadUrl.java    ///////
import java.io.*;
import java.net.*;

public class ReadUrl
{   public static void readOut(String url, OutputStream out)
    {    try
        {   URL urlobj = new URL(url);                   // (1)
            InputStream in = urlobj.openStream();         // (2)
            int c;
            while ( (c = in.read()) > -1 ) out.write(c);  // (3)
            in.close();
        }   catch (MalformedURLException e) { JavaSystem.error(e); }
            catch (IOException e) { JavaSystem.error(e); }
    }

 // other methods ...
}
```

The static method readOut takes a URL string and an OutputStream as arguments. It forms a URL object (line 1), creates an InputStream object (line 2), then reads and outputs each byte (line 3). Appropriate exceptions are caught and processed. This method is useful for retrieving data from a URL for local display or storage.

Add the following `main` method to test the code:

```
public static void main(String[] args) throws IOException
{   if ( args.length < 1 || args.length > 2 )
    {   System.err.println("Usage: ReadUrl URL [output-file]");
        System.exit(1);
    }
    if ( args.length == 1 )
        readOut(args[0], System.out);
    else
    {   OutputStream out = new FileOutputStream(args[1]);
        readOut(args[0], out);
    }
}
```

To experiment with this code, you can run it with the command

java ReadUrl "http://SymbolicNet.org/index.html"

which should display all lines in the file `index.html` to standard output. You can use the command

java ReadUrl *someURL file*

to save any URL-identified resource into the given *file*.

Instead of displaying or saving to a file, you may want to read textual data from a URL into a string buffer. The following method does just that:

```
public static StringBuffer readString(String url)
{   try
    {   URL urlobj = new URL(url);
        InputStreamReader in = new
            InputStreamReader(urlobj.openStream());
        int c;
        StringBuffer buf = new StringBuffer();
        while ( (c = in.read()) >= 0 )
            buf.append((char)c);
        return buf;
    } catch (MalformedURLException e) { JavaSystem.error(e); }
      catch (IOException e) { JavaSystem.error(e); }
    return null;
}
```

The method returns either a buffer with the desired text or `null`, indicating an error.

The URL class makes reading any resource identified by a URL (usually served by a Web server) anywhere on the Internet as easy as constructing a file name and opening it for reading.

10.4 COMMUNICATING WITH A URL

The openStream described in the previous section is used for reading a URL that locates a resource via a GET query. To send a POST query (Section 10.7), you must also send the query body before retrieving the results from the URL. For such applications, you should (Figure 10.2):

1. Establish a URLConnection object.
2. Set desired connection parameters for the connection.
3. Connect to the target URL.
4. Write query data to the connection.
5. Read the response.

The URL method openConnection creates and returns a URLConnection object for reading and/or writing the target URL:

```
URLConnection connection = urlobj.openConnection();
```

Set the doOutput connection parameter if you wish to enable output to the URL:

```
connection.setdoOutput(true);
```

Then make the connection:

```
connection.connect();        // throws IOException
```

Figure 10.2   I/O VIA URLCONNECTION

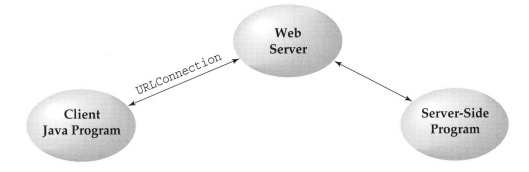

Now you can write to the URL, using the connection's `OutputStream`

```
OutputStream out = connection.getOutputStream();
```

and read from the URL using the connection's `InputStream`:

```
InputStream in = connection.getInputStream();
```

Reading via `openStream` (Section 10.3) and via a `URLConnection` are the same—data located by the URL are retrieved. A URL connection also allows you to access *message headers* sent by the server.

Writing to the URL is also simple: just output to the `OutputStream` of the connection. What to write and the exact data format depend on the protocol of the given URL. The `URLConnection` class supports mainly HTTP, the *hypertext transfer protocol* used by Web servers and clients. The class is most convenient for dealing with HTTP URLs.

A basic understanding of HTTP will help you use `URLConnection` effectively.

10.5 HTTP BASICS

When a program communicates with an HTTP URL, it becomes a client of an HTTP server (Web server) identified by the URL. The HTTP protocol governs how the client and the server exchange information. Knowing HTTP enables you to write code for Web clients and servers. Basics of HTTP are introduced here so that you can take full advantage of Java networking tools.

HTTP usually employs the connection-oriented TCP/IP (Section 7.1). Following is the framework of an HTTP transaction:

1. Connection—A client opens a connection to a server.
2. Query—The client requests a resource controlled by the server.
3. Processing—The server receives and processes the request.
4. Response—The server sends the requested resource or an error back to the client.
5. Transaction complete—The transaction is done and the connection may be closed.

HTTP is *stateless*, meaning each request is independent and assumed to have no relation with any prior request. The resource sent back can be a file or the output of a server-side program (Section 10.7). The data content can be one of many types, including text, HTML, image, sound, and video.

HTTP governs the format of the query and response messages (Figure 10.3). The header part is textual, and each line in the header should end in RETURN and NEWLINE. However, it may end in just NEWLINE. The initial line identifies the message as a query or a response.

Figure 10.3   HTTP QUERY AND RESPONSE FORMATS

```
initial line              (different for query and response)
HeaderKey1: value1        (zero or more header fields)
HeaderKey2: value2
HeaderKey3: value3
                          (an empty line with no characters)
Optional message body contains query or response data.
The amount and type of data in the body are specified
in the headers.
```

A query line has three parts, separated by spaces: a *query method* name, a local path to the requested resource, and an HTTP version number. For example:

```
GET    /path/to/file    HTTP/1.1
```

or

```
POST    /path/script.cgi    HTTP/1.1
```

The GET method requests the specified resource and does not allow a message body. In Java, when you read a URL without first writing to it, the GET method is used. There is also a HEAD query method, which is like GET but requests only the header part of the response. Unlike GET, POST allows a message body and is the preferred method for contacting a server-side program.

A response (or status) line also has three parts separated by spaces: an HTTP version number, a status code, and a textual description of the status. Typical status lines are:

```
HTTP/1.1    200    OK
```

for a successful query, or

```
HTTP/1.1    404    Not Found
```

when the requested resource cannot be found.

HTTP headers are textual and are KEY: value pairs. HTTP/1.0 defines 16 headers, although none are required. HTTP/1.1 defines 46 headers, and one (Host:) is required for queries because multiple Web sites can be at the same IP address. Header keys are case insensitive. Table 10.1 lists usual headers.

HTTP/1.1 also allows persistent connections and the sending of the body of a long response in chunks for better performance.

Table 10.1   HTTP HEADERS

Header	Meaning
`HOST:`	Host and port part of the URL, required for queries under HTTP/1.1
`FROM:`	Email address of user sending query
`User-Agent:`	Name/version of program sending query
`SERVER:`	Name/version of server sending response
`Last-Modified:`	Last modification time of resource retrieved
`Content-Type:`	The type of the body in the message
`Content-Length:`	Length in bytes of the body
`Location:`	URL to retrieve

10.6   A URL DOWNLOADER

Now let's apply knowledge of Java I/O and networking with URLs to write a program that's useful in practice. The Downloader class downloads from a URL (Figure 10.4). To use it simply do

java Downloader *SomeURL*

and data will be retrieved across the network into a local file with an appropriate name derived from the given URL string or the content type.

```
///////    Downloader.java    ///////
import java.io.*;
import java.net.*;
import java.util.StringTokenizer;

public class Downloader
{ public Downloader(String url)  // constructor
   {   try
      { URL urlobj = new URL(url);                        // (1)
        String file = simpleFilename(urlobj.getFile()); // (2)
        ser = urlobj.openConnection();                   // (3)
```

Figure 10.4   WEB DOWNLOADER

```
            if ( file == null )
            {   file = ser.getContentType();                 // (4)
                file = "download." + file.replace('/','-');   // (5)
            }
            fileobj = new File(file);
            out = new FileOutputStream(fileobj);              // (6)
            fileCreated = true;                               // (7)
            System.runFinalizersOnExit(true);                // (8)
        } catch (MalformedURLException e)
          { JavaSystem.error(e); }
          catch (IOException e) { JavaSystem.error(e); }
        }
 // other methods ...
        protected File fileobj = null;
        protected URLConnection ser = null;
        protected OutputStream out = null;
        protected boolean fileCreated = false;
        protected boolean done = false;
}
```

The constructor forms a URL object (line 1), obtains the simple file name from the given URL string (line 2), and establishes the URL connection (line 3). In case the URL string does not yield a file name, a name is constructed based on the content type detected (lines 4–5). After a FileOutputStream is successfully opened, the fileCreated flag is set to true (lines 6–7). The class has a finalize method, which should be run at the end of the program (line 8).

```
public String filename() { return fileobj.getName(); }

public boolean isReady()
{   return ( ser != null && out != null ); }

public boolean isDone() { return done; }
```

The file name used can be retrieved, and the isReady predicate should be called before actual downloading performed by:

```
public void download()
{   if ( ! isReady() ) return;
    try
    {   InputStream in = ser.getInputStream();        // (A)
        int c;
        while ( (c = in.read()) > -1 ) out.write(c);  // (B)
        in.close();
        out.close();
        done = true;                                  // (C)
    } catch (IOException e) { JavaSystem.error(e); }
}
```

The download method obtains the InputStream in the URL connection ser (line A) and reads every byte into the ready FileOutputStream out (line B). Reading a URL connection without first writing to it sends an HTTP GET query automatically. The method then closes both input and output streams and sets the done flag (line C). The flag is used in the finalize method

```
public void finalize()
{   if ( ! done && fileCreated ) fileobj.delete(); }
```

to ensure that no empty file is left around if downloading failed. The auxiliary method simpleFilename extracts a simple file name from the file part of a URL string:

```
String simpleFilename(String s)
{   String a = null;
    StringTokenizer t = new StringTokenizer(s,"/");
    while ( t.hasMoreTokens() )
        a = t.nextToken();
    return a;
}
```

A main method finishes the implementation. It takes one command-line argument, a URL to download. The file name for the downloaded data is also displayed.

```
public static void main(String[] args)
{   if ( args.length != 1 )
    {   JavaSystem.err.println("Usage: Java Downloader URL");
        System.exit(1);
    }
    Downloader d = new Downloader(args[0]);
    if ( d.isReady() )
    {   d.download();
        if ( d.isDone() )
            JavaSystem.out.println("Downloaded file: "
                + d.filename());
        else
            JavaSystem.err.println("file: " + d.filename()
                + " may be incomplete.");
    }
    else
        JavaSystem.err.println("Downloader failed");
}
```

This example can be used to download URLs without accessing a Web browser. It illustrates many Java features covered so far and demonstrates the power of Java networking.

10.7 THE POST QUERY

By writing to a URLConnection, you are sending data to a Web server via a POST query (Figure 10.5). The URLConnection constructs a POST query and encloses the data you write as the body of the query. A Web server usually processes the incoming data by calling a CGI program, a Java servlet, or an *active page*.

A POST query includes:

- A URL, which specifies a server-side program
- Content-Type and Content-Length headers
- A message body

A CGI program receives the message body through standard input and processes it. The Web server to CGI program interface is explained later (Section 10.12).

The POST query content type is usually

application/x-www-form-urlencoded

which means that the content body is *URL-encoded* (Section 10.8).

Following is a sample HTTP POST query:

```
POST /cgi-bin/register-user HTTP/1.1
HOST: SymbolicNet.org
From: jDoe@great.enterprise.com
User-Agent: JavaHTTPTool/1.1
Content-Type: application/x-www-form-urlencoded
Content-Length: 132

name=John+Doe&address=678+Main+Street&...
```

Figure 10.5   POST **QUERY BY JAVA**

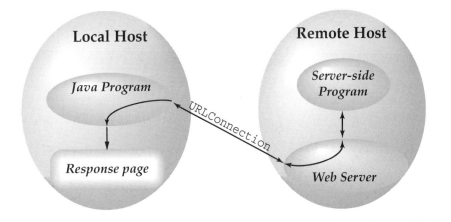

When you write to a URLConnection, you supply only the properly encoded message body; the other parts of the POST query are automatically sent for you. For sending custom headers yourself, you must use the socket mechanism (Section 10.14).

10.8 QUERY BODY ENCODING

When you write to a URLConnection, the message body follows the encoding convention used by the HTML forms: the message body is a series of entries separated by &. Each entry is a *name=value* pair. The name and value parts are encoded as follows:

1. Each nonalphanumeric character that is not a SPACE is replaced by a three-character sequence %*xx*, where *xx* is its ASCII code in hexadecimal.
2. Each SPACE is coded as a +.

For example:

Character	URL Encoding	Character	URL Encoding
:	%3a	?	%3f
~	%3e	@	%40
$	%24	;	%3b

This encoding can be done easily with the Java class java.net.URLEncoder. Following is a simple class to show the encoding:

```
///////    ShowURLCode.java    ///////
import java.net.URLEncoder;

class ShowURLCode
{  public static void main(String[] args)
   {   String to = URLEncoder.encode(args[0]);
       System.out.println(to);
   }
}
```

You can find a URLDecoder in Section 3.5.

10.9   A POST-QUERY CLIENT

The URLConnection is very useful for writing Web clients. We first establish an interface PostClient to specify the required methods:

```java
///////    PostClient.java    ///////
import java.io.InputStream;

/**
 * An interface for POST-query clients that
 * make a post query and receive the server response
 * @author Paul S. Wang
 */

public interface PostClient
{
 /** Sends POST query to Web server.
  *  Gets ready for reading response.
  *  This method can be called only once.
  *  @param msg the URL-encoded POST query body to send.
  */
  void post(String msg);

 /** Reads entire textual response body.
  *  @return TextLines object containing response body.
  */
  TextLines bodyText();

 /** Reads next text line of response body.
  *  @return String object.
  */
  String readNextLine();

 /** Reads the headers of the server response.
  *  @return TextLines object containing response headers.
  */
  TextLines responseHeader();

 /** Gets input stream useful for reading nontext content types.
  *  @return InputStream to read server response.
  */
  InputStream getInputStream();
```

```
/** Closes down the client.
 */
  void close();
}
```

Documentation comments (Section 12.10) are included. Now we can implement a URL-based PostClient, UrlClient, as follows. Later (Section 10.15) a socket-based implementation SocketClient will also be given (Figure 10.6).

```
public class UrlClient implements PostClient
{  public UrlClient(String url)
   {    try
        {  URL urlobj = new URL(url);                    // (i)
        }  catch (MalformedURLException e)
           { JavaSystem.error(e); }
           catch (IOException e) { JavaSystem.error(e); }
   }

   public void close() {}
 // other methods ...

   protected URL urlobj;
   protected BufferedReader in;
   protected InputStream ins;
   protected PrintWriter out;
   protected URLConnection ser;
}
```

A UrlClient is instantiated with a URL string of a server-side program (line i). The UrlClient object is now ready to post a query via the post method

```
public void post(String msg)
{   try
    {   ser = urlobj.openConnection();                   // (ii)
        ser.setDoOutput(true);                           // (iii)
        out = new PrintWriter(ser.getOutputStream());    // (iv)
        if (out != null)
```

Figure 10.6   POST **CLIENTS**

```
    {  out.println(msg); out.close();              // (v)
        ins = ser.getInputStream();
        in = new BufferedReader (new InputStreamReader (ins));
     }
    } catch (IOException e) { JavaSystem.error(e); }
}
```

which follows these steps:

1. Opens a URLConnection (lines i–ii)
2. Enables writing to the connection (line iii)
3. Gets the output stream, calling connect() implicitly, then writes the message body (lines vi–v)

The msg string is assumed to be properly URL-encoded already. The post method of a PostClient can be called only once. Establish a new client to send another query. After posting the query, the response becomes available. To read textual responses use:

```
public TextLines bodyText()  // reads all lines
{   if ( ins != null )
    {  TextLines from = new TextLines();
        int len = from.input(ins);
        if ( len > -1 ) return from;
    }
    return null;
}

public String readNextLine()     // reads one line
{   try
    {    return in.readLine();
    } catch (IOException e) { JavaSystem.error(e); }
    return null;
}
```

The method bodyText makes reading textual responses from a server-side program even more convenient. It returns a TextLines object (Section 4.20) containing the lines of text produced by the target server-side program or null for failure.

To read nontextual data, use

```
public InputStream getInputStream()
{   return ins;  }
```

to obtain the input stream and read bytes from it.

10.10 A SPECIFIC URL CLIENT

Applying the general `UrlClient` to access a real server-side program should be interesting. The Institute for Computational Mathematics (ICM/Kent) Web site provides demonstrations of inspiring and nontrivial mathematical computations by computers. Let's see how the `RemoteFactor` class sends a user-specified polynomial to ICM for factoring over the integers.

The command

```
java RemoteFactor '27*y^3-8*x^3'
```

displays this result:

```
<html>
<h1>Answer Computed:</h1>
<p>
<pre>
(C3)  factor(27*y^3-8*x^3);
                                  2                 2
(D3)          (3 Y - 2 X) (9 Y  + 6 X Y + 4 X )
</pre>
</p>
</html>
```

In `RemoteFactor`, the `main` method first checks the command-line arguments. Then it prepares the `POST` query message with a single name/value pair:

```
factor=URL-encoded integer polynomial in infix notation
```

A `PostClient` object is used to send the `POST` query and obtain the response (lines 1–2):

```
///////   RemoteFactor.java    ///////
import java.net.URLEncoder;

class RemoteFactor
{ public static void main(String[] args)
  {   if ( args.length != 1 )
      {  System.err.println( "Usage: RemoteFactor poly");
         System.exit(1);
      }
      String msg = URLEncoder.encode("factor", "UTF-8") +
               "=" + URLEncoder.encode(args[0], "UTF-8");
      PostClient cc = new UrlClient(protocol + "://" +
            server + ":" + port + path);            // (1)
      cc.post(msg); TextLines ans = cc.bodyText();   // (2)
      cc.close();
      ans.output(System.out);
  }
```

```
static String protocol = "http";
static int port = 80;
static String server = "icm.mcs.kent.edu";              // (3)
static String path = "/cgi-bin/icm.demo";               // (4)
}
```

The ICM/Kent server host address is on line 3. The server-side program location is on line 4. The path string identifies the program icm.demo.

Try to remotely factor your favorite polynomial with this program.

10.11 NETWORKING IN APPLETS

An applet is able to network with its codebase host computer. For example, an applet for accessing the factoring demo (Figure 10.7) can also be found on a server at Kent.

```
///////    Factor.java    ///////

public class Factor extends JApplet
{  public void init()
   {    browser = getAppletContext();
        server = "http://ox.cs.kent.edu" + path;
        tf = new JTextField(20);
        tf.setBackground(Color.cyan);
        JButton s = new JButton(" Submit ");
        Container cp = getContentPane();
        cp.setLayout(new FlowLayout());
        cp.add(tf); cp.add(s);
        s.addActionListener(new SubmitHandler());
   }

// other methods ...
```

Figure 10.7   A NETWORKING APPLET

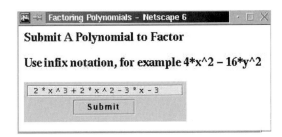

```
    protected JTextField tf;
    protected AppletContext browser;
    protected String server;
    static String path = "/cgi-bin/jfac";
}
```

A JTextField receives the input polynomial in infix notation. A Submit button posts the query and obtains the URL of a file containing the computational result. The result is then displayed by the applet context:

```
private final class SubmitHandler implements ActionListener
{   public void actionPerformed(ActionEvent e)
    {   factor(tf.getText()); }
}
```

The submit action is to call factor on the polynomial entered in the JTextField. The factor method prepares the POST query, creates a PostClient to send the POST query (A–B), reads one line which should be a valid URL string (C), then asks the applet context to display the URL in a separate top-level window (D):

```
protected void factor(String poly)
 { try
   { String to = URLEncoder.encode("factor", "UTF-8")
            + "=" + URLEncoder.encode(poly, "UTF-8");   // (A)
     UrlClient cc=new UrlClient(server); cc.post(to);   // (B)
     String msg = cc.readNextLine();                    // (C)
     URL url = new URL(msg);
     browser.showDocument(url, "_blank");               // (D)
   } catch(java.io.UnsupportedEncodingException e) {}
     catch(MalformedURLException e) { JavaSystem.error(e); }
     catch(IOException e) { JavaSystem.error(e); }
 }
```

To try this applet, visit the following Web page:

```
http://ox.cs.kent.edu/factor/Factor.html
```

10.12 CGI SCRIPTS

When accessing a URL for CGI, a client obtains service provided by a CGI program through a Web server (Figure 10.8). The RemoteFactor example (Section 10.9) accesses the CGI program icm.demo through the Web server http://icm.mcs.kent.edu/.

Figure 10.8   CGI: COMMON GATEWAY INTERFACE

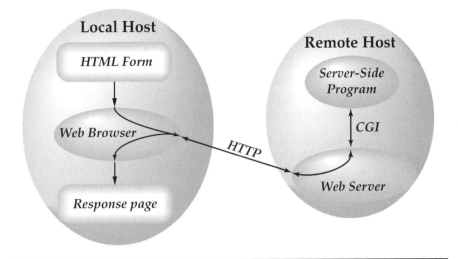

CGI programs are simple and usually written in high-level scripting languages such as UNIX Shell or Perl, but they can be in any language, including Java. Following are the interface considerations for a CGI program:

- A CGI script must usually be placed in a special directory, commonly known as a *cgi-bin*, where programs accessible through the Web server are placed.
- A CGI script obtains the specially formatted and URL-encoded message body from a query (usually POST) through standard input.
- A CGI script can access command-line arguments.
- A CGI script can access environment-variable settings transmitted to it by the Web server.
- A CGI script's standard output goes to the Web server, which relays the data back to the CGI client.

Typically, a CGI program follows this outline:

1. Determines request method and receives input data—The request method is given by the REQUEST_METHOD environment variable. For a POST query the data are read from standard input and the length of the data is indicated by the CONTENT_LENGTH environment variable. For a GET query, the input data is from the QUERY_STRING environment variable.

2. Decodes and checks input data—The URL-encoded input data is decoded and the name-value pairs recovered. The presence and correctness of the input data are checked. Incomplete or incorrect input results in a request to the end-user to resubmit the information.

3. Performs tasks—The input data is complete and correct. The program now processes the information, completing what the program is supposed to do.

4. Produces output—A generated response is sent to standard output. The response is usually in HTML format.

Steps 2 and 4 follow the CGI protocol and are described further.

The query body received by a CGI script is usually a set of name-value pairs in the form:

```
name1=value1&name2=value2&name3=value3
```

When the input comes from an HTML form, the names are specified in the `input`, `select`, or `textarea` tags. The values are entered by the user. But when the input is generated by a program, such as a Java applet, it must be URL-encoded. The input is a long coded string with no white spaces or line breaks.

Follow these simple steps to decode the input:

1. Break the input at places marked by `&`, and treat each part with steps 2 and 3.

2. Convert each `+` character to a SPACE.

3. Convert each `%`*xx* sequence to a single character with ASCII value *xx* in hexadecimal.

The `FormData` class (Section 9.2) implements this input-unpacking procedure. To send back a response, first, output the content-type line

```
Content-Type: text/html
```

to standard output, *followed immediately by an empty line*. Then send the complete document in the indicated content type. The CGI program now terminates.

10.13 WEB SERVER-SIDE PROGRAMMING

Java can also be useful for writing Web server-side programs. A Java servlet is a special class that can be loaded and run in a servlet-capable Web server such as Apache. CGI programs work with any Web server and can also be written in Java. For example, a Java CGI program `NewMember` to support an HTML form (Figure 10.9) may send email to a designated person about new members joining a Web site. Then it can confirm success by sending a simple reply:

```
void reply(String msg)
{    StringBuffer buf = new StringBuffer(front);
```

Figure 10.9   HTML FORM FOR NewMember

```
Join club.com

Full Name: [                              ]
Email:     [                              ]
           [ Join Now ]
```

```
        buf.append(msg);
        buf.append(back);
        System.out.print("Content-Type: text/html\r\n");        // (1)
        System.out.print("Content-Length: " +
                        buf.length() + "\r\n");                 // (2)
        System.out.print("\r\n");    // empty line
        System.out.print(buf);                                 // (3)
}
```

The reply method sends the content type (line 1) and length (line 2) before sending the response page (line 3). NewMember uses the getInput method to obtain the query data:

```
void getInput() throws IOException
{   String msg, method =
        System.getProperty("REQUEST_METHOD");
    if (method.equals("GET") || method.equals("get"))
    {   msg = System.getProperty("QUERY_STRING");            // (4)
        form = new FormData(msg);
    }
    else if (method.equals("POST") || method.equals("post"))
    {   int c, len = Integer.parseInt(
            System.getProperty("CONTENT_LENGTH"));           // (5)
        StringBuffer buf = new StringBuffer(len);
        while ( len > 0 )                                    // (6)
        {   c = System.in.read();
            buf.append((char) c);
            len--;
        }
        msg = buf.toString();
        form = new FormData(msg);                            // (7)
    }
    else reply("<p>Error: unsupported method " +
                method + "</p>");
}
```

For a GET request, input is from the query string (line 4). For a POST request, a given number of bytes (line 5) is read from standard input (line 6). The FormData class (Section 9.2) is handy for unpacking and decoding the query input (line 7).

Follow these steps to install NewMember.class as a CGI program accessible via a Web server:

1. Place NewMember.class in the *cgi-bin* directory of the Web server.

2. Make the .class file readable and executable by everyone.

3. Place in the *cgi-bin* a UNIX shell script that executes the Java interpreter on a given Java class. The shell script also transmits CGI command-line arguments and environment variables to the Java program.

Servlets

Java *servlets* offer another, more efficient way to supply server-side programming to the Web. A servlet is a Java program, in the form of a class, that is loaded and executed by a Web server to perform specific tasks. Once loaded, a servlet stays in its executing environment and can be invoked time and again. Compared to CGI, where a program is created and destroyed for each invocation, servlets can be much more efficient. The *servlet API*, defined by the Java servlet interface, governs the way any server program interacts with a servlet. Detailed coverage of servlets is beyond the scope of this text.

10.14   NETWORK COMMUNICATION WITH SOCKETS

The term *networking* refers to communication between programs running on different host computers. Independent processes must be able to initiate and/or accept communication requests in an asynchronous manner. A *socket* is a software mechanism representing a *communications entry point* on the Internet. A client process uses its own socket to communicate with another socket belonging to a server process. Different *Internet Protocols* (TCP/IP, UDP/IP, etc.) are supported by different types of sockets. The role of a socket on the Internet is not unlike that of a telephone on a phone network.

Communication using URL and URLConnection is internally implemented using sockets. The two classes provide convenient facilities to access well-established Internet services. The URLConnection is especially useful for accessing Web servers. Other networking activities such as accessing other types of services, writing custom-designed servers, and enabling one-on-one direct communication between remote processes are performed using sockets directly.

Each host computer on the Internet creates its own sockets to communicate with other sockets on the Internet. A socket address consists of the following:

- The numerical IP address of the host computer
- An integer port number

Through its own socket, a process communicates with another socket belonging to a remote process. Thus network communication is conducted through a pair of cooperating sockets, each known as the *peer* of the other.

Processes connected by sockets can be on very different computers that may use different data representations. A long is 32 bits on some systems but 64 bits on others, for example. Even when the data sizes agree, systems may still use either the high or the low byte to store the most significant part of a number. In this *heterogeneous environment*, data are sent and received at the socket level as a sequence of bytes. Thus a sequence of ASCII characters can usually be sent and received directly through sockets. Other types of data must be *serialized* into a sequence of bytes before sending and *deserialized* from a byte sequence into the local data type at the receiving end.

As stated in Chapter 7, a network service involves a *server* and a *client*. A server process, such as a Web server, provides a specific service accessible through the network communications mechanism. A client process, such as a Web browser, provides user access to a particular network service. A well-defined set of conventions must exist to govern the way services are located, requested, accepted, and terminated. This set of conventions comprises a protocol that must be followed by both server and client. Standard Internet services such as World Wide Web, Telnet, and FTP usually use sockets with preassigned port numbers: 80 for HTTP, for example.

Different types of sockets support different protocols (Figure 10.10). Communication takes place between sockets of the same type. Two important types are:

- Stream socket—With a stream socket, a process can *dial another stream socket's address and make a connection*. A pair of connected stream sockets supports bidirectional, reliable, sequenced, and unduplicated flow of data without record boundaries. Stream sockets use the *Transmission*

Figure 10.10   JAVA CLIENT SOCKETS

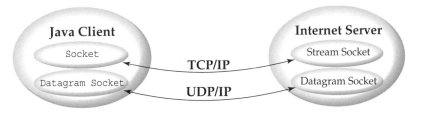

Control Protocol (TCP/IP). The Java `Socket` and `ServerSocket` classes provide the client- and server-side stream socket mechanisms.

- Datagram socket—With a datagram socket, a process can *send a data packet with the receiving socket's address*, like sending a letter. Datagram sockets provide bidirectional flow of data packets called *messages*. The communications channel is not promised to be sequenced, reliable, or unduplicated. That is, a process receiving messages on a datagram socket may find messages duplicated and, possibly, not in the order in which they were sent. Datagram sockets use the *User Datagram Protocol* (UDP/IP). The Java `DatagramSocket` and `DatagramPacket` provide mechanisms for datagram-based communications.

10.15 STREAM SOCKET CLIENTS

Internet client programs use stream sockets to access TCP-based servers. The Java `Socket` class provides easy access to stream sockets. The line

```
Socket soc = new Socket(String host, int port);
```

opens a stream socket `soc` connected to a server at the given *port* on *host*. The call may throw `IOException` or `UnknownHostException`. When `soc` is established,

```
OutputStream out = soc.getOutputStream();
InputStream in = soc.getInputStream();
```

produce I/O streams for communicating with the target server. When two-way communication is finished, use the code

```
out.close();
in.close();
soc.close();
```

to close the socket connection.

The Internet standard *Echo service* (TCP) uses port 7. It echoes back every line of text received. Let's write a stream socket client to experiment with this service:

```
public class Echo
{ public static void main(String[] args)
  {   try
      {   Socket soc = new Socket("monkey.cs.kent.edu", 7);  // (1)
          PrintWriter out = new                              // (2)
              PrintWriter(soc.getOutputStream());
          InputStream in = soc.getInputStream();             // (3)
          for (int i=0; i < args.length -1 ; i++)            // (4)
              out.print(args[i] + " ");
          out.println(args[args.length-1]);                 // (5)
```

```
            int c;
            while ( (c = in.read()) != -1 )                        // (6)
            {    System.out.print((char)c);
                 if ( (char)c == '\n' ) break;                     // (7)
            }
            System.out.println();                                  // (8)
            out.close(); in.close();  soc.close();                 // (9)
        } catch (UnknownHostException e) { JavaSystem.error(e); }
          catch (IOException e) { JavaSystem.error(e); }
    }
}
```

The stream socket soc connects to the Echo server running on the host
monkey.cs.kent.edu (line 1). The I/O streams out and in are obtained from soc
(lines 2–3). The command-line arguments are sent to the Echo server (lines 4–5)
and the return message is received and displayed (lines 6–8). Then the socket
connection is closed (line 9).

Try the program with

java Echo It is OK.

and you'll see this display:

It is OK.

As another example, let's implement a PostClient (Section 10.9) using the
lower-level socket rather than a URLConnection. The SocketClient class makes
a stream socket connection to a Web server and sends the query header and
body explicitly.

```
public class SocketClient implements PostClient
{   public SocketClient(String server, int port, String cg)
    {   host = server; path = cg; port = pt;  }

    public TextLines responseHeader()        // HTTP response header
    {   return header;  }

 // other methods ...

    protected Socket sin;
    protected int port;
    protected BufferedReader in;
    protected InputStream ins;
    protected PrintWriter out;
    protected String host;
    protected String path;
    protected TextLines header = null;
    protected BufferedReader hr;
}
```

With a `SocketClient` object, a client program calls the `post` method to send a `POST` request that is already formatted and encoded as needed. The `post` method opens the stream socket (line A) and gets the I/O streams as usual (lines B–C). The method now sends the header, then the body. The response head is stored in `header`, a `TextLines` object (line E).

```
public void post(String msg)
{   try
    {   sin = new Socket(host, port);                            // (A)
        if ( sin == null ) System.err.println("socket failed");
        out = new PrintWriter(sin.getOutputStream());            // (B)
        ins = sin.getInputStream();                              // (C)
        if (out != null)
        {   postHeader(msg);                          // header
            out.println(msg); out.flush();            // msg body  (D)
        }
        setHeader();    // response header
    } catch (UnknownHostException e) { JavaSystem.error(e); }
      catch (IOException e) { JavaSystem.error(e); }
}


protected void setHeader()      // records HTTP response header
{   if ( ins != null && header == null )
    {   header = new TextLines();                                // (E)
        hr = new BufferedReader(new InputStreamReader(ins));
        String line;
        try
        {   do
            {   line = hr.readLine();
                if ( line.length() != 0 )
                    header.addLine(line);
            } while ( line.length() != 0 );
        } catch ( IOException e) { }
    }
}


public TextLines bodyText()
{   if ( ins != null )
    {   TextLines from = new TextLines();
        int len = from.input(ins);
        close();
        if ( len > -1 ) return from;
    }
    return null;
}
```

After making the call to post, the client calls the method bodyText to receive the response from the server-side program. The postHeader method sends the header part of the query (lines F–G), followed by an empty line and the message body (line D). The POST query header is sent following the HTTP protocol:

```
static void postHeader(PrintWriter out, String host,
               String path, String msg)
{   out.print("POST " + path + " HTTP/1.0\r\n");    // request  (F)
    out.print("HOST: " + host + "\r\n");            // host
    out.print("User-Agent: JavaSocketClient\r\n");  // agent
    out.print("Content-Type: +
       "application/x-www-form-urlencoded\r\n");
    out.print("Content-Length: "
       + msg.length() + "\r\n");                     // length   (G)
    out.print("\r\n");                               // empty line
}
```

A client finally can call the close method, which will shut down the stream socket. Do not close the I/O streams of a Java stream socket until you are done.

```
public void close()
{   try
    { if ( sin != null ) sin.close();
    } catch (IOException e) { JavaSystem.error(e); }
}
```

Because SocketClient is a PostClient, the same RemoteFactor code, with UrlClient replaced by the plug-compatible SocketClient, can be used to test SocketClient.

10.16 DATAGRAM SOCKETS

Java also supports datagram sockets:

- DatagramSocket—class to create server or client datagram sockets, and to provide send and receive methods
- DatagramPacket—class to construct and manipulate datagram messages sent and received via datagram sockets

Network services following the UDP protocol use datagrams. With a good understanding of the stream socket descriptions and examples, you'll be able to handle datagram applications by reading the API.

An efficient and general purpose *sh* (UNIX shell) script is:

```
#!/bin/sh
## File name:  java.cgi
```

```
## Usage:  java.cgi ClassName args ...
CGI_DIR=/usr/local/WWW/scripts   ## use correct cgi-bin

## set environment variables CLASSPATH and
## LD_LIBRARY_PATH also when necessary

cd $CGI_DIR
exec java -DCONTENT_TYPE=$CONTENT_TYPE \
          -DCONTENT_LENGTH=$CONTENT_LENGTH \
          -DREQUEST_METHOD=$REQUEST_METHOD \
          -DQUERY_STRING=$QUERY_STRING \
          -DSERVER_NAME=$SERVER_NAME \
          -DHTTP_COOKIE=$HTTP_COOKIE \
          -DHTTP_HOST=$HTTP_HOST \
          -DHTTP_REFERER=$HTTP_REFERER \
    $* ## the class name of the CGI program to invoke
```

Note that only a few important CGI environment variables are shown transmitted to the Java program. The *sh*-shell notation `$*` stands for all the command-line arguments `java.cgi` receives.

With this arrangement, the URL to access the `NewMember` program becomes

`http://`*host*`/`*cgi-bin*`/java.cgi?NewMember`

The `sendEmail` method is shown in Section 12.4. The complete `NewMember.java` can be found in the example package.

10.17 CREATING NETWORK SERVERS

You usually access existing servers, but you can also write your own to supply customized services. A stream socket server in Java first creates a server-side stream socket with

`Serversocket listen = new ServerSocket(`*port*`);`

on the local host at the given *port*. The socket `listen` is used to listen and wait for incoming connections:

`Socket s_soc = listen.accept();`

A new `Socket` object is returned when an incoming connection is made. The socket s_soc is the peer of the connecting client socket and is used by the server to communicate with the client. The socket s_soc can be closed when the client is finished. The `listen` socket remains available for another `accept()` call.

Accepting and servicing multiple incoming clients can be complicated, especially in Java. Fortunately, servers can be written without such complications by using the **inetd**, the *internet services daemon* (Figure 10.11).

Figure 10.11   JAVA SERVER UNDER inetd **CONTROL**

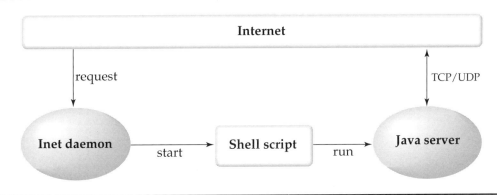

Following is the process:

1. Implement a server, to serve one client, that reads from the client via standard input and writes to the client via standard output. This server does not need any socket code at all.

2. Register the server program, the service protocol, and the port number with the inetd by placing an appropriate entry in the inetd configuration file.

The inetd waits for an incoming connection (stream socket) or data (datagram socket) and then takes appropriate action:

- When a connection request (stream socket) at your designated port is detected, it invokes your registered server program, passing to it the connected socket for standard I/O.

- When incoming data is detected (datagram socket) at your designated port, it invokes your registered server program, passing to it the datagram socket for standard I/O.

The inetd then goes back to monitoring designated ports, ignoring activity on any datagram socket still being serviced.

10.18 STREAM SOCKET SERVER EXAMPLE

A remote file service is implemented in Java, showing the following features:

- A file server performs file storage or retrieval for remote clients, based on client-specified file names.

- The file server communicates with clients through standard I/O.
- The server is put under **inetd** control.

Both server and client code are presented. Client input to the file server is in the following format:

```
filename= string mode= r        (first line)
<empty line>                     (second line)
```

or

```
filename= string mode= w
<empty line>
byte stream of file to store
```

Here is the server code:

```
public class FileServer
{   public static void main (String[] args) throws IOException
    {    String filename, rw, dir = "/tmp/";
         BufferedInputStream in = new
                 BufferedInputStream(System.in);
         String line = getLine(in);                         // (A)
         StringTokenizer tk = new
                 StringTokenizer(line, " \r\t=&");           // (B)
         int c = tk.countTokens();
         if ( c != 4  ) return;
         filename = tk.nextToken();
         if ( filename.equals("filename") )
             filename = tk.nextToken();
         else return;
         rw = tk.nextToken();
         if ( rw.equals("mode") )
             rw = tk.nextToken();
         else return;                                       // (C)
         line=getLine(in);                                  // (D)
         if ( line.equals("") || line.equals("\r") )
            if ( rw.equals("r") ) readBack(dir + filename);  // (E)
            else writeTo(dir + filename, in);               // (F)
    }

    // other methods ...
}
```

The FileServer main method reads the first line from standard input (line A) and extracts tokens (lines B–C). After reading the second input line (line D), which must be empty, the server retrieves (line E) or stores (line F) a file as appropriate.

Files are stored and retrieved on the server host. The /tmp directory is used in this example.

```
static String getLine(InputStream in) throws IOException
{   int c;
    StringBuffer buf = new StringBuffer();
    while ( (c = in.read()) > -1 && c != '\n' )
        buf.append((char) c);
    return buf.toString();
}

static void readBack(String file) throws IOException
{   int c;
    FileInputStream infile = new FileInputStream(file);
    while ( (c = infile.read() ) > -1 )
        System.out.write(c);
}

static void writeTo(String file, InputStream in)
            throws IOException
{   int c;
    FileOutputStream ofile = new FileOutputStream(file);
    while ( (c = in.read() ) > -1 )
        ofile.write(c);
}
```

Installing a Server

On a UNIX machine, follow these steps to install the preceding server:

1. Compile FileServer, and place FileServer.class in a suitable directory, for example,

   /usr/local/bin

2. Create an executable sh shell script that sets up environment variables and invokes FileServer.
3. Register the shell script with **inetd**.

Here is a sample sh script (filesvr.sh) for step 2:

```
#!/bin/sh
### filesvr.sh

cd /usr/local/bin    ## directory of FileServer.class
exec /usr/java/bin/java FileServer
```

To register `filesvr.sh` (located in /usr/local/bin, for example) add a line similar to the following entry to the `inetd.conf` file (normally in /etc):

```
javafilesvr   stream   tcp nowait  pwang   /usr/local/bin/filesvr.sh
```

And add a line similar to

```
javafilesvr   3298/tcp javafilesvr   # Experimental Java file server
```

in the system file /etc/services that lists network servers and their port numbers. Note that we used port 3298 for our Java file server. A system manager should enter these entries and signal **inetd** to process the revised configuration file. After these steps are performed, `FileServer` is active.

A File Server Client

Let's establish a client program to test the file server. The class `FileTest` allows you to store or retrieve a remote file conveniently with commands in the following form:

java FileTest *remote_file* r > *local_file*
java FileTest *remote_file* w < *local_file*

```
public class FileTest
{  public static void main(String[] args)
   {    try
       {  if ( args.length != 2 ) err();
          String filename = args[0];
          String mode = args[1];
          if ( !mode.equals("r") && !mode.equals("w") ) err();
          Socket soc
             = new Socket("monkey.cs.kent.edu", 3298);          // (1)
          OutputStream os = soc.getOutputStream();              // (2)
          PrintWriter out = new PrintWriter(os);
          InputStream in = soc.getInputStream();                // (3)
          out.println("filename="+filename + "    "             // (4)
                + "mode=" + mode);
          out.println();                                        // (5)
          out.flush();
          int c;
          if ( mode.equals("w") )                               // (6)
             while ( (c = System.in.read()) != -1 )
                 os.write(c);
          else // mode.equals("r")                              // (7)
          {   while ( (c = in.read()) != -1 )
                 System.out.write(c);
          }
          out.close(); in.close();  soc.close();                // (8)
```

```
        } catch (UnknownHostException e) { JavaSystem.error(e); }
          catch (IOException e) { JavaSystem.error(e); }
    }
}
```

After checking command-line arguments, FileTest.main sets up a stream socket connected to the experimental file server at port 3298 on the indicated host (line 1). The stream out (in) is used to write (read) the server (lines 2–3). A file request is then sent to the server (lines 4–5). The client proceeds to either send (line 6) or retrieve (line 7) a file as appropriate. The I/O streams and the stream socket are closed at the end (line 8).

The err method follows:

```
static void err()
{    JavaSystem.err.println("Usage: FileTest filename r or w");
     System.exit(1);
}
}
```

10.19   REMOTE METHOD INVOCATION

Through networking, a Java program running on any host can locate *remote objects* running on other hosts (*remote objects*) and call their methods, passing arguments and receiving results. After being set up, remote objects are used as if they were local objects. This *remote method invocation* (RMI) capability makes Java a powerful platform for writing client and server applications. For example, an applet can be an RMI client that uses remote objects running on its codebase server.

Remote Objects

The Java RMI feature is supported by the java.rmi package. A *remote object* is one whose class implements either the java.rmi.Remote interface or a subinterface of it. A remote object r_obj in one JVM running on *server host* can be used by a client from another JVM running on *client host* as if r_obj were running locally on the client host. This is arranged by having a *stub object* on the client side and a *skeleton object* on the server side to hide the networking details of RMI. You generate stubs and skeletons for a remote class by using the **rmic** (RMI stub compiler) tool.

A stub is the client-side proxy of the remote object, and the skeleton is the networking front end of the remote object. When a method in the stub is invoked, it does the following:

1. Initiates a connection with the remote JVM containing the remote object

2. Marshals (serializes and transmits) the arguments to the remote JVM

3. Waits for the result of the method invocation

4. Unmarshals (receives and deserializes) the value or exception returned

5. Returns the value or exception to the caller

On the server side, networking with the stub and invoking the r_obj is handled by a skeleton, which does the following:

1. Unmarshals the arguments

2. Invokes the method in r_obj

3. Marshals the result (return value or exception) to the caller

Within Java 2 and later environments, skeletons are eliminated by generic code in the JVM.

Because Java can easily load classes across a network and run its objects efficiently within the same JVM, the decision to keep the class remote through RMI must be based on the infeasibility of the load-and-run approach. For example, a remote object may be a database agent or may represent an extensive, complicated, or proprietary computation.

The Java RMI Architecture

Java RMI provides a framework within which to develop and deploy client-server applications. RMI supports the creation of remote objects, stubs, and skeletons. It also provides ways to register, locate, and launch remote objects as well as transmit remote method call arguments and results.

The RMI architecture (Figure 10.12) involves these elements:

• Remote object—An instance of a class that implements the Remote interface and supplies well-defined functionalities from a server host

Figure 10.12   RMI ARCHITECTURE

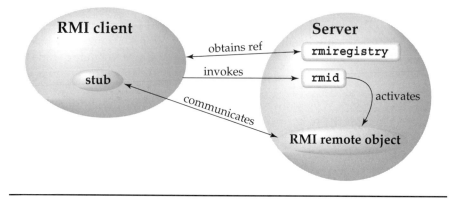

- Client—An application that obtains services from remote objects
- Registry (**rmiregistry**)—A daemon that registers and associates names to remote objects available on a server host
- RMI daemon (**rmid**)—A daemon that activates, on demand, remote objects on the server host

The java.rmi.Naming class supplies static methods to register and look up remote objects with the registry

```
static Remote lookup(String location)
static void bind(String name, Remote obj)
static void rebind(String name, Remote obj)
```

where the string location is in the form

```
//serverhost/name
```

and name is any string chosen to identify a remote object.

A Factorial Server by RMI

Let's illustrate RMI with a simple example in which an applet uses a remote object at its codebase to compute *n*! (*n* factorial). The client is the applet, and the remote object is one that can compute the factorial. This example is placed in a package myrmi/demo.

The FactorialApplet obtains a remote object and casts it into a known type (line 1) then uses it normally to perform a computation (line 2). The result is displayed in a JLabel (line 3).

```
///////    FactorialApplet.java    ///////
package myrmi.demo;

import java.rmi.Naming;
import java.rmi.RemoteException;
import javax.swing.*;

public class FactorialApplet extends JApplet
{  public void init()
   {   try
       {   obj = (Factorial)Naming.lookup("//" +        // (1)
                     getCodeBase().getHost() +
                     "/FactorialServer");
           ans = obj.factorial(7);                      // (2)
       } catch (Exception e)
         { System.out.println("FactorialApplet" +
               " exception: " + e.getMessage());
           e.printStackTrace();
         }
```

```
        getContentPane().add(new JLabel(              // (3)
            "Factorial 7 = " + ans, JLabel.CENTER));
    }

    int ans;
    Factorial obj = null;
}
```

The Factorial is an interface that extends Remote:

```
///////    Factorial.java    ///////
package myrmi.demo;

import java.rmi.Remote;
import java.rmi.RemoteException;

public interface Factorial extends Remote
{
    int factorial(int i) throws RemoteException;
}
```

This is all the client-side code you need to write. The Factorial interface is used on the server side as well as the client side.

For the server side, we program the actual factorial computation as an *activatable* remote object (line 4) that implements Factorial (line 5). An activatable remote object can be activated on demand by the RMI daemon when a client requires its services. The constructor is typical (6). The factorial computation is as expected (line 7). Note that a remote object throws RemoteException (line 8).

```
///////    FactorialImpl.java    ///////
package myrmi.demo;

import java.rmi.*;
import java.rmi.activation.*;

public class FactorialImpl extends Activatable    // (4)
        implements Factorial                      // (5)
{
  public FactorialImpl(ActivationID id,           // (6)
                     MarshalledObject data)
        throws RemoteException
    {
      super(id, 0);
    }
```

```
public int factorial(int n)                          // (7)
       throws RemoteException                         // (8)
{   if ( n < 0 ) throw(new RemoteException(
       "Arg to factorial cannot be negative."));
    return ( n == 0 ) ? 1 : n*factorial(n-1);
  }
}
```

Note that we simply defined the factorial method. Other methods required by the Remote interface are supplied by Activatable. Alternatively, a server-side remote class, such as FactorialImpl, can extend UnicastRemoteObject, instead of Activatable, in which case the remote object must run as a daemon ready to provide service. It is simpler to take the Activatable approach.

The server side also needs a set-up program that sets up the security policy (line 9) for an activation group created using system defaults (line 10). It registers with the RMI daemon (**rmid**) an activation descriptor containing information on the activation group ID, the class file for the remote object, its location, and any initialization data (lines 11–12). The remote object returned by Activatable.register (line 13) is then bound with the name FactorialServer (line 14) through the **rmiregistry**.

This all may seem complicated. But for typical RMI applications, this set-up program can be used as a template:

```
///////    Setup.java    ///////
package myrmi.demo;

import java.rmi.*;
import java.rmi.activation.*;
import java.util.Properties;

public class Setup
{ public static void main(String[] args) throws Exception
   {   // Create and install a security manager
       System.setSecurityManager(new RMISecurityManager());

       Properties props = new Properties();
       props.put("java.security.policy", path + "policy");    // (9)

       ActivationGroupDesc.CommandEnvironment ace = null;
       ActivationGroupDesc gd = new                           // (10)
                   ActivationGroupDesc(props, ace);
       ActivationGroupID agi =
          ActivationGroup.getSystem().registerGroup(gd);

       String location = "file:" + path;                      // (11)
```

```
        MarshalledObject data = null;
        ActivationDesc desc = new ActivationDesc          // (12)
            (agi, "myrmi.demo.FactorialImpl",
             location, data);

        // Register with rmid
        Factorial mri = (Factorial)Activatable.register(desc); // (13)
        System.out.println("Got the reference for FactorialImpl");

        // Bind the reference to a name in the registry
        Naming.rebind("FactorialServer", mri);            // (14)
        System.out.println("Exported FactorialServer");
        System.exit(0);
    }

    // you need to customize the path
    static String path ="/home/smith/javaWang/ex11/myrmi/demo/";
}
```

See Section 12.13 for information on Java security and policy files.

Deploying the Client and the Server

To deploy RMI applications, several steps are needed:

1. Run the RMI registry **rmiregistry** on the server host.
2. Compile the RMI client and place it on the client host.
3. Compile the RMI server and place it on the server host.
4. Use the RMI compiler **rmic** to generate the stub (part of the client) and skeleton (part of the server) files. Place one file with the client and the other with the server. To generate the files, run **rmic** on the class that implements Remote. For example:

   rmic myrmi.demo.FactorialImpl

   generates FactorialImpl_Skel.class and FactorialImpl_Stub.class for the server and client side respectively.
5. Start the RMI daemon **rmid** on the server host.
6. Run the setup program on the server host.

The example package contains the complete remote factorial example in the directory:

javaWang/ex11/myrmi/demo/

This is where we will keep the class files for the server also. The client is an applet, and it will be deployed in the personal Web space of the user smith at:

~smith/public_html/applet/

This is a typical situation on UNIX systems. The following UNIX shell script, also contained in the example, can be used to deploy the RMI application:

```
#!/bin/csh

### run registry
unsetenv CLASSPATH
rmiregistry &

### copy html file to web space
set adir = ~smith/public_html/applet
cp Factorial.html $adir
chmod o+r $adir/Factorial.html

### compile RMI client:
### compile applet classes and place in web space
javac -d $adir  Factorial.java FactorialApplet.java

### compile server in source directory
setenv CLASSPATH .:$adir
javac Factorial.java  FactorialImpl.java Setup.java

### generate and position stub and skeleton files
###      FactorialImpl_Skel.class
###      FactorialImpl_Stub.class
cd ../..
rmic myrmi.demo.FactorialImpl
mv myrmi/demo/FactorialImpl_Stub.class $adir/myrmi/demo
chmod o+x $adir/myrmi $adir/myrmi/demo
chmod o+r $adir/myrmi/demo/*

### start rmi daemon, the policy is a toy policy
rmid -J-Djava.security.policy=myrmi/demo/policy &

sleep 5

### run Setup (on one line)
java  -Djava.rmi.server.codebase=
         http://server-name/~smith/applet/
      -Djava.security.policy=
         myrmi/demo/policy myrmi.demo.Setup &
```

To experiment with this program on your computer, the user, host, and domain names as well as file locations must be customized to your own settings.

When deployed the ~smith/public_html/applet/myrmi/demo directory contains these files:

```
Factorial.class
FactorialApplet.class  FactorialImpl_Stub.class
```

The stub class is generated by the **rmic** tool. The applet HTML file is in ~smith/public_html/applet/. These files constitute the client part.

For the server part, the two files, FactorialImpl.class and FactorialImpl_Skel.class, are kept in the source directory where all of the .java files are. The skeleton file is not necessary for Java 2 and later environments.

Building an RMI Application

Let's summarize the steps for building an RMI application:

1. Define an interface *RemoteTask* by extending the Remote interface and specifying descriptors for remote methods. These are the methods to be invoked remotely. The RemoteTask interface is used on both the server and the client sides.

2. The client-side code obtains a *stub* object by

   ```
   RemotTask stub = (RemoteTask)Naming.lookup( "//" + server-host
   + "/" + serviceName);
   ```

   and then makes remote method calls with

   ```
   stub.remote-method(...);
   ```

3. On the server side, write a class *TaskImpl* that implements *RemoteTask* and extends Activatable.

4. Use **rmic** to generate the stub and skeleton classes from the file *TaskImpl*.class.

5. For the server side, write code to set up and register the service under *serviceName*.

6. Deploy the service on the server host and run the compiled client on any client host.

Argument Passing in RMI

When a call is made to a remote method, arguments are passed from the client to the server over the network. Similarly, the returned values are also passed back to the client across the network. Primitive data can be passed and returned without any concern. When objects are passed and returned, we have to pay more attention.

An ordinary object, one that does not implement the java.rmi.Remote interface, can be passed and returned as long as it implements the Serializable interface. Serializable is an interface without methods. Simply declaring a class to implement Serializable will allow its object to be marshaled and unmarshaled and therefore used as arguments or return values in remote method invocations. For the same reasons, serializable objects can be input and output directly with object I/O streams (Section 6.13).

A remote object, one whose class implements java.rmi.Remote, can be passed and returned also. In this case, only a stub object will be passed and returned for the other side to access the remote object through the RMI mechanism.

The example package also contains a fraction server that passes Fraction objects to a remote object. For more information, see the *RMI Guide* in the Java documentation.

10.20 SUMMARY

Networking enables processes on the server side and the client side to communicate and exchange information. Java supports basic networking in the java.net package at two levels: the higher URL level and the lower socket level. A URL identifies a server and a resource controlled by that server. The *scheme* part of the URL identifies the server type and usually also the protocol to use. An HTTP URL indicates a Web server that uses the HTTP protocol.

In a URL object, the openStream() method gets you an InputStream to read the content of the target URL. The URL object is convenient for sending an HTTP GET request. In a URLConnection object, the openConnection method establishes a connection to read the header and body of an URL or to send an HTTP POST query and read the response. URL and URLConnection make writing clients for standard networking services simple. With these, an applet can easily network with its codebase server.

Understanding the HTTP query and response formats is necessary for Web server-side and client-side programming. In Java, you may write CGI and servlet programs on the server side. CGI programs work with all Web servers. Because a Java program runs under an interpreter, a CGI program written in Java normally must be activated by a shell-level front end. Servlets are more efficient but work only with enabled servers.

A socket is a communications end point on the Internet. A network client establishes an appropriate socket to communicate with its peer socket on the server side. An Internet socket address consists of a host IP address and a port number.

Java supports both stream (TCP/IP) and datagram (UDP/IP) sockets. The Socket and ServerSocket classes support stream sockets on the client side and server side, respectively. The DatagramSocket and DatagramPacket classes support datagram sockets and the manipulation of messages. The facilities allow the building of custom clients and servers that use their own, usually ad hoc, protocols. An applet storing files to and retrieving files from its codebase host is an example.

Remote Method Invocation (RMI), in the `java.rmi` package, is a higher-level networking mechanism that masks lower-level details of networking and supports the ability of invoking methods in objects running on remote hosts. To this end, RMI provides ways to locate, activate, pass arguments to, and receive results from remote objects. Ordinary objects are passed by serialization, and remote objects are passed by sending stubs.

EXERCISES

Review Questions

1. Explain the parts of a URL. Why is the port number part optional? What is `PATH_INFO`? `QUERY_STING`?

2. List the sequence of steps in a Java program for retrieving a URL-specified file. What exceptions can occur? What about making a `GET` request?

3. List the steps in a Java program for sending a `POST` query and receiving a response. What exceptions can occur?

4. What are the different HTTP query and response formats? What is the difference between a `GET` and a `POST` query?

5. With a URL, when should you use the simpler `openStream` method of `URL` and when should you use the more complicated `openConnection` method of `URLConnection`?

6. What is URL encoding? Explain the encoding and decoding process. What Java classes help URL encoding?

7. What information transfers from a Web server to a CGI program? From a CGI program back to the Web server?

8. Explain why a shell front end is needed to launch a CGI program written in Java.

9. Why does a CGI program written in Java need a shell script to launch it? How does such a shell script transmit CGI environment variables to the Java program?

10. What is the purpose of a socket? What is the difference between a stream socket and a datagram socket?

11. When should sockets be used instead of URLs for networking?

12. What are the steps for creating and installing a network server written in Java? How does the `inetd` get involved?

13. Consider RMI. In what situation would one prefer the `unicastRemoteObject` option? Revise the `Factorial` application given in Section 10.19 from the activation model to the always-running model.

14. What does serialization mean? Why does an object have to be serialized before being transmitted across a network?

15. What is the difference between a remote object and an ordinary object?

Programming Assignments

1. Consider the `UrlClient` implementation of the `PostClient` interface. Write the `responseHeader` method that is required but has not been shown in the text.

2. Write an applet that collects user data such as name, address, phone number, and email address and sends the information back to a server-side CGI program for processing.

3. An applet cannot read or write files on a client system, but it can network with its codebase server. Write an applet that uses a server-side *file saver* (Section 10.13) to store and retrieve information.

4. Write a *talk* application in which two people can join in a chat session from different hosts. This problem requires a clear overview of the problem and a careful design before implementation.

5. (Term Life-5) Refer to exercise Term Life-4 in Chapter 8. Turn the premium calculator GUI (Section 8.7) into an applet, and connect it to a remote term life calculator automatically activated at the codebase host.

6. Follow the `DownLoader` example (Section 10.6) and write a `WebRetriever` that, when given a URL, will download all files recursively reachable from the contents of that page into a local file hierarchy. Limit the downloading to the pages on the same Web site as the given URL.

7. The RMI client `FactorialApplet` is an applet. Convert this program into a regular application and test it.

8. Write a Java `telnet` client for remote login. Can this be done with `URLConnection`? With stream socket?

## CHAPTER ELEVEN

Threads and Concurrent Programming

When a computer is running, multiple tasks are being performed simultaneously. Hence the computation environment (the operating system) and programming languages (such as Java) have features to support the performing of independent tasks in parallel.

Java provides *threads* for concurrent programming. We will explain the concept of threads, the added dimensions of programming in the presence of threads, and the Java constructs that supports them. You'll also see how threads are put to use in practical applications, such as a 60-minute timer.

The application of threads to decouple image drawing and image loading shows their benefits and power.

11.1 WHAT IS A THREAD?

In a sequential computer, there is only one program being executed at any given time. The computer has only one CPU, or *processing element (PE)*, and it runs one program at a time. A program under execution is called a *process*. A process consists of routines, data, stack, and operating system code and structures. When the Java Virtual Machine interprets your program, it executes as a process. A sequential computer can perform *multiprogramming* by rapid reassignment of the PE among many processes, giving the appearance of parallelism. Such processes run *concurrently*. True parallelism is achieved by a computer with multiple PEs.

Within a process, control usually follows a single *execution thread*, typically starting with the first statement of the main method, stepping through a sequence of statements, and ending when main returns. This is the familiar *single thread* programming model. Java also supports multiple concurrent *threads of execution* or *multithreading*. A Java process can create and manage, within itself, multiple execution sequences concurrently. Each execution sequence is an independent *thread*. All threads in a process share the same address space and operating system resources of the process. Therefore each thread can access all of the data and procedures in the process, but each thread has its own program counter and procedure call stack. As an independently running entity, a thread is much easier to create than a new process. Hence a thread is sometimes known as a *lightweight process*.

Advantages of Multithreading

Single-threaded programs are good for simple calculations. Dynamic, inter-active, or event-driven programs usually consist of multiple active parts that naturally perform independently and interact or cooperate in some way to achieve the intended goals. For example, a video game program has inde-pendent parts for user controls, graphical rendering, motion generation, score keeping, and so on. A single-threaded video game would be enormously com-plicated, if not impossible. A multithreaded program (Figure 11.1) can model each of these parts with a different thread.

Furthermore, graphical rendering and user control processing take place si-multaneously. Responsive handling of such concurrency is difficult in a single-threaded program. A 60-minute timer example (Section 11.13) shows how a GUI program can count the timer down and respond to user control (e.g., pausing the timer) effectively with multithreading.

You can also use threads to decouple activities with very different process-ing speeds. The Java image loader and image observer setup (Section 11.15) is a clear example of this technique.

Figure 11.1   MULTITHREADED PROGRAM

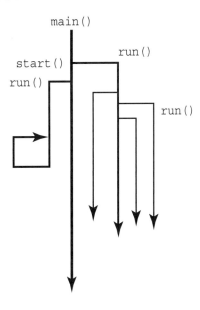

Concepts and techniques for writing multithreaded programs in Java are introduced. Examples show how to apply them in practice.

Challenges of Multithreading

Basically, a multithreaded program has to coordinate several independent activities and avoid the possibility that they will *trip over one another*. Multithreaded programs involve four important new aspects not present in ordinary single-threaded programs: *mutual exclusion, synchronization, scheduling,* and *deadlock*. A good understanding of these concepts will help you write correct multithreaded programs.

Mutual Exclusion

Threads in a program usually have to cooperate to achieve a certain task. Cooperation typically involves different threads accessing the same program constructs. When multiple threads share a common resource (field, array, object, or file), simultaneous access by more than one thread can take place. Such simultaneous accesses usually result in erroneous or unpredictable results. For example, if a field `flag` is read by one thread as it is being assigned a value by a second thread, the value read can be either the old value or the new value. Worse yet, if two threads assign values to `flag` simultaneously, one of the values is lost. Because the relative speeds of concurrent threads can never be known, the outcome of multithreaded programs can depend on *which thread gets where first*. This *race condition* should be avoided if your multithreaded program is to work correctly every time.

To avoid simultaneous access, it is possible to arrange *mutually exclusive access* to shared quantities. When programmed correctly, only one thread at a time can access the same quantity protected by *mutual exclusion (mutex)*.

Consider a team of programmers working on a project. If two programmers work on the same file from different workstations concurrently, disaster strikes. Mutual exclusion in this case can be arranged by having a programmer *lock* a file before working on it. No one else can obtain access to the file until it is *unlocked*.

With OOP, the shared resource and operations on it can often be encapsulated in an object. All critical operations lock and unlock the host object to enforce mutual exclusion. Access to an already locked object causes the thread to wait until the object is unlocked.

Synchronization

Mutual exclusion avoids having threads trip over one another, but you still need a way for threads to communicate and coordinate their actions in order to cooperate. Threads make progress through their code at independent and unpredictable rates. Thus it is necessary to coordinate the order in which some tasks are performed. If a task must not be started before other tasks are finished, it is important to make sure that this is the case. For example, imagine each thread is a worker in a factory. A thread must wait until another thread has finished a part it needs. Such time-related coordination of concurrent activities is called *synchronization*. Thread synchronization usually involves delaying a thread until certain conditions are met or certain computations by other threads are done.

A thread is said to be *blocked* if its continued execution is delayed until a later time. There are several ways to block a thread. A thread can *spin* in a loop, checking a condition repeatedly until it becomes true (or false). Here is the top-level analogue of a spin block loop

```
while ( flag != true ) { sleep(t); }
// now perform task knowing flag is true
```

where `flag` is a shared variable. While a thread is *sleeping*, other threads can execute.

Thread Scheduling

When a process involves multiple threads, the available PE executes all threads in rapid succession. Exactly when the current thread gives up the PE and which thread is run next depend on the *scheduling policy* of the thread system. Java threads have a *priority* attribute that affects scheduling, as will be explained.

Deadlock

When multiple threads are interdependent in many ways, with resources shared under mutual exclusion and subtasks under synchronization, there is the possibility of *deadlock*. Deadlock happens when threads are waiting for events that will never happen. For example, thread A is waiting for data from thread B before producing output for B. B is waiting to receive some output from A before it can produce data for A. When writing multithreaded programs, one must be very careful to avoid such problems.

11.2   THREADS IN JAVA

A Java program begins execution with a *main thread*—the `main` of the Java application or the applet control thread. The main thread can spawn other threads to run concurrently. When the main thread finishes, the Java program terminates. Ways to create, coordinate, and control threads will be described. Examples are given to illustrate thread usage.

Here are the principal things to learn about threads:

- Writing programs for individual threads

- Launching and controlling new threads
- Arranging mutual exclusion for threads
- Coordinating thread interactions
- Closing down threads
- Putting threads to good use in practice

11.3 PROGRAMMING THREADS

A thread is a separate control flow that runs its own code. In Java, a thread is an object of a class that either extends the Thread class or implements the Runnable interface. A thread's entry point is its run method:

```
public void run();
```

A thread terminates when run returns.

When extending Thread, you simply override the run method to perform desired functions. Following is a simple example thread program that displays even or odd integers from a given starting point up to 100:

```
class EvenOdd extends Thread
{   public EvenOdd(int first, int interval)
    {   i0 = first;  delay = interval; }

    public void run()
    {   try
        {   for (int i=i0; i <= 100; i += 2 )
            {   System.out.println(i);      // (A)
                sleep(delay);               // (B)
            }
        } catch (InterruptedException e)  // (C)
            {   return;  }
    }
    private int i0, delay;
}
```

The run method of EvenOdd pauses momentarily (line B) after displaying an integer (line A). The Thread method sleep(n) suspends execution of the current thread for n milliseconds, giving other threads a chance to run. The sleep method throws an exception (caught on line C) if the pause is interrupted.

In addition to extending Thread, you can write thread code by implementing the Runnable interface, as explained in Section 11.12.

11.4 LAUNCHING THREADS

An executing thread can *launch* or *spawn* other threads (Figure 11.1) by creating thread objects and invoking their start methods to start them running independently.

Following is a simple program that puts EvenOdd threads to work:

```
class ThreadTest
{  public static void main(String[] args)
               throws InterruptedException
   {   EvenOdd thread1 = new EvenOdd(1, 20);  // (1)
       EvenOdd thread2 = new EvenOdd(0, 30);  // (2)
       thread1.start();
       thread2.start();
       thread1.join();                        // (3)
       thread2.join();                        // (4)
       System.out.println("Main thread done");
   }
}
```

Two instances of EvenOdd are created (lines 1–2). These are threads that can run independently. The Thread method start() launches a thread and makes it ready to run. A ready thread competes for available PE service. When it gets the PE for the first time, its run() method is called. After starting thread1 and thread2, the main thread goes on to wait for the child threads to finish (lines 3–4). The call thread1.join() will return when thread1 dies (runs to completion or otherwise terminates).

Running ThreadTest produces the following sequence of numbers:

```
1  0  3  2  5  4  7  9  6  11  8 13 15 10
17 12 19 21 14 23 16 25 27 18 29 20 31 33
```

As you can see, both threads run concurrently. The shorter delay used for odd numbers causes that thread to progress that much faster.

11.5 THREAD CONTROL

A parent thread spawns a child thread by creating a Thread object and invoking its start method. The start method causes the object to become a new thread, ready to run. The JVM calls the run method when it is that thread's turn to execute for the first time. A thread can be in one of five states:

1. Newborn—The thread is newly created.
2. Ready—The thread is ready to run or continue.

3. Running—The thread is being executed.

4. Blocked—The thread is waiting for an event and not receiving PE service.

5. Dead—The thread is finished and can no longer run.

A thread is *alive* if it is ready, running, or blocked.

A thread t1 can be controlled by another thread (t0), usually the parent thread, through the following Thread methods:

- t1.checkAccess()—Determines whether the current thread (t0) has permission to control t1. This is done implicitly for many control methods listed below.

- t1.start()—Makes a newborn thread t1 ready.

- t1.stop()—Makes t1 go from alive to dead. It causes t1 to throw a newly created ThreadDeath exception, which causes the Java run time to kill the thread. This is abnormal termination of a thread from the outside and a drastic measure used as a last resort to kill a thread. Avoid using stop() to terminate a thread.

- t1.isAlive()—Tests whether t1 is alive.

- t1.suspend()—Makes t1 go from ready or running to blocked.

- t1.resume()—Makes t1 go from blocked to ready.

- t1.interrupt()—Sends an interrupt signal to t1, which can detect it by calling interrupted(). An interrupt is like an external event and can trigger preprogrammed responses in a thread.

- t1.join()—Suspends the current thread and waits for t1 to terminate. Throws InterruptedException if t0 is interrupted while executing t1.join().

- t1.destroy()—Kills t1 without cleanup. The method is normally not used.

Note that a dead thread cannot be started; only a newborn thread can.

The preceding methods provide external control. A thread can also control itself internally through these Thread methods:

- sleep(int t)—Suspends the current thread for t milliseconds

- yield()—Makes the current thread go from running to ready, giving other threads a chance to run

- run() returning—Makes the current thread go from running to dead

11.6 MUTUAL EXCLUSION FOR JAVA THREADS

To illustrate mutual exclusion for threads, consider a program designed to find the maximum element in an integer array. Several threads can be used, each looking for a maximum element in a subrange of the array. Each thread then deposits its local maximum in a shared variable maxValue which, at the end, holds the answer. The threads in this simple example work largely independently. However, simultaneous access to maxValue is a potential problem and must be avoided. If multiple PEs are available to run the threads, the program can actually be faster than the sequential solution.

To arrange mutual exclusion for the threads on maxValue, we will use a *mutual exclusion object*. For our example, the mutual exclusion object is an instance of the class MaxGuard that encapsulates the maxValue field with special *get* and *set* methods.

```
class MaxGuard
{      public MaxGuard(int e)
       {    maxValue = e;  }

       public synchronized int getMax()
       {     return maxValue;     }

       public synchronized void setMax(int e)
       {     maxValue = Math.max(maxValue, e);    }

       private int maxValue;
}
```

The keyword synchronized is used to mark mutually exclusive methods within the host mutual exclusion object. When a thread calls a synchronized instance method, it operates as follows (Figure 11.2):

1. Waits (blocked) for the host object to be unlocked if it is already locked by another thread
2. Locks the host object

Figure 11.2   MUTUAL EXCLUSION OBJECT

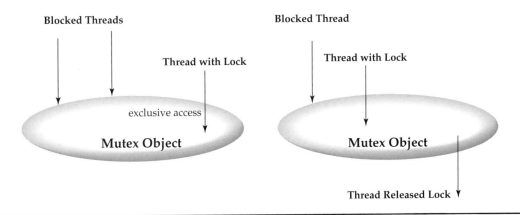

3. Executes the body of the method

4. Unlocks the host object just before returning from the method

Thus, threads are mutually exclusive in time when calling synchronized methods in a mutual exclusion object. With this mechanism, mutual exclusion is achieved for multiple threads getting and setting `maxValue` contained in a `MaxGuard` object (a *mutual exclusion object*).

It is possible to call a synchronized method within a synchronized method. Such nested calls are handled in a straightforward way: When a synchronized method is called on an object locked by the same thread, the call proceeds, but the lock is released only when the outermost synchronized method returns.

With `MaxGuard` in place, we can use multiple `FindMax` threads safely:

```
class FindMax extends Thread
{   public FindMax(int[] ar, int l, int h, MaxGuard m)
    {   arr = ar;   low = l+1; high = h;
        l_max = arr[l];   xobj = m;
    }
 // run method later
    private int l_max;       // local maximum
    private int low, high;   // array range
    private int incr = 10;   // increment
    private int[] arr;       // array ref
    private MaxGuard xobj;   // mutual exclusion object
}
```

Each `FindMax` thread looks for a local maximum in a subrange of the given integer array. The thread examines `incr` array elements at a time (line 1), pausing to give other threads a chance to run. The local maximum found is deposited into a mutual exclusion object `xobj` (line 2) which holds the current overall maximum.

```
public void run()
{   try
    {   while ( low < high )
        {   int n = Math.min(incr, high-low);
            for (int i=low; i <= low+n; i++)
                l_max = Math.max(l_max, arr[i]);   // (1)
            sleep(5);
            low += n;
        }
    } catch(InterruptedException e)
        {   return ;   }
    xobj.setMax(l_max);                            // (2)
}
```

An object that can be used by multiple threads safely is said to be *thread-safe*. Thread safety of objects in a multithreaded program is a concern not to be taken lightly.

We write a simple test for this example. An array of 1024 randomly generated integers is used (line A). The number of slave FindMax threads used either is 4 or is given on the command line (line B). Each slave thread gets a fair subrange of the array (line C) and access to the mutual exclusion object ans (line D).

```
class MaxTest
{ public static void main(String[] args) throws InterruptedException
   {    int[] a = new int[1024];
        for (int i=0; i < 1024; i++)                         // (A)
            a[i] = (int) (100000*Math.random());
        int nt=0;
        if ( args.length == 1 )
            nt = Integer.parseInt(args[0]);
        if ( nt <= 0 ) nt = 4;                               // (B)
        MaxGuard ans = new MaxGuard(a[0]);
        FindMax[] slave = new FindMax[nt];
        int range = 1024/nt;                                 // (C)
        int high, low = 0;
        for (int i=0; i < nt-1; i++)
        {    high = low + range -1;
             slave[i] = new FindMax(a, low, high, ans); // (D)
             low = high + 1;
        }
        slave[nt-1] = new FindMax(a, low, 1023, ans);
        for (int i=0; i < nt; i++) slave[i].start();    // (E)
        for (int i=0; i < nt; i++) slave[i].join();     // (F)
        System.out.println("Maximum = " + ans.getMax());
   }
}
```

All threads are launched (line E), and the desired result is finally obtained by the main thread after all slave threads have finished (line F).

Synchronized Methods

To summarize, mutual exclusion for threads can be arranged by encapsulating a shared quantity such as MaxValue in a *mutual exclusion object*, which guards against simultaneous access by different threads. The mutual exclusion object keeps the guarded data private and provides synchronized get and set methods. A program may use multiple mutual exclusion objects, and they do not interfere with one another.

In addition to instance methods, you may declare static methods synchronized. A synchronized static method locks the class and achieves mutual exclusion with other synchronized static methods in the same class. This is done by using the unique Class object for the class as a mutual exclusion object. Instance and static synchronized methods do not interfere with each other.

If you override a synchronized method in a subclass, the overriding method may or may not be declared synchronized. The subclass declaration does not affect the synchronized property of a superclass method.

Synchronized Statements

With synchronized methods, the host object is the mutual exclusion object. To provide more flexibility, Java also allows you to name a *mutual exclusion object* in front of a set of statements within any method:

```
synchronized ( mutex_obj )
{      statements under control      }
```

A thread executing the statement above will first lock mutex_obj and then proceed to execute the controlled statements only after the lock is acquired. This construct supports the *critical sections* concept of concurrent programming. Different parts of a program that have to be mutually exclusive are called *critical sections*. Synchronized statements in Java are just right for this purpose. Use the same mutual exclusion object in front of all sections of code that are mutually critical. Use different mutual exclusion objects for unrelated critical sections. Synchronized statements and synchronized methods may use the same mutual exclusion object to become mutually exclusive.

A simple mutual exclusion object can come from a class that has no members:

```
class MyLock {  }
```

Let's see a critical-sections version of *finding the minimum element in an integer array*:

```
class FindMin extends Thread
{ public FindMin(int[] ar, int l, int h)
   {   arr = ar;   low = l+1; high = h;
       l_min = arr[l];
   }
   public void run()
   {   try
      {   while ( low < high )
         {   int n = Math.min(incr, high-low);
             for (int i=low; i <= low+n; i++)
                 l_min = Math.min(l_min, arr[i]);
             sleep(5);
```

```
                low += n;
            }
        }  catch(InterruptedException e)
            {   return ;   }
        synchronized ( MinTest.lock )     // critical section
        {  MinTest.min = Math.min(MinTest.min, l_min);
        }
    }
    private int l_min;         // local minimum
    private int low, high;   // array range
    private int incr = 10;   // increment
    private int[] arr;         // array ref
}
```

The threads will update the static member MinTest.min, using code in critical sections guarded by the lock MinTest.lock.

The test program MinTest is very similar to MaxTest but uses a static lock and a static min value. These are made accessible by the slave threads employed.

```
class MinTest
{ public static void main(String[] args) throws InterruptedException
    {    int[] a = new int[1024];
        for (int i=0; i < 1024; i++)
            a[i] = (int) (100000*Math.random());
        int nt=0;
        if ( args.length == 1 )
            nt = Integer.parseInt(args[0]);
        if ( nt <= 0 ) nt = 4;
        lock = new MyLock();            // lock object
        min = a[0];
        FindMin[] slave = new FindMin[nt];
        int range = 1024/nt, high, low = 0;
        for (int i=0; i < nt-1; i++)
        {   high = low + range -1;
            slave[i] = new FindMin(a, low, high);
            low = high + 1;
        }
        slave[nt-1] = new FindMin(a, low, 1023);
        for (int i=0; i < nt; i++) slave[i].start();
        for (int i=0; i < nt; i++) slave[i].join();
        System.out.println("Minimum = " + min);
    }

    public static MyLock lock;
    public static int min;
}
```

Java-supplied containers in the collections framework (Chapter 9) are not thread-safe for efficiency in single-thread programs. For multithreading, synchronized containers that are thread-safe can easily be obtained by factory methods in the `Collection` class (Section 9.9).

11.7 COORDINATING THREADS

Synchronized methods and statements take care of mutual exclusion, but you still need a way to communicate between threads to coordinate interdependent activities. Consider two threads cooperating. Thread A bakes a cake in the oven, and thread B takes it out of the oven to serve. Thread A bakes another cake after thread B removes the cake. This is the typical *producer-consumer* relationship in concurrent programming. It is obvious that the two threads should access the oven with mutual exclusion, but it is also clear that thread B has to wait until thread A has finished baking the cake before serving it. We must arrange for the communication of the *cake ready* and *oven empty* information and coordinate certain actions of the otherwise independently running threads. In concurrent programming, achieving such coordinations is often called *synchronization*, not to be confused with the Java keyword `synchronized`.

To coordinate, a thread can usually check an appropriate condition contained in a mutual exclusion object. The thread will not proceed until the condition is satisfied. In Java, such thread coordinations are achieved with the help of `wait` and `notify` methods inherited from the `Object` class. When executing code under the control of a mutual exclusion object (in a synchronized method or statement), the mutual exclusion object (Section 11.6) also functions as a *monitor*[1] for thread coordination. In Java, every object and class can potentially function as a mutual exclusion object and a monitor. A thread can call monitor methods `wait` and `notify` to achieve coordination.

When a thread calls `wait()` the following happens:

1. The execution of the current thread is suspended and blocked.
2. The lock on the mutual exclusion object is released.
3. The thread is placed on the *monitor queue* of waiting threads to be resumed by some other thread with a `notify` call on the same monitor.

These actions are performed *atomically*—no other thread's code can come between them. Other forms of the `wait` method can block the current thread for up to a given time interval.

When a thread calls `notify()` of an object, the thread at the head of the monitor queue, if any, is resumed (becomes ready). The `notifyAll` method resumes all threads on the monitor queue.

---

[1] The term *monitor* refers to a well-defined concept in concurrent programming.

In our example, thread B would `wait` on a monitor associated with the oven mutual exclusion object until thread A performs a `notify` just after completing the cake in the same oven. Keep in mind that `wait` and `notify` methods *can be used only within synchronized methods or statements.*

To further illustrate thread coordination, let's look at a typical consumer-producer example next.

11.8   CONSUMER AND PRODUCER

For a typical consumer-producer example, let's revisit the circular buffer example first discussed in Section 3.6. Here the circular buffer is used by two co-operating threads. The producer thread deposits characters into the buffer, and the consumer thread extracts characters from the buffer. They access the buffer with mutual exclusion and must also coordinate their actions (Figure 11.3):

- The producer checks to see whether the buffer is full before depositing more characters into it. If the buffer is full, it waits for notification from the consumer thread, which can create space in the buffer by consuming characters.
- The consumer checks to see whether the buffer is empty before extracting characters from it. If the buffer is empty, it waits for notification from the producer thread, which can supply more characters into the buffer.

The mutual exclusion circular buffer is described first, followed by code for the producer and consumer threads. A main method that puts everything to use wraps up this example.

Figure 11.3   CONSUMER-PRODUCER SYNCHRONIZATION

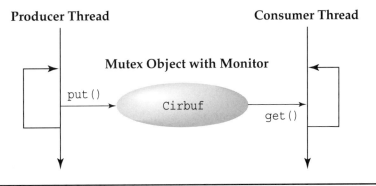

Circular Buffer with Mutual Exclusion

```java
public class Cirbuf
{   public Cirbuf() { this(D_SIZE);}

    public Cirbuf(int s)
    {   head = tail = length = 0;
        fin = false;
        size = s;
        cb = new char[s];
    }
 // other methods ...
    private static final int D_SIZE = 16;
    private volatile boolean fin = false;
    private volatile int head;          // 1st char in buffer
    private volatile int tail;          // 1st empty slot in buffer
    private volatile int length;        // length of chars in buffer
    private int size;                   // buffer capacity
    private char[] cb;                  // character buffer
    private int mod(int x)
    { return(x >= size ?  x - size : x); }
}
```

Declaring a field `volatile` tells the compiler that the field's value may change even if the current thread does not set it, because another thread may do so. Certain optimizations that avoid retrieving values from memory are disabled by `volatile`. The field `fin` is used by the producer thread to signal its completion. Mutually exclusive access to a `Cirbuf` object is achieved with `synchronized` instance methods:

```java
public synchronized boolean is_empty()
{   return length==0; }

public synchronized boolean is_full()
{   return length==size;}

public synchronized boolean finished()
{   return fin; }

public synchronized void finished(boolean v)
{   fin=v;  notify(); }
```

To produce into the buffer a thread calls `put`. Note that a `while` loop (line 1) is used for the test condition (line 2). It is always better to test the condition after a thread is resumed after a `wait` call. This way the thread is assured that the green light is on. In certain situations, another thread can cause the condition to change between the time a thread is resumed and the time it runs.

The producer notifies any waiting consumer at the head of the monitor queue (line 3) just before returning from put.

```
public synchronized void put(char c)
{   while ( is_full() )  // test condition  (1)
        try
        {   wait();        // wait on monitor (2)
        } catch (InterruptedException e){ }
    cb[tail++] = c;
    length++;
    tail = mod(tail);
    notify();   // resume waiting consumer  (3)
}
```

To consume from the circular buffer, a thread calls get. The character extracted is placed in the return parameter c[0], and get returns false if the buffer is empty and the producer has completed (line A). The consumer notifies any waiting producer just before returning from get (line B).

```
public synchronized boolean get(char[] c)
{   while ( is_empty() )
    { if ( fin ) return ( false );    // (A)
      else
        try
        {   wait();   // wait on monitor
        } catch (InterruptedException e){}
    }
    c[0] = cb[head++];
    length--;
    head = mod(head);
    notify(); // resume waiting producer (B)
    return true;
}
```

The Cirbuf class here shows a complete example for defining a mutual exclusion object with synchronized methods and thread coordination with wait and notify.

The Producer Thread

A producer thread is initialized with a circular buffer to use. It deposits characters read from standard input into the buffer until there is no more input (line a). Then it signals producer completion (line b). The produce method performs input reading and buffer stuffing.

```
class Producer extends Thread
{   public Producer(Cirbuf b) { buffer = b;}
```

```
    public void run()
    {   produce();                  // (a)
        buffer.finished(true);   // (b)
    }

    private void produce()
    {   int c;
        while ( true )
            try
            {   if ( (c = System.in.read()) >= 0 )
                    buffer.put((char)c);   // deposit into buffer
                else
                    return;                  // no more input
            } catch(IOException e) { JavaSystem.error(e); }
    }

    private Cirbuf buffer;        // mutual exclusion object
}
```

The Consumer Thread

The consumer thread reads from the given circular buffer and counts the total number of words until there is no more input.

```
class Consumer extends Thread
{   public Consumer(Cirbuf b)
    {   buffer = b; c = new char[1]; }

    public int count() { return wcnt; }

    public void run() {   consume();  }
// consume method later

    private boolean word= false; // partial word indicator
    private int wcnt= 0;           // whole words counted so far
    private Cirbuf buffer;
}
```

The partial word indicator is set to true after the start but before the end of a word. Words are separated by SPACE, TAB, RETURN, or NEWLINE characters.

```
public void consume()
{   char[] c = new char[1];
    while ( buffer.get(c) )      // while more input
        switch(c[0])
        {   case ' ' : case '\t':
```

```
         case '\r': case '\n': // word delimiters
            if ( word )
            {   wcnt++;          // word ends
                word = false;
            }
            break;
         default:
            word = true;        // word begins
      }
   if ( word ) wcnt++;
}
```

Multithreaded Word Counting

Now a main method can be written that employs two independent threads: a consumer and a producer to perform word counting:

```
class WordCount
{  public static void main(String[] args)
   {   Cirbuf buf = new Cirbuf();      // the mutual exclusion object
       Producer pd = new Producer(buf);
       Consumer cs = new Consumer(buf);
       pd.start();          // producer thread now running
       cs.start();          // consumer thread now running
       try
       {   pd.join();
           cs.join();
       }   catch(InterruptedException e) { }
       System.out.println("total " + cs.count() + " words");
   }
}
```

11.9 I/O BETWEEN TWO THREADS

Cirbuf demonstrates data transfer from one thread to another. In practice, it may be more convenient to use the Java supported classes PipedInputStream, PipedOutputStream, PipedReader, and PipedWriter for I/O between two threads.

A PipedOutputStream connected to a PipedInputStream (or PipedWriter to a PipedReader) forms a FIFO byte (character) *pipe* from a producer thread to a consumer thread (Figure 11.4).

Figure 11.4   PIPED I/O

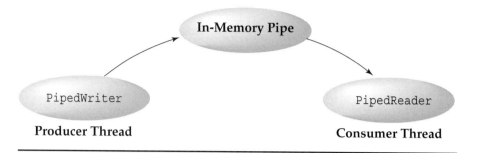

To establish a piped reader-writer pair, for example, use the following:

```
PipedReader reader = new PipedReader();        // not yet connected
PipedWriter writer = new PipedWriter(reader);  // connected now
```

Be sure to treat any IOException that may result. The reader can be given
to a consumer thread and the writer to a producer thread. For example, the
Consumer class (Section 11.8) can be modified to use the reader end of a pipe.
The modifications turning Consumer into PipeConsumer are shown below:

```
public PipeConsumer(PipedReader r) { in = r; }

public void run()
{   try
    {   consume();
        in.close();
    } catch ( IOException e ) { JavaSystem.error(e); }
}

public void consume() throws IOException
{   char[] c = new char[1];
    while ( in.read(c,0,1) > 0 )  // reading one char from pipe
    {   switch(c[0])
        /*  code same as before */
    }
    if ( word ) wcnt++;
}

private PipedReader in;
```

11.10 THREAD PRIORITIES

When created, a thread has the same priority as its parent thread. In Thread, the static integer constants MIN_PRIORITY, NORM_PRIORITY, and MAX_PRIORITY specify the minimum, default, and maximum priority for a thread. Typical values are 1, 5, and 10 respectively. The Java interpreter executes all ready threads according to their *priority setting*. The thread with the highest priority is run, and all threads with that priority will receive some PE time. Lower-priority threads are guaranteed to run only when all higher-priority threads are blocked.

Use getPriority() for the priority of a thread, and setPriority(p) to set a new priority. To make a multithread program run more responsively and efficiently, you may want to set the continuously running part of a program to a lower priority so that event-handling threads are more responsive. For example, the animation thread in Section 11.16 runs at a low priority.

A thread can also call sleep, yield, or suspend to give other threads a chance to run.

11.11 TERMINATING THREAD EXECUTION

A thread terminates normally when its run method returns. Often the best way to terminate a thread is to cause its run method to return. This is especially important if run executes an infinite loop. The recommended method is for run to check a continuation condition periodically and return when the condition is no longer true. The Quartz thread for the 60-minute timer (Section 11.13) and the consumer-producer threads (Section 11.8) work this way.

A customary way of stopping a thread that performs repeated tasks is to record a reference for the thread itself in a field, for example me, and control the thread with the code:

```
while (Thread.currentThread() == me)
{    //  continue to run
}
```

The me field can be set, by this or another thread, to null to stop the thread. The technique will be demonstrated again in the 60-minute timer example (Section 11.13).

A parent thread can call child.join() to wait for the termination of a child thread. It can also stop a child directly by calling child.stop(). A thread can stop itself by calling stop() from any method. The stop() call actually causes a ThreadDeath exception, which causes the JVM to kill the thread. Another form of stop() can throw a user-supplied exception, which can be caught in the thread code for special processing. This mechanism can be a general way to send signals from parent to child threads.

A thread can be either a *user thread* or a *daemon thread*. A daemon thread works in the background. A multithreaded program terminates only when its last *user thread* terminates. Use `setDaemon(true)` to make a thread daemon. A thread inherits the user/daemon status from its parent thread. If you want a program to terminate when `main` returns, you must mark other threads in your program as daemon.

11.12 RUNNABLE CLASSES

In addition to subclassing `Thread`, you may turn any class into an independently executable thread by implementing the `Runnable` interface. If a class is already a subclass of something else, subclassing `Thread` is not possible. In this case, you can instead implement runnable, which requires a single method:

```
public void run();
```

Following is the general form:

```
class Abc extends Xyz implements Runnable
{   Abc(...) {  ... }  // constructor

    public void run ()
    {   ...   }

    // other members ...
}
```

With `Runnable` you can turn any class with a `main` into a thread by adding a method `run` to do what `main` does or even to call `main`.

Here is how to launch a runnable:

```
Runnable runMe = new Abc(...);
new Thread(runMe).start();
```

When you create a `Thread` object with a `Runnable` argument, the thread's `start` method invokes the `run` method of the runnable.

Not subclassing `Thread` means that a runnable does not inherit methods from the `Thread` class. Luckily, `Thread` provides `static` constants and methods that can be used. Some of these are listed here:

```
Thread.MIN_PRIORITY  Thread.NORM_PRIORITY  Thread.MAX_PRIORITY
Thread.yield()
Thread.currentThread()
Thread.sleep(long millis)
Thread.interrupted()
```

An example `Runnable` class can be found in Section 11.16, where we show how to perform animation.

11.13 MULTITHREADED GUI APPLICATIONS

GUI applications run in an event-driven environment in which the program must respond quickly to each event received. An event handler must return directly to preserve the responsiveness of the GUI. But what if some functions take longer to perform? In such cases, the program can *spawn an independently running thread* to perform the time-consuming functions while the main part of the program continues to respond to events. A real-life example can help illustrate the situation. A taxi dispatcher answers phone calls (events) from clients and sends drivers (independent threads) out to pick up passengers. The dispatcher remains ready to answer calls. The alternative, the dispatcher driving off to pick up rides, would be unworkable. For this reason, the Java windowing environment draws widgets and graphics in a separate thread.

Let's see how a GUI program can use threads to perform time-consuming tasks.

A 60-Minute Timer

Consider a GUI application implementing a 60-minute timer not unlike those found on kitchen ovens (Figure 11.5). A user sets and starts the timer, which performs the countdown and sounds a buzzer as the time expires. Such a timer can be handy when you need to leave your workstation within the next hour, to see your dentist, for example. Here is the object-oriented design of this program (Figure 11.6):

- Display—A `TimerFace` object displays the timer setting or time remaining as countdown progresses.
- User control—A `TimerControls` object provides convenient means for the user to set, start, and stop the timer.
- Timing mechanism—A `Quartz` object, running as an independent thread, performs continuous countdown by seconds.
- Overall management—The `Timer60` object manages and oversees the entire timer operation.

Figure 11.5   A 60-MINUTE TIMER

Figure 11.6   OO DESIGN OF 60-MINUTE TIMER

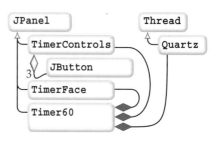

This example illustrates the following:

- Creating, launching, stopping, and restarting a thread
- Performing tasks (countdown) at regularly scheduled intervals
- GUI with complicated user controls
- Changing the name and function of a button dynamically
- Using BoxLayout
- Setting font and foreground and background colors

Class TimerFace

A TimerFace is a JPanel that contains a JLabel (line 1) to display the time digits in a prescribed color (line 2), using 36-point boldface Courier font (line 3). Whenever the minute and second reading is set (line 4), the label string is updated.

```
public class TimerFace extends JPanel
{   public TimerFace(Color c)
    {    setup();
         String time = ""+ m1 + m2 + ":" + s1 + s2;
         face = new JLabel(time, JLabel.CENTER);           // (1)
         face.setForeground(c);                            // (2)
         face.setFont(f);                                  // (3)
         setLayout(new BorderLayout());
         add(face, BorderLayout.CENTER);
    }

    protected TimerFace() { }

    public void set(int min, int sec)                      // (4)
    {    m = min; s = sec;
         setup();
```

```
            String time = ""+ m1 + m2 + ":" + s1 + s2;
            face.setText(time);
        }

    protected void setup()
    {   m1 = m/10; m2 = m % 10;
        s1 = s/10; s2 = s % 10;
    }

    protected JLabel face;
    protected int m=0, s=0;         // time displayed
    protected int m1, m2, s1, s2;   // digits
    protected Font f = new Font("Courier", Font.BOLD, 36);
}
```

The timing mechanism of the timer is considered next.

Class `Quartz`

A `Quartz` object serves as the timing mechanism for the timer program. To run
it as an independent thread, `Quartz` extends the Java-supplied class `Thread`. As
a thread, `Quartz` must implement the `run` method, which is the entry point of
the thread as it starts execution.

```
public class Quartz extends Thread
{   Quartz(Timer60 a)  { tm = a; }
    Quartz(Timer60 a, int d)                              // (i)
    {   tm = a; delay = d; }

    public void tref(Thread t)                            // (ii)
    {   me = t; }  // set self reference

    public void run()
    {   while ( me == Thread.currentThread() )            // (iii)
        {   try
            {    Thread.sleep(delay);                      // (iv)
            } catch (InterruptedException e) { break; }
            tm.countDown();                                // (v)
        }
        tm.pause();                                        // (vi)
    }

    Timer60 tm;            // timer object
    Thread me = null;      // thread of self
    int delay = 1000;      // default 1-sec delay
}
```

A Quartz ticks after a one-second or a specified delay (line i). The Quartz object also keeps a reference to the timer to which it belongs and a reference to its own thread.

The run method continues to trigger countDown() (line v) in the timer tm after each delay period (line iv). The loop stops only when the field me is different from the current running thread (line iii). The program can stop the Quartz timing thread by calling tref (line ii) to set me to null. This is a typical way to stop a thread. The timing thread tells the timer just before terminating (line vi).

Class TimerControls

A TimerControls object provides convenient GUI elements to use to set and start or stop the timer. A horizontal BoxLayout (lines A and B) is used to arrange three buttons: min, sec, and go (lines C–E) to set the minutes and the seconds, and to start and stop the timer. The buttons use a specified background color (line F).

```
public class TimerControls extends JPanel
{   public TimerControls(Timer60 t, Color bg)
    {    tm = t;
         setLayout(new BoxLayout(this, BoxLayout.X_AXIS));    // (A)
         add(Box.createHorizontalGlue());                     // (B)
         add(m = new JButton("min"));                         // (C)
         add(s = new JButton("sec"));                         // (D)
         add(ss = new JButton(" go "));                       // (E)
         s.setActionCommand("sec");
         m.setActionCommand("min");
         ss.setActionCommand(" go ");
         s.setBackground(bg);                                 // (F)
         m.setBackground(bg);
         ss.setBackground(bg);
         s.addActionListener(new SetHandler());
         m.addActionListener(new SetHandler());
         ss.addActionListener(new SsHandler());
    }

    protected TimerControls() { }

    void startButton()
    {    ss.setText(" go ");    }

    protected int minute=0, second=0;
    protected JButton m,s,ss;
    protected Timer60 tm;
```

```
        protected boolean stopped=true;

 // event handlers ...
 }
```

Clicking the min (sec) button advances the minute (second) reading on the timer display. The inner class SetHandler reacts to events from these two buttons:

```
private final class SetHandler implements ActionListener
{  public void actionPerformed(ActionEvent e)
    {    second = tm.getSecond();
        minute = tm.getMinute();
        if ( e.getActionCommand().equals("sec") )   // seconds
        {   if ( ! stopped )
            {  tm.pause();                           // (G)
               stopped = true;
            }
            second = (second + 1)%60;
        }
        if ( e.getActionCommand().equals("min") )   // minutes
        {   if ( ! stopped )
            {  tm.pause();                           // (H)
               stopped = true;
            }
            minute = (minute + 1)%61;
            if ( minute == 60 ) second = 0;
        }
        tm.set(minute, second);                      // set timer
        if ( ss.getText().equals("stop") )           // ready to go
        {   ss.setText(" go ");                       // (I)
        }
    }
}
```

SetHandler also makes sure to stop the timer while setting it (lines G and H) and to display go on the start/stop button (line I).

The SsHandler (start-stop handler) starts and stops the timer by calling the beginEnd() method of the Timer60 object (line J):

```
private final class SsHandler implements ActionListener
{  public void actionPerformed(ActionEvent e)
    {   if ( tm.beginEnd() ) ss.setText("stop");    // (J)
        else ss.setText(" go ");
    }
}
```

The `Timer60` Panel

`Timer60` is a `JPanel` that manages the timing, display, and user-control widgets, described in prior subsections, to make the timer work. The timing element runs continuously in a separate thread. A buzzer sounds when the time expires.

Here we use an `init` method to perform the initializations usually performed by a constructor. This makes it easier for a subclass to add other initializations. Here `init` creates a `TimerControls` (line 1) and a `TimerFace` (line 2) widget and places one above the other in the `Timer60` panel, which has a nice border (line 3). A `Toolkit` object (line 4) is needed for sound effects, as you will see.

The fields `m` and `s` keep the current minute and second settings for the timer.

```
public class Timer60 extends JPanel
{   protected void init()
    {    tmt = null;
        if ( cntl == null )
            cntl = new TimerControls(this, Color.cyan);   // (1)
        if ( face == null )
            face = new TimerFace(Color.blue);             // (2)
        face.set(m,s);
        myBorder();                                       // (3)
        setLayout(new BorderLayout());
        add(face, BorderLayout.CENTER);
        add(cntl, BorderLayout.SOUTH);
        if ( tk == null )
            tk = Toolkit.getDefaultToolkit();             // (4)
    }

    private void myBorder()
    {    setBorder(BorderFactory.createCompoundBorder
        ( BorderFactory.createEmptyBorder(20, 10, 10, 20),
            BorderFactory.createLineBorder(Color.blue)
        ));
    }

    public int getMinute() {   return m;  }
    public int getSecond() {   return s;  }

  // other methods ...

    protected TimerFace face;
    protected TimerControls cntl;
    protected int m=0, s=0;         // min, sec, counter
```

```
    protected Quartz tmt = null;   // timing thread
    protected Toolkit tk;          // for sound
}
```

The method set is called by the cntl object to set the timer to a user-specified time interval. The method enforces a 60-minute maximum setting. It also makes sure that the timer is stopped before setting it.

```
public void set(int min, int sec)
{   if ( min < 0 || sec < 0 ) return;
    pause();
    m = Math.min(min, 60);
    if ( m == 60 ) s = 0;
    else s = Math.min(sec, 59);
    face.set(m,s);    // update display
}
```

The method countDown is called to *tick away* one second by calling the method tick and then to set the time displayed to the current time remaining. The countDown method is called once by the timing thread tmt after each elapsed second:

```
public void countDown()
{   tick();           // down one second
    face.set(m, s);   // redisplay
}
```

When the time remaining is zero, tick sounds the buzzer, stops the count-down, and shows go on the start button. Otherwise the time is decreased by one second.

```
protected void tick()
{   if ( s <= 0 )
    {   if ( m <= 0 )
        {   ring();     // buzzer
            pause();
            cntl.startButton();
            return;
        }
        s=59;  m--;
    }
    else s--;
    return;
}
```

The ring() method beeps three times via the Toolkit object:

```
protected void ring()
{   try        // 0.4-sec interval between sounds
```

```
    { tk.beep();    Thread.sleep(400);
      tk.beep();    Thread.sleep(400);
      tk.beep();
    } catch( InterruptedException e) { }
}
```

The beginEnd method is called by the cntl object to start or stop the countdown. If the timer is currently not running (line 5) and the setting is not zero (line 6), a new Quartz timing thread tmt is created (line 7) and started (line 9) after its self-reference field is set (line 8). Otherwise the pause method is called to stop the timing thread and to set tmt to null (line 10):

```
// returns true if timer is started else false
public boolean beginEnd()
{   if ( tmt == null )                       // (5)
    { if ( s <=0 && m <=0 ) return false; // (6) nothing to do
      tmt = new Quartz(this);              // (7)
      tmt.tref(tmt);                       // (8)
      tmt.start();                         // (9) starts Quartz thread
      return true;
    }
    pause();
    return false;
}

public void pause()                            // (10)
{   if ( tmt != null )
    { tmt.tref(null); tmt = null; }
}
```

The main method instantiates a Timer60, initializes it, and launches the GUI in the usual manner:

```
public static void main(String[] args)
{   Timer60 tm = new Timer60();
    tm.init();
    tm.go(new JFrame("Timer"));
}

protected void go(JFrame win)
{   win.setContentPane(this);
    win.addWindowListener(new WindowHandler(win));
    win.setSize(220, 136);
    win.validate();
    win.setVisible(true);
}
```

11.14　TIMER WITH IMAGES

Java uses threads to decouple image loading from drawing. But first let's look at an application involving images. The basic 60-minute timer becomes more impressive with simple improvements to its appearance (Figure 11.7). Here we change the dull character string timer display to a graphics display with `.gif` images for the digits.

With subclassing the improvement is easy to make (Figure 11.8):

1. Extend `TimerFace` to establish an `ImageFace` class.
2. Extend `Timer60` to get `ImageTimer`, which simply uses an `ImageFace` object in place of a `TimerFace` object.

The main purposes of this example are:

- Illustrating image loading and drawing
- Motivating discussions on image manipulations
- Demonstrating OOP techniques

Class `ImageFace`

Although `ImageFace` extends `TimerFace` (a `JPanel`) to become a kind of `TimerFace`, it works very differently. `ImageFace` custom draws image digits to form the timer display. The digit images and the display background are

Figure 11.7　TIMER WITH DIGIT IMAGES

Figure 11.8　OO DESIGN OF TIMER WITH DIGIT IMAGES

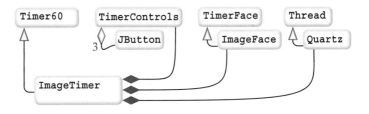

creator-supplied arguments (line 1). The set method requests repainting after
setting up the digits to display (line 2).

```
public class ImageFace extends TimerFace
{  public ImageFace(Image[] im, Color c)          // (1)
   {   setup();  bg = c;
       dig = im;    // dig[10] is colon (:)
   }

   protected ImageFace() {}

   public void set(int min, int sec)              // (2)
   {   m = min;  s = sec;
       setup();  repaint();
   }

// paintComponent later ...

   protected Color bg;
   protected int x, y, w, h;
   protected Image[] dig;  // timer digits
   protected boolean success;
}
```

The paintComponent method clears the background (line 3) and draws a
rectangular window with rounded corners to fit just in the display area of
this widget (line 4). The window has a decorative border in the designated
background color, enclosing a solid black area (line 5) to showcase the timer
digits (Figure 11.9).

```
public void paintComponent(Graphics g)
{   super.paintComponent(g);                      // (3)
    w = getWidth();
    h = getHeight();
    g.setColor(bg);
    g.fillRoundRect(3, 4, w-6, h-4, 10, 6);       // (4)
    g.setColor(Color.black);
```

Figure 11.9   DIGIT IMAGES

```
    g.fillRect(10, 8, w-20, h-12);                          // (5)
    w = (w-26)/5; h -= 16;                                  // (6)
    x = 15; y = 9;
    success =                                               // (7)
     (g.drawImage(dig[m1], x,       y, w, h, this) &&  // (8)
      g.drawImage(dig[m2], x+w,     y, w, h, this) &&
      g.drawImage(dig[10], x+2*w, y, w, h, this) &&
      g.drawImage(dig[s1], x+3*w, y, w, h, this) &&
      g.drawImage(dig[s2], x+4*w, y, w, h, this));   // (9)
}
```

A Java Graphics object supplies many methods for common drawing needs. The fillRoundRect method of Graphics

```
void fillRoundRect(int x, int y, int width, int height,
                   int arcWidth, int arcHeight)
```

draws a filled rectangle with rounded corners, locating the upper-left corner at (x, y), and uses arcWidth and arcHeight as horizontal and vertical arc diameters to round the corners. The drawRoundRect method draws the same shape without filling the area with the current foreground color.

The paintComponent method then computes the width and height (line 6) of the display space for each digit and the separating colon (mm:ss). Images for the minute digits m1 and m2, the second digits s1 and s2, and the separating colon are displayed with calls to drawImage (lines 8–9). The flag success (line 7) records true only if all five drawImage calls succeed. The success flag is handy for future refinements of ImageFace (Section 11.16).

The Graphics class supplies a variety of overloaded drawImage methods. They all work under the same principles. The method

```
boolean drawImage(Image img, int x, int y, int width, int height,
                  ImageObserver observer)
```

draws the given image img inside the specified rectangle, scaling the image to fit if necessary. Java uses the ImageObserver parameter to decouple image drawing and image loading for better performance (Section 11.15). The drawImage method returns false if the image has not been loaded completely and will draw it when loaded.

Class ImageTimer

To make use of the new ImageFace, the Timer class is extended. The init method is redefined to create images from files (line i) and to use an ImageFace timer display (line ii). The `Timer.init()` method then performs the remaining initializations. The call `super.init()` (line iii) can be placed anywhere, whereas the call `super()` must occur at the very beginning of a subclass constructor.

```
public class ImageTimer extends Timer60
{  protected void init()
   {    tk = Toolkit.getDefaultToolkit();
        img = new Image[11];
        for ( int i=0; i < 10; i++ )                        // (i)
            img[i] = tk.createImage( "images/0"+ i + "green.gif");
        img[10] = tk.createImage("images/cogreen.gif");
        if ( face == null )
            face = new ImageFace(img, Color.cyan);          // (ii)
        super.init();                                       // (iii)
   }

   protected Image[] img;

   public static void main(String[] args)
   {    ImageTimer tm = new ImageTimer();
        tm.init();
        tm.go(new JFrame("ImageTimer"));
   }
}
```

In the init methods, checking to see whether a reference is already set before initializing it allows a subclass first to initialize certain fields, then to call a superclass init method. The ease with which the `ImageTimer` is implemented testifies to the power of class extension.

11.15 DECOUPLED IMAGE LOADING AND DRAWING

Java uses multithreading to help decouple image loading and image drawing for better performance. Image files, usually in GIF, JPEG, or PNG format, can be large and time-consuming to load, especially across a network. After loading, the image often must also be *converted* to a suitable format for the particular graphics output device. To avoid long delays, Java decouples image loading and conversion from drawing. An applet, `getImage` call or a `Toolkit` `createImage` call (line i of `ImageTimer` in Section 11.14), creates an `Image` object and returns immediately without attempting to load the image. Loading of the image data is triggered by an attempt to use it, such as a `drawImage` call.

The Graphics method

```
boolean drawImage(Image img, int x, int y,
                          int width, int height,
                          ImageObserver observer)
```

specifies an ImageObserver, the widget that will draw the image. An initial drawImage call triggers the loading of the image data. The drawImage call always returns false immediately if the image is not yet ready (Figure 11.10). Because the image-drawing thread is the same as the event-dispatching thread, it is important to perform the time-consuming image loading and conversion in a separate thread.

An *image producer*, working independently of the image-drawing thread, loads and converts the image. Multiple drawImage calls on different images trigger multiple producer threads.

The ImageObserver is the widget that performs the drawing, in the drawing thread, after the image has been loaded. The image producer reports progress to the image observer at various stages of image loading/conversion. The reporting is done by calling the imageUpdate method of the ImageObserver interface. The Component, and therefore the JComponent, implements this interface and defines an imageUpdate method that triggers repaint() in the observer when the image can be displayed. The imageUpdate method can be overridden to achieve other image-drawing behaviors.

For a program dealing with multiple images, a MediaTracker object can be employed to initiate and track the loading of groups of images (Section 11.16). The ImageIcon class automatically uses a MediaTracker to load an image.

The Graphics class also provides drawing methods to render a subarea of an image or to flip an image horizontally or vertically.

Figure 11.10   DECOUPLED IMAGE PROCESSING

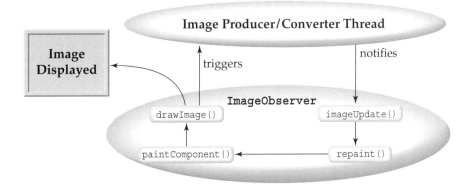

In-Memory Image Manipulations

If an image is already in a memory buffer, it can be manipulated, transformed, and rendered immediately. JFC supports this *immediate-mode imaging* based on `BufferedImage`, a subclass of `Image`.

You usually create a `BufferedImage` from within a widget with:

```
BufferedImage bImg = (BufferedImage) createImage(width, height);
```

You get a blank opaque image with the foreground and background colors of the widget.

With a blank `bImg`, you can now draw graphics and/or desired images into it. Then you can easily make transformations on `bImag` and render it immediately at any time. Basically you compose the image you desire in `bImg` and then display it.

You draw into a `bImg` as if drawing onto the screen:

```
Graphics2d g2 = bImg.createGraphics();    // graphics context
g2.drawImage(img2, ...);                  // draw image into bImg
g2.draw(...);                             // draw graphics into bImg
```

Displaying a `BufferedImage` is no different from drawing an `Image` object:

```
g.drawImage(bImg,0, 0, this);             // in paintComponent
```

You can also use `BufferedImageOp` objects to perform well-defined image transformations such as sharpen and blur.

11.16 ANIMATION

One frequent application of threads is animation, where a number of images are displayed in rapid succession to produce perceived motion. Each image is called a *frame*. Animation ordinarily varies from 8 to 24 frames per second (*fps*) for poor to realistic motion. A GUI program, whether an applet or regular application, performs animation in a separate thread. The animation thread implements an *animation loop*, which draws the sequence of frames, possibly repeatedly. To avoid taking over the drawing and event-handling thread, which calls `update/paintComponent`, the animation loop should not be placed within the `paintComponent` method.

Important aspects for a well-written animation program to manage are the following:

- Coordination of image loading and display—Using separate threads to load the images can save time, but the program must wait for all images to finish loading before displaying them. The `MediaTracker` class can do this and detect errors during image loading.

- Maintenance of frame rate—The animation should display frames at a constant rate. The fps can be specified as a parameter.
- User control—By clicking the mouse over the image, a user can stop and start the animation. A mouse-event handler can take care of this.
- The animation is stopped (started) in reaction to window iconification (deiconification) events.

We present a general-purpose animation program with the following main features:

- Dual purpose—The program runs as an applet or as a regular application.
- Arbitrary image sequences—Given user-specified quantities $file$ (file name), n (number of frames or files), and $extension$ (file name extension), the image files are $filej.extension$, with j between 0 and $n-1$.
- Transparent loading and tracking of images—The images are assumed to be located at codebase or the current directory. Tracking of asynchronous loading is done transparently.
- Flexible looping—The animation loop can be executed one or more times, or it can run continuously.
- Standard animation control—Standard starting and stopping of the animation by the Web browser and by mouse clicks are supported.
- Flexible image handling—A separate class stores and produces images for any renderer. This allows the handling of either fixed images or dynamically computed images.
- Settable animation speed—The fps can be set to desired rates.
- Iconification control—The animation stops or restarts as the window is iconified or de-iconified.

The following example shows concrete techniques for achieving these goals. The program consists of three parts:

1. AnimatorPanel—The widget that uses a javax.swing.Timer object and an ImageSequence to perform animation.
2. Animator—An applet that instantiates an AnimatorPanel and controls its actions. The applet also has a main method and can run as a regular application.
3. ImageSequence—A manager for the sequence of images that tracks asynchronous loading and provides the next image for display. Image tracking details are encapsulated.

11.17 `AnimatorPanel`

The `AnimatorPanel` controls the animation display and is the heart of the animation program. It is instantiated from either an applet (line 1) or an application (line 2). The object is initialized with the number of image frames, the frame rate (line 3), the file name of the images (lines 4–5), and the delay (in milliseconds) between frames (line 6).

```
class AnimatorPanel extends JPanel implements ActionListener
{  public AnimatorPanel(URL cb, JApplet a,                    // (1)
          int n, int ps, String fname, String ext)
   {   app = a;
       codeBase = cb;
       init(n, ps, fname, ext);
   }

   public AnimatorPanel(Toolkit t,                            // (2)
          int n, int ps, String fname, String ext)
   {   tk = t;
       init(n, ps, fname, ext);
   }

   protected void init(int n, int ps, String fname, String ext)
   {   nf = n; fps = ps;                                      // (3)
       filename = fname;                                      // (4)
       extension = ext;                                       // (5)
       interval = 1000/fps;                                   // (6)
       timer = new Timer(interval, this);                     // (7)
       timer.setInitialDelay(0);                              // (8)
       timer.setCoalesce(true);                               // (9)
       img = new ImageSequence(codeBase,                      // (10)
               filename, extension, nf, app, tk, this);
       addMouseListener(new MouseHandler());                  // (11)
   }

   public void actionPerformed(ActionEvent e)                 // (12)
   {   showFrame(); }

   private final class MouseHandler extends MouseAdapter      // (13)
   {   public void mouseClicked(MouseEvent e)
       {   sr();  }
   }
// other methods ...

   protected URL codeBase=null;          // applet codebase
```

```
    protected boolean frozen=false;        // frozen by user request
    protected Image frame=null;            // current frame
    protected ImageSequence img;           // image manager
    protected boolean nonstop =false;      // continuous loop or not
    protected Timer timer = null;          // javax.swing.Timer
    protected int nf;                      // number of frames
    protected int fps;                     // frames per second
    protected int interval=0;              // time interval of a frame
    protected String filename, extension;  // image files
    protected JApplet app = null;          // applet
    protected Toolkit tk = null;           // local image loader
}
```

The `javax.swing.Timer` class is handy for animation. It runs in a separate thread and sends an action event, after each given time interval, to the `ActionListener` specified in the constructor (line 7). Here the `AnimatorPanel` itself is the action listener (line 12). Because multiple images are always involved in an animation, we use an `ImageSequence` object to manage the loading and sequencing of the animation sequence (line 10). The `MouseHandler` enables the user to stop and resume the animation with mouse clicks (lines 11, 13, and 14).

Starting and stopping the animation (lines 15–16) is just a matter of starting and stopping the `Timer` object, which triggers the display of the next frame when the action event handler (line 12) calls `showFrame()` (line 17).

```
public synchronized void sr()            // (14)
{   if ( frozen ) start();  // resume
    else stop();
}

public synchronized void start()         // (15)
{   if ( !timer.isRunning() )
    {   timer.start();
        frozen = false;
    }
}

public synchronized void stop()          // (16)
{   if (timer.isRunning())
    {   timer.stop();
        frozen = true;
    }
}

protected void showFrame()               // (17)
{   frame = img.next(nonstop);           // (18)
    if ( img.ERROR ) return;
```

```
        if ( ! nonstop && frame == null )
        {   stop();  }
        repaint();
}
```

Animation Drawing

The showFrame method sets frame, the next image frame to be displayed, to the next image in the sequence img, which returns null after returning the last frame in the sequence. If nonstop is true, the animation will be shown continuously (line 18).

The paintComponent method defines custom painting. It computes the display area and draws the current image frame in it.

```
public void paintComponent(Graphics g)
{   Insets insets = getInsets();
    int w = getWidth() - insets.left - insets.right;
    int h = getHeight() - insets.top - insets.bottom;
    if ( frame != null )    // draws a frame
       g.drawImage(frame, 2, 2, w-4, h-4, Color.white, this);
    else                    // image not ready or error
    {  g.drawRect(0, 0, w, h);
       if (img.ERROR) g.drawString("Error loading images!", 0, h/2);
    }
}
```

11.18 Animator APPLET-APPLICATION

Animator is an applet that also has a main method to be used as a stand-alone GUI application. The init method (line i) records the applet codebase, and sets the animation-specific parameters such as number of frames, frame rate, and file names. The image file names are assumed to be in the following form:

```
filename0.extension
filename1.extension
```

The JFC supports the popular GIF, JPEG, and PNG image formats. In this example, extension is gif. The applet sets its content pane to an instance of AnimatorPanel (line ii). The applet life-cycle methods start and stop simply start and stop the animation (lines iii–iv).

```
public class Animator extends JApplet
{  public void init()                                    // (i)
   {   URL codeBase = getDocumentBase();
       int nf = 10; int fps = 16;
       String filename = "images/T";
```

```
            String extension = ".gif";
            an = new AnimatorPanel(codeBase, this,
                    nf, fps, filename, extension);
            setContentPane(an);                          // (ii)
        }

        public void start()          // starts animation (iii)
        {   an.start(); }

        public void stop()           // stops animation  (iv)
        {   an.stop(); }

        protected AnimatorPanel an;

        public static void main(String[] args)
        {   Toolkit tk = Toolkit.getDefaultToolkit();
            int nf = 10; int fps = 16;
            String filename = "images/T";
            String extension = ".gif";
            AnimatorPanel an = new AnimatorPanel(tk, nf, fps, filename,
                                                        extension);
            JFrame frame = new JFrame("Animator");
            an.setPreferredSize(new Dimension(59, 72));
            frame.setContentPane(an);
            frame.addWindowListener(new AnimatorWindowHandler(frame,
                                                        an));
            frame.pack();
            frame.setVisible(true);
            an.start();
        }
    }
```

To run the program as a GUI application, the main method sets up a JFrame to hold the AnimatorPanel. It also has a window handler that stops and resumes the animation upon window iconification and deiconification.

```
/////// 	AnimatorWindowHandler.java 	///////
import java.awt.event.*;
import javax.swing.JFrame;

public class AnimatorWindowHandler extends WindowAdapter
{   AnimatorWindowHandler(JFrame f, AnimatorPanel an)
    {   fr = f;  anm = an; }

    public void windowIconified(WindowEvent e)
    {   anm.stop();  }
```

```
public void windowDeiconified(WindowEvent e)
{   anm.start();  }

public void windowClosing(WindowEvent e)
{   anm.stop();
    fr.setVisible(false);
    fr.dispose();
    System.exit(0);
}

private JFrame fr;
private AnimatorPanel anm;
}
```

11.19 THE IMAGE MANAGER

An ImageSequence object isolates image management and can be very useful
for any animation program based on a sequence of images. An animation
program simply creates an ImageSequence object by supplying a few arguments
to the constructor. The object then encapsulates the asynchronous loading,
tracking, storing, and retrieving of the sequence of animation images.

```
class ImageSequence
{   public ImageSequence(URL location, String img_file, String ext,
                   int dim, JApplet app, Toolkit tk, JComponent wg)
    {   pic = new Image[dim];
        app = p;  n = dim;
        tracker = new MediaTracker(wg);                     // (A)
    // get animation frames (id == 0)
        for (int i = 0; i < n; i++)
        {   pic[i] = (tk != null)
                ? tk.createImage(img_file+i)+"."+ext)
                : app.getImage(location, img_file+i+"."+ext);    // (B)
            tracker.addImage(pic[i], 0);                        // (C)
        }
        tracker.checkID(0, true);          // starts image loading (D)
    }
// other methods ...

    public static boolean ERROR = false;
    protected boolean ready=false;
    protected Applet app;
    protected Image[] pic = null;
    protected int n;         // dimension of pic
```

```
      protected MediaTracker tracker;
      protected int index=-1;
  }
```

The constructor uses a `MediaTracker` to perform asynchronous image loading (line A). The `MediaTracker` can initiate and track the loading of a number
of media objects, including images as well as audio clips.[2] A media object
to be tracked can be *added* to a tracker object under a designated integer ID.
Media objects under the same ID can be tracked as a group. The `MediaTracker`
`CheckID` methods are convenient for initiating and checking for completeness
of the loading of all objects under a given ID. The `checkAll` method does the
same for all media objects added to the tracker. You can also check to see
whether any errors occurred. For example,

```
isErrorID(int ID)
```

returns `true` if any image with the specified ID had an error during loading.
In the constructor, `Image` objects are created. If a `Toolkit` argument is
supplied, images are loaded from the local file system. If not, images are
loaded from the given URL location (line B). The `Image` objects are added to
the tracker object (line C), then started to load (line D).
A client of `ImageSequence` does not need to worry about details of image
loading and tracking. They are taken care of by `ImageSequence`. All a client
does after creating an `ImageSequence` is to call `next` to get the next frame. The
method `next` takes care of tracking the loading (line E). The argument `cycle`
controls whether `next` cycles back to the first frame at the end of the sequence
(line F).

```
public Image next(boolean cycle)
{    if ( loaded() )                     // waits         (E)
     { if ( ! cycle && index == n-1 ) // end reached (F)
       { index=-1;   return null; }
       index = (index+1) % n;
       return pic[index];
     }
     return null;                        // error
}
```

The `next` method returns `null` if a loading error has occurred. The private method `loaded` checks that images are all loaded correctly with the

---

[2]Current (SDK 1.4) Java media trackers support only images.

MediaTracker. The `waitForID` method returns when the media objects under the given ID are loaded, successfully or otherwise (line G). The `isError` method tells whether an error has occurred (line H).

```
private boolean loaded()
{   if ( ready ) return true;
    try
    {   tracker.waitForID(0);     // loading terminated (G)
    } catch (InterruptedException e)
      { ERROR = true;   return false; }

    if ( tracker.isErrorID(0) )   // check for error      (H)
    {   ERROR = true;   return false;  }
    else
        return (ready = true);
}
```

The `ImageSequence` class also provides access to the width and height of the images:

```
public int width()
{   if ( loaded() ) return pic[0].getWidth(null);
    else return -1;
}

public int height()
{   if ( loaded() ) return pic[0].getHeight(null);
    else return -1;
}
```

This example shows thread usage and provides the essentials of a general animation engine. The use of the Swing `Timer` class makes animation easy. The `ImageSequence` demonstrates good OOP in separating image management from animation control. It also provides another concrete case for applet-application dual-purpose programs. Some improvements can make this animator program even more useful (see programming assignments 5 and 6 at the end of this chapter).

11.20 SUMMARY

A thread is a single line of control flow within a process. A sequential program has a single thread represented by the control flow specified by the `main` method. Java offers multithreading, allowing easy support of event-driven and concurrent programming and providing facilities to manage multiple independent threads.

A multithreaded program has independently running threads sharing the same address space (classes and objects). Concurrent programs involve programming concerns: mutual exclusion, synchronization, scheduling, and deadlock.

Java threads are represented by objects of type Thread and objects that implement the Runnable interface. The start method causes the Java virtual machine to launch a new thread and to call its run method. A thread terminates when its run method returns. A parent thread controls child threads that it has launched.

Threads run asynchronously or at unpredictable relative speeds. In a single-CPU environment, a thread must yield or be blocked before another thread can run. In Java, threads can be assigned different priorities for receiving CPU service. Piped byte and character streams are available for threads to perform I/O with each other.

Synchronized methods and *synchronized statements* based on the same mutual exclusion object are mutually exclusive in time. This achieves mutual exclusion. The mutual exclusion object also serves as a *monitor* for coordinating time-sequenced activities of related threads. Use the wait and notify methods to achieve coordination.

To preserve the responsiveness of event handling, GUI programs avoid time-consuming tasks in the event dispatching and drawing thread by performing them in other threads. A Timer (javax.swing) object can provide a background thread to trigger events in other threads at regularly scheduled intervals.

Consumer and producer mutual exclusion and synchronization provide an important model for multithreading. Java decouples image loading, conversion, and drawing by employing image producer and observer threads. A general animator illustrates how to apply multithreading in practice.

 EXERCISES

Review Questions

1. What methods in the Object class help multithreading? Why are these methods placed in the root superclass Object?

2. What is mutual exclusion? What is synchronization? Are these different?

3. What Java constructs support mutual exclusion? Synchronization?

4. Different processes also run concurrently. What is the major difference between a thread and a process?

5. What are the different states of a Java thread? Indicate all possible state transitions.

6. Take the maximum integer example in Section 11.6 and modify the MaxGuard class to use static synchronized methods.

7. List the program steps for creating and launching a child thread and waiting for it to finish.

8. Follow the maximum integer example in Section 11.6 and write a multi-threaded program that counts the number of even and odd integers in an array.

9. Convert the classes Consumer, Producer, and WordCount so that they use a reader-writer pipe instead of a circular buffer. Establish PipeConsumer, PipeProducer, and PipeWordCount according to the description in Section 11.9.

10. List the ways that a thread can terminate.

11. Find out more about the javax.swing.Timer class used in the AnimatorPanel (Section 11.16). Compare it with the java.util.Timer class. Discuss the differences and discuss pros and cons. In particular, what does the setCoalesce method do?

12. What relation is there between Thread and Runnable?

Programming Assignments

1. (ImgT-1) Make the 60-minute timer (Timer60) into an applet-application dual-purpose program. Use the tool **jar** to pack all files for the applet and make sure that its Web page uses the .jar file.

2. (ImgT-2) Instead of a Quartz object, use a Swing Timer object in the 60-minute timer.

3. Write a clock applet to display time. How much code can you reuse from the 60-minute timer?

4. (ImgT-3) Apply the information on media tracking to the ImageTimer (Section 11.14). Define FastImageFace by extending ImageFace to use a MediaTracker to load all images used for the timer face. FastImageFace will also avoid drawing digits that have not changed. The resulting program should become faster and more efficient. This is especially true if you turn this application into an applet.

5.   (Animator-1) Consider the animator program of Section 11.16. The program uses hard-coded parameters: `nf`, `fps`, `filename`, `extension`, `nonstop`, and `times`. Improve the program by allowing these parameter values to be set by `<PARAM>` or command-line supplied values. Add the applet method `getParameterInfo`, too. The result should remain working as a dual-purpose program.

6.   (Animator-2) Consider the animator program of Section 11.16. The program uses hard-coded window dimensions as both an applet and a GUI application. There is little we can do for the applet case, but as an application, we can make the size of the `AnimatorPanel` automatically adjust to be just right for the size of the images.

7.   (Animator-3) Consider adding sound effects to the animator. Each image potentially has an associated sound file. Add a sound manager class to the previous exercise. Modify the animation program so that it will play the audio clips while showing the images.

8.   Write a toy Web server using a stream socket at a non-privileged port, such as 8234. The server spawns a new thread to service each new incoming HTTP request.

## CHAPTER TWELVE

Advanced Topics

Java is a widely used system with many features. Most basic and intermediate topics have been covered in previous chapters. Here a select set of advanced topics is introduced so that you can get even more out of Java. Even if you don't use these features immediately, you may find them handy in the future.

Java provides the Class class, whose objects represent the various classes in a Java program. With Class objects, you can compute and manipulate classes themselves—pass classes as arguments to methods, check the type of objects, inquire what methods are available in a class, and so on at run time. Combining Class and other classes that represent methods, constructors, fields, and so on, you get *reflection*, the ability of Java to inspect and manipulate its own programming.

While running, a Java program can also initiate class loading requests to incorporate additional classes into the program. This facility is especially useful for loading classes across the network. We'll show how remote classes can be loaded and run.

In practice, the ability for a Java program to interact with other programs can be important. We'll see how a Java program can execute other programs as processes and communicate with them on your system.

It is also possible to combine a Java program with code written in a *native language* such as C or C++. The *Java Native Interface* (*JNI*) defines a systematic way to interface Java with native code. A sequence of examples shows how to use JNI.

The success of programming projects can depend significantly on the accuracy and completeness of documentation for users and programmers. With *doc comments*, you can embed well-formed comments right where the source code is. Then the `javadoc` tool can be used to generate HTML documents from the source code.

The way Java transfers information among widgets via clipboards and the way applets communicate through their execution context are also introduced. The chapter concludes with a discussion of the Java security model and some details on preparing and using signed applets.

12.1 REFLECTION

Reflection is a unique Java feature that allows an executing program to examine or *introspect* upon itself, and manipulate internal properties of the program. For example, the names of all members of a class can be obtained. With reflection, you can dynamically load a class, find out what it does, and use it accordingly.

Classes as Objects

In OOP, classes are for building objects. At run time, objects interact to achieve computational goals. But what if one also wishes to compute with the classes themselves at run time? For example:

- To check whether a class (given by a name string) is there and, if not, to load it under program control
- To see whether a class has a certain constructor or method
- To get the string name of the class of an object
- To obtain a superclass or a superinterface of a class
- To get a list of all members in a class and use the members discovered

More generally, it would be nice to have run-time access and manipulation of all types. This is exactly what Java provides through the classes `Class`, `Member`, `Method`, `Constructor`, and `Field`.

In a running Java program, there is *a unique instance* of `Class` for each class and interface defined in the program. Let's call a `Class` object a *cbj*. Primitive types (and `void`) are represented by predefined *cbj*s created by the Java Virtual Machine and stored as static `TYPE` fields in the corresponding wrapper classes. Examples are `Integer.TYPE` (the *cbj* for `Integer`) and `Double.TYPE` (the *cbj* for `Double`). There is also a different *cbj* for each set of arrays with the same element type and number of subscripts.

Run-time type manipulations are done with *cbj*s. To obtain a *cbj*, use one of the following:

```
Class cbj = obj.getClass()         (class of an object)
Class cbj = Class.forName(str)     (class with name str)
```

When you have a `Class` object *cbj*, you can use its methods to obtain information about the class. For example:

- `cbj.isInstance(obj)` returns `true`/`false`.
- `cbj.getName()` returns the class name string.
- `Method[] ma = cbj.getDeclaredMethods()` returns all methods declared in this class.
- `Method[] ma = cbj.getMethods()` returns all methods, including inherited ones.

- Constructor[] ctor = getDeclaredConstructors() returns all constructors declared in this class (also getConstructors()).
- Class sup = cbj.getSuperclass() returns the superclass of this class or null.

Similar methods exist in Class to inspect fields and inner classes.

Given a fully qualified class name *str*, forName returns its *cbj*. It locates, loads, and links the class first if necessary. For example, we can display the methods in any given class as follows:

```
import java.lang.reflect.*;                    // reflection package

public class DisplayMethods
{  public static void main(String[] args)
   {   try
       { Class cbj = Class.forName(args[0]);
                                        // loads class if necessary
         Method m[] = cbj.getDeclaredMethods();
         for (int i = 0; i < m.length; i++)
         System.out.println(m[i].toString());
       } catch (Throwable e) { System.err.println(e); }
   }
}
```

The methods obtained by getDeclaredMethods() do not include constructors or inherited methods.

Running the code

```
java DisplayMethods java.util.Stack
```

produces the following output, showing four declared methods:

```
public java.lang.Object
java.util.Stack.push(java.lang.Object)

public synchronized
java.lang.Object java.util.Stack.pop()

public synchronized
java.lang.Object java.util.Stack.peek()

public boolean java.util.Stack.empty()
```

To support reflection, these Java features are important:

- Each class loaded into a Java program is represented by a unique object, (its *cbj*) belonging to the java.lang.Class class.
- The *cbj* has useful methods for extracting info about the class.

- The Member, Method, Constructor, Field, Array, and Modifier classes from the java.lang.reflect package provide representation and manipulation of class members.

Here is how to use reflection:

1. Get the Class object of the class in question.

```
Class cbj = Integer.TYPE;
Class cbj = obj.getClass();
Class cbj = Class.forName("java.lang.String");
```

2. Discover superclass, method, constructor, and/or field information about the class.

3. Use the information to invoke methods, create new objects, or set field values.

As another example, consider a method that displays the class/interface hierarchy (inheritance chain) for any given type represented by *cbj*:

```
public static void
displayType(Class cbj, int level, boolean cl)
{   if ( cbj == null || cbj == root ) return;              // (A)
    if ( level == 0 )                                      // (B)
    {   out.println((cbj.isInterface() ?  "interface "
                          : "class ") + cbj.getName() );
    }
    else
    {   for (int i=0; i < level; i++) out.print("    ");    // (C)
        out.println( (cbj.isInterface() && cl ?  "implements "
                          : "extends ") + cbj.getName() );  // (D)
    }
    if ( cbj.isArray() ) return;                           // (E)
    Class[] faces = cbj.getInterfaces();
    if ( faces != null )
    {   for (int i =0 ; i < faces.length ; i++)            // (F)
            displayType(faces[i], level+1, !cbj.isInterface());
    }
    displayType(cbj.getSuperclass(), level+1,
                  !cbj.isInterface());                     // (G)
}
```

The recursive method stops when cbj is root (Object) or null (line A). It begins by displaying the class or interface name (line B). Unless cbj is an array (line E), the method continues to display all superinterfaces (line F) and superclasses (line G) recursively. The level parameter controls the amount of indentation (line C). The cl parameter (line D) is true if a recursive call is coming from a subclass, not a subinterface.

The class `DisplayType` contains the preceding method and a main method to test it:

```
/////// DisplayType.java ///////
import java.io.*;

public class DisplayType
{  public static void main(String[] args)
   {   try
       {   out = new PrintWriter(System.out);
           root = Class.forName("java.lang.Object");
           for (int i =0 ; i < args.length ; i++)
               displayType(Class.forName(args[i]),0,false);
           out.close();
       } catch (ClassNotFoundException e)
       {   System.err.println(e.getMessage());  }
   }

 // put method displayType here

   private static PrintWriter out;
   private static Class root;
}
```

Running the command

java DisplayType java.awt.event.MouseAdapter

produces the following output:

```
class java.awt.event.MouseAdapter
   implements java.awt.event.MouseListener
      extends java.util.EventListener
```

The `newInstance` method of a *cbj* creates a new object by calling the null constructor of the class represented by *cbj*.

Use the `getMethod` and `getConstructor` methods to obtain a method or constructor taking specified argument types. Call `invoke` (`newInstance`) of a `Method` (`Constructor`) object to execute it. With these, you can write programs that take class names supplied on the command line and instantiate and run them, as will be demonstrated presently. But first let's see how to inspect methods.

Inspecting Methods

As stated earlier, using a *cbj*, the call

```
Method ma[] = cbj.getDeclaredMethods();
Constructor ct[] = cbj.getDeclaredConstructors();
```

returns methods or constructors declared in the class. For a `Method` or `Constructor` object mc, you can use:

- `mc.getName()` to get the method name string
- `mc.getDeclaringClass()` to get the *cbj* of the class where the method or constructor is declared
- `mc.getParameterTypes()` to obtain a `Class` array of parameter types that this method or constructor takes
- `mc.getExceptionTypes()` to obtain a `Class` array of the types of exceptions that this method or constructor may throw
- `mc.getModifiers()` to get an integer representing the method declaration modifiers (`public`, `static`, `synchronized`, etc.) for this method
- `mc.getReturnType()` to get the *cbj* for the return type of a method

The class `Modifier` has constants and methods to help decode and recognize the meaning of the returned integer code. For example:

```
Modifier.isStatic(int_code)
Modifier.isPublic(int_code)
Modifier.isFinal(int_code)
Modifier.isAbstract(int_code)
```

Also, `Modifier.toString(int_code)` returns the string representation of the type modifiers.

Fields of a class are inspected in a similar way.

Invoking an Inspected Method

When we know the return type and argument types of a method through inspection, we can make a call to it, using `invoke` in the class `Method`. For illustration purposes, let's write a simple class Xyz with a made-up instance method myTimes that also uses a private field factor:

```
///////    Xyz.java    ///////

public class Xyz
{   public double myTimes(int a, float b)
    {   return a * b * factor; }

    private float factor=0.5f;
}
```

Now we will apply reflection to inspect and invoke Xyz.

The main method of TestInvoke takes command-line supplied arguments as follows

java TestInvoke Xyz

and inspects Xyz and its method myTimes. It then calls myTimes with arguments entered interactively by the user.

```
///////    TestInvoke.java    ///////
import java.io.*;
import java.lang.reflect.*;

public class TestInvoke
{  public static void main(String[] args)
   {  try
      {  Class type;
         Class cbj = Class.forName(args[0]);           // (1)
         Method[] ms = cbj.getDeclaredMethods();       // (2)
         Method mtd = ms[0];                           // (3)
         Class[] argTypes = mtd.getParameterTypes();   // (4)
         Object[] carg = new
                 Object[argTypes.length];              // (5)
         for (int i=0;
              i < argTypes.length; i++)
         {   type = argTypes[i];                       // (6)
             carg[i] = getNumberObject(                // (7)
                       type.toString());
         }
         Constructor ctor =
                 cbj.getConstructor(null);             // (8)
         Object host =  ctor.newInstance(null);        // (9)
         Object val =  mtd.invoke(host, carg);         // (10)
         System.out.println(val.toString());
      }
      catch (Throwable e)
         { System.err.println(e); }
   }
// ...
}
```

The main method obtains the *cbj* for the given class (line 1), gets the declared methods (line 2), obtains the first method (line 3) which happens to be myTimes, and inspects the argument types of the method (line 4). Arguments of the required types are obtained from user input (lines 6 and 7) and placed in an argument array (line 5). In order to invoke an instance method, we need to create an object of the target class. This is done here by obtaining the no-args constructor (line 8) to create an instance (line 9). With all that preparation (or introspection), we are now ready to invoke the method (line 10) and display the result. Note, invoke needs the host object and the array of arguments.

The static method getNumberObject, in TestInvoke, makes a numeric object from user input by calling getInput of MyUtil (Section 3.2).

```java
public static Number getNumberObject(String s) throws IOException
{   String number = MyUtil.getInput("Input " + s + " :");
    if (s.equals("int"))
        return new Integer(Integer.parseInt(number));
    if (s.equals("short"))
        return new Short(Short.parseShort(number));
    if (s.equals("long"))
        return new Long(Long.parseLong(number));
    if (s.equals("float"))
        return new Float(Float.parseFloat(number));
    if (s.equals("double"))
        return new Double(Double.parseDouble(number));
    if (s.equals("byte"))
        return new Byte(Byte.parseByte(number));
    return null;
}
```

Compile both Xyz.java and TestInvoke.java, run,

javac Xyz.java TestInvoke.java
java TestInvoke Xyz

and respond to prompts:

```
java TestInvoke Xyz
Input int : = 100
Input float : = 4.5
225.0

java TestInvoke Xyz
Input int : = 150
Input float : = 0.04
3.0
```

Because TestInvoke.java does not refer to the class Xyz statically, compiling TestInvoke.java will not compile Xyz.java automatically.

Some other things to know about reflection:

- Use null as the first argument to invoke to call a static method.
- Use ctor.newInstance(arglist); to call a constructor and instantiate an object.
- Use the following to get and set a field:

```java
Field fld = cbj.getField("field_name");
Class cbj = fld.getType();    // type of field
```

```
fld.setDouble(obj, 12.34);    // sets field value in obj
fld.getDouble(obj);           // gets instance field value
fld.getDouble();              // gets static field value
fld.set(obj, valObj);         // sets Object-type value
```

12.2 DYNAMIC CLASS LOADING

Before your program starts, the Java Virtual Machine loads all necessary .class files. Normally, the bytecode files are found on the local file system by following the CLASSPATH environment variable. The default class loader loads only from the local file system.

After starting, a program may load additional classes from local or nonlocal sources. Nonlocal classes are loaded by user-defined ClassLoader objects, allowing you to load classes on the fly from any given location, even across networks. For example, an applet may load one of several animations on a choice list.

The class ClassLoader provides for class loading. The method

```
Class loadClass(String className, boolean resolve)
    throws ClassNotFoundException
```

loads the given className from the local file system. If resolve is true, the class is also linked with classes it needs, recursively loading them when necessary.

The loadClass method performs a sequence of actions:

1. Calls findLoadedClass to make sure the target class has not been loaded yet. If the class is already loaded, loadClass returns.

2. Calls super.loadClass or the JVM class loader to search for the target class on the local host. If found, the class is loaded and loadClass returns.

3. Calls findClass to find and load the target class. The LoadClass default implementation of findClass throws ClassNotFoundException.

4. Calls resolveClass to link the new class with other classes it needs if resolve is true. The resolveClass call recursively loads, defines, and resolves all classes required to link the new code.

5. Returns the new cbj of the class loaded.

Once a class is loaded and resolved, its cbj can be used for instantiation and method calls.

To load local classes dynamically, simply obtain an instance of ClassLoader and call its loadClass method. To load nonlocal classes on the fly, you need to extend ClassLoader and override the method findClass to retrieve the class byte codes and to call defineClass. You may use different subclasses of ClassLoader for loading different remote classes. To load a remote class, obtain an appropriate extended class loader object and call its loadClass method.

Loading Remote Classes: An Example

To illustrate the dynamic loading of classes, let's write a `UrlClassLoader` to load a `.class` file from any given URL. The loader can be used readily by an applet to load classes from its codebase.

```
///////    UrlClassLoader.java    ///////
import java.net.*;
import java.io.*;
import java.util.HashMap;
import java.lang.reflect.Method;

public class UrlClassLoader extends ClassLoader
{  public UrlClassLoader(String url)   // constructor
   {   urlstr = url;    }

   protected UrlClassLoader() {}

   public Class findClass(String name)
        throws ClassNotFoundException
   {   byte[] b = loadFromUrl(name);              // (1)
       return defineClass(name, b, 0, b.length);  // (2)
   }

 // loadFromUrl  and other methods ...

   private String urlstr;
}
```

A `UrlClassLoader` object, `urlLoader`, is initialized with a URL string. The object can then be used to load any *name*`.class` located at the given URL. You simply call

```
urlLoader.loadClass(name);
```

to load a remote class. The call leads to the invocation of the overriding `findClass`, which gets the byte array of the `.class` code (line 1) and then defines the class (line 2).

The private `loadFromUrl` method applies Java networking. It opens the URL input stream (line A) and reads the data into a byte array (line B), which is returned. If something goes wrong, it throws a `ClassNotFoundException`.

```
private byte[] loadFromUrl(String name)
              throws ClassNotFoundException
{   try
    {   URL urlobj = new URL(urlstr+name+".class");
        BufferedInputStream in = new
            BufferedInputStream(urlobj.openStream());       // (A)
```

```
        int len = in.available();
        if ( len <= 0 )
            throw new ClassNotFoundException("Empty Class");
        byte[] buf = new byte[len];
        in.read(buf);                                        // (B)
        in.close();
        return buf;
    } catch (IOException e)
        { throw new ClassNotFoundException(e.toString()); }
}
```

Loading and Running Remote Classes

The `UrlClassLoader` is complete. Now we can put it to use and implement a program that loads and runs any given remote class (invoking its `main` method). The intended usage is

java UrlClassLoader *URL TargetClass arg1 arg2* ...

where *TargetClass*`.class` is the class to load at the *URL* location (lines i–ii).

```
public static void main(String[] args)
{   if ( args.length < 2 )
    {   System.err.println(
            "Usage: Java UrlClassLoader url ClassName arg1 ...");
        System.exit(1);
    }
    try
    {   UrlClassLoader loader = new UrlClassLoader(args[0]); // (i)
        Class cbj = loader.loadClass(args[1], true);        // (ii)
        System.out.println("class loaded: "+cbj.getName());
        Class[] param = new Class[1];                       // (iii)
        param[0] = args.getClass();        // parameter type
        Method tm = cbj.getMethod("main", param);           // (iv)
        int n = args.length-2;                              // (v)
        String[] arg = new String[n];
        if ( n > 0 ) System.arraycopy(args, 2, arg, 0, n);  // (vi)
        Object[] argArray = new Object[1];                  // (vii)
        argArray[0] = arg;
        tm.invoke(null, argArray);                          // (viii)
    } catch (Exception e)
        { System.err.print(e.getMessage()); System.exit(1); }
}
```

After the remote class is loaded, its `main` method is obtained (lines iii–iv) as a `Method` object `tm`. The argument for the `TargetClass main` is set up (lines v–vi) and stored in the `Object` array `argArray` used to invoke `tm` (lines vii–viii).

To experiment with this program, we can locate `Factorial.class` at the URL:

`http://SymbolicNet.mcs.kent.edu/Factorial.class`

Then, the command

java `UrlClassLoader "http://icm.mcs.kent.edu/research/" Factorial 6`

loads and executes the target class and produces the display:

```
class loaded: Factorial
factorial(5)= 720
```

Because remote and local classes are never in the same package, only `public` classes can be run by remote loading.

In summary, the `java.lang.Class` class, together with classes in the `java.lang.reflect` package, provides the *reflection* capability that allows a Java program to dynamically discover field and method information about a class. The reflection facility forms the foundation of *introspection*. Discovering the public interfaces of unknown local or remote classes helps make portable and reusable Java components, called *Java Beans*, possible.

12.3   THE JAVA RUN TIME

When the Java Virtual Machine runs, an instance of the class `Runtime` records the status of the running system and provides execution control operations: managing memory, loading classes, tracing method calls, creating and using processes, and so forth.

The static method call

```
Runtime rt = Runtime.getRuntime();
```

returns the current `Runtime` object rt. With rt you may perform, for example, these operations:

`rt.gc()`	(runs garbage collector now)
`rt.runFinalization()`	(runs any pending finalize methods now)
`rt.freeMemory()`	(gets number of bytes free)
`rt.totalMemory()`	(gets total bytes of memory)
`rt.traceMethodCalls(boolean)`	(starts/stops method call tracing)

Method call trace can also be turned on and off from a Java debugger (Appendix I) with commands `trace on` and `trace off`.

You can also initiate other programs on your platform from Java (Figure 12.1). Create a process, an instance of `Process`, with an exec method call:

`Process p = rt.exec(str);`	(executes the command string)
`Process p = rt.exec(strArray);`	(executes the command string array)

Figure 12.1   SPAWNING PROCESSES FROM JAVA

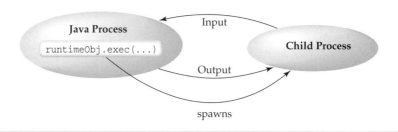

The *child process* created runs independently on the host platform. The Process object allows you to control and communicate with the child process.

12.4 RUNNING OTHER PROGRAMS FROM JAVA

Consider invoking the command

ls -l   (on UNIX)
dir   (on PC)

from Java. This is relatively simple to do. The Exec class here can run any given program available on your system and display its output:

```
public class Exec
{  public static void main (String[] args)
        throws IOException
   {    Process child = Runtime.getRuntime().exec(args);  // (1)
        InputStreamReader in =
            new InputStreamReader(child.getInputStream()); // (2)
        OutputStreamWriter out =
            new OutputStreamWriter(System.out);            // (3)
        int c;
        while ( (c = in.read()) != -1 )                    // (4)
            out.write((char) c);
        out.flush();
   }
}
```

The child process executes the command specified on the command line (line 1), and the textual output of the child process is read (line 2) and displayed (lines 3–4). To run this program, you can give a command such as:

java Exec ls -l

The parent process can also read the error output stream of the child with the method child.getErrorStream and send data to the child via the method child.getOutputStream, wait for the child to finish (child.waitFor()), get its exit status (child.exitValue()), or kill the child (child.destroy()).

For example, the sendEmail method of the class NewMember (Section 10.13) sends data to a mail process:

```
// in class NewMember
  void sendEmail() throws IOException
  {    cmd[4]=email;    // sets cc address
       Process child = Runtime.getRuntime().exec(cmd);
       PrintWriter out = new PrintWriter(
                 child.getOutputStream());
       out.println("name=" + name);
       out.println("email=" + email);
       out.close();
  }

  String[] cmd = {"/bin/mail", "-s", "New Member",
                  "-c", "email", recipient};
```

The static methods in class System

```
public static void setIn(InputStream in)
public static void setOut(PrintStream out)
public static void setErr(PrintStream err)
```

reassign the standard input, output, and error output streams, respectively. These can be used in combination with child processes to achieve I/O redirection. For example the code

```
Process child = Runtime.getRuntime().exec(args);
System.setIn(child.getInputStream());    // redirect
```

makes System.in read output produced by child.

12.5 THE JAVA NATIVE INTERFACE

It is possible to interface Java code with *native language* code, primarily in C or C++, within the same program. The capability allows you to combine Java code with programs written in native languages, to call native routines from Java, and to call Java methods from native code. The native code may be a legacy system that is large or difficult to reprogram in Java, or a routine whose execution speed is critical.

The *Java Native Interface* (*JNI*) defines and supports a Java-to-native and a native-to-Java interface:

- JNI specifies a standard naming and calling convention for implementing *native methods*—methods declared in Java but implemented in a native language.

- JNI provides a set of standard interface functions for native code to call Java methods and access and manipulate Java objects.

Combining programs in different languages requires substantial programming experience. We'll describe the JNI and give detailed examples to show how programs are interfaced.

12.6 JNI EXAMPLE: BASIC

A *native method* is declared in Java but implemented in a native language. You declare a native method just like an abstract method but with the `native` keyword instead of `abstract`. Both instance and static methods can be `native`. At run time, the code for a native method must be loaded and linked by the Java interpreter before it can be called.

Let's demonstrate the interface with a twist to the `Average.java` (Section 1.2) program: A C-coded method computes and displays the average of two integers.

We follow four typical steps:

Step 1: Write the Java Code

```
///////    Average.java    ///////

class Average
{  private static native void myAverage();  // (1)

   static { System.loadLibrary("ave"); }     // (2)

   public static void main(String[] args)
   {   myAverage();  }                        // (3)
}
```

The native method `myAverage` (line 1) is declared simply by a method descriptor. This example uses a static native method, but it could use an instance native method just as easily. When the class `Average` is loaded by the Java interpreter, the static initialization block (line 2) causes the loading and linking of the specified *shared library*, which should contain code for the native method `myAverage`. The precise name of the shared library loaded is dependent on the host operating system. The method call

```
System.loadLibrary("xyz")
```

loads the shared library file

```
libxyz.so    (on Sun Solaris and on Linux)
libxyz.sl    (on HP-UX)
xyz.dll      (on PC Win32)
```

After being loaded, a native method is called and used just like any other Java method (line 3).

If this method of loading fails, try the alternative

```
Runtime.getRuntime().load("file_to_load");
```

where you give the absolute pathname of the shared library to load.

Step 2: Generate the Header File

First compile Average.java to obtain Average.class. Then, use the **javah** tool

```
javah -jni -o myAverage.h Average
```

to create the header file myAverage.h specified by the -o option. This header gives you the correct ANSI C (or C++) declarations for implementing the needed native method myAverage. Here **javah** is given one class (Average.class) that contains a native method, although **javah** can process multiple classes.

Following is the generated myAverage.h:

```
/* DO NOT EDIT THIS FILE - it is machine generated */
#include <jni.h>                              /* (A) */
/* Header for class Average */

#ifndef _Included_Average
#define _Included_Average
#ifdef __cplusplus
extern "C" {
#endif
/*
 * Class: Average
 * Method: myAverage
 * Signature: ()V
 */
JNIEXPORT void JNICALL                        /* (B) */
Java_Average_myAverage(JNIEnv *, jclass);   /* (C) */

#ifdef __cplusplus
}
#endif
#endif
```

The header jni.h (line A) is supplied by JNI. Note the standardized return type (line B) and function name (line C) encodings. The extra arguments passed to the function (line C) enable it to access Java objects and methods (Section 12.8).

Step 3: Implement Native Codes

The header file myAverage.h can be used for implementing the function

Java_Average_myAverage

either in C or C++. Here we'll define the function in C:

```
/*******    myAverage.c     *******/
#include "myAverage.h"                          /* (i) */
#include <stdio.h>

JNIEXPORT void JNICALL
Java_Average_myAverage(JNIEnv *env, jclass cls) /* (ii) */
{   int i = 11, j = 20;
    double a = (i + j)/2.0;
        printf("i is %d and j is %d\n", i, j);
        printf("Average is %f\n", a);
}
```

Note the inclusion of the **javah**-generated header (line i) and the conforming function header (line ii).

Step 4: Create a Shared Library

With myAverage.c and Average.h in place, we are ready to compile the C code and create a shared library that will be loaded into Java to support the native method myAverage. This step is not difficult, but it is dependent on the operating system and the C compiler.

For example, on Solaris you simply use

```
cc -G -I/usr/java/include -I/usr/java/include/solaris \
   myAverage.c -o libave.so
```

to get the desired shared library libave.so. Of course, you have to specify, with -I, the correct include directories for the JNI header files on your system.

On Linux use:

```
gcc -I/usr/java/j2sdk1.4.0/include \
    -I/usr/java/j2sdk1.4.0/include/linux \
    -shared myAverage.c -o libave.so
```

On HP-UX you issue two commands. First use

```
cc -Ae +z -c -I/opt/java/include \
   -I/opt/java/include/hp-ux myAverage.c
```

to get myAverage.o, and then use

```
ld -b myAverage.o -o libave.sl
```

to combine .o files into a shared library libave.sl on HP-UX.

On Win32 with Microsoft Visual C/C++, you use:

```
cl -Ic:\jdk1.4.0\include -Ic:\jdk1.4.0\include\win32
                    -LD myAverage.c -Feave.dll
```

Now you are ready. To run the program, simply invoke the Java interpreter as usual:

java Average

and you'll get the following display:

```
java Average
In C code
i is 11 and j is 20
Average is 15.500000
```

If an error is caused by a failure to load the shared library, you should make sure that the directory containing the desired library is on the *shared library load path*. If not, add the directory to the UNIX Shell environment variable:

```
SHLIB_PATH              (for HP-UX)
LD_LIBRARY_PATH     (for Solaris and Linux)
```

For Win32, the System.loadLibrary() searches for DLLs in the usual way.

To summarize: This example demonstrates (1) writing Java code for JNI, (2) generating the JNI header file, (3) implementing C code, and (4) creating a shared library to load into Java. Figure 12.2 shows the files involved and their relationships.

Figure 12.2   FILE RELATIONSHIPS UNDER JNI

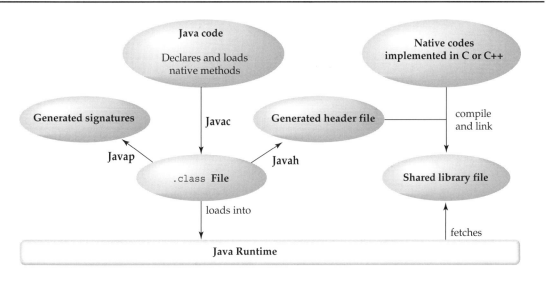

The example did not show how to:

- Pass arguments to and receive return values from native code
- Call Java methods from native code
- Create Java data and objects in native code
- Access Java objects and fields from native code
- Interface to Java when the program entry point is on the native side

Many of these are described in the following sections.

12.7 JNI EXAMPLE: ARGUMENT PASSING

Let's modify the preceding example slightly. The Java code now passes two integers to the native method, which computes their average and returns a Java double (lines 1–2):

```
///////    Arg.java    ///////

class Arg
{   private native static
        double newAverage(int i, int j);          // (1)

    static { System.loadLibrary("nave"); }

    public static void main(String[] args)
    {    double a = newAverage(12, 17);          // (2)
         System.out.println("Got average = "
                             + a + " from native method.");
    }
}
```

The C implementation file is now as follows:

```
/******    newAverage.c    ******/
#include "newAverage.h"
#include <stdio.h>

JNIEXPORT jdouble JNICALL
Java_Arg_newAverage(JNIEnv *env, jclass cls, jint i, jint j)
{   return (i + j)/2.0;    }
```

A native method can directly access Java primitive types passed from Java programs. Each Java primitive "*type*" has a corresponding C typedef "j*type*" that is an appropriate primitive C type. For example, jchar is unsigned short and jint is int. These mappings are platform dependent and defined in the jni.h header file. Table 12.1 shows a typical mapping.

Table 12.1   TYPICAL JNI-COMPLIANT typedefs

JNI typedef	C type
jboolean	unsigned char (8 bits)
jbyte	unsigned char (8 bits)
jchar	unsigned short (16 bits)
jshort	short (16 bits)
jint	int (32 bits)
jlong	long (64 bits)
jfloat	float (32 bits)
jdouble	double (64 bits)
void	void (n/a)

Native methods can also access and manipulate Java objects, as explained next.

12.8   JNI EXAMPLE: STRINGS

This example passes a String argument to the native method, which appends it to the String field str1 in the host object and returns a String to the Java code. Here the native method myAppend is an instance method just to provide variation.

```
///////    Str.java    ///////

class Str
{  private native String myAppend(String a);

   static { System.loadLibrary("app"); }

   private String str1 = "abc";

   public static void main(String[] args)
   {   Str obj = new Str();
       String value = obj.myAppend("XYZ");
       System.out.println(obj.str1);
       System.out.println(value);
   }
}
```

The C implementation of the native instance method includes `myAppend.h` (line A), generated by **javah**. Incoming arguments (line B) are the Java `String` object a, the host object `this`, and a pointer `env` to the JNI-supplied environment. The JNI environment provides C functions to access and manipulate Java objects, including strings and arrays. The call

```
(*env)->GetStringUTFChars(env, str, 0)
```

converts the Java string `str` to a C character array (lines C and G). The dynamic stores used are freed later (lines J and K).

```c
/******     myAppend.c     ******/
#include "myAppend.h"                                    // (A)
#include <string.h>

JNIEXPORT jstring JNICALL
Java_Str_myAppend(JNIEnv *env, jobject this, jstring a)  // (B)
{
   const char* s= (*env)->GetStringUTFChars(env, a, 0);  // (C)
   jclass cls= (*env)->GetObjectClass(env, this);        // (D)
   jfieldID fid= (*env)->GetFieldID(env, cls, "str1",    // (E)
                           "Ljava/lang/String;");
   jstring b= (*env)->GetObjectField(env, this, fid);    // (F)
   const char* t= (*env)->GetStringUTFChars(env, b, 0);  // (G)
   char buf[64]={'\0'};
      strcat(buf,t);                             // (H)
      strcat(buf,s);                             // (I)
      (*env)->ReleaseStringUTFChars(env, a, s);  // (J)
      (*env)->ReleaseStringUTFChars(env, b, t);  // (K)
      a= (*env)->NewStringUTF(env, buf);         // (L)
      (*env)->SetObjectField(env, this, fid, a); // (M)
      return a;
}
```

To access the field `str1`, you first obtain the class of its host object (line D) and the ID of the desired field (line E). Then the value of `str1` can be obtained (line F). After building C strings in `buf` (lines H and I), you can create a Java `String` object (line L), set the field `str1` (line M), and return the `String`.

A native method obtains an instance field (instance method) ID before being able to access the field (method). The call

```
jfieldID fid= (*env)->GetFieldID(env,cls,"field_name","type_code");
```

returns a particular field ID given a string name and a type code. The call

```
jmethodID mid= (*env)->GetMethodID(env,cls,"method_name",
                              "signature");
```

returns a particular method ID, given a string name and a signature. The rules for field type code and method signatures are well defined in Java (see JNI documentation). But an easier way is to use the `javap` tool

```
javap -s -p ClassName
```

to display all of the field code and signatures in the given class.

After getting a method ID (`mid`), you can call the method with

```
(*env)->CallrtypeMethod(env,obj,mid,args);
```

where *rtype* is the return value type of the method and *obj* is the host object (`jobject`) of the method. Use

```
GetStaticMethodId
CallStaticrtypeMethod
```

for static methods; the calls are similar for static fields.

12.9   JNI EXAMPLE: ARRAYS

Here an integer array is passed to a native method (line 1), which displays it and then calls a Java method (line 2) to increment each array element by one. The native method displays the array again.

```
///////    Array.java    ///////

class Array
{   private native void myDisplay(int[] a);        // (1)

    static { System.loadLibrary("arr"); }

    private int[] ia = {1,3,5,7};

    private void add1(int[] a)                      // (2)
    {    for (int i=0; i < a.length; i++) a[i]++; }

    public static void main(String[] args)
    {    Array obj = new Array();
         obj.myDisplay(obj.ia);
    }
}
```

The C implementation of the native method obtains the length and body of the Java array object arr (lines 3–4) and the method ID of add1 (lines 5–6). It then displays the array in C (line 7), calls add1 from C (line 8), and displays the array again.

```
/******    myDisplay.c    ******/
#include "myDisplay.h"
#include <stdio.h>

JNIEXPORT void JNICALL Java_Array_myDisplay
  (JNIEnv *env, jobject host, jintArray arr)
{
    jsize len = (*env)->GetArrayLength(env, arr);    // (3)
    jint *b = (*env)->GetIntArrayElements           // (4)
                  (env, arr, 0);
    jclass cls = (*env)->GetObjectClass(env, host);  // (5)
    jmethodID mid = (*env)->GetMethodID             // (6)
                  (env, cls, "add1", "([I)V");
    int i;
       for (i = 0; i < len-1; i++)                   // (7)
           printf("%d  ", b[i]);
       printf("%d\n",b[len-1]);
       (*env)->CallVoidMethod(env, host, mid, arr);  // (8)
       for (i = 0; i < len-1; i++)
           printf("%d  ", b[i]);
       printf("%d\n",b[len-1]);
       (*env)->ReleaseIntArrayElements(env, arr, b, 0);
}
```

The JNI provides additional support for arrays, exceptions, and threads. Complete information on the current JNI can be found at the Java Web site. The same procedures described here can be used to interface Java and C++. It is also possible to interface to f77 programs by connecting through a C program.

Examples available from the code site show details of Java-C++ and Java-f77 interface techniques.

12.10 GENERATING JAVA DOCUMENTATION IN HTML

The tool **javadoc** takes Java source code files containing *doc comments* and generates API documentation in HTML. The doc comments follow a well-defined format and can contain HTML constructs. A doc comment is in the following general form:

```
/**
 * Summary line.
 * more
 *       lines of comment
```

```
* @tag line (optional)
* @tag line (optional)
* @tag line (optional)
*/
```

A doc comment starts with /** and ends with */ The summary line should concisely describe the purpose of the construct. The summary line ends with a period followed by white space or end-of-line. Other comment lines can be given freely as indicated. HTML constructs can be given and will be included *as is* in the generated document. Do not use header tags (<H1>, <H2>, <H3>,...) in doc comments.

To place doc comments in a Java source file, follow these rules:

- One doc comment is allowed per construct: class, interface, method, constructor, or field.
- A doc comment is placed immediately in front of the construct, with no other intervening Java code whatsoever.
- To supply individual doc comments, fields must be declared separately.
- Avoid header tags and horizontal rules in doc comments (<H1>, <HR>,...)

A number of special *doc comment tags* are keyed by the character @ after a single SPACE from the starting * character.

- @see—Indicates a cross-reference to a class, interface, method, constructor, field, or URL. For example:

```
@see BankAccount
@see Vector2D#toString
@see java.io.Cloneable
@see Character#toLowerCase(char)
@see <A HREF="..."> Some text </A>
@see "This article"
```

Note the use of # to separate a class from a member.

- @param—Describes a method parameter. For example:

```
@param amt  the amount to deposit
```

- @return—Describes the return value of a method (not void). For example:

```
@return  <tt>true</tt>, or <tt>false</tt> for failure
```

- @exception—Indicates a specified exception for a method. Use this to list one exception class followed by a short description.
- @author—Indicates the author of a class or interface.

The BankAccount class with doc comments is listed here as an example:

```
///////    BankAccount.java    ///////

/**
 * Superclass of bank account hierarchy.
 * @author Paul S. Wang
 */
public class BankAccount     // class name
{   public BankAccount() {}
/**
 * Constructor.  Initializes a new account.
 * @param id     BankAccount number
 * @param amt    Initial balance amount
 * @param ss     Social security number as string
 */
    public BankAccount(int id, String ss, double amt)
    {   acct_no = id;
        owner = ss;
        acct_bal = (amt > 0) ? amt : 0.0;
    }
/**
 * Retrieves the account balance.
 * @return the <tt>balance</tt>
 */
    public double balance()
    {   return acct_bal;   }
/**
 * Retrieves the account number.
 * @return the <tt>acct_no</tt>
 */
    public int id()
    {   return acct_no;   }
/**
 * Deposits into account.
 * @param amt   the amount to deposit, if <tt>amt <=0</tt> no effect
 */
    public void deposit(double amt)
    {   if ( amt > 0 )
            acct_bal += amt;
    }
/**
 * Withdraw from account.
 * @param amt     the amount to deposit
 * @return        <tt>false</tt> if <tt>amt <=0</tt>
 *                or insufficient balance
 */
```

```
    public boolean withdraw(double amt)
    {   if( amt <= 0 || amt > acct_bal )
          return false;   // failure
        acct_bal -= amt;
        return true;
    }
/**
 * The account number.
 */
    protected int  acct_no;     // account number
/**
 * The social security number of owner.
 */
    protected String owner;     // owner ss no.

// private fields
/**
 * The account balance.
 */
    private double   acct_bal; // current balance
}
```

Use the command

javadoc BankAccount.java

to generate API documentation. Several .html files will be produced, including BankAccount.html.

The following is a portion of the generated BankAccount.html. The code site contains the complete file.

```
<body>
<h1>
  Class BankAccount
</h1>
<pre>
<a href="java.lang.Object.html#_top_">java.lang.Object</a>
    |
    +----BankAccount
</pre>
<hr>
<dl>
  <dt> public class <b>BankAccount</b>
  <dt> extends <a href="java.lang.Object.html#_top_">Object</a>
</dl>
Superclass of bank account hierarchy.
<hr>
```

`javadoc` Generated Files

For larger projects, use the command

`javadoc` *package-dir1 package-dir2...*

to generate Java documentation. The `javadoc` tool will generate the following:

- One *name*`.html` file per class or interface.
- One package page (`package-summary.html`) for each package it is documenting. `javadoc` will include any HTML and `javadoc` text provided in a file named `package.html` in the package directory.
- One overview page (`overview-summary.html`) for the entire set of packages. This is the front page of the generated document.
- Other cross reference and helper pages.

Doclets

By default, `javadoc` generates HTML documentation based on doc comments inserted in Java source files. However, it can be more general.

A *doclet* is a program that is written in Java and uses the doclet API to specify the content and format of the output of the `javadoc` tool. By default `javadoc` uses a standard doclet that generates API documentation in HTML. You may write doclets to modify how the standard doclet works or write new doclets to generate documentation in other formats, such as MIF.

12.11   CLIPBOARDS

An important windowing system feature is the ability to transfer user-selected data from one application to another. For this purpose, most window systems support a *system clipboard* as an information way station. You *copy* information from a *source* application onto the clipboard and then *paste* the information from the clipboard into a *target* application. The source and target can be the same or different applications (Figure 12.3). All applications share the same clipboard. Thus, a copy operation replaces information on the clipboard with new information. On the PC, MS/Windows applications usually provide copy and paste through the `Edit` menu and/or mouse clicks. On UNIX, X-window applications normally support copy and paste with mouse-based operations. Text-oriented widgets have the ability to receive text from the system clipboard.

Data Transfer Support in Java

The `java.awt.datatransfer` package supports a *system clipboard* for copy and paste between a Java program and other processes under the same window

Figure 12.3   DATA TRANSFER VIA CLIPBOARD

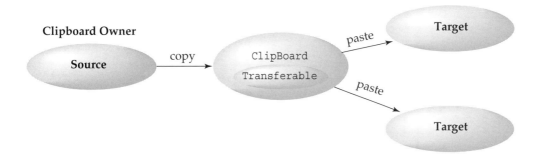

system. It is also possible to establish local clipboards for internal use within a Java program.

A Clipboard object supports data transfer by providing three methods:

1. getName()—Returns the string name of the clipboard.

2. getContents(*target*)—Returns the clipboard contents, in the form of a Transferable, to the requesting *target* object. This is the *paste* operation.

3. setContents(*data, source*)—Sets *data* supplied by *source* as the new contents of the clipboard. The *data* must be prepared as a Transferable and the *source* object must implement the ClipboardOwner interface. This is the *copy* operation.

Pasting from a Clipboard

Follow these simple steps:

1. Obtain a reference to the desired clipboard.

2. Determine whether the clipboard contents can be produced in a format you can use.

3. Retrieve the contents in an indicated format.

Let's look at an example applet that pastes (obtains) a string from the system clipboard and displays the data in a JTextArea:

```
///////    ClipReceiver.java    ///////
import java.awt.*;
import java.io.*;
import java.awt.event.*;
import java.awt.datatransfer.*;
import javax.swing.*;
```

```
public class ClipReceiver extends JApplet
{  public void init()
   {    sysClip = Toolkit.getSystemClipboard();        // (A)
        JButton pb = new JButton(" Paste ");           // (B)
        receiver = new JTextArea(3, 50);
        Container cp = getContentPane();
        cp.add(receiver, BorderLayout.CENTER);
        cp.add(pb, BorderLayout.SOUTH);
        pb.addActionListener(new PasteHandler());      // (C)
   }

  // PasteHandler shown later

   protected JTextArea receiver;
   protected Clipboard sysClip;
}
```

The system clipboard is obtained (line A) by calling

```
Toolkit.getSystemClipboard();
```

The Paste button (line B) triggers PasteHandler (line C), which retrieves data from the system clipboard.

The listener obtains the system clipboard contents (line D), makes sure that the contents can be retrieved as a string (line E), gets the contents in string form (line F), then adds the string to the JTextArea (line G).

```
private final class PasteHandler implements ActionListener
{  public void actionPerformed(ActionEvent ev)
   {  Transferable content = sysClip.getContents(this);      // (D)
      if ( content != null &&
        content.isDataFlavorSupported(DataFlavor.stringFlavor) // (E)
      )
      {  try
         {  String s =(String) content.getTransferData        // (F)
                        (DataFlavor.stringFlavor);
            receiver.append(s);                                // (G)
         } catch ( IOException e )
           {  e.printStackTrace();  }
           catch ( UnsupportedFlavorException e ) { }
      }
   }
}
```

Because data transfer via the clipboard may involve different program elements, in one or several applications, that support different data formats, a Transferable object is used as a data delivery vehicle that can ship data in its original format but deliver it to a target program in possibly one of several other formats. These possible formats are called *data flavors*, or simply *flavors*. For example, an incoming character string must be converted to a Java String object before a Java program can use it. The DataFlavor class provides constants to indicate various standard data formats.

Copying to a Clipboard

Follow these simple steps:

1. Obtain a reference to the desired clipboard.
2. Create a Transferable object with the data to be copied onto the clipboard.
3. Deposit the Transferable object on the clipboard.

Note that an object that copies to a clipboard must implement the Clipboard-Owner interface.

Let's look at an example in which the ClipSource applet copies text in a JTextArea onto the system clipboard:

```
public class ClipSource extends JApplet
{   public void init()
    {   sysClip = getToolkit().getSystemClipboard();
        JButton pb = new JButton(" Copy ");
        source = new JTextArea(3, 50);
        Container cp = getContentPane();
        cp.add(source, BorderLayout.CENTER);
        cp.add(pb, BorderLayout.SOUTH);
        pb.addActionListener(new CopyHandler());
    }

 // CopyHandler shown later

    protected JTextArea source;
    protected Clipboard sysClip;
}
```

The CopyHandler also implements the ClipboardOwner interface, which requires one method:

```
public void lostOwnership(Clipboard c, Transferable t)
```

This method allows an arrangement in which the data to be placed on the clipboard is held by the source object (the clipboard owner) until an actual paste operation takes place. The source object loses its ownership of a clipboard when another object performs a copy onto the clipboard.

The lostOwnership method is usually a no-op.

```
private final class CopyHandler
        implements ActionListener, ClipboardOwner
{
   public void lostOwnership(Clipboard c, Transferable t) { }

   public void actionPerformed(ActionEvent ev)
   {   StringSelection ct =
               new StringSelection(source.getText());      // (I)
         sysClip.setContents(ct, this);                    // (II)
   }
}
```

The copying action creates a string-type transferable object (line I), where StringSelection is a Java-supplied class that implements Transferable and then copies the object onto the system clipboard (line II).

Although our examples deal with the system clipboard, the use of local clipboards is similar. The StringSelection transferable works for the stringFlavor (Java character strings).

Java also has a *Drag and Drop* subsystem, which allows Java GUI programs to participate in the familiar drag-and-drop operations on different platforms including Win32, CDE/Motif, and Mac OS. An extensible data type system based on the MIME standard is used to describe flavors in transferables.

12.12 INTERAPPLET COMMUNICATION

Applets contained in the same .html file and displayed on the same page can communicate with one another and cooperate to achieve certain goals. Many browsers limit such communications to applets originating from the same Web server.

An applet looking to communicate with another will simply:

1. Obtain an object representing the execution context (usually a Web browser) of the applet.
2. Obtain the target applet reference from the applet context.
3. Use the reference to call public methods in the target applet.

The code

```
AppletContext browser = getAppletContext();
Applet ap = browser.getApplet( target );
```

returns an Applet-type reference of an applet named by the string *target*. An applet's name is specified by the name attribute (Section 7.13) in its Web page. To illustrate applet cooperation, let's revisit the Tic Tac Toe game. Now it is organized as two applets: One plays the game and the other provides an unmove button. When a player clicks the unmove button, the button applet contacts the game-playing applet to undo a move.

The HTML page contains two applets TicUnButApplet and TicApButton.

```
<html><head><title>Tic Tac Toe</title></head>
<body>
<H1>Tic Tac Toe Game</H1>
<H3>Unmove by Another Applet</H3>
<p>
Play Tic Tac Toe.
<p>
You and the computer alternate playing first.
<p>
<applet width=140 height=140  name="gameApplet"
        code="TicUnButApplet.class"
        archive="TicUnButApplet.jar">
First Java Applet here
</applet>
<br>
<applet width=140 height=25
        code="TicApButton.class"
    <param name="game" value="gameApplet">
Second Java Applet here
</applet>
</body></html>
```

The former is given a name, "gameApplet". The latter is given the game parameter value "gameApplet" in order to reach the former.

```
///////    TicApButton.java     ///////
import java.awt.BorderLayout;
import java.awt.event.*;
import javax.swing.*;

public class TicApButton extends JApplet
{  public void init()
   {   b = new JButton(" Unmove ");
       getContentPane().add(b, BorderLayout.CENTER);
       String tg = getParameter("game");                    // (1)
       JApplet t = (JApplet)                                 // (2)
                   getAppletContext().getApplet(tg);
       tap = (TicUnButApplet) t;                             // (3)
       b.addActionListener(new ActionHandler());             // (4)
   }
```

```
    private final class ActionHandler
               implements ActionListener
    {   public void actionPerformed(ActionEvent e)
        {   tap.unMove(); }                                    // (5)
    }


    JButton b;
    TicUnButApplet tap = null;                                 // (6)
}
```

The `TicApButton` applet has an unmove button and a reference to the game-playing applet (line 6). The name of the game-playing applet is obtained (line 1) using `getParameter` (Section 7.13). The string name is used to obtain the `JApplet` reference (line 2) with the following call:

```
getAppletContext().getApplet(tg);
```

The field `tap` is initialized by appropriate casting (line 3). The event listener registered with b will trigger unmoves by calling `tap.unMove()` (line 5). The inner `ActionHandler` is defined as usual.

Java also has the call

```
Enumeration en = getAppletContext().getApplets()
```

which returns all applets on the same page in an `Enumeration` object.

An applet can also request the browser to display any HTML document by giving it a URL. The calls

```
browser.showDocument(java.net.URL url)
browser.showDocument(java.net.URL url, window)
```

request that the `AppletContext` browser display the document given by the `url`. The optional *window* can specify what window to use. For example, the window "_blank" displays the document in a new, nameless window.

12.13 JAVA SECURITY MANAGER

Applets and dynamically loaded remote classes make Java very useful for network-based applications. However, an application program must be able to guard against unwanted, undesirable, or even malicious behaviors in external code. Without good security measures, such an application can be dangerous. No wonder security problems relating to executable content for Web browsers are taken very seriously.

Java offers mechanisms that help maintain security. When a Java application starts, it is running *trusted code*. Before the execution of *untrusted code*, such as an applet or nonlocal class, the application can install a *security manager*. The security manager guards a predefined list of critical operations and enforces application-defined access controls over these operations. When installed, the security manager takes effect for the entire duration of the application's execution and cannot be removed or replaced. Security managers in HotJava and Netscape typically use the contents of the method call stack to deduce whether trusted or untrusted code is accessing a guarded operation. The in-memory security manager is tamper-proof due to Java's type system.

Security Checks

Java recognizes a well-defined list of security-critical operations, including file system access, networking, class loading, external program execution, system properties access, and so on. A security manager defines check*xxx* methods to guard low-level operations on the list. Here are some check methods:

```
checkAccess(Thread)
checkAwtEventQueueAccess()
checkConnect(String, int)
checkCreateClassLoader()
checkExec(String)
checkPropertiesAccess()
checkRead(FileDescriptor)
checkWrite(FileDescriptor)
```

Built-in Java classes and the JVM consistently access critical operations only after checking with the security manager (Figure 12.4). A check method either throws a SecurityException or returns to allow the particular access. Application code cannot get around the security checks.

Figure 12.4   JAVA SECURITY MODEL

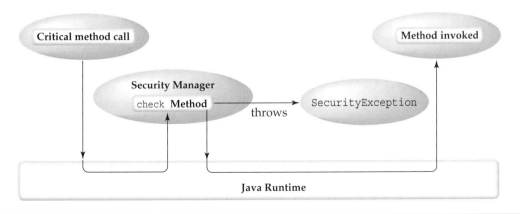

Writing a Security Manager

The SecurityManager is an abstract class that defines the interface and provides partial implementation for user-defined security managers. The default implementation of all check*xxx* methods throws an exception. You subclass SecurityManager and override desired check methods to implement a custom security policy. For example, each file access from untrusted code may require interactive user approval.

```
class MySecurityManager extends SecurityManager
{   . . .
}
```

To install a security manager, use something like the following:

```
try
{   SecurityManager sm = new MySecurityManager();
    System.setSecurityManager( sm );
} catch (SecurityException e)
    {   System.err.println("Failed to install MySecurityManager");
        e.printStackTrace();
    }
```

To get the current security manager use

```
System.getSecurityManager()
```

which returns null if no security manager has been installed.

Security Policy Files

Java supports a fine-grained access control scheme in which different permissions can be granted to code from local or remote sources. Application programs from the local file system normally have few restrictions. Remote applets will typically run in the severely restrictive security sandbox (Section 7.14). But, Java users and developers can fine-tune security restrictions by setting up security policies.

Remotely loaded programs such as applets and remotely accessed programs such as RMI remote objects and the RMI daemon usually get more restricted permissions than local programs. When code is loaded or remotely accessed, it is assigned *permissions* based on the *security policy* currently in effect for the code and access. Each permission grants a particular resource, for example, reading or writing files, obtaining system properties, or making network connections. A policy specifies what permissions are assigned for code and access from given signers and locations. In a policy file, unless a permission is explicitly granted, the resource is off limits.

By default the system-wide policy file is located at

```
java.home/jre/lib/security/java.policy
```

and provides the normal permissions for Java code. Per-user policy files are located at

```
user.home/.java.policy
```

A policy file contains a number of *grant* entries and an optional *keystore* entry. The keystore specified in a policy file is used to look up the public keys of the signers specified in the grant entries. A keystore entry must be included if a policy file specifies signers. A keystore entry is in this form:

```
keystore "keystore_url", "keystore_type";
```

Each grant entry establishes a *security domain* of programs with assigned privileges. A grant entry is in the following form

```
grant signedBy "signer_names", codeBase "URL"

permission-entry
...
permission-entry
```

It grants the specified permissions to codes signed by the given signers and from the given codebase. The signedBy and codeBase attributes are optional.

A codeBase value indicates the code source location and the permissions are granted to code from that location. If codeBase is not specified, the code can originate from any source location. A signedBy value indicates the alias for a certificate stored in a keystore. The public key within that certificate is used to verify the digital signature on the code. Permissions are granted only to code signed by the private key corresponding to the public key in the keystore entry specified by the alias. If signedBy is not specified, the code need not be signed.

Each permission entry is in the form

```
permission permission_class
              "target_resource",
              "action_allowed",
              signedBy "signer_names";
```

where *permission_class* indicates the type of permission (for example, java.io.FilePermission), *target_resource* is the resource to be accessed (e.g., /tmp), *action_allowed* lists the action permitted (e.g., read or write), and *signer_names* name required signers, if any. Not all parts are required for certain permissions.

Policy files are best prepared with the **policytool**, which provides a visual environment for creating and editing security policy files.

12.14 SIGNED APPLETS AND DYNAMIC TRUST MANAGEMENT

The JAR file of an applet can be *digitally signed* by its creating entity (person or organization). An application, such as a Web browser or the Java Plug-in, may give more leeway to code signed by known and trusted entities.

Digital signature can be achieved with *public key encryption*[1] where a signing entity obtains an encryption key pair—a public key and a private key. The private key is used to sign a document or a program, such as an applet, and is held by the signing entity and revealed to no one else. The public key is made available to anyone who wishes to verify a signed file from the entity. The RSA is a widely used public-key encryption system. Even though DSA (digital signature algorithm) can be used, RSA remains the most popular method for digital signature.

Support for applets, especially Swing applets, is non-uniform across different Web browsers. Security and treatment of signed applets are also different. It is highly advisable to deploy applets to run under the Java Plug-in from Sun. The Java Plug-in follows the Netscape signing model to support standard VeriSign and Thawte RSA certificates. It provides identical RSA signed applet support in Internet Explorer and Netscape Navigator.

The Java Plug-in can rely on the policy files, which provide static and preassigned security domains. In practice, it is often difficult or impossible for applet users to preconfigure the permissions and indicate the signers, especially when users may not know which applets will be used or available in the future. To overcome this difficulty, the Java Plug-in now provides *dynamic trust management* and prompts the user for permissions right after a signed applet is loaded and verified.

Dynamic trust management uses information stored in an *identity database* to grant or deny access to critical operations by applets. The database stores *identity certificates* and user-supplied access control information for code signed by the identified entities. A certificate identifies a signing entity and contains its public key. Formal identity certificates are issued by *certifying authorities* that can vouch for the identities of organizations and individuals. The certificate allows a browser to verify the authenticity of the signature and the entity who signed it. When verified, a signed applet can be afforded degrees of freedom outside of the *sandbox* (Section 7.14).

We will describe how to accept and deploy signed applets for the Java Plug-in.

Accepting Signed Applets

When an RSA signed applet JAR file is loaded by the Java Plug-in, it verifies the signature on the RSA certificate. Successful verification results in a pop-up security dialog telling the user who signed the applet and providing four options:

---

[1] A very effective technology for the secure digital transmission of information.

- Grant always—To grant the applet and all identically signed applets *AllPermission* in the future automatically
- Grant this session—To grant the applet and all identically signed applets *AllPermission* for the current browser session
- Deny—To treat it as an untrusted applet
- More Info—To allow the user to examine the attributes of each certificate in the certificate chain in the JAR file

The applet will then be run in the corresponding security context selected from the security dialog. The scheme requires no preconfiguration of security preferences and is easy to use.

Creating Signed Applets

To create your own signed applets you need to obtain two items first:

1. The Netscape Signing Tool
2. A Netscape Object Signing Certificate from an RSA Certificate Authority (CA) such as VeriSign or Thawte

After you have installed the Netscape Signing Tool and a Netscape Object Signing Certificate (a practice certificate can be generated by the signing tool), you are ready to sign applets, as follows:

1. Create an empty directory/folder

   `mkdir myapplet`

   and move all files for the applet to this new directory.

2. Create a signed JAR file:

   `signtool -k MyCertificate -Z myapplet.jar myapplet`

   This command will query you for a password to your protected private-key database. Only you know that password, and therefore only you can sign applets using your object signing certificate. The signed applet is in the `myapplet.jar` file.

3. Test the JAR file created

   `signtool -v myapplet.jar`

   to ensure that it is signed correctly.

After an applet is thus signed, you can deploy it in a Web page, using the HTML code given in Section 7.13. This applet will work when downloaded by a browser with the Java Plug-in installed.

12.15 SUMMARY

Each class in your Java program is represented by a unique instance of the class `Class`. The arrangement allows the treatment of classes as objects and runtime manipulation of classes. The Class class is the cornerstone of the Java *reflection* feature, which allows programs to instrospect upon themselves. At run time, a program can load a class; discover its methods, constructors, and fields; and then put them to use.

The JVM loads classes on the local machine automatically (using CLASSPATH). Remote classes can be loaded with application-defined class loaders (by subclassing ClassLoader) and overriding findClass. After loading, a remote class can be executed just like any other class.

The Java run time is represented by an object retrieved by the call Runtime.getRuntime(). The run-time object supplies methods that examine available memory, trigger garbage collection, trace method calls, and launch other programs. A Java program can communicate directly with a launched program to supply data and receive results.

It is possible to interface and combine a Java program with programs written in *native languages* such as C and C++. JNI and the tools **javah** and **javap** support making such interfaces: writing Java code, creating native code, and linking and loading them together to run.

The Java tool **javadoc** can extract information from Java source code files (with doc comments) and produce API documentation in HTML.

The Clipboard class provides a way for transferring data of various formats among JFC widgets and to other applications through the system clipboard.

Java uses a security manager to guard critical operations. *Check methods* serve as gatekeepers for critical operations and will allow or disallow access to these operations according to a default or user-configured security policy. The **policytool** helps create and edit policy files.

The Java Plug-in follows the Netscape signing model to support signed applets using dynamic trust management. It provides identical RSA signed applet support in Internet Explorer and Netscape Navigator. The signature allows verification of the origin of the applet code and grants permissions obtained by prompting the user.

An applet has special methods for communicating with its execution context (**appletviewer** or a Web browser). Applets on the same Web page and coming from the same codebase can communicate and cooperate.

EXERCISES

Review Questions

1. Consider reflection in Java. What classes are involved in the support of reflection?

2. How does one call a method and a constructor, through reflection?

3. Given any object, can you obtain the object representing its class? Can you obtain the string name of its class? How?

4. Given a string, can a Java program find out whether there is a class by that name? If there is, can the program proceed to create an instance of that class?

5. When `cbj.getSuperclass()` returns `null`, what does it mean?

6. What are the steps for class loading?

7. What is a Java doc comment? What is the general form of a doc comment? Where should a doc comment be placed? Name and describe five doc comment tags.

8. Explain how `System.setIn`, `System.setOut`, and `System.setErr` are used for I/O redirection with child processes launched by the `exec` method of the Java run time.

9. Take the `Account.java` program with doc comments and use **javadoc** to produce API documentation in HTML.

10. List and explain the major steps for interfacing a Java program that uses a native method with the native code that implements the method.

11. What is the utility of the tool **javah** for interfacing a Java program with native code?

12. What role does the tool **javap** play in interfacing Java programs with native code?

13. Under JNI, what scheme is used to pass Java and native data types?

14. Is it possible to interface Java code with a native program that contains the `main` function and therefore the starting point of execution?

15. Explain how signed applets work.

16. What is a `securityException`? What are security check methods?

17. What constitutes a digital signature? List and explain major steps for creating signed applets.

Programming Assignments

1. Write a QuickAPI class that uses reflection to display API information. The command

   java *ClassName methodName*

   displays the API information for the given method in the specified class. If the method name is not given, all the declared methods in the class are listed.

2. Write a class MatchFiles so that the command

   java MatchFiles *dir str*

   displays all file names, in the given directory *dir*, that contain *str* in the name. (Hint: Make use of MatchingLines in the exercises of Chapter 8.)

3. Create a GUI for the DisplayType application in Section 12.1.

4. Download the Java documentation, and install it on your computer locally. Add an applet in the Java API document index page. The applet receives a class or package name and displays directly its .html page. (Hint: Use a command such as the UNIX ls or DOS dir from Java.)

5. Take the Fraction class (Section 2.4) and add Java doc comments to it. Then run **javadoc** to generate API documentation files and use a Web browser to view the .html files.

6. Refer to the sendEmail method (Section 12.4). Improve the method to use any designated mailing program, such as **sendmail**, and to send the email with supplied Subject, To, Cc, and Bcc values.

7. (Bookmark-4) Take the Bookmark-3 (Exercises, Chapter 8) solution and add an Open feature: (A) If matching lines in the List contain only one URL, this Web page is opened and displayed. (B) Otherwise the user may select any URL from the List to open. (Hint: Launch a browser.)

8. (Bookmark-5) The Bookmark program's JTextArea already has the ability to receive text from the system clipboard. Now we will make it possible to copy from the Bookmark program to the system clipboard. Add a Copy button that copies a selected string in the Bookmark's JList component to the system clipboard. This feature is useful for transferring a URL to the system clipboard.

9. It is possible to interface f77 code into Java through C. Assuming that you already know how to interface C and f77 code, all you need to do now is compile the C and f77 programs into position-independent .o code. Then use the link loader to collect all .o files into a shared library. Try this on your system. If you get stuck, find a full example in the example package.

## CHAPTER THIRTEEN

Object-Oriented Design

Java provides excellent support for OOP. However, simply using Java constructs does not automatically lead to well-organized, object-oriented programs. On the contrary, without a good design created with an object-oriented view, the resulting program will most likely be a procedure-oriented program written in Java. Worse yet, it could be such a program bent out of shape to give rise to classes!

Object orientation requires its own approach to software design. The well-known life cycle model divides software construction into several phases:

1. Requirement analysis
2. Design specification
3. Implementation
4. System testing
5. System maintenance

The first two phases produce a set of design specifications that guide the implementation (actual coding) phase. The life cycle model gives a somewhat rigid sequential view of the software creation process. Producing an OO program usually involves an incremental and iterative process in which each of the listed steps are done with object orientation.

One technique shared by all software engineering methodologies is "divide and conquer," whereby the problem at hand is decomposed into smaller and more manageable pieces. The individual pieces are made and then put together to achieve the overall goal. Starting with large pieces and breaking them down into smaller ones is considered a *top-down* approach. Collecting small chunks and combining them into larger chunks of the solution follows the *bottom-up* style. The way a problem is broken apart is limited only by the experience, creativity, and ingenuity of the designers.

In object-oriented design (OOD), the given problem is broken into self-contained, interacting objects that correspond to actual or logical entities in the problem domain. A detailed study of OOD would take us beyond the scope of this book. This chapter will, however, provide some basic principles, suggest concrete steps to follow to identify objects, introduce the design pattern concept, show UML (Unified Modeling Language) diagrams, describe the CRC design method, discuss the model-view-controller (MVC) design paradigm and the Swing MVC architecture, and provide examples.

469

13.1 DECOMPOSITION APPROACHES

Before the design process begins, there must be a clear understanding of the requirements and purposes of the software to be constructed. The first step of the design effort usually involves breaking down the whole problem into manageable chunks and defining the interrelationships among them. Decomposition forms a basis for design specifications that in turn govern implementation. The three major decomposition methods are listed here:

1. Procedural decomposition
2. Data decomposition
3. Object-oriented decomposition

Procedural Decomposition

One way to solve a problem is to look at the steps required for its solution. This method of decomposition produces interrelated procedures that combine to form the desired solution.

Taken from the top down, a problem is divided into several major procedures. Each procedure is then decomposed in the same manner. Common procedures are identified, and eventually the procedures are implemented as functions. The bottom-up approach to procedural decomposition considers the basic steps necessary in the solution and how they combine to form larger procedures.

With any methodology, after a problem is decomposed sufficiently, we always arrive at a point where procedures are necessary to carry out the computation. The design of efficient procedures (*algorithms*) to solve given problems is a major topic in computer science.

Data Decomposition

Another way to break up a problem is to look at the usage of data. This method of decomposition considers which parts of the solution system deal with which data, how data flow through the system, and which pieces of data are shared by which parts. The data considered include input to the system, information generated for internal use, and results for output. This analysis identifies self-contained pieces and defines their interrelationships.

A need-to-know view should be applied to data decomposition. A system component possesses knowledge of only required data and nothing else. This design principle helps isolate data to restricted parts of the system and therefore reduces the overall complexity.

Object-Oriented Decomposition

The OO view is to decompose a system into autonomous computing agents that correspond to the interacting mechanisms in the problem. These agents are then modeled by software objects. In a banking system, for example, the objects are customers, accounts, loans, CDs, passbooks, statements, and so on. At a finer level, objects could be addresses, charges, credits, overdrafts, payments, and interests.

Each object represents some tangible entity and behaves in a well-defined way. The internal organization of the object can be anything that supports its external behavior. The major advantage of OO decomposition is its flexibility and close relationship to the problem domain. Clearly, once objects are identified and put into place, they can support, for example, one particular banking system just as easily as another.

Procedural decomposition and OO decomposition take orthogonal views: One highlights the sequencing of logical solution steps; the other focuses on the interacting entities. Both views are important for the overall design process, but it is perhaps best to first apply the OO view to identify the objects and define their behaviors. Then the sequencing-of-events view can be applied to the interactions of these objects.

The data decomposition view can also help identify the objects, define their relationships, and set limits on knowledge and the access of data. The need-to-know principle of data decomposition is enforced very well with OO decomposition. Protected and hidden from unnecessary outside view are not only data structures but also internal procedures. To the rest of a program, an object is completely characterized by its behavior, which is important to good design.

Thus, in one sense, the OO organization is like setting up a company that contains a number of autonomous divisions, departments, factories, centers, and so on. Some of these entities contain other entities, and all have well-defined external behaviors and internal organizations. A company can adapt to many different tasks and react to a changing marketplace because these entities can adapt to different patterns of interaction without major reorganization.

13.2 OBJECT-ORIENTED DESIGN PRINCIPLES

Ideally, an *object-oriented analysis (OOA)* phase produces a set of requirement specifications. The requirement specifications become input to the design stage. The design stage, in turn, produces a software architecture to achieve the goals and conditions set forth in the specifications. After an OO architecture is achieved, OOP, the actual implementation using an OO language, follows (Figure 13.1).

Figure 13.1 **OBJECT-ORIENTED SOFTWARE CONSTRUCTION**

OOD, like other creative activities, does not follow any fixed recipe. There is no magic formula for creating a software design. The recommended approach involves an iterative process called the *round-trip gestalt design,* a style that views the system as a whole and emphasizes incremental development and stepwise refinement. A preliminary design is based on what is known and doable; improvements, modifications, and redesigns take place thereafter.

This does not mean that OO design is completely unstructured. Although the design follows an evolutionary path, the design effort usually involves a sequence of tasks:

1. Identify classes and objects in the entire system.
2. Characterize the external behavior of each object.
3. Specify the data and operations within each object.
4. Identify requests answered by each object.
5. Identify services required of other objects by each object.
6. Establish the visibility of each object in relation to other objects.
7. Group similar objects, and develop inheritance relationships and class hierarchies.
8. Produce system architecture.

Often the most crucial step is the first one—in this case, to identify classes and objects.

Identifying Classes and Objects

Software designers examine and reexamine the requirement specifications at hand; become familiar with the terminologies, conventions, assumptions, and solution methods in the problem domain; and, through discussions and consultations, form a high-level computation model of the architecture. Interacting problem-domain entities (real and logical) become candidates for objects, and the nouns used in the problem description, such as account, loan, and mortgage, are considered as potential class names.

At this point, the problem decomposition is in the early stages and the boundaries are not yet fixed. Often, the closer the computation model is to reality, the better the decomposition. The design process not only formulates a high-level abstract view of the software to be constructed, but also sharpens the specifications and the attributes of the final software product. Frank

discussions among the designers provides checks, balances, and different per-
spectives.

External Behavior of Objects

After classes and objects are identified and listed, each object on the list must
be characterized by its external behavior. In other words, each object is considered a "black box," and its actions and reactions to the outside world are
prescribed. To do this, the designer acts like a detached customer, demand-
ing functionalities from these black boxes, with little concern over how the
functions are achieved.

To help the design, a script can be written for each object, describing its
role in the overall scenario, including creation, typical actions, and demise.
It is also important to look at various scenarios and how the objects interact
through their external interfaces in each scenario. These activities may suggest
modifications or refinements of the OO decomposition produced earlier.

Finally, a list of objects with external behavior descriptions is produced.

Designing Objects

With the external behavior defined, an object's public interface functions, data
structures, and internal workings are then considered. When an object represents a high-level abstraction, it can often be further decomposed, using the
same OO design methods. Additional objects are then introduced into the
evolving design. For each object, a class is specified to support data hiding
and encapsulation. Arguments for public function members should reflect the
information necessary to achieve the functionality at hand. Requiring too little
information will obviously not work. However, requiring too much information will lead to unreasonable designs.

The design produced at this stage serves as a blueprint for the eventual
implementation of classes.

Relationships among Objects and Classes

The goal now is to obtain a comprehensive picture of how the objects in the
system interact to perform the desired overall functionalities. Almost always,
objects naturally fall into groups. Within each group, objects are heavily dependent on one another and closely related. The behavior patterns and characteristics of objects and classes are then compared to detect any additional is-a,
has-a, uses-a, and can-be-implemented-as-a relationships. Objects that can be
made plug-compatible are identified. The visibility and invisibility of objects
help package classes into files and modules.

In the process of discovering such relationships, certain adjustments of
the characterization of the objects may suggest themselves. Thus the design
process is evolutionary.

Implementation

The design process produces a software system architecture including classes, objects, relationships among them, object grouping, and interaction scenarios. Each class is characterized by its external behaviors and internal organization. Then we enter the implementation phase.

Implementation is the coding phase. The designed classes, modules, and objects are set down in Java or some other OO language. However, this process is not a simple transcription of the design specifications into codes. Often implementation exposes unforeseen problems and opportunities that make rethinking parts of the design necessary or desirable. Thus the design process is iterative.

13.3 DESIGN PATTERNS

Among the multitude of OOD literature, one of the most useful is *design patterns*, cataloging a variety of OOD solutions for frequently encountered problems in practice. Design patterns describe and solve recurring problems in software design and construction. A design pattern is a recipe for solving a certain type of design problem that captures the high-level objects, their interactions, and their behaviors. Each design pattern is characterized by the following:

- Pattern name, motivation, purpose, and intended application
- Classes, their relationships, structure, and collaborations
- Consequences of the pattern
- Implementational issues
- Other related patterns

There are three large categories of patterns:

1. Creational patterns—Solutions for creating and building objects with flexibility. An *object factory* allows polymorphic programs to instantiate objects without knowledge of how they are created. For example, in Java the Swing package (Chapter 8) has a `BorderFactory` class that helps create window borders, a `JOptionPane` class that makes dialog widgets, and `NumberFormat`, which creates formatter instances.

2. Structural patterns—Innovative ways to organize classes and hierarchies, mix-in interfaces, and apply inheritance. A *composite* pattern, for instance, addresses the need to treat components and the whole as objects of the same type. The fact that a document can be a single word, a diagram, a sentence, a paragraph, a section, a chapter, and so on, illustrates the composite idea. In Java, the GUI widget is a composite and is represented by the super class `Component` (for AWT) or `JComponent` (for Swing).

Figure 13.2   THE ITERATOR PATTERN

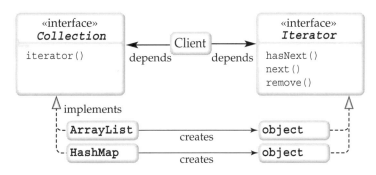

3. Behavioral patterns—Setting up objects and collaborators to achieve well-defined overall behaviors for certain goals. An example is iterators and how they glue containers and algorithms. Another example is the model-view-controller pattern explained in more detail in Section 13.7.

For example, the iterator concept (Section 9.3) can be captured as a behavioral pattern depicting how iterators are established and operate in relation to container classes that implement iterators. Figure 13.2 is a typical design pattern diagram.

Different generic containers such as ArrayList and HashMap (Section 9.1) implement the iterator method that returns iterator instances conforming to the java.util.Iterator interface. A concrete iterator supplies the methods hasNext(), next(), and remove(). A client class can treat containers that supply iterators in a polymorphic way. Such pattern diagrams, when combined with descriptions, examples, applicability, implementation techniques, and critical evaluations, can be valuable tools for object-oriented design and programming. A good book in this area is *Design Patterns: Elements of Reusable Object-Oriented Software*, by Gamma et. al. Addison Wesley (1995).

13.4 UNIFIED MODELING LANGUAGE (UML)

For larger OOD projects, many classes will be involved. There are standard ways to diagram these relationships so that the overall architecture can be captured, presented, and discussed clearly. The Unified Modeling Language (UML)[1] is an industry-standard language for specifying, visualizing, constructing, and documenting the artifacts of software systems. It simplifies the software design process and provides standard notations for making a *blueprint*

---

[1]See *Communications of the ACM*, Oct. 1999, for more information on UML.

for construction. Among other things, the UML offers ways to specify and diagram classes and their relationships. Software tools are available for creating the classes, their attributes, and the relationship diagrams. The encoded design can be transferred directly to other implementation software.

The UML Class Relation Diagrams are very useful for OOD. Typically, boxes represent classes with a name, key components, and attributes. A box is connected to other boxes by lines to denote relationships: instantiates, has an integral part (composition), has-a component (aggregation), uses-a, has reference/pointer to, inherits, and so on (see figure page **??**). Text labels on these lines can indicate whether the relationship is one-way or mutual, and how many objects may be involved. Figures 13.2, 7.11, 8.9, and 3.2 are samples of UML class diagrams we have used.

The UML also has a formalism for describing *use cases* (or usage scenarios) of the system under consideration. It is good practice first to describe the main and typical uses of the system and write down those use cases. Then think also of the unusual ways the systems can be put to use. The use-case descriptions include *preconditions* (state of the system before use), *postconditions* (state of the system after use), *actors* (objects involved), and *sequence diagrams* (a timeline of interactions among the involved objects). Figure 13.3 shows the URL sequence diagram for the pocket calculator simulation program.

See

```
http://www.rational.com/uml/resources/
```

for a *UML Notation Guide* and other UML resources.

UML class relationship and sequence diagrams help render the big picture of an OO design. For performing the OO decomposition and identifying objects, the CRC method can be very effective.

Figure 13.3   SEQUENCE DIAGRAM

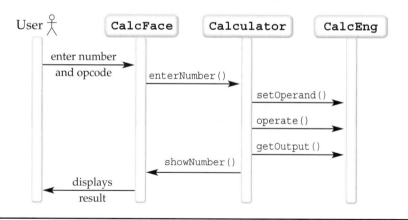

13.5   THE CRC METHOD

A particularly effective technique for identifying objects and defining their relationships is the CRC (class, responsibility, collaboration) method. It is especially good for helping beginning programmers learn OO design.

For CRC, a set of regular index cards is used. On each card, the name of a class, its responsibilities, and its collaborators (other classes and objects) are recorded (Figure 13.4). Completing these cards is an iterative and evolutionary process; many cards will be revised or rewritten before a design emerges.

- Class names—It is important to find the right names for the classes to be created. Names should be natural, conventional (using accepted terms from problem domain), and easy to understand and remember. They should not be misleading. Using nouns for class names is recommended.

- Responsibilities—These are actions assigned to an object. Responsibilities should be described with short verb phrases. Again, it is important to use the right words.

- Collaborators—For each class, names of related objects should be recorded. All objects required to fulfill the responsibilities are obvious collaborators. Classes that require or supply services or data from or to the class under consideration should also be recorded.

With a set of index cards so marked, the designers then proceed to play out execution scenarios and spot omissions or corrections for the descriptions. They also ask "what if" questions to anticipate all conditions that might arise. They can break up complicated classes into more components if necessary. A clear understanding of the problem domain is very helpful because domain knowledge should be used to check and verify the OO design.

Figure 13.4   A SAMPLE CRC INDEX CARD

Class: `CalcEng`	
Responsibilities	Collaborators
• Stores operands, opcode, result.	□ Calculator
• Performs arithmetic operations.	
• Carries out control operations.	□ Derived engines
• Produces quantity stored.	
• Reports error.	

13.6 POCKET CALCULATOR SIMULATION

For our design example, let's revisit the pocket calculator simulation. Since Chapter 3, we have considered many aspects of this problem. Now we are interested in designing and implementing a more realistic pocket calculator with error checking, memory, square root, and percent functions, as well as a GUI (Figure 13.5). By applying the design principles explained in this chapter and following the CRC method, we can formulate a design.

CRC Design

Extensibility is central to our design. The program must allow the easy addition of new features and functions to the calculator. In OOP this means designing the parts of the calculator to be plug-compatible objects, each of which can be improved and extended through inheritance.

Basic Calculator

At the base are these superclasses that combine into a basic calculator with error checking. User interaction is through standard I/O.

- `CalcEng`—Calculator engine that receives operands and opcodes, performs the computation, and provides the results. The public methods are `setOperand`, `operate`, `getOutput`, `getOpcode`, and `status`,

Figure 13.5   POCKET CALCULATOR WITH GUI

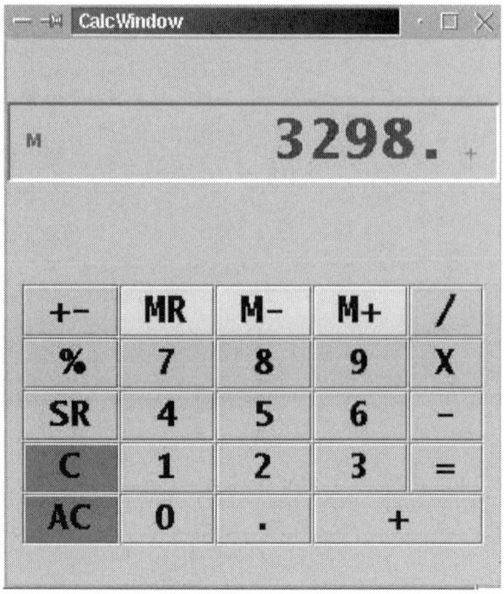

which returns a well-defined engine status string indicating errors or some other status information. The basic engine keeps an internally set computation precision (number of significant digits within a range that can be supported by arithmetic with `double`) and performs error checking.

- `CalcFace`—Calculator user interface that obtains input through the keyboard and displays to standard output. It reports to a `Calculator` object settable with the method `setCalc`. Other public methods are `showNumber`, `showOp`, `showStatus`, `errorInput`, and `input`. The basic prompt `Calc:` changes to `Calc [Error}:` to show error status. The interface operates in two modes: normal and error, set by the `errorInput` method. Under error mode, only the clear and all-clear operations are allowed as input.

- `Calculator`—Calculator manager that coordinates between the `CalcEng` and `CalcFace` objects. This organization affords the maximum independence for engine and interface objects and flexible coordination by a manager. The `on` method outputs an initial display and activates the input loop in `CalcFace`, using the `enterNumber` and `enterOp` methods in the calculator manager to transmit user input. The manager then extracts and formulates engine output for display, checking engine status and showing status through the user interface object as appropriate.

This design follows the *model-view-controller* pattern.

Memory and Scientific Engines

Extending the basic `CalcEng`, we add memory (`M+`, `M-`, `MR`), square root, and percent operations.

- `MemoryEng`—Extending `CalcEng`, the memory engine adds a memory register and memory operations, as well as square root and percent functions. The percent functions work only with opcodes for times and divide. The new *memory-in-use* and *memory-error* statuses are put in place. The `getMemory` method returns the value of the memory register. The `isError` and `getKeys` methods are redefined.

```
public boolean isError()
{   return statusFlag.equals(ERROR) ||
            statusFlag.equals(MEMORY_ERROR);
}
```

- `ScientificEng`—Extending `MemoryEng`, the `ScientificEng` adds trignometry and log calculations (Section 5.2).

Further developing the calculator simulation, we define a window calculator with a GUI, using Swing widgets.

Window Calculator

The CRC descriptions for the window calculator contain four classes:

1. `MemoryEng` (*Compute Engine*)

   - Responsibilities: stores operands, operation codes, and results; performs arithmetic operations; carries out control functions such as clear, all clear, and sign change; produces quantities (result, status, memory) stored in the compute engine upon request; keeps an internal state for status reporting
   - Collaborators: `CalcEng` (superclass), `Calculator`, `CalcFace`, `WinCalculator`, plug-compatible subclass engines with additional features

2. `WinFace` (*GUI*)

   - Responsibilities: receives input character for the calculator under normal and error modes; shows operands, computation results, statuses, and opcodes
   - Collaborators: `CalcFace` (superclass), any engine, `CalcWindow` (a Swing widget), derived plug-compatible user interface classes

3. `CalcWindow` (*Display Window*)

   - Responsibilities: establishes a GUI with a simulated LCD window and graphical buttons for the calculator keys; shows given string in the LCD window; shows given single-character opcode; shows calculator status; receives button events and sends appropriate characters to `WinFace`
   - Collaborators: `WinFace`, Swing widgets

4. `WinCalculator` (*Calculator Control*)

   - Responsibilities: runs any plug-compatible compute engine (type `MemoryEng`) and user interface (type `WinFace`); enters operands and opcodes into engine; extracts engine status and results for display; controls interface input modes (normal/error); formats floating-point numbers for correct LCD display
   - Collaborators: `Calculator` (super class), `MemoryEng`, `WinFace`, and their plug-compatible derivations

Figure 13.6 shows the class relationships.

Implementation

The full implementation of the calculator simulation program can be found in the example package. Let's describe some key implementation features here.

Figure 13.6   CALCULATOR DESIGN

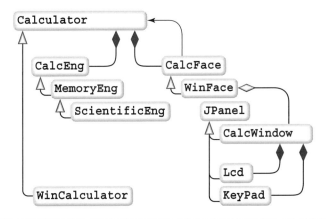

Class WinCalculator

The WinCalculator class supplies critical output formatting to make sure that the output fits in the LCD window and the display is a true simulation of a pocket calculator. If *prec* is the number of significant digits supported by the calculator,

- The LCD window has *prec*+2 positions, its width, for the significant digits, a decimal point, and a possible leading minus sign.
- A number without a fractional part is displayed with an ending decimal point.
- A positive number is displayed without a leading sign.

```
///////     WinCalculator.java     ///////

public class WinCalculator extends Calculator
{   public WinCalculator(MemoryEng e, WinFace f)
    {    super(e,f);
         setFormat(e.precision());
         width = f.getWidth();
    }

    protected WinCalculator() {}

    protected void output()
    {    String e = eng.status();
         if ( e.indexOf('E') != -1 ) return;    // error
         double n = eng.getOutput();
         String a = MyUtil.doubleFormat(n, format);      // (1)
```

```
        if (a.indexOf('.') == -1) a = a+".";          // (2)
        if ( a.length() > width )                      // (3)
            a = a.substring(0, width);
        cf.showNumber(a);
    }

    protected void setFormat(int prec)                 // (4)
    {   int len = 2*prec+1;
        StringBuffer b = new StringBuffer(len);
        for ( int i=0; i < len; i++ )
        {   b.append('#');   }
        b.setCharAt(len/2, '.');
        format= " " + b.toString() + ";" + "-" + b.toString();
    }

    protected int width;
    protected String format;
}
```

The format pattern is set based on *prec* to have a leading sign (or blank), up to *prec* digits in the integral part, a possible decimal point, and up to *prec* digits in the fractional part (line 4). The engine output is formatted by calling the static doubleFormat method (line 1) of our MyUtil class. If the decimal point is not part of the formatted result, add it to the end (line 2). If the formatted string is long, it is truncated to a length of width (line 3).

The static MyUtil.doubleFormat method follows:

```
public static String doubleFormat(double p, String format)
{   Locale us = new Locale("en", "US");
    NumberFormat nf = NumberFormat.getNumberInstance(us);
    DecimalFormat df = (DecimalFormat)nf;
    df.applyPattern(format);
    return df.format(p);
}
```

Class WinFace

The class WinFace instantiates a CalcWindow object with just enough LCD window width to accommodate *prec*+2 positions for displaying numbers with a decimal point and a possible leading sign (line A). The input method is disabled because the reading of standard input is not needed (line B). Show number and show status requests are passed to the CalcWindow object directly (lines C and D).

```
///////    WinFace.java    ///////

public class WinFace extends CalcFace
{   public WinFace(String k, int prec)
```

```
    {    super(k, pr);
         width= pr + 2;   // LCD window width
         cw = new CalcWindow(width, this);      // (A)
         cw.go();
    }
    protected WinFace() {}

    public int getWidth() { return width; }

    public void input() {}                      // (B)

    public void showNumber(String s)            // (C)
    {    cw.showStr(s);  }

    public void showStatus(String e)            // (D)
    {    cw.showStatus(e);  }

// more methods ...

    protected boolean leading_0 = false;
    protected CalcWindow cw;
    protected int width;
}
```

The showOp method checks the opcode and shows or hides it accordingly:

```
public void showOp(char op)
{    switch(op)
     {    case '+': case '-': case '*': case '/':
             cw.showOp(op);      break;
          case 'A':
             cw.showOp(' ');     break;
          case 'S': case '%': case '=':
             cw.showOp(' ');
     }
}
```

The enter method is called by event handlers in CalcWindow to enter digits and opcodes. When the calculator is in error mode, all but the active opcodes (clear and all-clear) are ineffective (line E).

```
public void enter(char c)
{    if ( errMode )                             // (E)
     {    if ( active.indexOf(c) == -1) return;
          else errMode = false;
     }
     super.enter(c);
}
```

```
protected void reset()
{   super.reset();
    leading_0 = false;
    nbuf.append('0');
    nbuf.append('.');
}
```

We override the reset method called by super.enter() so that nbuf and leading_0 are reset correctly. They are used in an overriding buildNumber method that updates the LCD display as the calculator receives input (line F).

```
protected void buildNumber(char c)
{   int i = nbuf.length();
    if ( before_point )
    {   if ( c == '.' )
        {   before_point = false;
        }
        else if (i == 2 && nbuf.charAt(0) == '0')  // 0. case
            nbuf.setCharAt(0, c);
        else
        {   nbuf.setCharAt(i-1, c);
            nbuf.append('.');
        }
    }
    else  // after point
    {   if ( c == '.' ) return;
        nbuf.append(c);
    }
    cw.showStr(nbuf.toString());    // (F)
}
```

Class CalcWindow

The Swing-based GUI for the calculator consists of a CalcWindow widget that contains Lcd (line 1) and Keypad (line 2) child widgets that are positioned with a vertical BoxLayout (line 3). Rigid areas and vertical glue are used to space the widgets in a nice way.

```
public class CalcWindow extends JPanel
{  public CalcWindow(int size, WinFace f)
    {   lcd = new Lcd(size);                                        // (1)
        keypad = new Keypad(f);                                    // (2)
    // vertical box
        setLayout(new BoxLayout(this, BoxLayout.Y_AXIS));          // (3)
        add(Box.createRigidArea(new Dimension(0,40)));
        add(lcd);
```

```
        add(Box.createRigidArea(new Dimension(0,60)));
        add(Box.createVerticalGlue());
        add(keypad);
        add(Box.createRigidArea(new Dimension(0,20)));
    }

    protected CalcWindow() {}

    public void showStatus(String s)
    {   lcd.showStatus(s);    }

    public void showStr(String s)
    {   lcd.showStr(s);    }

    public void showOp(char op)
    {   lcd.showOp(op);    }

    public void go()
    {   JFrame win = new JFrame("CalcWindow");
        win.addWindowListener(new WindowHandler(win));
        win.setContentPane(this);
        win.pack();
        win.setVisible(true);
    }

    protected Lcd lcd;
    protected Keypad keypad;
}
```

CalcWindow employs a Keypad object and an Lcd object. These classes are internal to CalcWindow and are placed in the same source file.

Class Keypad

The Keypad widget (Figure 13.7) creates the calculator buttons with familiar names (line 4) and action commands (line 5) recognized by the calculator engine. Keypad implements ActionListener (line 7) and handles events for all buttons in the Keypad (line 6). The buttons are then added to the Keypad, using a GridBag layout (lines 8 and 9).

```
class Keypad extends JPanel implements ActionListener
{   Keypad(WinFace f)
    {   face = f;
        setBorder(BorderFactory.createEmptyBorder(5,10,5,10));
    // create buttons
        Font g = new Font("Courier", Font.BOLD, 22);
```

Figure 13.7   KEYPAD `GridBag` **LAYOUT**

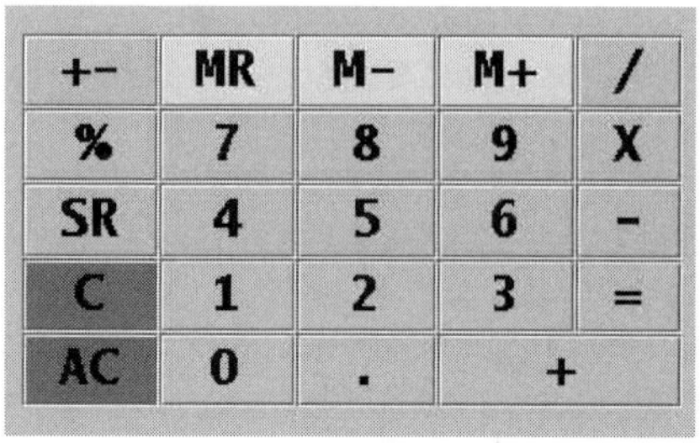

```
        for (int i=0; i < name.length; i++)
        { b[i] = new JButton(name[i]);                        // (4)
          b[i].setVerticalTextPosition(JButton.CENTER);
          b[i].setHorizontalTextPosition(JButton.CENTER);
          b[i].setActionCommand(cmd[i]);                      // (5)
          b[i].addActionListener(this);                       // (6)
          b[i].setFont(g);
        }
        b[1].setBackground(Color.cyan);
        b[2].setBackground(Color.cyan);
        b[3].setBackground(Color.cyan);
        b[15].setBackground(Color.red);
        b[20].setBackground(Color.red);
        layout_buttons();
    }

    public void actionPerformed(ActionEvent e)                // (7)
    {   String cmd = e.getActionCommand();
        face.enter(cmd.charAt(0));
    }

    void layout_buttons()                                     // (8)
    {   setLayout(gridbag);
        c.fill = GridBagConstraints.BOTH;
        c.weightx = 1.0;   // full size cell
        e.fill = GridBagConstraints.BOTH;
        e.weightx = 1.0;   // full size cell
        e.gridwidth = GridBagConstraints.REMAINDER; //end row
        add_buttons(0,4);
        add_buttons(5,9);
        add_buttons(10,14);
        add_buttons(15,19);
```

```
        add_buttons(20,23);
    }

    void add_buttons(int s, int f)                              // (9)
    {   for (int i=s; i < f; i++ )
        {   gridbag.setConstraints(b[i], c);
            add(b[i]);
        }
        gridbag.setConstraints(b[f], e);
        add(b[f]);
    }

    WinFace face;
    JButton[] b = new JButton[name.length];
    static String[] name
        = {"+-", "MR", "M-", "M+", "/", "%", "7", "8", "9", "X",
           "SR", "4", "5", "6", "-", "C", "1", "2", "3", "=",
           "AC", "0", ".", "+" };
    static String[] cmd
        = {"N", "R", "m", "M", "/", "%", "7", "8", "9", "*",
           "s", "4", "5", "6", "-", "C", "1", "2", "3", "=",
           "A", "0", ".", "+" };
    private GridBagLayout gridbag = new GridBagLayout();
    private GridBagConstraints c = new GridBagConstraints();
    private GridBagConstraints e = new GridBagConstraints();
}
```

Note how the GUI widgets are isolated from the application event logic. The `actionPerformed` method calls the `enter` method in the `WinFace` object to handle any button event. There is no other complication.

Class `Lcd`

The `Lcd` widget handles the display of number, opcode, and status code. Two `JLabel`s, one for the calculator status and the other for the number and the opcode, are connected by horizontal glue in a `BoxLayout` (lines i–ii). Figure 13.8 shows the layout of the `Lcd` panel.

```
class Lcd extends JPanel
{   Lcd(int len)
    {   size =len;
        status = new JLabel(" ", JLabel.LEFT);
        num_op = new JLabel(str, JLabel.RIGHT);
        setBorder(BorderFactory.createCompoundBorder
        ( BorderFactory.createLoweredBevelBorder(),
          BorderFactory.createEmptyBorder(5,10,5,10)));
```

Figure 13.8   LCD BoxLayout

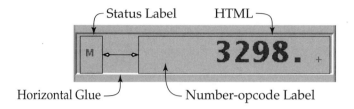

```
        setLayout(new BoxLayout(this, BoxLayout.X_AXIS));    // (i)
        add(status);
        add(Box.createHorizontalGlue());
        display();
        add(num_op);                                          // (ii)
    }

    void showStatus(String s)
    {    status.setText(s);    }

    void showStr(String s)
    {    str = s;    display();    }

    void showOp(char c)
    {    op = c; display();    }

    void display()
    {    num_op.setText(hl+str+ht+op+ot);    }                // (iii)

    int size;
    String str = "0.";
    char op = ' ';
    JLabel status;        // status
    JLabel num_op;        // number-opcode

    String hl="<html><p align=right>"+
                    "<font color=blue size=+3><tt><b>";
    String ht="</b></tt></font>" +
                    "<font color=red size=+0><tt> ";
    String ot="</tt></font></p></html>";
}
```

Methods for showing the display simply set the text in the corresponding labels. Note the use of HTML in the number-opcode label (line iii).

13.7 THE MVC DESIGN PATTERN

As stated, a design pattern is a recipe for solving a certain type of design problem that captures the high-level objects, their interactions, and their behaviors. The *model-view-controller* pattern is a particularly useful one for any application that involves interactive usage. Figure 13.9 illustrates the MVC design pattern. The three high-level objects are as follows:

1. Model—The compute engine or heart of the program. It performs necessary computations and maintains the state and data required. The model provides methods for appropriate external control and manipulation as well as state reporting methods to extract values from the model. It also notifies and updates known views of any state changes within the model that may affect the view.

2. Controller—The interface through which users manipulate, control, and use the program.

3. View—The display that informs users about the state of the model. In order to obtain change notifications or updates, a view must register with the model.

The MVC pattern brings a number of advantages:

• Clear division of functions—A program involving interactive usage always has one part that performs the internal computations and another that deals with users. These two parts ought to interact through well-designed APIs. Within the user interface, the presentation of information and the user control of the application are also clearly distinct functions.

• Independence of the objects—The model, controller, and view can be made independent of one another through well-defined interfaces. This allows any and all of the objects to evolve in a plug-compatible manner and be replaced without affecting the other objects.

Figure 13.9   MVC DESIGN PATTERN

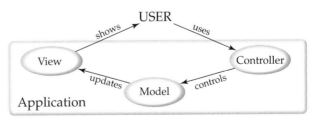

- Multiple views—It is possible to supply various different views based on the same model. For example, a bar chart view, a pie chart view, and a listing view are all possibilities for a population distribution model. Making multiple views easy increases the usability and flexibility of the application.

- Ready for distribution—With the MVC design, the application can move easily into a client-server mode, in which the server takes care of the model and the client runs the view(s) and the controller.

- Multiple models—A presentation can easily combine data from multiple model objects. Thus information from several related models can be shown in an integrated fashion, and a view can be constructed based on data from a number of models.

In practice, the view and controller are sometimes combined into one object because they both use the same UI and because some control functions directly affect the view, and vice versa. Looking at the pocket calculator simulation from the MVC viewpoint, we see that the CalcEng is the model, while the CalcFace and Calculator combine to provide the view and controller funcitons. The CalcEng, however, supports neither view registration nor view notification. It is a good exercise to consider a strict MVC design for the pocket calculator program.

13.8   SWING WIDGET ARCHITECTURE AND MVC

Swing employs the MVC paradigm to provide these features:

- Separation of model from view/controller for certain Swing widgets
- *Pluggable look and feel* (*plaf*) for all Swing widgets

The *look and feel* of each Swing widget is provided by a *UI delegate*, which is replaceable dynamically. The javax.swing.plaf package defines look-and-feel (laf) delegate classes that extend ComponentUI, which contains basic rendering methods such as paint(), getPreferredSize(), and getMinimumSize(). Specific delegates such as ButtonUI and ListUI build on these view methods and add component-dependent controller aspects as well.

For a Swing widget, the delegate is accessed through the setUI and getUI methods. For JButton, for example, the Java supplied delegates include:

```
BasicButtonUI
WindowsButtonUI
MotifButtonUI
MetalButtonUI
MacButtonUI
```

Although it is possible, an application normally does not have to set individual delegates. Instead, the entire look and feel of the GUI can be switched at once at run time. This is the major advantage of this architecture. The LookAndFeel object maintains a mapping of Swing widgets with their UI delegates. Setting LookAndFeel for an application then switches the entire GUI from one laf to another. Typically, you will work with either the laf for your particular platform (SystemLookAndFeel) or the cross-platform laf (CrossPlatformLookAndFeel). The UIManager class has helpful methods for dealing with laf. For example, to set the system-specific laf use

```
UIManager.setLookAndFeel(UIManager.getSystemLookAndFeelClassName());
```

and to switch to the cross-platform laf use:

```
UIManager.setLookAndFeel(UIManager.
                    getCrossPlatformLookAndFeelClassName());
```

Another MVC aspect of Swing is that a number of key widgets, including JButton, JList, and JTree, support external models. This means that such Swing widgets can be used as view/controllers for existing and user-defined models. Separating complicated models from view/controllers achieves good OO design.

MVC Structure of JList

Let's take a closer look at JList and its architecture (Figure 13.10). The other MVC-wise Swing widgets work in similar ways.

- A JList uses two models: an object implementing the ListModel interface for storing and manipulating a list of items and an object implementing the ListSelectionModel interface for storing and manipulating selection indices.
- The JList methods setModel, setSelectionModel, getModel, and getSelectionModel serve obvious functions. For JList, the default models are DefaultListModel and DefaultListSelectionModel.
- A look-and-feel object ListUI is responsible for rendering the JList widget.

Figure 13.10   JList MVC ARCHITECTURE

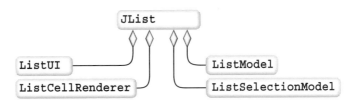

- Yet another object implementing the ListCellRenderer interface is used by JList to render list cells. The default used is DefaultListCellRenderer.

- JList, as a view, registers a ListDataListener (ListSelectionListener) with the ListModel (ListSelectionModel) to receive value-changed notifications.

Lunch Menu: An MVC Example

LunchOrder (Figure 13.11) is a simple example that illustrates independent views and models in a Swing application. LunchMenu, extending JList, presents the lunch menu items as a selection list for users. Multiple selections are allowed. The ListModel and ListSelectionModel used by the LunchMenu view are obtained, and a PriceView object uses these two models to display the total price for the lunch ordered. Figure 13.12 shows the MVC architecture of this example.

Figure 13.11   MVC EXAMPLE IN SWING

Figure 13.12   LunchOrder MVC ARCHITECTURE

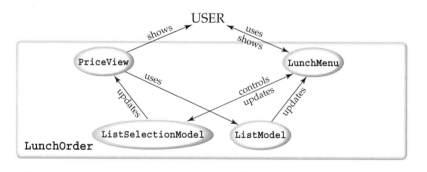

To reflect this architecture, we can construct a UML Class Relation Diagram (Figure 13.13) for the OO design. Following are the CRC descriptions for the three classes involved.

- LunchMenu—Extends Jlist to display a menu given as an array of strings, each carrying the prices at the end of the string; allows multiple user selections.
  Collaborators: ListModel and ListSelectionModel used by JList, also LunchOrder the main application object.
- PriceView—Extends JLabel to display the total lunch order price, registers a SelectionListener with the ListSelectionModel object, and computes the total pricing by querying the ListSelectionModel for items selected and obtaining the prices from the ListModel.
  Collaborators: ListModel, ListSelectionModel.
- LunchOrder—Instantiates a LunchMenu, extracts the ListModel and the ListSelectionModel from the LunchMenu. Gives both models to a new PriceView, lays out these widgets and a menu title, and displays the GUI for the application.
  Collaborators: none of any substance.

The LunchOrder constructor uses the following code to instantiate a LunchMenu and a PriceView:

```
LunchMenu menu = new LunchMenu();
PriceView pv = new PriceView(menu.getSelectionModel(),
                                       menu.getModel());
```

The PriceView class shows how it presents the total price view from two model objects.

The PriceView constructor sets up the initial display by setting the correct price total (line 1), then registers a ListSelectionListener to receive ListSelectionEvents from the ListSelectionModel (line 2). The valueChanged

Figure 13.13   OO DESIGN OF LunchOrder

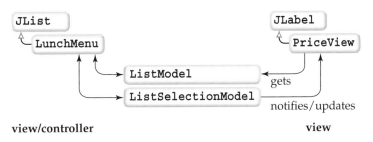

event-handling method (line 5) calls setTotal in PriceView to compute a new price total, which is done by adding the prices of all selected items (lines 3–4).

```
class PriceView extends JLabel
{  PriceView(ListSelectionModel m, ListModel l)
   {   super("", JLabel.CENTER);
       setAlignmentX(Component.CENTER_ALIGNMENT);
       sm = m;
       lm = l;
       setTotal();                                              // (1)
       sm.addListSelectionListener(new SelectionHandler());  // (2)
   }

   protected void setTotal()
   {   String s;
       float total = 0f;
       int first = sm.getMinSelectionIndex();                   // (3)
       if ( first > -1 )
       {   int last = sm.getMaxSelectionIndex();
           for (int i=first; i <= last; i++)
           {   if ( sm.isSelectedIndex(i) )
               {   s = (String) lm.getElementAt(i);
                   total += amount(s);                          // (4)
               }
           }
       }
       setText(p1+nf.format(total)+p2);
   }

   private final class SelectionHandler
           implements ListSelectionListener
   {  public void valueChanged(ListSelectionEvent e)            // (5)
      {   setTotal();   }
   }

   protected float amount(String s)
   {   String a = s.substring(s.lastIndexOf(' ')+1);
       return Float.parseFloat(a);
   }

   protected ListModel lm;
   protected ListSelectionModel sm;
   protected String p1 = "<html><font size=+1>Total: <b>";
   protected String p2 = "</b></font></html>";
   NumberFormat nf=NumberFormat.getCurrencyInstance();
}
```

The complete LunchOrder example can be found in the example package.

This example shows the use of views and models as separate objects. The key is to have models follow well-defined interfaces for control, value access, and view registration. We used ready-made models here, but any model implementing the required interfaces can be used. The ListModel does not change in this example. However, it could, and everything would still work. The MVC design pattern thus enables plug-compatible models and views to be used in very flexible ways.

13.9 SUMMARY

Good OO programs require a combination of thoughtful design and skillful implementation. The two processes form a feedback loop and help programs evolve. The central issue in OO design is the identification of objects and classes in a given system. Decomposition methods break up the entire problem into easier-to-handle pieces. OO design class diagrams, following the UML notations, can capture a global view of the design and make deliberations and communications much easier. The UML use-case sequence diagrams help capture interactions among objects in the program and in their executing environment.

Design patterns represent well-developed solutions to recurring software design problems. A pattern can be useful in many situations. The model-view-controller pattern is an example. It is useful for the 60-minute timer, the term life premium calculator, the pocket calculator simulation, and certain Swing widgets.

The CRC method is particularly helpful during the OO design process. The effective use of the CRC method has been demonstrated with the pocket calculator simulation program design. Design patterns offer descriptions and solutions for common programming problems.

The UML diagrams and CRC design for the pocket calculator simulation program, together with the Java implementation, offer a small but complete example of OOD and OOP.

The MVC design pattern has many advantages and is very useful for writing GUI applications. The Java Swing package puts MVC to work in delegating duties to models and in supporting the dynamically settable look-and-feel feature.

 EXERCISES

Review Questions

1. What are OOA, OOD, and OOP?

2. Describe the class and use-case UML diagrams.

3. What is a design pattern? How can it be useful?

4. In OOD, how are the needed classes identified?

5. Experiment with the dynamic change of look and feel for a GUI program.

6. What are design patterns? CRC method? UML? UML sequence diagrams?

Programming Assignments

1. Consider the `CalcWindow` class and the `Lcd` class. Currently each extends `JPanel` and sets a `BoxLayout`. Modify the code so that they extend `Box` instead, which uses a `BoxLayout` by default.

2. (Calc-MVC) Consider the the design of the pocket calculator simulation, and rework it so that it follows the MVC design pattern:
    - The `CalcModel` is the compute engine. It has a method to register views and notifies all registered views whenever its state has changed.
    - The `CalcModel` has *get methods* for appropriate attributes.
    - The `CalcModel` has a controller interface for controlling its operations.
    - `CalcController` allows users to enter input and control the computation.
    - `CalcView` displays information from the model.

3. Extend the `ArrayList` class (Section 9.1), and implement the `ListModel` interface. Then follow the MVC pattern to design and implement an application that can add, delete, and modify entries in the list and that displays at least two views, based on the list model.

4. (Calc-5) Make the GUI work for a scientific calculator supported by the `ScientificEng` (Section 5.2). (Hint: Write `ScientificWindow`.)

5. The `JTree` class in Swing also has an MVC architecture. Fint out how it works.

6. Modify the `PriceView` class so that the event handler is defined by an inner class.

7. Add a discount feature to the `LunchMenu` example. Any lunch order exceeding a set price, for example, $12, receives a 10% discount.

8. Reorganize the `PieChart` example (Section 8.8) so that it follows the MVC pattern. In addition to the pie chart view, add a bar chart view. Also give the program the ability to receive text input that defines the percentages.

9. Apply the CRC method and the OO design approaches suggested in this chapter to design a program for playing Othello. Identify the objects in this game, and write the CRC cards for them. Think about the game pieces, game board, moves, board positions, players, move generator, user interface, board display, and so on. Make the design general so that it works for most board games.

10. Consider the implementation of the Othello program design. Apply inheritance planning and polymorphism. Take into account future extensions and modifications to create other games. Do you find points overlooked in the design phase? Fix the design and start over.

APPENDIX A

Java Tools

A.1   THE SDK DISTRIBUTION

You'll find these subdirectories in the Java SDK:

- bin—executable programs supplying various tools for Java, including **javac**, **java**, **appletviewer**, **jar**, **javadoc**, **rmid**, and so on
- demo—example applets and applications with Java source code
- doc—documentation (downloaded separately)
- include—C header files that support native-code programming using the JNI
- jre—runtime environment, including the JVM and libraries, for executing Java programs
- lib—additional libraries for Java tools
- src.zip—compressed archive file containing Java source code files

The Java environment gives you a set of tools to compile, execute, document, and otherwise manage Java programs. After downloading and installing Java, you'll find it in the *javaHome* directory, typically C:\jdk1.4.0 on PC or /usr/java/j2sdk1.4.0 on UNIX. Make sure your *command search path* contains the directory where these tools are located. On a PC, it is *javaHome*\bin. Edit the autoexec.bat file (use **SysEdit**, for example) to add this directory to the end of the **SET** PATH statement. On UNIX systems, the Java tools may be in /usr/local/java/bin, /usr/bin, or *javaHome*/bin. Make sure your shell environment variable PATH contains this directory.

Some common Java tools are:

- **java**—The Java interpreter loads .class files and executes a Java program. The command line

  java *ClassXyz arg1 arg2...*

  loads *ClassXyz*.class and all other necessary .class files into the interpreter. A JDK-supplied tool can locate JDK-supplied classes. The CLASSPATH environment variable lists the default directories that Java tools search for user-defined classes. If your program depends only on JDK-supplied classes, you don't have to set the CLASSPATH variable. If you do use library classes that you have developed, you can set CLASSPATH (to be be described shortly). You also may give the -classpath option to a Java tool to specify a custom class search instead of the default search.

After loading bytecode, the interpreter invokes the main method in *ClassXyz*, passing to it any arguments given on the command line. When the main method returns, the interpreter terminates. An *exit status* code is returned to the invocation environment (UNIX or DOS shell). A zero exit status indicates normal termination of execution. The interpreter takes various options.

While interpreting a program, a Java interpreter may further rewrite the bytecode into platform-dependent native code for much increased speed. The *just-in-time* compilation is performed on the parts of the bytecode as they are invoked.

- **javac**—The java compiler compiles .java files and produces Java bytecode (.class) files that can be executed by any Java interpreter on any platform.

- **appletviewer**—The viewer is used to view an HTML document (.htm or .html) that contains Java applets.

- **javadoc**—The Java document generator automatically produces HTML pages of API documentation from source files. It takes a package name or names of source files and extracts *doc comments* and other information to produce HTML pages (Section 12.10).

- **jdb**—The Java debugger helps you locate and fix bugs. **jdb** is similar to the popular **dbx** debugger. To debug ClassName.java, first compile it into ClassName.class with the debugging option of the Java compiler **javac_g** -g), then issue the command:

jdb *ClassName*

See Appendix I for details on **jdb** usage.

- **javap**—The Java disassembler takes one or more .class files and displays source code information such as class names, fields, and methods.

- **javah**—The header generation tool creates header .h files needed to interface Java code with C or C++ coded programs.

To get a list of available command-line options, give no arguments to **java** or **javac**:

java   (lists **java** command-line options)
javac   (lists **javac** command-line options)

This convention works for most Java tools that take command-line arguments.

A.2   USING THE JAVA COMPILER

The Java compiler is very simple and easy to use once you understand the basic code structure conventions that it assumes:

- Java source files use the .java extension. A .java source file is compiled into a corresponding bytecode file with the .class extension. The .class file is placed in the same directory as its source file unless the -d option of the compiler indicates a different location.
- A public class *Xyz* is contained in its own file *Xyz*.java.
- When **javac** compiles a file *Abc*.java, it must access the .class files of all classes *Abc* uses, including all Java built-in and user-defined classes. Needed .class files are located through the usual class search procedure. A required .class file will be loaded automatically. If the .class file cannot be found or the source file is more recent than the existing .class file, the .class file is re-created (Figure A.1).
- Compiling a source code file with multiple classes produces .class files for each class.

Library classes supplied by Java are loaded automatically, but loading of user-defined classes can depend on the CLASSPATH. If you have to set CLASSPATH, set it to include all directories in which classes you developed and need are located. Make sure that the current directory symbol (.) is included on the CLASSPATH you set.

Figure A.1   FINDING CLASSES

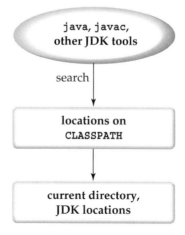

On a PC, enter a line similar to

```
SET CLASSPATH=.;C:\javaWang2\ex06;C:\javaWang2\ex08
```

in your `autoexec.bat` file. Note that the directories are separated by semicolons (;). On UNIX systems, enter a line similar to

```
setenv CLASSPATH \
        ".:$HOME/javaWang2/ex06:$HOME/javaWang2/ex08
```

in your `.login` file. Note that here the directories are separated by colons (:).

The `-classpath` *path* option can specify a classpath for a particular invocation of any of the Java tools. Here are some other useful options for **javac**:

- `-nowrite`—The compiler simply checks syntax but does not create `.class` files.
- `-nowarn`—The compiler does not generate the normal warning messages.
- `-verbose`—The compiler displays source-file and class names as well as timing information.
- `-d` *dir*—The compiler uses the given *dir* as the root directory of a package and deposits all generated `.class` files there.
- `-O`—The compiler optimizes the code by making method calls *inline* to avoid the run-time call overhead.
- `-deprecation`—The compiler checks and displays messages for *deprecated* (outdated) constructs in source code.

Syntax errors in a Java program are reported by displaying the file name, the line number, and the location in the source code line in which the error is found.

Other Java tools include the debugger **jdb**, the archiver **jar**, the API documentation generator **javadoc**, and the **appletviewer**.

A.3   JAVA IDES

Although the SDK provides basic tools for programming in Java, a professional *Integrated Development Environment* (*IDE*) can make code development much faster and easier. Some well-known IDEs are available at the Java download page reachable from, for example:

```
http://java.sun.com/j2se/
```

The IDEs include:

```
Forte for Java
Borland JBuilder
```

```
WebGain VisualCafe
Oracle JDeveloper
Metrowerks CodeWarrior Professional
```

With an IDE you have an environment in which source code editing, API documentation, compile-run-debug, visual layout of widgets, and automatic generation of certain codes are all made available in one application.

Because IDEs are powerful, you need to take some time to learn how to use them effectively.

Java Keywords, Operators, and Packages

B.1 KEYWORDS

abstract	default	if	null	switch
boolean	do	implements	package	synchronized
break	double	import	private	this
byte	else	instanceof	protected	throw
case	extends	int	public	throws
catch	final	interface	return	try
char	finally	long	short	void
class	float	native	static	volatile
continue	for	new	super	while
Unused:	const	goto	transient	

B.2 OPERATOR PRECEDENCE

All Java operators are listed here according to their relative precedence. An operator on an earlier line takes precedence over any that come later. Operators on the same line have the same precedence. An expression involving operators of the same precedence is evaluated according to the *associativity* rule of the operators. Most operators associate left to right. The ones that associate right to left are indicated by ⟵ in the table.

Note also that unary operators + and - take precedence over the binary forms.

Operator Type	Operator	Associativity
Postfix	`()  []  .  ++  --`	
Unary	`!  ~  ++  --  +  -  &`	←
Cast and Creation	`(type)  new`	←
Multiplicative	`*  /  %`	
Additive	`+  -`	
Shift	`<<  >>`	
Relational	`<  <=  >  >=`	
Equality	`==  !=`	
Bitwise	`&`	
Bitwise	`^`	
Bitwise	`|`	
Logical	`&&`	
Logical	`||`	
Conditional	`?:`	←
Assignment	`=  +=  -=  *=  /=  %=  ^=  |=  &=  <<=  >>=  >>>=`	←

B.3   SDK PACKAGES

Standard Packages

```
java.applet                      java.lang.ref
java.awt                         java.lang.reflect
java.awt.color                   java.math
java.awt.datatransfer            java.net
java.awt.dnd                     java.nio
java.awt.event                   java.nio.channels
java.awt.font                    java.nio.channels.spi
java.awt.geom                    java.nio.charset
java.awt.im                      java.nio.charset.spi
java.awt.im.spi                  java.rmi
java.awt.image                   java.rmi.activation
java.awt.image.renderable        java.rmi.dgc
java.awt.print                   java.rmi.registry
java.beans                       java.rmi.server
java.beans.beancontext           java.security
java.io                          java.security.acl
java.lang                        java.security.cert
```

```
java.security.interfaces         java.util.jar
java.security.spec               java.util.logging
java.sql                         java.util.prefs
java.text                        java.util.regex
java.util                        java.util.zip
```

Standard Extension Packages

```
javax.accessibility              javax.security.cert
javax.crypto                     javax.sound.midi
javax.crypto.interfaces          javax.sound.midi.spi
javax.crypto.spec                javax.sound.sampled
javax.imageio                    javax.sound.sampled.spi
javax.imageio.event              javax.sql
javax.imageio.metadata           javax.swing
javax.imageio.plugins.jpeg       javax.swing.border
javax.imageio.spi                javax.swing.colorchooser
javax.imageio.stream             javax.swing.event
javax.naming                     javax.swing.filechooser
javax.naming.directory           javax.swing.plaf
javax.naming.event               javax.swing.plaf.basic
javax.naming.ldap                javax.swing.plaf.metal
javax.naming.spi                 javax.swing.plaf.multi
javax.net                        javax.swing.table
javax.net.ssl                    javax.swing.text
javax.print                      javax.swing.text.html
javax.print.attribute            javax.swing.text.html.parser
javax.print.attribute.standard   javax.swing.text.rtf
javax.print.event                javax.swing.tree
javax.rmi                        javax.swing.undo
javax.rmi.CORBA                  javax.transaction
javax.security.auth              javax.transaction.xa
javax.security.auth.callback     javax.xml.parsers
javax.security.auth.kerberos     javax.xml.transform
javax.security.auth.login        javax.xml.transform.dom
javax.security.auth.spi          javax.xml.transform.sax
javax.security.auth.x500         javax.xml.transform.stream
```

Other Packages

```
org.ietf.jgss                    org.omg.CORBA_2_3.portable
org.omg.CORBA                    org.omg.CORBA.DynAnyPackage
org.omg.CORBA_2_3                org.omg.CORBA.ORBPackage
```

org.omg.CORBA.portable
org.omg.CORBA.TypeCodePackage
org.omg.CosNaming
org.omg.CosNaming.NamingContextExtPackage
org.omg.CosNaming.NamingContextPackage
org.omg.Dynamic
org.omg.DynamicAny
org.omg.DynamicAny.DynAnyFactoryPackage
org.omg.DynamicAny.DynAnyPackage
org.omg.IOP
org.omg.IOP.CodecFactoryPackage
org.omg.IOP.CodecPackage
org.omg.Messaging
org.omg.PortableInterceptor

org.omg.PortableInterceptor.
  ORBInitInfoPackage
org.omg.PortableServer
org.omg.PortableServer.CurrentPackage
org.omg.PortableServer.POAManagerPackage
org.omg.PortableServer.POAPackage
org.omg.PortableServer.portable
org.omg.PortableServer.ServantLocatorPackage
org.omg.SendingContext
org.omg.stub.java.rmi
org.w3c.dom
org.xml.sax
org.xml.sax.ext
org.xml.sax.helpers

Common Java Constructs

Main Method

```
public static void main(String[] args)
```

Simple Class

```
[access] [final] class Name
{
      members
}
```

A member may be a constructor, a field, a method, or an inner class. A public class must be in its own file Name.java.

Method

```
[access] [static] [synchronized] ...           (Method header)
      valuetype name ( type arg1, type arg2...)
         [throws Exception_1,..., Exception_i]
{                                               (Body begin)
      declarations and statements
}                                               (Body end)
```

for Statement

```
for ( init ;
     cont condition ; update )     (Loop control)
         statement                 (Loop body)
```

The *init* part can be a single expression or a comma-separated list of expressions, as can the *update* part.

`if` Statement

```
if  ( condition )
       statement one
else
       statement two
```

`switch` Statement

```
switch ( int-expression )
{
       case constant-exp1 :
                    statements
       case constant-exp2 :
                    statements
       ⋱
       default:
                    statements
}
```

Statements usually end with a `break` to avoid fall through.

`label` Statement

```
labelname: statement

break labelname
continue labelname
```

`do-while` Statement

```
do  body  while ( condition )  ;
```

Member Access

Access instance member:

```
object . member
```

Access hidden inherited instance member:

```
super . member (cast-to-superclass) this.field
```

Access static member:

```
ClassName . member object . member
```

String Concatenation

```
a + b
```

where at least one of a and b is a string. A nonstring operand must be a primitive type or an object with toString() overloaded.

Exception Handling

```
try {    statements
      }
   catch(e-type₁ e)
   {    statements    }
   catch(e-type₂ e)
   {    statements    }
    . . .

   finally
   {    statements    }
```

Explicit Type Casting

```
( type-name ) expression
```

Class Extension

```
[access] [final] class Name extends superclass
{
      extended class body
}
```

Subclass constructor:

```
public ClassName(arg1, ...)
{    super(...);
     . . .
}
```

Defining and Implementing Interfaces

Defining an interface:

```
public interface InterfaceName

{

   . . .

}
```

- All members are public automatically
- All methods are abstract automatically
- All fields should be declared static and final

```
access class ClassX extends ClassY
      implements Interface_1, Interface_2, ...
{   class body
}
```

Anonymous Class

```
new superName() {   class body   };
```

Applet

```
import java.awt.*;
import javax.swing.*;

public AppletName extends JApplet
{   public void init()
    {  ...
       getContentPane().add( ... );
       // or setContentPane(...);
    }
    public void start() { ... }
    public void stop() { ... }
    public void destroy() { ... }
}
```

GUI Application main

```
public static void main(String[] args)
{ // process command-line args

    JFrame win = new JFrame("Title");  // top-level window

   // set up win with menubar etc. ...

   // establish other components

    win.getContentPane().add(...);
   // or win.setContentPane(...);

   // window event listener
    win.addWindowListener( ... );
```

```
        win.setSize(width, height);
        win.setVisible(true);
    }
```

Reading and Writing Text

```
    BufferedReader rdr = new BufferedReader
            (new InputStreamReader(in));
    String line = rdr.readLine();
    char c = rdr.read();

    PrintWriter wtr = new PrintWriter(new BufferedWriter
            (new OutputStreamWriter(out)), true);
    wtr.println(...);
    wtr.print(...);
```

Overriding `equals`

```
    public boolean equals(Object y)              // override
    {   return ( y == this ||                    // same reference
                (this.getClass() == y.getClass() // same class
                && num == ((Fraction)y).num      // compare equal
                && denom == ((Fraction)y).denom )
            );
    }
```

Major Differences between Java and ANSI C/C++

What Java Does Not Support or Have

- Implementation-dependent features
- Pointers or pointer arithmetic or `->`
- Need to recompile on different platforms
- Preprocessor, `#include`, or header files
- Unattached functions
- Operator overloading
- Need to free memory manually or the `delete` operator
- Multiple inheritance or multiple base classes
- Bit fields, `struct`, `union`, or `typedef`
- `enum`, `inline`, `register`, `friend`, or `template`
- Pointer to member or operators `->*` or `->`
- Keyword `virtual`
- Comma operator (`,`) or scope operator (`::`)
- Optional or variable-length parameters for methods
- Templates or `template` keyword
- Init list for constructors
- Reference variable or reference parameter declarations
- `sizeof` operator
- `extern` declarations
- `protected` or `private` superclasses
- Destructor name depending on class name
- User-defined type conversions
- Implicit copying of objects
- Explicit casting notation `type(arg1, arg2, ...)`

Java Features Not Found in C/C++

- Run-time interpreter
- Automatic garbage collection
- Support for Web applets
- Support for platform-independent GUI programming
- Support for event-driven programming
- Support for multithreading, synchronized methods, and statements
- Support for networking
- Dynamic and automatic loading of classes on `CLASSPATH` for compilation and execution
- Interfaces and the keywords `interface` and `implements`
- Code organization by packages, the `package` and `import` keywords
- Automatic *virtual* instance methods
- Methods that throw or specify checked exceptions
- `Object` root superclass
- Wrapper classes for primitive types
- All object creation at run time through `new`
- Programs and characters in 16-bit Unicode
- Primitive types `boolean` and `byte`
- Strings and arrays as objects
- Object variables and parameters as references
- Access protection category `package`
- Each class represented by a unique object to allow computing with types
- Additional keywords: `boolean`, `final`, `finalize`, `null`
- Single inheritance and keywords `super`, `extends`
- Use of + for conversions to `String`
- Keywords `abstract`, `synchronized`, and `instanceof`
- Security manager
- Final methods that cannot be redefined and final classes that cannot be extended
- Field initializers
- Static initialization blocks
- Support for native language interface and `native` keyword

Features That Work Differently

- Instead of an absolute entry point `main`, each Java class may contain a special `main` method that can be invoked by the interpreter to run that class.
- Java uses `true/false` instead of nonzero/zero for boolean.
- Java has no `unsigned` declaration, and all integer types use signed twos complement representation.
- Java supports both `>>` and `>>>` shift operators.
- Java has no default return type for methods.
- Java allows `break/continue` to a labeled outer loop.
- Java requires explicit casting from `int` to `char`.
- Each class member must have its own explicit access specifier; otherwise the member is considered `package`.
- Java has access to only a predefined set of environment variables through system properties.
- The Java `%` operator works for integers and floating-point numbers.
- Resolution of a call to an overloaded method in Java is very different from that of C++.
- In Java, generic programming is done using the `Object` class rather than `void *` or template.
- Java does not use the keywords `const` or `goto`. The keyword `final` can be used to declare constant fields.
- Java classes use `finalize` methods instead of destructors.
- Java type compatibility can be done through both class extension and interface implementation.

Layout Managers and Swing Widgets

E.1 LAYOUT MANAGERS

The layout of child components depends on the layout manager set for the container. Containers have default layout managers. Set layout managers of your choice with the setLayout method. JFC layout managers include the following:

```
java.awt.BorderLayout
java.awt.FlowLayout
java.awt.GridLayout
java.awt.GridBagLayout
java.awt.CardLayout
javax.swing.BoxLayout
```

It is also possible to define your own layout managers.

BorderLayout

With BorderLayout you can place components in a container at positions known as "North," "South," "East," "West," and "Center." Components on the four sides are laid out according to their preferred sizes and the constraints of the container's size. The "Center" component gets any space left over. The code that produced the layout in Figure E.1 is as follows:

```
public class Border
{  public static void main(String[] args)
    {   JFrame win = new JFrame("Border Layout");
        Container cp = win.getContentPane();

    // default BorderLayout
        cp.add(new JButton("North"), BorderLayout.NORTH);
        cp.add(new JButton("East"), BorderLayout.EAST);
        cp.add(new JButton("South"), BorderLayout.SOUTH);
```

Figure E.1 BORDER LAYOUT

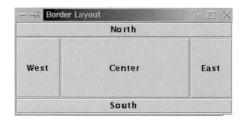

```
        cp.add(new JButton("West"), BorderLayout.WEST);
        cp.add(new JButton("Center"), BorderLayout.CENTER);

        win.addWindowListener(new WindowHandler(win));
        win.setSize(360, 180);
        win.setVisible(true);
    }
}
```

FlowLayout

Flow layout makes it easy to lay out buttons in a panel. It arranges buttons left to right until no more buttons fit on the same line. Each line is centered. Following is the code that produced the layout in Figure E.2:

```
public class Flow
{   public static void main(String[] args)
    {   JFrame win = new JFrame("Flow Layout");
        Container cp = win.getContentPane();
        cp.setLayout(new FlowLayout());

        cp.add(new JButton("111"));
        cp.add(new JButton("222"));
        cp.add(new JButton("333"));
        cp.add(new JButton("444"));
```

Figure E.2 FLOW LAYOUT

```
            win.addWindowListener(new WindowHandler(win));
            win.setSize(360, 180);
            win.setVisible(true);
        }
    }
```

GridLayout

With GridLayout you arrange components in a rectangular grid of rows and columns, each grid cell holding one component. As components are added, they are placed in the grid in a row-major order. Following is the code that produced the layout in Figure E.3:

```
public class Grid
{   public static void main(String[] args)
    {   JFrame win = new JFrame("Grid Layout");
        Container cp = win.getContentPane();
        cp.setLayout(new GridLayout(0,3));

        cp.add(new Button("1"));
        cp.add(new Button("22"));
        cp.add(new Button("333"));
        cp.add(new Button("4444"));
        cp.add(new Button("A"));
        cp.add(new Button("BB"));
        cp.add(new Button("CCC"));
        cp.add(new Button("DDDD"));

        win.addWindowListener(new WindowHandler(win));
        win.setSize(360, 180);
        win.setVisible(true);
    }
}
```

Figure E.3   GRID LAYOUT

GridBagLayout

`GridBagLayout` arranges components in a dynamic grid of cells. Each component has a display area that may occupy multiple row/column cells and can be placed flexibly within its display area. You specify constraint parameters as you add each component to the container. The number of cells in a row/column and the relative sizes of the cells are determined from the totality of constraint parameters for the components.

The steps for adding each component are as follows:

```
setLayout(bag = new GridBagLayout());
GridBagConstraints c = new GridBagConstraints();
c.parameter1 = value1;
   . . .
c.parameterk = valuek;
bag.setConstraints(myComponent, c);
add(myComponent);
```

`GridBagConstraints` parameters :

- `weightx` and `weighty`—Control relative sizes of the width and height of the cells. Only the settings of `weightx` (`weighty`) for components on the first row (column) affect the cell sizes.
- `gridwidth` and `gridheight`—Specify number of cells to occupy in the x and y directions.
- `gridx` and `gridy`—Position the upper-left corner of the component on the given cell position. The upper-leftmost cell is (0, 0).
- `fill`—Determines whether a component will expand in the x and/or y direction to take up available space in its display area.
- `anchor`—Positions a component inside its display area.
- `ipadx` and `ipady`—Define internal padding in the x and y directions.
- `insets`—Specifies external padding for a component.

Figure E.4   GRIDBAG LAYOUT

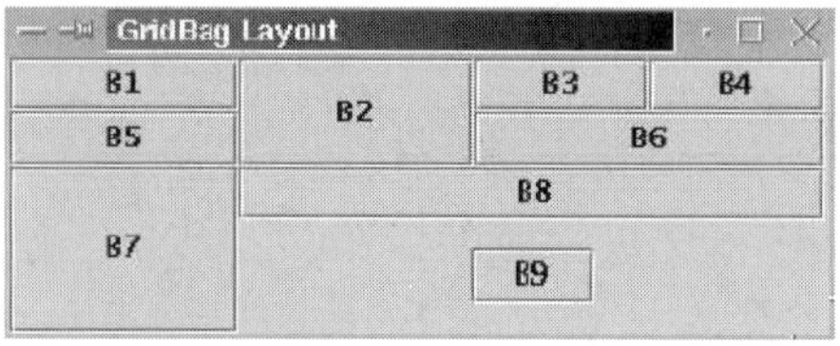

The code that produced the layout in Figure E.4 is as follows:

```
public class GridBag
{ public static void main(String[] args)
   { JFrame win = new JFrame("GridBag Layout");
      Container cp = win.getContentPane();

   // set GridBagLayout
      GridBagLayout gridbag = new GridBagLayout();
      GridBagConstraints c = new GridBagConstraints();
      cp.setLayout(gridbag);

      c.fill = GridBagConstraints.BOTH;
      c.weightx = 1.0;   // full size cell
      makebutton("B1", gridbag, c, cp);
      c.gridheight = 2;                // height occupies two rows
      makebutton("B2", gridbag, c, cp);
      c.gridheight = 1;
      c.weightx = 0.5;                        // half size cell
      makebutton("B3", gridbag, c, cp);
      c.gridwidth = GridBagConstraints.REMAINDER; //end first row
      makebutton("B4", gridbag, c, cp);

      c.weightx = 0.0;                 // reset to the default
      c.gridwidth = 1;   c.gridx=0;      // manual placement
      makebutton("B5", gridbag, c, cp);
      c.gridx= 2;                      // manual placement
      c.gridwidth = GridBagConstraints.REMAINDER; // end row
      makebutton("B6", gridbag, c, cp);
      c.gridx=GridBagConstraints.RELATIVE;
      c.gridwidth = 1;                       //reset to the default
      c.gridheight = 2;
      c.weighty = 1.0;
      makebutton("B7", gridbag, c, cp);

      c.weighty = 0.0;                       //reset to the default
      c.gridwidth = GridBagConstraints.REMAINDER; //end row
      c.gridheight = 1;                     //reset to the default
      makebutton("B8", gridbag, c, cp);
      c.fill = GridBagConstraints.NONE;
      c.anchor = GridBagConstraints.CENTER;
      makebutton("B9", gridbag, c, cp);
```

```
        win.addWindowListener(new WindowHandler(win));
        win.setSize(360, 180);
        win.setVisible(true);
    }

    protected static void makebutton(String name,
                        GridBagLayout gridbag,
                        GridBagConstraints c,
                        Container cp)
    {   JButton button = new JButton(name);
        gridbag.setConstraints(button, c);
        cp.add(button);
    }
}
```

BoxLayout

Use the general purpose BoxLayout provided by Swing to arrange widget windows either vertically or horizontally. The Swing container Box uses BoxLayout by default. If you set another container to use BoxLayout, using Box directly may be a good alternative.

With several containers that use BoxLayout, you can achieve some layouts without resorting to the complex GridBagLayout. BoxLayout is also useful in some situations where you might consider using GridLayout or BorderLayout. BoxLayout also respects each child widget's maximum size and x/y alignment. Horizontal spacing between child widgets can be easily adjusted with lightweight fillers (Section 8.11).

See the Lcd class (Section 13.6) for an application of BoxLayout with fillers (Figure 13.8).

CardLayout

Use CardLayout to control several alternative layouts for a container widget. (Figure E.5) Use a JPanel to lay out each alternative *card*. Only one card is visible at a time. The CardLayout method

show(*Container*, *String*)

is used to switch to a card identified by the given *string*. The *string* is a user-defined name for a card when it is added to the *container*.

Figure E.5   CARD LAYOUT

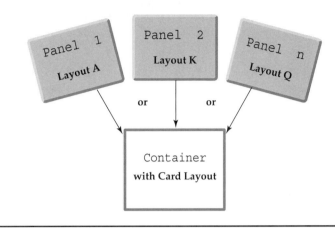

E.2 SWING WIDGETS

For a visual index of Swing widgets see

```
http://java.sun.com/docs/books/tutorial/
                uiswing/components/components.html
```

Table E.1   LIST OF SWING WIDGETS

JApplet	JInternalFrame	JPopupMenu.Separator	JTable
JButton	JLabel	JProgressBar	JTextArea
JCheckBox	JLayeredPane	JRadioButton	JTextField
JCheckBoxMenuItem	JList	JRadioButtonMenuItem	JTextPane
JColorChooser	JMenu	JRootPane	JToggleButton
JComboBox	JMenuBar	JScrollBar	JToolBar
JDesktopPane	JMenuItem	JScrollPane	JToolBar.Separator
JDialog	JOptionPane	JSeparator	JToolTip
JEditorPane	JPanel	JSlider	JTree
JFileChooser	JPasswordField	JSplitPane	JViewport
JFrame	JPopupMenu	JTabbedPane	JWindow

Colors in JFC

Color Specifications

Modern graphics displays use a *frame buffer* consisting of multiple *bit planes*. Each bit plane has one bit for each pixel on the screen. All bits for a particular pixel combine to specify the color or gray level for that pixel. The pixel bit pattern usually serves as an index to a memory area called a *color map*, which is simply a table of *color cells*. Each cell contains a specific RGB (red-green-blue) value for color or gray level. For *n* bit planes there can be up to 2^n cells in the color map. This is the maximum number of different colors available at any given time for the display. The 2^n colors available depend on the contents of the color map in use.

Fortunately, Java allows you to specify color independently from the target platform or display. The actual color used in rendering is the closest color in the color space available on the actual output device.

Use the class Color to create colors. The Color class specifies colors in the default *sRGB color space*,

```
http://www.w3.org/pub/WWW/Graphics/Color/sRGB.html
```

or in any given ColorSpace.

Every color has an implicit transparency setting, the *alpha value*, ranging from 0.0–1.0, or 0–255. An alpha value of 1.0 or 255 means that the color is completely opaque, and an alpha value of 0.0 or 0 means that the color is completely transparent. By default, the alpha value of a color is 1.0.

The following static fields make common colors easy to specify:

```
Color.black   Color.blue    Color.cyan      Color.darkGray
Color.gray    Color.green   Color.magenta   Color.orange
Color.pink    Color.red     Color.white     Color.yellow
```

Colors can also be specified by their RGB values. Use any of these constructors:

- Color(int red, int green, int blue, [int alpha])—creates a color with the specified red, green, and blue values in the range (0–255)

- `Color(float red, float blue, float green, [float alpha])`—creates a color with the specified red, green, and blue values in the range (0.0–1.0)
- `Color(int argb, boolean hasalpha)`—creates a color with the specified combined RGB-Alpha value consisting of the alpha component in bits 24–31, the red component in bits 16–23, the green component in bits 8–15, and the blue component in bits 0–7

If the alpha value is not given, the color is completely opaque. Given any color object, you can obtain its RGB components as follows:

`obj.getBlue()`	(gets the blue component)
`obj.getGreen()`	(gets the green component)
`obj.getRed()`	(gets the red component)
`obj.getAlpha()`	(gets the alpha component, 0–255)

A color can be brightened or darkened by scaling its RGB values up or down together.

It is also possible to create a color from a numerical string representing bits 0–23 of a color value:

`decode(String value)`   (gets the string-specified color)

The `Color` class also supports color specification using the HSB (*hue-saturation-brightness*) model. See the API for `Color` for more details.

Java I/O Classes

Input Streams

Subclasses of `java.io.InputStream`:

- `javax.sound.sampled.AudioInputStream`
- `java.io.ByteArrayInputStream`
- `java.io.FileInputStream`
- `java.io.FilterInputStream`
  - `java.io.BufferedInputStream`
  - `java.util.zip.CheckedInputStream`
  - `java.io.DataInputStream` (implements `java.io.DataInput`)
  - `java.security.DigestInputStream`
  - `java.util.zip.InflaterInputStream`
  - `java.util.zip.GZIPInputStream`
  - `java.util.zip.ZipInputStream` (implements `java.util.zip.ZipConstants`)
  - `java.io.LineNumberInputStream`
  - `javax.swing.ProgressMonitorInputStream`
  - `java.io.PushbackInputStream`
- `java.io.ObjectInputStream` (implements `java.io.ObjectInput`, `java.io.ObjectStreamConstants`)
- `java.io.PipedInputStream`
- `java.io.SequenceInputStream`
- `java.io.StringBufferInputStream`

Output Streams

Subclasses of `java.io.OutputStream`:

- `java.io.ByteArrayOutputStream`
- `java.io.FileOutputStream`
- `java.io.FilterOutputStream`
  - `java.io.BufferedOutputStream`
  - `java.util.zip.CheckedOutputStream`

  – `java.io.DataOutputStream` (implements `java.io.DataOutput`)
  – `java.util.zip.DeflaterOutputStream`
    * `java.util.zip.GZIPOutputStream`
    * `java.util.zip.ZipOutputStream` (implements
      `java.util.zip.ZipConstants`)
  – `java.security.DigestOutputStream`
  – `java.io.PrintStream` (deprecated)
    * `java.rmi.server.LogStream`
* `java.io.ObjectOutputStream` (implements `java.io.ObjectOutput`,
  `java.io.ObjectStreamConstants`)
* `java.io.PipedOutputStream`

Random Access File

`java.io.RandomAccessFile` (implements `java.io.DataOutput`,
`java.io.DataInput`)

Readers and Writers

Subclasses of `java.io.Reader`:

* `java.io.BufferedReader`
  – `java.io.LineNumberReader`
* `java.io.CharArrayReader`
* `java.io.FilterReader`
  – `java.io.PushbackReader`
* `java.io.InputStreamReader`
  – `java.io.FileReader`
* `java.io.PipedReader`
* `java.io.StringReader`

Subclasses of `java.io.Writer`:

* `java.io.BufferedWriter`
* `java.io.CharArrayWriter`
* `java.io.FilterWriter`
* `java.io.OutputStreamWriter`
  – `java.io.FileWriter`
* `java.io.PipedWriter`
* `java.io.PrintWriter`
* `java.io.StringWriter`

Mathematical Computations

H.1 CLASS Math

Math is a class in the core java.lang package. Static methods in class Math perform basic mathematical computations such as maximum, minimum, absolute value, and numeric operations including exponential, logarithm, square root, and trigonometric functions. Floating-point computations are performed using double and standard algorithms given by the *Freely Distributable Math Library* (fdlibm) of Netlib.

The following methods work on any numeric type:

```
Math.abs(exp)
Math.max(exp)
Math.min(exp)
```

Floating-Point Methods

Math.pow(double a, double b)	a^b
Math.exp(double a)	e^a
Math.ceil(double a)	$\lceil a \rceil$
Math.floor(double a)	$\lfloor a \rfloor$
Math.log(double a)	$\ln(a)$ (natural log)
Math.sqrt(double x)	$\sqrt{x}$
Math.round(float f)	Round to nearest int
Math.round(double d)	Round to nearest long
Math.random()	A random number between 0.0 and 1.0

Floating-Point Constants

Math.E	Base of the natural logarithms
Math.PI	π

Trigonometric Functions

`sin(double `θ`)`	$\sin(\theta)$
`cos(double `θ`)`	$\cos(\theta)$
`tan(double `θ`)`	$\tan(\theta)$
`asin(double `x`)`	$\frac{-\pi}{2} \leq \arcsin(x) < \frac{\pi}{2}$
`acos(double `x`)`	$0 \leq \arccos(x) < \pi$
`atan(double `x`)`	$\frac{-\pi}{2} \leq \arctan(x) < \frac{\pi}{2}$
`atan2(double `a`, double `b`)`	$\pi \leq \arctan(b/a) < \pi$

H.2 PACKAGE `java.math`

The package `java.math` supports extended-precision integer (`BigInteger`) and floating-point (`BigDecimal`) operations.

The Java Debugger: jdb

Syntax problems in a program are identified by **javac**. Straightforward execution problems can be spotted by placing System.err.println() statements in your code and by reading the exception stack traces displayed. For more subtle bugs, consider using the **jdb** debugging tool.

I.1 STARTING AND EXITING **jdb**

With **jdb**, debugging is performed with two cooperating processes: a Java interpreter that runs the program in question and a **jdb** debugger that controls the way the execution proceeds (Figure I.1). Before starting, make sure that files to be debugged are compiled with the -g option of **javac**.

Use one of the following forms to start **jdb**

```
jdb
jdb options TargetClass arg1...
```

and get a > prompt. Now you can debug interactively by loading and running classes. The second form simply tells **jdb** the **java** command line you wish to use ahead of time.

To debug applets, use the -debug option of **appletviewer**:

```
appletviewer -debug file.html
```

Figure I.1   DEBUGGING ARCHITECTURE

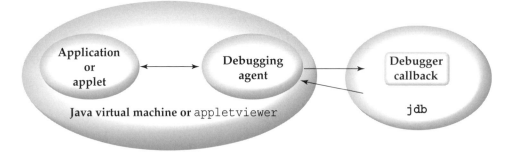

You may also first run a program to be debugged, using **java_g** -debug, which causes the display of a generated password:

```
% java_g -debug WordCount
  Agent password=3ab7ur
```

Then, from a different window on your system, start **jdb** with

```
jdb -host hostname -password password
```

to attach **jdb** to the running Java program. Use localhost as the host name if debugger and program are on the same host computer. Otherwise you must indicate the host on which the program being debugged is running. One advantage of this attachment method is the ability to separate the standard I/O of the program and **jdb**.

To exit **jdb**, use exit or quit.

I.2   HOW **jdb** HELPS DEBUGGING

When started, **jdb** allows you to load classes interactively, run them, stop the execution at selected *breakpoints* to display the source listing, and examine method arguments, local variables, the host object, and the sequence of calls (a backtrace) leading to the breakpoint. Computation can be continued after breaking, and breakpoints can be moved to different places to isolate the bug.

I.3   DEBUGGING STEPS

A typical debugging session should follow these steps:

1. Start **jdb**.
2. Load class to debug (if not already given on command line).
3. Set current thread group to main (threadgroup main).
4. Set current thread (thread t@1).
5. Install breakpoints (stop in *ClassName.method*).
6. Run the program (from **jdb** window or application window as appropriate).
7. Examine values of objects, variables, arguments, and call stacks.
8. Install new breakpoints to zero in on the bug, clearing old breakpoints as appropriate.
9. Continue or restart execution.
10. Repeat steps 5–9 until satisfied.

I.4 SAMPLE DEBUGGING SESSION

Here **jdb** is applied to control the execution and examine the run-time quantities of TestFract, the simple test program for the Fraction class (Section 2.4).

Output lines are indented for easier reading. Comments are added.

```
C:\javawang\ex3> javac -g *.java  /* compiles for debugging */

C:\javawang\ex3> jdb TestFract   /* starts jdb on class TestFract */
   Initializing jdb...
   0xe747f8:class(TestFract)
> threads                        /* displays all threads */
   Group system:
   1. (java.lang.Thread)0xe600d0   Finalizer thread   cond. waiting
   2. (java.lang.Thread)0xe65578   Debugger  agent     running
   3. (sun.tools.debug.BreakpointHandler)0xe72398
                                   Breakpoint handler cond. waiting
   Group main:
   4. (java.lang.Thread)0xe600a8 main cond. waiting
> threadgroup main               /* sets current group to main */
                                 /* this is a must */
> threads                        /* displays threads */
   Group main:                   /*    in current group */
   1. (java.lang.Thread)0xe600a8 main cond. waiting
> thread t@1                     /* sets current thread to main
                                    this is a must */
main[1] stop in Fraction.plus    /* sets breakpoint on method */
   Breakpoint set in Fraction.plus
main[1] clear                    /* displays all breakpoints */
   Current breakpoints set:
   Fraction:98
main[1] run                      /* runs TestFract */
   Breakpoint hit: Fraction.plus (Fraction:98)
main[1] locals                   /* displays local variables */
   Method arguments:             /* args to plus() */
   this = 1/20
   y = -1/60
   Local variables:
main[1] print this               /* displays host object */
   this = 1/20
main[1] dump this                /* shows details of object */
   this = (Fraction)0xe764c0 {
   private int num = 1
   private int denom = 20
   }
```

```
main[1] list                          /* lists 10 source lines around
                                          current position  (98) */
    94    public Fraction times(Fraction y)
    95    {   return( new Fraction( num * y.num,
                                    denom * y.denom ) ) ); }
    96
    97    public Fraction plus(Fraction y)
    98 => {   if ( num == 0 )
    99            return(makeFraction(y.num, y.denom));
   100        else if ( y.num == 0 )
   101            return(makeFraction(num, denom));
   102        else
    /* line numbers are from source file of class */
main[1] up                            /* moves up one frame on stack */
main[2] locals                        /* shows local variables on frame 2*/
    Method arguments:
    args =
    Local variables:
    x = 1/20
    u = -1/60
    v = 1/30
    y is not in scope
main[2] up
main[3] locals
No local variables: try compiling with -g
main[3] down                          /* moves down one frame on stack */
main[2] down
main[1] where                         /* shows stack backtrace */
    [1] Fraction.plus (Fraction:98)
    [2] TestFract.main (TestFract:10)
    [3] sun.tools.debug.MainThread.run (MainThread:55)
main[1] cont                          /* continues execution */
1/20 + -1/60 - 1/30 = 0/1main[1]  /* output is from TestFract */

TestFract exited
```

I.5 COMMANDS

When using **jdb**, you are always working within a current group and a current thread. These are usually the main group and the main thread. You then set breakpoints with stop in and stop at and run a class so that control reaches a breakpoint. At the breakpoint, you have a current class and a current method, as well as a current stack frame. You then use locals, list, print, where, and dump to examine the suspended thread. You may then clear certain breakpoints and install new ones before continuing the computation (cont).

A number of frequently used commands are listed here. In these commands, an object ID is a hexadecimal integer. A class or variable can usually be given by a simple name.

- Help—The help command lists a brief summary of available commands. The doc/javatools directory contains a manual page for jdb.

- Breakpoints—Breakpoints are set in classes. Use stop in *ClassName.methodName* just after a call to the method. The command methods *ClassName* lists all methods of the given class. If a method is overloaded, stop in only puts the breakpoint on the first method. Use stop at for other methods with the same name. The command stop at *ClassName*:101 installs a breakpoint on a line of code in that class. Line count begins on the first line in the source code file. At a breakpoint, use list to list ten lines around the current line and list *n* to list ten lines around line *n*. Use clear to remove breakpoints, and cont to continue execution. Single stepping is available via step.

- Displaying classes, variables, and objects—Use print *name* to display the given quantity and see the toString() representation of the object. Classes are specified either by their object ID or by name. If a class is already loaded, a substring can be used. Java expressions such as print *ClassName.staticVar* can be used.

- Displaying details of classes, variables, and objects—Use dump to display an object's instance variables. Objects are specified by their object ID; classes are specified by name or object ID. The dump command supports Java expressions such as dump this and dump 0x12345678.myArray[3].

Index of Classes

A list of *classes* and *interfaces* mentioned in the text, with section numbers to help you find them quickly:

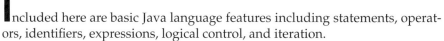

APPENDIX K

Basic Background

Included here are basic Java language features including statements, operators, identifiers, expressions, logical control, and iteration.

Basic constructs of Java are very similar to those in C++. Reading this appendix before starting Chapter 1 is recommended for beginners who are not familiar with C++.

If you know C or C++, you can read this appendix very quickly or use it as a reference. Appendix D lists differences between C++ and Java.

K.1 STATEMENTS

A method body contains statements. A statement specifies program actions at run time. The computational steps in a method are expressed by a sequence of statements that perform in ways predefined by the language. The statements are *executed* one by one in the given order when the program runs.

Java provides a full complement of statements that will be described shortly. Generally, statements fall into two categories:

1. Simple statement—One statement terminated by a semicolon (;).
2. Compound statement—Zero or more statements grouped together by { and }. A compound statement has the same structure as a method body. In fact, the method body is itself a compound statement. A compound statement can be used anywhere a simple statement can.

For example, each statement in the main method of class Average is a simple statement. Together they form the compound body of main. A compound statement is sometimes also referred to as a *block*.

A common programming mistake is to forget the semicolon terminator. When this happens in a program, because the compiler cannot easily determine that a semicolon is missing, it will almost always complain about some other alleged syntax problem. These erroneous complaints can be very confusing, so be sure to use the semicolon where it is needed:

1. A declaration always ends with a ; .
2. A simple statement is terminated by a ; .

3. There is no ; after a compound statement—in other words, after the closing } of a block.

4. There is no ; after a class definition.

For an example of item 3, see the `while` statement used by the `factorial` method in Section K.2.

K.2 THE `while` STATEMENT

Let's consider another simple program—in this case, one that computes n factorial for a nonnegative integer n. Recall that n factorial is $n! = n * (n-1) * \cdots * 3 * 2 * 1$. Hence $1! = 1$, $2! = 2$, $3! = 6$, and so on. We define a class Factorial that contains two `static` methods: `factorial` and `main`. The first is shown here.

```
public static int factorial(int n)
{    int ans = 1;
     while (n > 1)
     {    ans = ans * n;
          n = n - 1;
     }
     return ans;
}
```

The method `factorial` is defined with one formal parameter n of type `int`. The return value is of type `int` also. If control flows off the end of a method or returns through a `return` with no argument, the return value is undefined and the method return value type must be `void`.

In this `factorial` method, the `while` statement

```
while (n > 1)
{    ans = ans * n;
     n = n - 1;
}
```

specifies the repeated execution of two statements forming a *loop*. The *condition* n > 1 (enclosed in parentheses) produces a `boolean` value (`true` or `false`) and controls the number of times the body of the `while` loop (enclosed in braces) is executed.

Here is the way `while` works (Figure K.1):

1. Test the condition. If n is greater than 1 (the condition is true), the body of `while` is executed once. If the condition is false, then the body is not executed, the `while` statement is finished, and control goes to the next statement.

2. Go back and execute the previous step.

Figure K.1   THE `while` **LOOP**

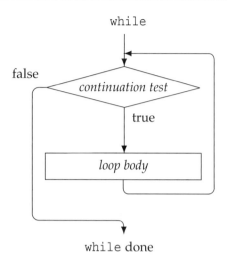

Because the continuation of the loop depends on the condition being true, such a condition is known as a *continuation condition*. The variable n in this example is called a *loop control variable* because its value changes for each repetition of the loop and it determines when the loop stops.

Take a particular value for n, for example, 4, and follow the actions of this while loop to see how the variable ans actually becomes *n*! (24 in this case).

K.3 A COMPLETE `factorial` PROGRAM

The method `factorial` is a member of the `Factorial` class whose complete listing follows:

```
///////    Factorial.java    ///////

/**
 * Lists n factorial for n from 0 to 12.
 * Usage:  java Factorial
 */
class Factorial
{   public static int factorial(int n)
        {    int ans = 1;
            while (n > 1)
                {    ans = ans * n;
```

```
                n = n - 1;
            }
        return ans;
    }

    public static void main(String[] args)
    {    int n = 0;
        while ( n < 13 )
        {     System.out.print(n + "! = ");
              System.out.println(factorial(n));
              n = n + 1;
        }
    }
}
```

Three forms of comments are possible in Java source files. The Java compiler ignores all characters starting from the two-character sequence // to the end of the line. Also ignored are all characters or lines enclosed in /* and */. Comments supply auxiliary information, documentation, and descriptions to make the program easier to use and understand. A comment given between /** and */ is a special *documentation comment*, or doc comment. A doc comment typically describes the purpose and usage of a class, method, or field that comes next. Doc comments in a source file help generate documentation for using the code (Section 12.10).

Compile and run the program with the following:

```
javac     Factorial.java     (to compile)
java      Factorial          (to execute)
```

Compilation results in a `Factorial.class` file, which contains the *Java bytecode* that is platform independent. The **java** command is given the name of the class, `Factorial`, to load and execute.

K.4 SIMPLE CONDITIONAL STATEMENTS

The if ... else statement provides *conditional branching* and can be used in the simple form:

```
if  ( condition )
        statement one
else
        statement two
```

The parentheses around the *condition* are mandatory. The condition is first tested to decide which one of the two given statements will be executed. If the condition is true, only *statement one* is executed; otherwise only *statement two* is executed. Because a statement, by definition, can be either simple or compound, statement one or two here can be compound in the form $\{ st_1; \ldots st_n; \}$.

The `else` part can also be omitted, resulting in this form:

```
if ( condition )
    statement
```

The effect is to execute the given *statement* only if the *condition* is true. Failing this, *statement* is skipped over, and control flows to the next statement after the `if` statement. The following statement

```
if ( n > 0 )
        m = m + n;
else
        m = m - n;
```

assigns to m the absolute value of n plus m. The condition

```
n > 0
```

is a *relational expression* that produces a `boolean` value. Its value is `true` only if the current value of n is greater than zero; otherwise its value is `false`. The operator > is a relational operator. Table K.1 shows a list of relational operators for numeric comparisons.

The `for` Statement

Java has the usual arithmetic operators +, -, *, and /. In addition there is the integer remainder operator % (for example 15 % 6 is 3). But there is no power or exponentiation operator. The `for` statement can be used in a power method to raise integers to integer powers.

```
static int power(int a, int n)
{    int i, ans = 1;
```

Table K.1   RELATIONAL OPERATORS

Operator	Meaning
>	Greater than
<	Less than
==	Equal to
!=	Not equal to
>=	Greater than or equal to
<=	Less than or equal to

```
        for (i = 1 ; i <= n ; i = i + 1)
                ans = ans * a;
        return ans;
}
```

The `for` statement specifies a loop and takes the following general form:

```
for ( init ; cont condition ; update )        (Loop control)
    statement                                  (Loop body)
```

The loop body can be a simple or a compound statement. The loop control consists of an initialization part, a continuation condition, and an update part, separated by semicolons. The `init` and `update` parts can be a single expression or a comma-separated list of expressions.

In the method `power`, the `init` part

```
i = 1
```

is executed before the `for` loop starts. The `cont condition`

```
i <= n
```

is tested. If true, the `statement`, or body, of the `for` loop is executed once. The `update` part

```
i = i + 1
```

is then executed, followed by a reexamination of the continuation condition. If it is true, the body is executed once again. If it is false, the `for` statement is finished. Figure K.2 further illustrates the control flow of `for`.

The `for` is a specialized `while`, and the iteration continues only while the test condition remains true. Thus it is possible for the body of the `for` to be *skipped without ever being executed* if the continuation condition is false to start with. It is also worth noting that only two semicolons are used in the loop control part of the `for`. (Details on the forms of expressions themselves are discussed in Section K.5.)

If `init` is not given, it specifies a no-op, or no operation. It is also possible to omit one or more parts in the `for` loop control. The absence of a part indicates a no-op. Thus an infinite loop can be written as follows:

```
for (;;) { loop body }       // infinite loop
```

It is also possible to write a `for` with a body that is empty or a *null statement*:

```
for ( control ) { }          //  empty loop body
for ( control );             //  null statement loop body
```

In this case, the loop body is a no-op and the effective computations are contained in the loop control.

Figure K.2   THE for **LOOP**

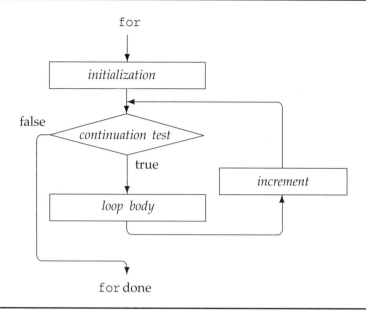

for

initialization

false

continuation test

true

loop body

increment

for done

Instead of declaring the loop control variable i outside the for construct, it is common practice to move the declaration statement for i inside the for, if possible:

```
for (int i = 1 ; i <= n ; i = i + 1)
    ans = ans * a;
```

Here the variable i is local to the for loop and cannot be used after the loop.

The method power assumes that the exponent n is non-negative. It does not work for a negative n. Strictly speaking, there should be a check for the sign of n before the for loop is entered. Another concern is the size of the answer. If the answer exceeds the maximum size for the type int, power will fail. In Java, as in C and C++, integer arithmetic overflow is undetected and results in an answer modulo the size of the type.

Increment and Decrement Operators

The unary operators ++ (increment) and -- (decrement) are used to increase or decrease the value of an integer variable by 1 (especially useful in loops). Applied to a variable i, these special operators perform four separate operations in a single step:

1. Access the current value of i

2. Add or subtract 1 from this value

3. Assign the new value to i

4. Return the i value, before or after the assignment, as the value of the expression

Specifically, we can use:

```
i++     (increment after) Gives value of i, then adds 1 to i
++i     (increment before) Adds 1 to i, then gives value of i
i--     (decrement after) Gives value of i, then subtracts 1 from i
--i     (decrement before) Subtracts 1 from i, then gives value of i
```

The idea is to combine referencing the value of a variable with assigning a new value to the variable to get shorter, more concise code. For example

```
j = 2 * i++;
```

means use the current value of i in the multiplication with 2, then change the value of i by adding 1 to it. Thus, it is shorthand for

```
j = 2 * i;
i = i + 1;
```

but more concise. Similarly, the increment before usage in

```
j = 2 * ++i;
```

is short for

```
i = i + 1;
j = 2 * i;
```

which is very different from the increment after operation.

Following is the power method with the increment operator:

```
static int power(int a, int n)
{       int ans = 1;
        for (int i = 1 ; i <= n ; i++)
            ans = ans * a;
        return ans;
}
```

Note that here ++i may be used instead of i++ in the loop control of the for because the value of this increment expression is not used.

An even more efficient implementation of power combines n-- with while, a construct explained in Section K.2.

```
static int power(int a, int n)
{       int ans = 1;
        while (n-- > 0)
```

```
        ans = ans * a;
    return ans;
}
```

Note the n-- in the `while` condition here cannot be replaced by --n.

Use of the increment and decrement operators can sometimes make code more difficult to read and contribute to errors in a program. It is advisable to favor readability over terseness in programming.

The do-while Statement

The `while` and the `for` loops continue the continuation condition at the beginning of the loop. If the condition is false to begin with, the `while` or `for` loop body can be skipped without being executed. The `do-while` loop is the same as `while` except that it tests the continuation condition at the end of the loop (Figure K.3). Therefore a `do-while` loop body is executed *at least once*.

The general form of the do statement is

```
do body while ( condition ) ;
```

where the loop body is again a simple or compound statement.

Figure K.3   **THE do-while LOOP**

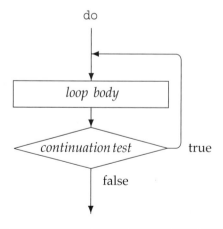

The Multiway `if` Statement

The simple `if-else` statement has been explained. The simple `if` provides a two-way branching of control flow. The `if` statement can be nested to perform multiway branching:

```
if ( exp1 )
            statement-1
else if ( exp2 )
            statement-2
...

            ...
else
            statement-i
```

There can be zero or more `else if` parts. As stated before, the final `else` part is optional.

This pattern specifies a multiway branching: If *exp1* is true, *statement-1* is executed; otherwise, if *exp2* is true, *statement-2* is executed; . . . ; if nothing is true, the last *statement-i* is executed. In other words, the logical expressions are examined in order, and the first true expression triggers the execution of the corresponding statement. Only one of the statements is executed. Control then goes to the next statement beyond the entire `if` statement.

Applying the `if` statement, the method `compare` takes two `int` quantities, a and b, and returns 1, 0, or −1, depending on whether a is bigger than, equal to, or less than b, respectively.

```
static int compare(int a, int b)
{    if ( a > b )
        return 1;
    else if (a < b )
        return -1;
    else
        return 0;
}
```

Actually, it is not necessary to insist on getting 1, 0, and −1 from `compare`. Following the convention established by the Java `String` method `compareTo` (string compare, Section 2.9), the return value can simply be positive, zero, or negative, depending on the relative size of the two quantities being compared. Hence the method `compare` can be simplified as follows:

```
static int compare(int a, int b)
{    return a - b;
}
```

A statement within an if can be another if to form a *nested if* statement. The following method evenOdd returns 2, 1, or 0 for a positive even, positive odd, or neither:

```
static int evenOdd(int a)
{   if ( a > 0 )                 // outer if
        if ( a % 2 == 0 )        // inner if begin
            return 0;
        else
            return 1;            // inner if end
    // outer if end
    return 0;
}
```

With nested if statements, a good question is to which if does the else belong. There are two logical possibilities: associate the else with the inner if, making the statement part of the outer if an if-else statement; or associate the else with the outer if. This potential ambiguity is known as the *dangling else* problem. In Java an else clause automatically goes with the immediately preceding open if. An if without an else can be closed off by enclosing the if statement in { }, making it a compound statement.

K.5 OPERATORS AND EXPRESSIONS

Constants, variables, and method invocations are the simplest sorts of expressions. When combined with operators, they form more involved expressions. Whether an expression is simple or complicated, it always gives a value.

An operator acts on operands. A *binary* operator takes two operands; a *unary* operator takes only one. In an expression involving multiple operators, the order in which the operations are carried out is very important. In the expression

```
a + b / c
```

the division is carried out before the addition. Thus, the operator / takes *precedence* over +. Generally, arithmetic operators take precedence over logical operators, which take precedence over assignment operators. Consider an expression involving operators with the same precedence:

```
a / b * c                // equivalent to (a / b) * c
```

Its value can depend on the *associativity* of these operators. Most operators associate left-to-right so the expression is evaluated from left to right. A few operators associate right-to-left. The relative precedence and associativity of all operators are shown in Appendix B. Parentheses can always be used to override the precedence and associativity rules, as follows:

```
(a + b) / c
a / (b * c)
```

The available operators and expressions are presented in the following subsections. The operators and expressions are also summarized in table form for easy reference (Tables K.2, K.3, K.4, K.5, and K.6).

Arithmetic Expressions

Table K.2 shows the variety of arithmetic expressions. When the divide operator / is used on two integers, an integer quotient is produced. Any fractional part is discarded. The increment and decrement operators can be used only on actual variables. Therefore an expression such as (a + b)++ is incorrect.

The arithmetic operator % provides the remainder or modulo operation for integer and floating-point operands. To compute a % b means to divide a by b and take the remainder. If both a and b are integers (b is not zero), the value computed satisfies the equality:

```
(a / b) * b + (a % b) = a
```

The remainder always has the same sign as a. Thus:

```
 7 % 5 is  2       7 % -5 is  2
-7 % 5 is -2      -7 % -5 is -2
```

For floating-point a and b, % computes the remainder r, satisfying $r = a - (b \cdot q)$ where q is an integer with a magnitude not larger than that of $\frac{a}{b}$ and the same sign as $\frac{a}{b}$. Thus:

```
 7.0 % 5.0 is  2.0       7.0 % -5.0 is  2.0
-7.0 % 5.0 is -2.0      -7.0 % -5.0 is -2.0
```

Table K.2   ARITHMETIC EXPRESSIONS

Expression	Description
i / 4	Integer division, truncating fractional part
a % b	Integer and floating-point remainder
x * x * x	Multiplication (no power operator)
++i, j++	Integer pre/post increment
--i, j--	Integer pre/post decrement
a/(3.4 + b)-3*c	Mixed operations with type conversions

The modulo operation (mod for short) is most often used for positive integers and is useful in many situations.

Consider computing the next tab position, given any current column position. On a typical CRT terminal, tab stops are set eight columns apart. So the next tab stop is given by

```
c - (c % 8) + 8
```

for any current column position c.

The operator + can be used to concatenate two strings. See Section 2.9 for details.

Relational and Logical Expressions

Some relational and logical expressions have been used already. The set of all relational operators is listed in Table K.1; logical operators are listed in Table K.3.

All forms of relational and logical expressions are shown in Table K.4.

The relational operators have higher precedence than the operator && (logical *and*), which takes precedence over || (logical *or*). *Evaluation of a logical*

Table K.3   LOGICAL OPERATORS

Logical Operator	Meaning
&&	Logical operator *and*
||	Logical operator *or*
!	Logical operator *not* (unary)
^	Logical *xor*

Table K.4   RELATIONAL AND LOGICAL EXPRESSIONS

Expression	Description
a > b, a < b, a >= b, a <= b	Relational expressions produce boolean values
a == b, a != b	Equal, not equal
a == true && b == false	True if first *and* second relations are true
a > 1 || a < -1	True if first *or* second relation is true
a || ! b && c	Logical expr: a or ((not b) and c)
a > b ? a : b	If (a > b) then value is a else b
str1 == str2	True if str1 and str2 refer to the same object

expression stops as soon as the logical value of the whole expression is determined. This may leave some operands unevaluated. For example, the expression

```
exp1 && exp2
```

is true only if both *exp1* and *exp2* are true. If *exp1* turns out to be false, the value of the whole must be false; therefore *exp2* is not evaluated. Similarly, in evaluating

```
exp1 || exp2
```

if *exp1* is true, the value of the whole expression is true, and *exp2* will not be evaluated.

When the logical operators & and ! are applied to `boolean` operands they compute logical *and* and logical *or* by always evaluating both arguments. Logical *xor* is achieved by ^. Thus

```
(x > 0) ^ (y > 0)
```

tests whether x and y have different signs. Because &, |, and ^ have higher precedence than relational operators, it is important to use parentheses appropriately, as shown here.

The unary operator ! (logical *not*) *negates* the `boolean` value of its operand. The negation turns `true` into `false` and vice versa. The operator ! has precedence over all relational and other logical operators.

Java also supports the *conditional expression* formed with the *ternary operator* ?:, which takes *three* operands:

```
exp0 ? exp1 : exp2
```

The expression has value *exp1* if *exp0* is true, and *exp2* otherwise. Thus, the expression

```
c = a > b ? a : b
```

sets c to max(a, b).

Assignment Expressions

An *assignment* is a statement as well as an expression because it produces a value: that of the left-hand side after the assignment is made. Hence, an assignment can be used anywhere an expression can. Furthermore, in the same spirit of the increment and decrement operators, the assignment operator = can combine with other operators to form efficient shorthand expressions. The allowable combinations are shown in Table K.5.

To see assignment expressions in action, consider a method that computes the sum of the squares of the first *n* odd integers.

```
static int sumSquares(int n)   // n is assumed positive
{   int sum = 1, i = 1;
    n *= 2;                     // n = n * 2
```

Table K.5   **ASSIGNMENT EXPRESSIONS**

Expression	Comment
`a = b = 1`	Same as a = (b = 1)
`(i=System.in.read()) != -1`	Assignment in relational expression
`a += b`	Shorthand for a = a + b
`a op= b`	Shorthand for a = a op b
	allowable ops: +, -, *, /, %, <<, >>, &, ^, |

```
    while ( (i += 2) < n )
         sum += (i * i);
    return sum;
}
```

In sumSquares the assumption is made that the argument n is positive. The while loop is completely bypassed for the case n equals 1. The parentheses around i += 2 in the while condition are necessary because assignment operators have lower precedence than almost all other operators. For the same reason, the parentheses around i * i are unnecessary but are included for readability.

Bitwise Operations

There is also a group of operators for dealing with data at the bit level. The shift operators

- <<—Shifts bits left, fills with zero
- >>—Shifts bits right, fills with highest (sign) bit
- >>>—Shifts bits right, fills with zero

work on integer types. The *signed shift*, $n >> i$, produces $\lfloor \frac{n}{2^i} \rfloor$ for n positive or negative.

The bitwise logical operators & (and), | (or), ~ (not), and ^ (xor) work on integer types. Table K.6 shows bitwise operations on integers where *ones complement* is obtained by flipping each and every bit of an integer.

Unlike increment and decrement operators, bitwise operations do not alter their operands. Thus j = i << 4 produces an integer value equal to left-shifting i by 4 bits without damaging the contents of i. If modifying i is actually desired, use:

```
i <<= 4;
```

Table K.6   **INTEGER BITWISE EXPRESSIONS**

Expression	Comment
n & 017	Bitwise logical and (4-bit mask)
i | j	Bitwise i or j
i ^ j	Bitwise i exclusive or j
i << 4	Bitwise left shift i
~n	**One**s complement

A one-bit left shift on a positive integer is normally equivalent to multiplying by 2. Thus the operation above results in a value 16 times that of i.

Bitwise operations provide an alternative way to compute the next tab stop. By zeroing out the last three bits of the current column position c, the expression

```
(c & ~07) + 8
```

produces the position of the next tab stop. The bit pattern ~07 (bitwise not applied to octal 7) is all 1s except for the lowest three bits. It is used as a *mask* by the bitwise & operation to produce the same value as c but with the last three bits blocked out (made 0).

Bitwise operations not only allow manipulations at the bit level, but also provide an efficient way to perform certain arithmetic operations involving positive integers. For example, left-shifting the number 3 by one bit gives 6. Conversely, right-shifting 6 by one bit gives 3.

K.6   ITERATION CONTROL

Iteration is the repeated execution of a set of statements in a program. Such repetitions make it possible for a short program to perform a very large number of operations. The constructs while, for, and do-while covered earlier in this chapter perform iterations.

An iteration is normally specified by the following components:

1. Initialization—Initial values are given to quantities used in the loop before any iteration begins.
2. Control variables—One or more variables that take on new values for each successive repetition.
3. Successor statements—One or more statements that assign new values to the control variables in preparation for the next repetition.

4. Loop body—A sequence of zero or more statements that is executed once for each repetition.

5. Continuation condition—A logical or relational expression tested before or after each repetition. If the condition is true, the next repetition is performed; otherwise control flows to the program statement just after the iteration construct.

In addition to normal termination via item (5), the loop body may contain statements that cause *early termination* of the iteration. An example is the method inString, which determines whether a string contains a particular character.

```
static int inString(char c, String str)
{    int i = 0;
     while ( i < str.length() )
     {   if (str.charAt(i) == c) return i;     // found c at index i
         i++;
     }
     return -1;                                // c not in string
}
```

The control variable i, initially zero, is incremented by 1 for each repetition. The call str.charAt(i) returns the *i*th character in str (indexing form 0). Normal termination comes when the string str has been completely examined and no match for c has been found. Early termination via the return statement occurs as soon as a match for c is found in str. Following are two calls to this method:

```
inString('g', "abcdefgh");
inString('/', filename);
```

A shorter implementation of inString uses the for construct:

```
static int inString(char c, String str)
{    for (int i = 0 ; i < str.length(); i++)
         if (str.charAt(i) == c) return i;
     return -1;
}
```

Statements break and continue

In the inString example, the return is used to terminate an iteration early. This technique is restrictive and cannot be used to break out of an iteration without causing the entire method to return. The statement break is used to break out of an iteration without returning from the method. When break is executed, control transfers immediately to the first statement after the current block or iteration. An application of break is found in the method monotonic, which examines an integer array and returns true or false depending on whether the sequence of integers is *monotonic* or not. A sequence of values is monotonically increasing if each value is no smaller than the previous one. Similarly, a sequence is monotonically decreasing if each value is no larger than the preceding one.

```
public static boolean monotonic(int[] a)
{   int n = a.length, i;
    for (i = 0 ; i < n - 1 ; i++)
        if (a[i+1] < a[i]) break;
    if (i == n - 1) return true;            // increasing
    if (i > 0 ) return false;
    for (; i < n - 1 ; i++)
        if (a[i+1] > a[i]) return false;
    return true;                            // decreasing
}
```

You should try this method with various increasing, decreasing, repeating, length-one, and other sequences of integers.

The break statement breaks out of the innermost block or iteration. To break out of nested blocks or loops, use

```
break labelname
```

which breaks out of a loop or block *labeled* by the identifier labelname. To label a *statement* simply use:

```
labelname: statement
```

Similar to break, the continue statement also shortens iterations. However, instead of breaking out of a loop entirely, continue *aborts the current iteration and starts the next one*. Within while or do-while, this means that control transfers immediately to the test condition part. Inside for, it transfers to the increment step. In other words, continue skips the rest of the loop body to reach the loop control of the next repetition. To demonstrate how this can be convenient, consider stringMatch, a method that determines whether a given string str is contained in another string line:

```
class StringMatch
{  public static int stringMatch(String str, String line)
   {   int n = str.length(), m = line.length();
       if (n == 0)  return 0;                   // str is empty
       for (int i = 0 ; i < m ; i++)
       {   if ( n > m - i ) return -1;
           if (line.charAt(i) != str.charAt(0))
                                        // first chars different
               continue;                // skip rest of loop body
       // compare remaining characters
       // until first mismatch or end of string
           int j, k;
           for (j = i + 1, k = 1;               // expression list
                k < n && line.charAt(j)==str.charAt(k);
```

```
                k++, j++)
            { /* empty loop body */ }
            if (k == n) return j-n;                // successful match
        }
        return -1;                                 // failed to match
    }
}
```

The method `stringMatch` uses a straightforward strategy. The string `str` is matched, in turn, with a series of substrings of `line`, starting at index 0, 1, and so on. A successful match returns an index of the matched position. Otherwise the next substring is used. The value −1 is returned when there is no match.

In `stringMatch`, a nested `for` loop is employed. The outer `for` iterates over the substrings of `line`. If the first character of the substring does not match the first character of `str`, the program skips the rest of the loop body to continue with the next substring. The inner loop matches the remaining characters after the leading character has been matched. Note that the inner loop has an empty loop body and it uses *expression lists* in the loop-control part of the `for` statement.

The algorithm in `stringMatch` is simplified, but it shows how to use `continue` to skip to the next iteration of the immediate enclosing loop. The statement

```
continue labelname
```

can be used to skip to the next iteration of a labeled outer loop. Note that there is no "goto" statement in Java.

K.7 MULTIPLE CHOICE

Although the `if . . . else if . . . else` construct remains the general-purpose decision-making mechanism, the `switch` statement provides a very handy way to select among a set of predefined choices. The syntax is as follows:

```
switch ( int-expression )
{       case constant-exp1 :
            statements
        case constant-exp2 :
            statements
        ·.·
        default:
            statements
}
```

The `switch` construct is like a structured multiple "goto." The switching *expression* is evaluated first. The resulting value is matched against each integer-valued constant case label. In a switch, all case labels must be distinct. Control is transferred to the matching case, or the default if nothing matches. There is no sequential, case-by-case matching at run time. Control is transferred directly. If the optional default case label is not given and if nothing matches, the execution of switch is successfully completed.

Following control transfer to a case label, the statements at the selected label *and all statements under other case labels after it* will be executed in sequence. This behavior is called *fall through*, and it makes switch very different from a multiple if. The break statement can also be used to break out of the switch statement. It is often the last statement for each case in order to prevent fall-through. With fall-through completely prevented, the order in which the case labels are given becomes unimportant. At each case label there can be zero, one, or more statements. This allows several case labels to precede one group of statements, making it convenient for certain situations.

Experimenting with the following test program can sharpen these concepts about switch:

```java
public static void main(String[] args)
{ int j = 4;
  System.out.println( "1: switch(" + j + ")");
  switch(j)
  {    case 1: case 3:
          System.out.println("A: case 1 or 3");
       case 5:
          System.out.println("B: case 5");
       default:    // deliberate
          System.out.println("C: case default");
       case 2:
          System.out.println("D: case 2");
  }
  j = 2;
  System.out.println( "2: switch(" + j + ")");
  switch(j)
  {    case 5:  System.out.println("E: case 5");
       default: System.out.println("F: case default");
       case 2:  System.out.println("G: case 2");
  }
}
```

The output produced is as follows:

```
1: switch(4)
C: case default
D: case 2
2: switch(2)
G: case 2
```

Index

+ operator, 14

Web Site and Code Example Package

WEB SITE

The book has a Web site useful for instructors and students. The site can be reached from

```
http://brookscole.com
```

or from

```
http://sofpower.com/booksites/
```

The open part of the site offers code examples, information updates, FAQs, resources, and useful links.

The protected instructor area offers online hands-on experiments, class notes, sample syllabus, homework instructions, and solutions to selected problems. Instructors may contact their Brooks/Cole representative for access information.

EXAMPLE PACKAGE

All examples in this book, and a few more, are contained in a code example package[1] The entire package can be downloaded from the website in one compressed file:

```
javaWang2.tgz          (for UNIX)

javaWang2.zip          (for PC and Mac)
```

The package contains the following files and directories

```
README.txt  ex01/ ex02/ ex03/ ex04/
            ex05/ ex06/ ex07/ ex08/
            ex09/ ex10/ ex11/ ex12/
            ex13/ exapp/
```

---

[1] This code example package is distributed under license from SOFPOWER. The code example package is for the personal use of purchasers of the book. Any other use, copying, or resale is prohibited.

corresponding to the chapters in the book.

To use these examples you need to set up your Java environment first. Simply download the lastest release of SDK from the website:

```
http://java.sun.com/j2se
```

or from your computer vendor and install it following instructions.

USAGE INSTRUCTIONS (UNIX)

Download the file `javaWang2.tgz` from the website into a destination directory, say `$home`, on your UNIX machine. Then unpack the file by:

cd $home
gunzip javaWang2.tgz

to make it into the `javaWang2.tar` file. Then do

tar xvf javaWang2.tar

to install the examples in the directory `$home/javaWang2`. You may now remove the `.tar` file if you wish.

Now you need to set the `CLASSPATH` environment variable by adding two lines to your shell start-up file (`.login`). First add these two lines

```
set loc = $home/javaWang2

set wp = $loc/ex06:javaWang2/ex08:
   $loc/ex04/textline:$loc/ex07/ticapplet:
   $loc/ex10/client:$loc/ex10/socket
```

Then add the third line

```
setenv CLASSPATH '.:'$wp
```

if your `.login` file does not have a previous setting for `CLASSPATH`; or the second line

```
setenv CLASSPATH "$CLASSPATH":$wp
```

if your `.login` file already has a previous setting for `CLASSPATH`.

Now you should issue the Shell-level command:

source $HOME/.login

to read in the `CLASSPATH` setting (or login again). You can check the `CLASSPATH` setting by typing the Shell command:

echo $CLASSPATH

Now you are ready to compile and run the code examples.

USAGE INSTRUCTIONS (PC)

Download the file `jvW2.zip` from the website and unpack with your WinZip tool and place the unzipped files in the `C:\` folder for example. And this will give you `C:\jvW` with all the example files in it. You may now delete `javaWang2.zip` if you wish.

Now, you need to modify your `CLASSPATH` by modifying your `AUTOEXEC.BAT` file. If your

AUTOEXEC.BAT file does not have a previous setting for `CLASSPATH` add the single line:

```
SET CLASSPATH= .;C:\jvW2\ex06;
  C:\jvW2\ex08;C:\jvW2\ex04\textline;
  C:\jvW2\ex07\ticapplet;
  C:\jvW2\ex10\client;C:\jvW2\ex10\socket
```

to the `AUTOEXEC.BAT` file using the Notepad tool, for example. Make sure the line has a line terminator at the end.

If your `AUTOEXEC.BAT` already has a setting for `CLASSPATH`, then simply add the above value to the end of the existing `CLASSPATH`.

Now, at the DOS prompt, issue the command:

`C:\>` **autoexec**

to read in the `CLASSPATH` setting. You can display the setting by giving the DOS command

`C:\>` **echo** %CLASSPATH%

Now you are ready to compile and run the code examples.